The
Diplomat-Scholar

The **ISEAS – Yusof Ishak Institute** (formerly Institute of Southeast Asian Studies) was established as an autonomous organization in 1968. It is a regional centre dedicated to the study of socio-political, security and economic trends and developments in Southeast Asia and its wider geostrategic and economic environment. The Institute's research programmes are the Regional Economic Studies (RES, including ASEAN and APEC), Regional Strategic and Political Studies (RSPS), and Regional Social and Cultural Studies (RSCS).

ISEAS Publishing, an established academic press, has issued more than 2,000 books and journals. It is the largest scholarly publisher of research about Southeast Asia from within the region. ISEAS Publishing works with many other academic and trade publishers and distributors to disseminate important research and analyses from and about Southeast Asia to the rest of the world.

The Diplomat-Scholar
A Biography of Leon Ma. Guerrero

ERWIN S. FERNANDEZ

First published in Singapore in 2017 by
ISEAS Publishing
30 Heng Mui Keng Terrace
Singapore 119614

E-mail: publish@iseas.edu.sg
Website: <http://bookshop.iseas.edu.sg>

All rights reserved. No part of this publication may be reproduced, stored in a retrieval system, or transmitted in any form or by any means, electronic, mechanical, photocopying, recording or otherwise, without the prior permission of the ISEAS – Yusof Ishak Institute.

© 2017 ISEAS – Yusof Ishak Institute, Singapore

The responsibility for facts and opinions in this publication rests exclusively with the author and his interpretations do not necessarily reflect the views or the policy of the publisher or its supporters.

ISEAS Library Cataloguing-in-Publication Data

Fernandez, Erwin S.
   The Diplomat-Scholar : A Biography of Leon Ma. Guerrero
   1. Guerrero, Leon Ma. (Leon Maria), 1915–1982.
   2. Authors, Filipino—Biography.
   3. Ambassadors—Philippines—Biography.
   I. Title.
DS686.6 G93F36   2017

ISBN 978-981-47-6222-9 (soft cover)
ISBN 978-981-47-6243-4 (e-book, PDF)

Cover photo: Ambassador Leon Ma. Guerrero poses in front of the Palacio de Oriente at the Plaza de Oriente where the statue of Felipe IV can be seen on the background. Reproduced with kind permission of Enrique L. Locsin and Teodoro L. Locsin Jr. of the Philippines Free Press.

Typeset by Superskill Graphics Pte Ltd
Printed in Singapore by Markono Print Media Pte Ltd

Engr Ely V. Fernandez tan Mrs Florida S. Fernandez

Contents

Preface	ix
Prologue	1
Chronology	11

I   Ermita and Santa Cruz to Intramuros: Between Literary and Legal Career

1	Bourgeois Ermita: Birth and Boyhood	19
2	Education under American Jesuits	30
3	The Humorist as Critic, Writer and Actor	39
4	Juggling Law and Journalism on the Eve of War	48

II   To Tokyo and Back: The Making of a Diplomat

5	The Assistant Solicitor	67
6	From Intelligence Officer in Bataan to the Return of Ignacio Javier	73
7	Second, then First Secretary	84
8	At the Home Office: The Diplomat as Historian	98

III   Going In, then Out of the Political Jungle: Padre Burgos to Arlegui

9	The Legal Counsel, Professor and Translator	107
10	The Foreign Policy Critic and Spokesman	119
11	"Asia for the Asians" or How to Leave Arlegui in Six Months	128

IV London and Madrid: The Philippines in a Resurgent Asia

12 At the Court of Saint James	153
13 A Verbal Tussle in the UN	172
14 The Biographer	178
15 At Franco Country	193
16 In Search of the Burgos Trial Records	202
17 Home Leave in Preparation for a State Visit	212

V New Delhi to Belgrade: The Philippines towards Non-Alignment

18 Homecoming to Asia at Nehruvian India	223
19 "Diplomacy of Development" and Other Speeches	233
20 The Foreign Policy Rescuer and Again, Critic	241
21 The Diplomat as Efficient Intellectual-Bureaucrat	252
22 Endorsing Non-alignment amid Personal Crisis	263
23 Flirting with Dictators	270
24 Martial Law Propagandist	281
25 At Tito's Pre-Balkanized Yugoslavia	288
Epilogue	295
Glossary	313
List of Abbreviations	317
Bibliography	319
Index	341
About the Author	360

Preface

Since 2010 when I finished an early version of my full-length work on Leon Ma. Guerrero, I managed to come up with a number of articles on Guerrero. In the meantime, the plan to publish the biography opened up after having submitted the manuscript for consideration by the Institute of Southeast Asian Studies (ISEAS) (now known as ISEAS – Yusof Ishak Institute) in Singapore and having received a favourable review in 2014. In 2015, Guerrero's family and heirs commemorated his birth centenary at a time when the revision process did not take off. Early in 2016 when I have the luxury of time to fine-tune and rework the manuscript, the outcome is this biography.

As the making of this biography is a journey in itself, I could not have arrived at my destination without the encouragement and help along the way of my family, especially my mom and dad, and relatives, especially Mrs Martha S. Rosa; my former teachers and colleagues, Dr Milagros C. Guerrero, Dr Ma. Bernadette G.L. Abrera, Dr Evelyn A. Miranda, Dr Ferdinand C. Llanes, Dr Bienvenido Lumbera, Dr Ricardo T. Jose, Prof Herman Joseph H. Kraft, Dr Maria Luisa T. Camagay, Dr Filomeno V. Aguilar, Dr Motoe Terami-Wada, Dr Floro C. Quibuyen, Dr Jaime B. Veneracion, Dr Jonathan Chua, Mr Phillip Ramirez, Prof. Elizabeth Siler, late Dr Josefina Cabigon, Dr Laura Lee Junker, Dr Rachel Harrison, Prof Henry David Burton; Mr Alfredo Liongoren and late Mrs Norma Liongoren; Mr Marciano de Borja; Guerrero's immediate family, Margaret Burke Guerrero and David Guerrero; Mrs Carmen Guerrero Nakpil, Mrs Gemma Cruz Araneta; Prof Ajit Singh Rye, late Fr John N. Schumacher, S.J., former Ambassador Juan A. Ona, late Fr. James Reuter, S.J., Mrs Ljiljana Plavsic, Mr Abelardo Caro, Ms Rahilah Yusuf and other helpful staff of the ISEAS – Yusof Ishak Institute.

Along the journey were crucial brief or long stopovers at the National Library of the Philippines, the National Archives of the Philippines in Paco, Manila; University of the Philippines Main Library and its constituent libraries headed at that time by Prof. Salvacion Arlante, Ateneo de Manila University Archives, De la Salle University Library; Far Eastern University library, Lyceum of the Philippines library, *Instituto Cervantes* library, the *Manila Bulletin* under its editor-in-chief, Dr. Crispulo J. Icban, the National Historical Institute, now the National Historical Commission of the Philippines, Jorge B. Vargas Museum and Filipiniana Research Center and the Lopez Museum and Library.

It could not have been bearable without the pleasant company of Marjorie D. Pamintuan, Manuel Paner, Albuen Jude Fiel, Deo Navaja, Jeoffrey Liboon, Rolando Esteban, Edwin Valientes, Renato Pelorina, Jaynee Tamboong, Jennifer Guman, Rosabella Mendez, Vincent Isles, Luis Lisa, Dido Miranda, Russel Lomboy and Rosabella D. Fernandez.

In the course of it, short trips were made when I read parts of Chapters 23, 24 and parts of the Epilogue at the first international conference on Philippine-Latin Americans relations hosted by the Philippine Academic Consortium on Latin American Studies (PACLAS) at the Pamantasan ng Lungsod ng Maynila and when I delivered at the National Conference on Rizal Law in Claro M. Recto Conference Hall, UP Diliman Campus an earlier version of Chapter 14, which was revised and published in *Philippine Studies*. Chapters 1 to 4 dealing with Guerrero's early years and Chapter 6 on his war-time years were not read in any conference but revised, submitted to and published respectively in *Asian Perspectives in the Arts and Humanities* by the Ateneo de Manila University and *South East Asia Research* by the School of Oriental and African Studies, University of London.

I might have missed people who were part of the making of this biography; I regret the omission. Nonetheless, I am grateful for all the support of those named and nameless. However, they do not bear any responsibility for all interpretive and factual errors, which I claim to be mine alone.

Prologue

On the morning of 19 June 1982, President Ferdinand E. Marcos awarded the *Gawad Mabini*, the highest decoration in the Foreign Service, to a shrunken man on his deathbed. The day was special for an avid Rizalist. That *barong*-clad man who once displayed his brilliance and audacity was Leon Ma. Guerrero III. He was far from his old self, the tall dashing man who had exchanged barbs with foreigners in defence of the Filipino. In that hospital room, close family, a few friends and himself listened to Prime Minister Cesar Virata declare that he had "helped set the tone of Philippine foreign policy" and that "many of his beliefs have become part of the parcel of the foreign policy of the Republic...."[1]

Being a writer was the other side of Guerrero. Shortly after his death, one author published an intriguing article on what he called "the great switcheroo of eighty-two", finding the National Artist for Literature award to Carlos P. Romulo unmerited and that Guerrero deserved it more than Romulo because of his lasting contributions to Philippine literature. To him, "the better writer got the award for diplomacy and the better diplomat got the award for writing", unaware that Romulo got his *Gawad Mabini* ahead of Guerrero.[2]

As a diplomat, how did Guerrero influence the template of Philippine foreign policy? What were those beliefs he held that became one of the features of Philippine foreign policy in the 1970s and 1980s? In any case, as a writer, how did Guerrero contribute to Philippine letters that he is said to deserve the highest honour in Philippine arts and what were these contributions?

Examining the life of a historical figure requires placing him in the context of his times. Acting not only on his own volition, he responds to the forces about him and the limitations of the environment where he lives. Leon Ma. Guerrero III, the subject of this biography, distinguished himself as a writer and as a diplomat. To understand him demands an examination of Philippine, particularly elite Hispanic Tagalog society and culture during the twentieth century. In addition, we must take into account the circumstances in which he finds himself in literature and in diplomacy.

Exploring Guerrero's life would uncover the significant events highlighting a career in writing and diplomacy. Today, Guerrero is relatively unknown as a writer and diplomat unlike in the 1980s when he ranked fourth among Filipino essayists in the choice of Filipino teachers, his essay "What are Filipinos Like?" garnering the first place in the list of best Filipino essays. This lack of appreciation of him is not surprising because more than two decades have passed since he died. The last anthology of his historical and diplomatic writings was published two years after his death. But if we dig deeper into his past, a colourful life, not only about his two careers, would surface. Unorthodox in his views and methods, he also made a career in translation becoming the focus of a recent study that provided a new interpretation of Filipino nationalism.[3]

If the history of the world is the biography of its great men, as English writer Thomas Carlyle said, then the history of Philippine literature and diplomacy is the biography of its distinguished writers and diplomats. Guerrero could claim to be one because, no doubt, he carved a significant niche in Philippine literary and diplomatic history. The task then of this biography is to describe and to determine Guerrero's niche in Philippine literary and diplomatic history, but it is not limited to highlighting these two main threads in his life.

The biography reveals the personal and social circumstances that shaped Guerrero's persona from his youth to adulthood, recognizes his accomplishments as a writer and his place in the Philippine literary scene, and highlights his contribution to Philippine diplomacy and his place in Philippine diplomatic history.

In a larger context, Guerrero was one among Southeast Asian intellectuals who grew up before the war and matured to witness his country's postwar independence. He belonged to this generation of Southeast Asian intellectuals who served his country both as intermediary and interlocutor between national and international political players. They were products of the Western educational system as most of Southeast Asia, with the exception of Thailand, underwent Western colonization. *Mision civilisatrice* moulded a generation of colonial wards in preparation for the eventual independence of each colony so that a new generation of educated class would man the bureaucracy necessary for nation-building alongside the charting of the respective nation's intellectual and literary development. To cite a few, Guerrero was in the same league as Soedjatmoko and Sumitro Djojohadikusumo from Indonesia, or Syed Hussein Alatas from Malaysia or Chit Phumisak from Thailand, who were intellectuals shaping their respective nation's history.

As a diplomat, Guerrero was like Sumitro. Born in 1917 in Kebumen, Central Java, Sumitro became the deputy head of the Indonesian delegation to the UN Security Council in 1948, member of the Indonesian delegation to the Round Table Conference in The Hague, Netherlands, and chargé d'affaires, Indonesian Embassy in Washington, D.C. in 1950. Unlike Guerrero who was a career diplomat and never a party politician, Sumitro first served Indonesian President Sukarno as Minister of Trade and Industry, then as Minister of Finance, before joining the PRRI/Permesta movement that opposed the Jakarta central government, causing him to live as an exile as economic consultant in a number of foreign countries. But in 1968 President Suharto appointed him Minister of Trade, and later, Research from 1973 to 1978. While serving as minister to these governments, Sumitro was a member of the Faculty of Economics in the University of Indonesia.

Again, Guerrero the diplomat could be seen in Indonesia's Soedjatmoko. Born in 1922 Soedjatmoko was sent in 1948 to New York as member of the Indonesian delegation to lobby for UN recognition of its country's sovereignty; to London in 1950 to establish the nucleus of Indonesia's embassy in that capital, and in Washington, D.C. to create the political desk of the Indonesian Embassy in the United States. He studied medicine in Batavia (later Jakarta) but was expelled by the Japanese for his subversive activities. After his stint in the United Nations, Soedjatmoko was elected member of the Constitutional Assembly of Indonesia; served as member of the Indonesian delegation in the Bandung Conference in 1955; and founded the Indonesian Institute of World Affairs and became its Secretary-General. Unlike Guerrero who was a loyal soldier of the state, Soedjatmoko was critical of Sukarno's authoritarian policies. He went abroad for two years and worked as guest lecturer at Cornell, followed by three years back in his country in voluntary unemployment. As a historian and scholar however, Guerrero was like Soedjatmoko who co-edited in 1965 *An Introduction to Indonesian Historiography*. But when Suharto assumed power, Soedjatmoko again served the government and was sent as envoy to the United Nations in 1966 and later as ambassador to the United States in 1968. Back in Indonesia in 1971, he became a member of various local and international think-tanks until he was framed as a mastermind of the Malari Incident in 1974 when students protested and rioted during the Japanese prime minister's state visit. Prohibited from leaving Indonesia for two-and-a-half years, he was awarded the Ramon Magsaysay Award for International Understanding in 1978. Two years later, in Tokyo he assumed the rectorship of the United Nations University and came out with two more books, *Primacy of Freedom in Development* and *Development and Freedom* —

again in contrast to Guerrero, who was a firm believer that curtailment of freedom was necessary to achieve development, thus his tacit support for Martial Law — before his death in 1989 when he suffered a cardiac arrest while he was on a lecture back in his home country. Guerrero was never an academic and political party organizer like Syed Hussein Alatas, who was born in 1928 in Bogor, Dutch East Indies, and a founding member of Parti Gerakan Rakyat Malaysia and Parti Keadilan Masyarakat Malaysia while working in a publishing house and later lecturer and full-time faculty at the University of Malaya, National University of Singapore and Universiti Kebangsaan Malaysia. But as a scholar, Guerrero shared interest with Alatas when the latter wrote his *The Myth of the Lazy Native*, which tackled and expanded on Rizal's splendid exposition on the indolence of the Filipino and in extension, of other Southeast Asian natives.

As a translator, Guerrero was like Chit Phumisak, a Thai philologist, born in 1930 in Prachantakham District, Prachinburi Province, who was asked to assist in the translation into Thai of *The Communist Manifesto* by Karl Marx. However in contrast to Guerrero who was a nationalist and anti-communist though he supported the opening of relations with communist countries, Phumisak was anti-nationalist and Communist, a member of the *Communist Party of Thailand*. A scholar like Guerrero, Phumisak wrote *The Face of Thai Feudalism* in Thai. He died young at age thirty-five when he was shot to death in 1966.

With the exception of Alatas who had a biography written by his daughter, the rest have no definitive biographies written about them. George McT. Kahin and Milton L. Barnett wrote a brief account of Soedjatmoko in memory of this Indonesian intellectual. Soedjatmoko as intellectual was also the subject of a recent forum at an Indonesian university but its proceedings are not yet available to my knowledge. J.D. Legge wrote about a circle of followers of Indonesian nationalist Sutan Sjahrir, among whom was Soedjatmoko, in the formation of Indonesian nationalism during the Japanese Occupation and years after. Thee Kian Wie wrote a biographical account of Sumitro in honour of his memory. Peter McCawley wrote a brief but lucid account of Sumitro's life for *Jakarta Post*. Craig J. Reynolds wrote a biographical introduction on Phumisak to his English translation of Phumisak's *The Face of Thai Feudalism*.[4]

Nonetheless, Guerrero's intellectual contemporaries in the Philippines have become the subject of biographies. The life of Renato Constantino (1919–99), historian and intellectual, was written by Rosalinda Pineda-Ofreneo. Armando J. Malay (1914–2003), the dean of Philippine journalists, was the subject of a biography by Marites N. Sison and Yvonne T. Chua.

PROLOGUE 5

Emmanuel Pelaez (1915-2003), former Vice President of the Philippines and Secretary of Foreign Affairs, was examined in a biography by Nelson A. Navarro, who also authored a biography of Maximo V. Soliven (1929-2006).[5]

Not unlike Edna Z. Manlapaz's approach to poet Angela Manalang-Gloria's biography, this is my account of Guerrero's story or my interpretation of his life, holding on to the precepts of traditional and modern life-writing, which means reliance on sources and the recognition of their limitations. For authenticity, Guerrero's voice — as long as it is possible, warranted and available in the sources — is re-echoed from his speeches and interviews. As much as a biographer would want to know all about his subject, it is inherent in a biography what John Worthen calls "the necessary ignorance of a biographer", which means that inasmuch as I would want to know all about Guerrero, I am unable to. There will be gaps in the narrative that even sources cannot supply.[6]

For a biography such as this, the historical descriptive approach suffices in telling Guerrero's life as culled from primary and secondary sources, supplemented by interviews because a biographer is first and foremost a historian. Nonetheless, Guerrero can be better understood if examined in the broader intellectual development at the time, thus the approach had to be widened by using transnational and comparative contextual analyses. Guerrero's literary works (for example, poems, short stories, essays, novelettes, serials, speeches, biography, translations, reports and letters) are examined; their consistencies are checked with other sources. Since Guerrero was a public figure, events in his life are recorded in diverse sources from the print media and government documents. The latter has been limited to available documents at the National Archives because Guerrero's diplomatic dispatches, the "literature of diplomacy" as the late Adrian Cristobal puts it, are confidential at the moment, under the custody of the Department of Foreign Affairs (DFA). An official request had been sent to access them but was denied as there is no law at that time governing the access of these records by the public. The breadth and scope of Guerrero's diplomatic activities presents a challenging but not insurmountable task; he was appointed as diplomat during his entire career to several countries in three different continents. Visits to these countries cannot be afforded due to financial and time restrictions. The use of Guerrero's personal papers in the form of private correspondences and newspaper clippings in scrapbooks in the possession of Guerrero family remedied this problem to a certain extent. The papers, however, are weak in documenting his life in his last two posts in Mexico and Yugoslavia, which other sources such as DFA publications tried to fill in the other factual details. Like any biography, certain conclusions and claims made here are bound to be tentative.

To reconstruct the narrative of Guerrero's life, the following primary sources were used. *The Guidon* and other Ateneo publications at the Ateneo de Manila University Archives provide the data on Guerrero's schooling from primary grades to college including his activities and achievements as a student, his early literary works, law studies and work before the war. The *Philippines Free Press* from 1934 to 1941 contains works written by and about him including short stories, verses, novelettes, letters to the editor, profiles, and essays among others. The *Japanese Occupation Papers*, the *People's Court Papers* at the University of the Philippines (UP) Main Library and the *Jorge B. Vargas Papers* at the Jorge Vargas Museum and Filipiniana Research Center, UP, have particular documents related to his activities during the war particularly his stint as second secretary in Tokyo, and his work as radio commentator for the Hodobu, the Japanese Department of Information. The *Leon Ma. Guerrero Personnel Data Papers* at the National Archives in Paco, Manila are documents detailing his appointments (1947–53) as technical assistant and legal adviser at the Philippine Senate. The *Leon Ma. Guerrero Papers*, kept by the Guerrero family, are scrapbooks on local and foreign newspaper clippings about him, his speeches, letters received, invitations, and other relevant papers but lacking information on his stints in Latin America and Yugoslavia as well as his pre-war activities. The *Horacio de la Costa Papers* at the Ateneo de Manila University Archives contain Guerrero's letters to Father de la Costa, which were indispensable in reconstructing Guerrero's scholarly undertakings, particularly his writing of the *The First Filipino*. The *Salvador P. Lopez Papers* and *Carlos P. Romulo Papers* at the University of the Philippines Main Library hold some correspondences between Lopez and Guerrero in the case of the former and exchanges between Romulo and other Filipino diplomats including Lopez relating to Guerrero in the case of the latter detailing politics in the Philippine Foreign Service. A protégé of Romulo, Lopez as a pre-war journalist was Guerrero's colleague. Romulo served as long-time Philippine secretary of Foreign Affairs, a position Lopez held for a time. The *DFA Review* and other DFA publications, for example, *Diplomatic Agenda of Philippine Presidents, 1946–1985*, provide information on his appointments as envoy and his activities in Latin America and Yugoslavia as well as the outline of the different foreign policies of each administration from Presidents Roxas to Marcos.

Beyond the bits and pieces written about Guerrero, there is no work that treats him in a full-length biography. Nick Joaquin made a *Free Press* article on him as "the Guerrero Family's Ambassador". Carlos Quirino wrote a brief biographical account on him as part of his introduction to *The First Filipino*. Doreen G. Fernandez and Edilberto N. Alegre conducted an interview with him several months before his death. Included in a book about Filipino writers, the interview was filled with personal tales and anecdotes about his life. On his death in 1982, the Ministry of Foreign Affairs (MFA, now the Department of Foreign Affairs) released a slim collection of eulogies by his colleagues. Wilfrido Ma. Guerrero, a cousin of Leon and a noted playwright, wrote about the Guerrero family history. Benedict Anderson wrote a brief account of his life but suffered from dubious assumptions on Guerrero's motives and life as a whole. Carmen Guerrero Nakpil published the trilogy of her autobiography and memoirs, relating vividly not only her life but also her relationship with and intimate knowledge about her brother Leon and the whole family before, during, and after the war. Recently, David Guerrero produced and edited an anthology about his father, Leon, which compiles news articles and recollections of Guerrero and his writings.[7]

The life story of Guerrero is best organized and studied by situating it through the intersections of family, literary, diplomatic and transnational history. Nakpil provides the necessary background on the Guerrero family apart from Wilfrido Ma. Guerrero's clan history. Bienvenido Lumbera, Cynthia N. Lumbera's and Asuncion D. Maramba's literary histories and anthologies are to some extent helpful in putting into context Guerrero's literary achievements. Lumbera husband and wife did not mention Guerrero as short story-writer and essayist but as a translator, with an excerpt of Guerrero's translation of Rizal's novels. Maramba mentioned him as an essayist but not as a short-story writer. More useful is Edilberto N. Alegre and Doreen G. Fernandez's oral histories collection cited above. Alegre and Fernandez were able to draw candid revelations about Guerrero's personal and public lives. The works of Milton W. Meyer, Lewis E. Gleeck Jr, Richard J. Kessler Jr, Jose D. Ingles and Malaya C. Ronas supplied the structure towards a better understanding of Guerrero's diplomatic activities in relation to a larger Philippine foreign policy. Meyer wrote a pioneering Philippine diplomatic history from 1946 to the end of Carlos P. Garcia's presidency. Gleeck examined Philippine foreign policy in the context of each presidency from Manuel A. Roxas to the first term of Ferdinand E. Marcos. Kessler discussed Philippine foreign policy under Marcos. From the perspective of a senior diplomat in Philippine Foreign Service, Ingles gave a nuanced viewpoint on Philippine foreign policy under Marcos. Ronas summarized Philippine foreign policy under Marcos in two chapters.

Relatively important are the volume edited by Aileen S.P. Baviera and Lydia Yu-Jose, and the works of Benjamin Domingo.[8]

Divided into twenty-five chapters in five parts, the narrative begins with a brief historical background of Ermita and the family. Then, it relates Guerrero's childhood and teenage years and recounts his education, tracing the development of his writing career seen in his literary involvements at the Ateneo de Manila and work at the *Philippines Free Press*. Events leading to his appointment as second secretary in Tokyo, and Assistant Chief of Division, then Chief of Protocol at the Department of Foreign Affairs are recounted in the second part giving first accounts of his activities prior to and during World War II. The third part opens with his application as legal adviser to the Philippine Senate, a position that lasted six years until appointed Undersecretary of Foreign Affairs. His ambassadorial stints in the Court of Saint James and Madrid are discussed in the fourth part. The fifth part tackles his postings in New Delhi, Mexico, and Belgrade. Finally, questions raised here are answered in the epilogue as it attempts to identify and describe the place of Guerrero in Philippine diplomacy and letters.

Notes

1. *In Memoriam: León Ma. Guerrero, Lawyer, Writer, Diplomat, Historian and Nationalist (1915–1982)* (Manila: Office of Press & Public Affairs, Ministry of Foreign Affairs, 1982), p. iii.
2. Alfrredo N. Salanga, "The Great Switcheroo of Eighty-Two: Was there a mistake about the Romulo & the Guerrero Awards?", *Mr & Ms*, 13 July 1982, p. 10.
3. Estrellita V. Gruenberg, "The canon of Philippine Literature according to teachers of Metro Manila", in *Manila: History, People and Culture, Proceedings of the Manila Studies Conference*, edited by Wilfrido V. Villacorta, Isagani R. Cruz and Ma. Lourdes Brillantes (Manila: De la Salle University Press, 1989), pp. 296–97; Benedict Anderson, "Hard to Imagine: A Puzzle in the History of Philippine Nationalism", in *Cultures and Text: Representations of Philippine Society*, edited by Raul Pertierra and Eduardo F. Ugarte (Quezon City: University of the Philippines Press, 1994), pp. 81–118.
4. Masturah Alatas, *The Life in the Writing Syed Hussein Alatas: Author of the Myth of the Lazy Native* (Marshall Cavendish, 2010); George McT. Kahin and Milton L. Barnett, "In memoriam: Soedjatmoko, 1922–1989", *Indonesia* 49 (1990): 133–40; "Contemplating Soedjatmoko's Thought about Intellectuals", <https://ugm.ac.id/en/news/5531-contemplating.soedjatmoko%E2%80%99s.thought.about.intellectuals> (accessed 1 February 2016); J.D. Legge, *Intellectuals and Nationalism in Indonesia* (Ithaca: Cornell University Press, 1987), pp. 53–55, 129–31; Thee Kian Wie, "In memoriam: Professor Sumitro Djojohadikusumo, 1917–2001", *Bulletin of Indonesian Economic Studies* 37, no. 2 (2001): 171–81; Peter McCawley, "Sumitro's

life mirrors the turbulence of Indonesian history" <http://www.thejakartapost.com/news/2001/03/31/sumitro039s-life-mirrors-turbulent-indonesian-history.html> (accessed 1 February 2016); Craig J. Reynolds, "Introduction", *Thai Radical Discourse: The Real Face of Thai Feudalism Today* (Ithaca: Cornell University, 1987).

5. Rosalinda Pineda-Ofreneo, *Renato Constantino: A Life Revisited* (Quezon City: Foundation for Nationalist Studies, 2001); Marites N. Sison and Yvonne T. Chua, *Armando J. Malay, a Guardian of Memory: The Life and Times of a Filipino Journalist and Activist* (Manila: Anvil, 2002); Nelson A. Navarro, *What's Happening in Our Country: The Life and Times of Emmanuel Pelaez* (Makati City: Emmanuel Pelaez Foundation, 2008); Nelson A. Navarro, *Maximo V. Soliven: The Man and the Journalist* (Manila: Solidaridad Publishing House, 2011).

6. Thomas Carlyle, "History as biography", in *The Varieties of History: From Voltaire to the Present*, edited by Fritz Stern (New York: Vintage Books, 1973), p. 103; Edna Z. Manlapaz, *Angela Manalang-Gloria* (Quezon City: Ateneo de Manila University Press, 1993), p. xii; Cristina Pantoja Hidalgo, *Creative Nonfiction: A Manual for Filipino Writers* (Quezon City: University of the Philippines Press, 2005; John A. Garraty, *The Nature of Biography* (New York: Alfred A. Knopf, 1957); Ira Nadel, *Biography: Fiction, Fact and Form* (New York: St. Martin's Press, 1984); John Worthen, "The necessary ignorance of a biographer", in *The Art of Literary Biography*, edited by John Batchelor (Oxford: Clarendon Press, 1995), pp. 227–44.

7. Nick Joaquin, "The Guerrero Family's Ambassador", in *Gloria Diaz and Other Delineations* (National Book Store, 1977), pp. 118–23; Carlos Quirino, Introduction to *The First Filipino* by Leon Ma. Guerrero (Manila: Guerrero Publishing, 1998), pp. xiv–xix; Edilberto N. Alegre and Doreen G. Fernandez, *The Writer and his Milieu: An Oral History of the First Generation Writers in English* (Manila: De la Salle University Press, 1984); *In Memoriam*, see note 1; Wilfrido Ma. Guerrero, *The Guerreros of Ermita (Family History and Personal Memoirs)* (Quezon City: New Day Publishers, 1988); Anderson, "Hard to Imagine", pp. 81–118; Carmen Guerrero Nakpil, *Myself, Elsewhere* (Metro Manila: Circe Communications, Inc., 2006); Carmen Guerrero Nakpil, *Legends & Adventures* (Metro Manila: Circe Communications, Inc., 2007); Carmen Guerrero Nakpil, *Exeunt* (Manila: Nakpil Publishing, 2009); David Guerrero, *LMG: The Leon Maria Guerrero Anthology* (Guerrero Publishing, 2010). In a series of emails in May 2014 which was shown to me, David Guerrero confronts the late Anderson about certain passages in the latter's work that are "defamatory" to his father's reputation.

8. Bienvenido Lumbera and Cynthia N. Lumbera, *Philippine Literature: A History and Anthology* (Manila: Anvil, 2005); Asuncion D. Maramba, *Early Philippine Literature: From Ancient Times to 1940* (Manila: Anvil, 2006); Milton W. Meyer, *A Diplomatic History of the Philippine Republic: The First Years 1946–1961* (Claremont, California: Regina Books, 2003); Lewis E. Gleeck, Jr, *The Third Philippine Republic, 1946–1972* (Quezon City: New Day Publishers, 1993); Richard J. Kessler, Jr, "Development Diplomacy: The Making of Philippine Foreign Policy under Ferdinand E. Marcos" (PhD dissertation, Fletcher School of Law and

Diplomacy, 1985); Jose D. Ingles, *Philippine Foreign Policy* (Manila: Lyceum of the Philippines, 1982); Malaya C. Ronas, "Philippine Foreign Policy, 1946–1972", pp. 487–500 and "Philippine Foreign Policy, 1972–1986", pp. 501–16, in *Philippine Politics and Governance: An Introduction*, edited by Teresa S. Encarnacion-Tadem and Noel M. Morada (Quezon City: Department of Political Science, College of Social Sciences and Philosophy, University of the Philippines Diliman); Aileen S.P. Baviera and Lydia Yu-Jose, eds., *Philippine External Relations: A Centennial Vista* (Pasay City: Foreign Service Institute, 1998); Benjamin Domingo, *The Making of Filipino Foreign Policy* (Quezon City: University of the Philippines Asian Center, 1983) and *The Re-Making of Filipino Foreign Policy* (Quezon City: University of the Philippines Asian Center, 1993).

Chronology

1915	**March 24.** Guerrero born in Ermita, Manila.
1918	His younger sister Gemma dies
1919	Birth of his brother Mario Xavier
1921	**June.** Admitted to St Paul Institution
1922	Birth of his sister Carmen
1923	**June.** Transfers to the Ateneo in Intramuros
	October. Admitted to the Sodality of the Virgin Mary
1924	**March.** Gets a bronze medal for highest general average
	September. Becomes associate promoter in the League of Sacred Heart
1927	**March.** Graduates from preparatory school second in batch
	June. Enrols for high school at the Ateneo
	Meets Horacio de la Costa
1928	**March.** Tops his class
1929	**July.** Begins writing for *Guidon* as feature writer
	Starts submitting his humorous column, "Totoy to Momoy" in *Guidon*
1930	**January.** Promoted to feature editor
1931	**February.** Elected editor-in-chief with "Skeezix" de la Costa his associate editor
	March. Sends his first short story to *Graphic*
	June. Enrols for university studies
	October. Writes poetry for *Wings*, a literary semi-annual
1932	**February.** Awarded Silver Medal for Oratorical Excellence in a public symposium-contest on modern literature
	March. Appointed associate editor of *Wings*
	mid-August. Fire gutted Ateneo. Transfers to *Calle* Padre Faura
	October. With Skeezix, criticizes Jose Garcia Villa's brand of poetry in letters to the *Philippines Free Press*
1933	**October.** Performs King Lear at the Manila Grand Opera House

1934	**April.** Starts his "The Times in Rhymes" at the *Philippines Free Press*
	July. Writes his first detective short story
1935	**February.** Publishes his first detective novelette
	March. Graduates with an Bachelor of Arts degree *summa cum laude*
	June. Enrols at Philippine Law School
1936	**October.** Becomes a charter-member of the Philippine Book Guild
1937	**July.** Broadcasts over KZRM on "Mummers of the Air"
	August. Starts writing on high personalities in government
1938	**31 March.** Marries Anita Corominas of Cebu
1939	**August.** Passes the bar and starts working as secretary at the Supreme Court
1940	**January.** Starts writing about movie stars
	April. Works as assistant city fiscal in Manila City Hall
	September. Promoted to assistant solicitor at the Bureau of Justice
	October. Handles the brief on the appeal case of Ferdinand E. Marcos
	Campaigns for Quezon's re-election
	December. His "Still Small Voice" listed in Villa's Annual Honour Roll for the Short Story
1941	Attacks Japanese imperialism in radio broadcasts
	8 December. Pearl Harbour bombed
1942	**January.** Flees Manila along with Salvador P. Lopez
	Enlists as first lieutenant at Military Intelligence Service camp in Bataan
	Edits a daily war news bulletin, *See You in Manila*
	April. Evacuates to Corregidor
	Participates in *Voice of Freedom* radio broadcasts
	9 April. Fall of Bataan
	6 May. Fall of Corregidor
	late May. Arrives as POW in Capas concentration camp
	July. Released from Bilibid Prison
	2 October. Works as private secretary to Executive Commission Chairman Jorge Vargas
	12 October. Anchors the programme "The Philippines Today" over KZRH

1943	**May to July.** Reminisces the last days and fall of Corregidor in two articles
	13 October. Resigns from the Hodobu
1944	**February.** Goes to Japan to work as Second Secretary in the Philippine Embassy in Tokyo
1946	**July.** Repatriated to Manila
	August. Works as assistant chief of division, Division of European and African Affairs, Department of Foreign Affairs at Arlegui
	November. Promoted to Chief of Protocol
	Writes and publishes the serial *Twilight in Tokyo*
1947	**9 May.** Releases to the press his serial *The Passion and Death of the USAFFE*
	Resigns from Arlegui due to congressional reaction to his serial
	1 September. Starts working at the Senate as legal adviser (technical assistant)
1948	**June.** Teaches law at Far Eastern University and Francisco Law School
	September. Appointed Secretary to the Senate delegation to the conferences in Italy
1949	**August.** Files a suit together with Attorney Claro M. Recto challenging President Elpidio Quirino's exercise of emergency powers
1950	**April.** Translates Rizal's boyhood memoirs
1951	**April.** Writes speeches for Recto
	Becomes Nacionalista Foreign Policy Spokesman
1952	**August.** Releases his first articles on Philippine relations with other countries
1953	**February.** Demands along with Senator Recto final verdict from the Supreme Court regarding Emergency Powers Act
	April–November. Supports and campaigns for Ramon Magsaysay for the presidency
1954	**1 January.** Appointed Undersecretary of Foreign Affairs
	7 February. Enunciates "Asia for the Asians" in Philippine foreign policy
	April. Appointed Acting Secretary
	Negotiates with the Japanese on war reparations

	July. Leaves for London as ambassador to the Court of Saint James
	13 October. Presents credentials to the Queen
1955	**March.** Organizes the Philippine Society of London
1956	**September.** Comes home to report on Suez Canal Crisis
1957	**March.** President Ramon Magsaysay dies from plane crash
1958	**February.** BBC invites him for the "Third Programme" talks
1959	**September–October.** Talks back to an American diplomat at UN
	December. Finishes translating the *Noli Me Tangere*
1960	**January.** Starts writing his Rizal biography
	Engages in an extramarital affair with Margaret Burke, his private secretary
	April. Defends "Filipino First" policy to *The Economist*
	19 June. Submits to the Jose Rizal National Centennial Commission biography contest
	October. Recto dies in Rome
1961	**5 April.** Birth of his son, Leon Xavier, later known as David
	August. Awarded first prize for his *The First Filipino*
	December. Speaks for Rizal Day lecture at the Luneta
1962	**April.** Departs for Madrid
	June. Prepares for the Macapagal state visit
1963	**November.** Organizes a party for the Bonifacio centenary
1964	**February.** Prepares a necrological service for Emilio Aguinaldo
	April. Awarded the Zobel Prize for his collection of Spanish speeches
1965	**February.** Arranges the state visit to the Philippines of Marquess and Marquesa de Villaverde, the son-in-law and only daughter of Generalissimo and Mrs Franco
	March. Talks before UP lessons from Spanish diplomacy regarding military bases
	Clarifies the statement on parity of a visiting U.S. diplomat
1966	**June.** Leaves for New Delhi
	1 August. Presents credentials to President Sarvepalli Radhakrishnan
	September. Admires India's policy of non-alignment
	Gets plans for the building of the Philippine Embassy chancery in New Delhi

1968	**February.** Co-chairs with India the UNCTAD II
	July. Arrives in Bangkok to beef up Philippine panel in Sabah talks with Malaysia
1969	**March.** Atomic agreement signed in Manila
	September. Foreign Affairs Secretary Carlos P. Romulo inaugurates the chancery
	Cultural agreement signed in New Delhi
1970	**June.** Flies home to attend the funeral of his mother
	President Ferdinand E. Marcos calls for the removal of "unequal" provisions in the military bases agreement
1971	**January.** Represents the country in the Asian-African Legal Consultative Committee in Colombo
	June. Prescribes non-alignment as development alternative
	Attends to his dying wife
	4 July. Anita dies of cancer
	October. Prepares the state visit to India of First Lady Imelda Marcos
1972	**30 November.** Marries Margaret Burke at a Catholic church in London before flying to Mexico with his second wife
1973	**January.** Presents credentials to President Luis Echeverría
	November. Defends martial law in a letter to *New York Times*
1974	**November.** Technical cooperation in commerce and trade agreement signed in Mexico
1975	**3 January.** Afro-Asian Writers Symposium in Manila begins
	12 June. Entertains for the first time a Chinese envoy in the embassy due to the opening of relations between Manila and Beijing
	June–August. Arranges visits of the First Lady to Mexico, Havana and Caracas
	25–29 August. Philippine application for observer status in the Non-Aligned Movement during the Non-Aligned Foreign Ministers' Meeting in Lima, Peru
	September. Releases *Today Began Yesterday*, a booklet justifying martial law
	October. Welcomes niece Gemma and her two children to his residence
1976	**March.** Flies to Havana to present credentials
	November. Leaves Mexico for Belgrade
1977	**March.** Comes home to attend the funeral of best friend de la Costa

	Addresses the graduation exercises at the Ateneo
	14 June. Presents credentials to the Yugoslav Vice President
	September. Cultural agreement between the Philippines and Yugoslavia signed in Manila
1978	**July**. Attends the Non-Aligned Foreign Ministers Conference in Belgrade
1980	**May**. Attends Marshal Tito's funeral ceremony
	October. Retires from the Foreign Service
1981	**October**. Allows interview by two writers
1982	**19 June**. President Marcos awards him the *Gawad Mabini*
	24 June. Dies of lung cancer

I

Ermita and Santa Cruz to Intramuros: Between Literary and Legal Career

"…Ermita became not just a hermit's retreat, but by the thirties, the gala suburb of Manila."

F. Sionil Jose, *Ermita*

Leon Ma. Guerrero is "called upon to aid in the shaping of the Philippines of the future".

The Guidon, 31 January 1941

1

Bourgeois Ermita: Birth and Boyhood

Before the coming of the Spaniards, there was Lagyo, a Tagalog coastal community. On the afternoon of 21 May 1571, Legazpi's armed expeditionary troop pacified it in the name of Spain. They stumbled upon a group of natives paying homage to a wooden *anito*, joined them in tribute and carried it to their camp claiming that it was the carved image of the Virgin Mary. The image became the *Nuestra Señora de Guía*, patroness of the coastal *arrabal* (later of the Manila-Acapulco galleons) where a Romanesque church was built from the sand of the seashore that saw fishermen unloading from their boats the day's catch. A hermit monk was said to have stayed and died there and, in his honour, the small fishing community was absorbed into a larger village named Hermita in 1591. Over time the "h" disappeared, and Hermita became Ermita.[1]

The coming of the Americans would bring more changes. Seventeen years after Dewey's naval squadron destroyed the Spanish flotilla on Manila Bay to annex the Philippines in 1898, the country continued to suffer from the ravages of the Philippine-American War. Officially declared over in 1902, the war continued in other parts of the archipelago including the island of Mindanao between 1903 and 1916. The war decimated the population, as did disease and famine, in the countryside. In Batangas where hamletting was employed, at least 100,000 died. In Manila, it was relatively peaceful. The Americans succeeded in courting the elite who cooperated in the establishment of a colonial government for eventual self-rule. The passage of the Philippine Bill of 1902 or the Cooper Act provided for the administration of civil government. The Filipino elite gained the power to run the affairs of the country, although the Americans still held sensitive positions in the government. In 1907, an elective Philippine Assembly was inaugurated with eighty-four members from the thirty-four provinces. Then, the Jones Law mandated the creation of a Philippine Senate in 1916, which superseded the Philippine Commission.[2]

At the turn of the twentieth century, Ermita, a genteel suburb of Manila south of Intramuros, was an enclave of the rich and educated class — the *mestizo* elite — the product of the miscegenation between native and Spanish aristocracies. Ermita was enclosed by San Luis (now T.M. Kalaw) Street on the north, Dewey (now Roxas) Boulevard on the west, Taft Avenue on the east and Herran (now Pedro Gil) Street on the south. Prior to the war that completely destroyed and transformed it into a red-light district, Ermita was a residential suburb facing Manila Bay. It was the smallest of the villages after Tondo, Malate or Santa Cruz.[3]

What differentiated Ermita from other districts was its bourgeois atmosphere. Known for its pious women and the fine embroidery they wove, it was said that the Spanish colonials settled there for relaxation. As Carmen Guerrero Nakpil put it, Quiapo was a trading centre; San Miguel was the district home to the aristocracy; Santa Mesa and Sampaloc were the preference of property buyers and developers; Santa Ana and Paco, like Tondo, had been pre-Hispanic kingdoms; Ermita had a unique character that lured sugar magnates from Pampanga and Visayas to buy houses and settle in. Ermita's beach disappeared when the Americans constructed a breakwater made of huge stones but the beautiful sunset remained, enticing the residents to the grand boulevard along the bay every afternoon.[4]

Following the Burnham Plan, Manila slowly metamorphosed into an American city, with Ermita playing a crucial part in the blueprint. Thus, a state university was built there beside a general hospital, which opened in 1910. A few blocks away were a baseball field, the Luneta Park, the Manila Hotel, the university and Army-Navy clubs, the post office, the Legislative Building — "all newly built and running like clockwork", and all, it may be added, serving as channels of Americanization. In Maramag's words, Manila "had become a socio-political nerve center under the new colonial masters, an enduring symbol of imperium". Such was the environment in which our protagonist, Leon Ma. Guerrero, would grow up.[5]

THE GUERREROS

For four generations, the Guerreros settled in an extensive tract of land in Ermita comprising Mabini, Isaac Peral (now United Nations Avenue), M.H. del Pilar (the former *Calle* Real) and the Ermita Church. Our story starts when Binondo-born León Jorge Guerrero, the patriarch of the family, married Clara Leogardo. The couple settled in Ermita. Eventually, their sons and daughters would have families of their own and settled there too.[6]

León María (1853–1935), one of their children, married Aurora Dominguez, eventually siring two sons. They lived on *Calle* Nueva, in a two-storey "wood-frame" house surrounded by the houses of their relatives. When their younger son, Alfredo León (1886–1962), married Filomena Francisco (1886–1970), daughter of the Tagalog novelist, Gabriel Beato Francisco of Sampaloc, León María and Aurora moved to a chalet on *Calle* Cortada so that the couple could stay in the ancestral house.[7]

In the ancestral house on *Calle* Nueva, renamed Mabini in 1913 after the great thinker and philosopher, Filomena bore and raised a son named after her father-in-law who had a distinguished career in public service and was at the end of his teaching career at the University of Santo Tomas (UST). On this same street, León María Ignacio Agapito Guerrero y Francisco, the child's full baptismal name, was born on 24 March 1915. He would be the first of four children; his siblings in order of birth, were Gemma (1917), Mario Xavier (1922), and Carmen María Vicenta (1922), who was nicknamed Chitang.[8]

THE PERSISTENCE OF THE HISPANIC PAST IN A U.S. COLONY

The see-sawing between Americanization and Hispanization was evident in the Guerrero household. This was not to be wondered at since Manila was a Hispanic city. Ermita for its part was home to some Spanish and Spanish *mestizo* residents. Before long, Americans would settle in Ermita. The clash between an ascendant culture and a culture on the wane affected to a certain degree the impressionable years of Guerrero.

Catholicism remained the strongest citadel of Hispanic values against the forces of Americanization. This is shown in the very spaces of the house of the Guerreros, spaces that preserved Catholic practices.

The ancestral house where Leoni — Leon's nickname — spent most of his childhood, stood out in the neighbourhood. The family would gather for family prayers and other church rituals in a private chapel with a regulation altar containing revered images of the *Santo Niño*, the Virgin Mary and Saint John the Apostle. It was here where Father Cesar, the elder brother of Alfredo and Leoni's uncle, would perform Holy Communion rites to his nephews and relatives. The family also owned a gramophone on which Alfredo played Gregorian chants to the admiration and at times irritation of American neighbours — it was to them deafening music.[9]

The house, built in the early 1900s to replace an earlier thatch-roofed structure, was periodically remodelled — an expense that Alfredo's well established clinic and teaching career at the Manila College of Pharmacy made affordable. By the 1930s or Leoni's teen years, it gained a third storey, which gave the family "three new bedrooms, baths and a roof garden ... with pots of rose plants and a jasmine vine on a trellis". A front patio, another addition, was watched over by a wooden statuette of Our Lady salvaged from the Manila Bay.[10]

The interior of the house reflected the family's upper middle-class standing and vestiges of the Old World. The stairs were carpeted and installed with brass rods. The second floor was English panelled, adorned with lamps, candelabra and Persian rugs. A Spanish screen made of elaborate ironworks enhanced the dining room. At the entrance hall, one would be greeted by a carved image of the Sacred Heart. In the living room were a piano, a small organ and wooden antique furniture sets. A library beside it contained some 5,000 books, a modest collection inherited from patriarch Leon. There, one could find Zola, Darwin, and Voltaire.[11]

There was a bar room; on its walls was a mural by Alfredo who was also a painter. Paintings decorated the walls. One was a large painting dedicated to Filomena by Alfredo's uncle, Lorenzo — *Santa Filomena* — a picture showing the saint's dead body adrift in the Tiber River. On the landing going to the third floor hung a Juan Luna sketch of an old man playing a cello. An exclusive room called *sala de armas* displayed Alfredo's collection of weapons ranging from bows and arrows; Cordillera bows, lances and shields; Mindanao-made *kris*, a samurai's armour and a German medieval warrior suit, which was a gift from his friend, Don Alfredo Carmelo.[12]

But pressing upon this world of the Hispanized elite like the Guerreros were the forces of Americanization. One of its channels was the public school system. As Nick Joaquin elegantly put it, "And yet it's just indubitable that during the 1900s the temper of our people underwent a change — from a loathing of the Gringo to a growing liking of him. And the villain responsible is: the public school." American teachers, the so-called Thomasites, imparted to their Filipino wards all over the country the values and attitudes necessary for the Americans to run and maintain the new colony, through the English language. The transition to English, however, was not easy. Manila newspapers and magazines had to use English and Spanish since the elite and the common people were more familiar with Spanish than with English. However, the Manila elite, although resistant at first, had to learn English and eventually did. Equally important was the opening of Manila to free trade with the United States after the passage of the Payne-Aldrich Act in 1909, later modified by the Underwood–Simmons Act in 1913. These acts facilitated the reception of American goods by Filipinos. An example was the importation of cotton and cotton-made goods (cloths whether unbleached, bleached, dyed, or printed; wearing apparel, handkerchiefs, thread, yarns, and other products), the bulk of which came from the United States and amounted to more than PHP41 million in 1918. The local elite, meanwhile, enjoyed the perks accorded them from the export of raw materials to an American market.[13]

Nevertheless, the Philippine Revolution, the execution of Jose Rizal and the Philippine-American War accounted for recent memories. Leoni had grandparents, parents, and uncles who participated in and who could vividly recall these tragic historical incidents. His grandparents on both sides were supporters of the revolution. His parents were in their teens during the revolution and the war against the Americans. As classmates in pharmacy at the *Liceo de Manila*, they would join other student demonstrators in presenting a manifesto on Philippine conditions to the anti-imperialist William J. Bryant on his visit to Manila in 1905. Leoni's uncle, Fernando María Guerrero, wrote for the revolutionary daily, *La Independencia*, under General Antonio Luna and was a noted poet in Spanish. Caught between tradition and modernity, young Leoni would grow up imbibing American culture as did others of his generation, but he would be no stranger to the Hispanic legacy of the revolution, whose records either in poetry or prose were written and remembered in Castillian, the language that was alive in the Guerrero home.[14]

The first language one learnt as a child in the doctor's house was Spanish. While everybody at the turn of the century in Manila was busy acquiring English, inside the house of Alfredo and the Guerrero compound in Ermita, people spoke Spanish. His mother, Filomena, read Russian and French literatures in Spanish. Besides Filomena, her cousins-in-law also took care of Leoni and his siblings, teaching them Spanish. The situation at home aided Leoni's interest in reading the novels of Rizal. In later life, he would recall that he had read Rizal's novels in his childhood, "only half-understanding them, and half secretly", for his mother, a devout Catholic, feared that they would make him lose his faith.[15]

Filomena appeared to be an agent of tradition. Although she herself was "modern", in that she was one of the first women pharmacists in the country, she also handed down the traditions — religious mostly — to Leoni. A devoted wife and mother, Filomena would teach her children at a tender age the rudiments of Catholic teachings. She insisted that Leoni be an altar boy and before long he was. Soon, Mario followed suit. After they outgrew being altar boys, they still had to be present at daily Mass, at the Dominican annual pilgrimage known as *Esclavos de María*, at the *Semana Santa* processions, and at other town festivities. Every night, the family would gather for the long evening prayers in Spanish and some in Latin. Every Sunday, the family would also attend Mass in the nearby church. When two more children were added to the family after Leoni, Filomena hired maids and houseboys. She employed kitchen maids so that she could attend to her lessons in English, French cooking, and crochet. A nanny, the family cook's niece, was employed to take care of Chitang when she was a baby until she got married.[16]

In contrast, Alfredo appeared to be the agent of modernity, the conduit of Americanization. For instance, he acquired the American accent from having stayed as a medical student at Washington University in Missouri. Every morning, Filomena would prepare an American breakfast of ham and eggs, and cereal — a diet Alfredo had been accustomed to when he was in the United States and disliked by everyone else. Alfredo would impart his smart ways to Leoni. Whenever he went to work, either to the clinic or to college, he would be dressed impeccably either in his "white alpaca or pearl grey Palm Beach wool" suit. He would put on French cologne, keep a flower in his lapel, and never forget his fedora. He never went to Mass or Holy Communion with the family. During his short siesta every day after lunch, he would smoke a cigarette. On evenings, he would visit a cabaret at Santa Ana. A man with varied interests, he was "a Sunday painter", "a deer hunter" and "a racing car aficionado".[17]

Grandfathers on both sides would become Leoni's role models too and they too were a mix of the "modern" and the "old". Grandfather León was olive-skinned and medium-built in height and physique. At every opportunity, at work or at home, he always put on a white suit paired with black belt, tie, and shoes. An avid newspaper reader, he was up-to-date on current affairs. A botanist, he maintained a herbarium and from time to time, he would engage in scientific experiments in Philippine pharmacopoeia. Curious about almost everything, he was considered not only the clan's adviser and counsellor but also of the town's. A fond grandfather, he used to tell three-year-old Leoni, curling up on bed beside him, fantastic tales about battles between red gnomes and yellow gnomes and between white ants and red ants. Meanwhile, Leoni's maternal grandfather, the Tagalog writer Gabriel Beato Francisco, or "*Lolo* Abeng", also made an impression on Leoni, even though he was rarely visited by his grandchildren in Sampaloc at *Calle* Lipa (now Jocson Street). A tall bespectacled man, he was a productive novelist, a "seditious" playwright and a historian in Tagalog. Leoni and his siblings' future literary inclinations might have come from him, although much of what the young Leoni would write, as will be shown, would be a far cry from what Lolo Abeng had written.[18]

TWO PRINCES AND AN ACCIDENTAL GIRL

Since Filomena chose to live with her husband, naturally their children were closer to relatives of their father than their mother's. Leoni would grow up in a neighbourhood where everyone was also a Guerrero. He played with his cousins. One of them was Lorenzo Ma. Guerrero, two years his senior, son of his uncle, Dr Manuel, and younger brother of Wilfrido Ma. or Freddie, the future playwright. Writing about the Guerrero family history, Freddie recalled: "Our houses were walking distance from one another, so we all attended baptisms, weddings, ordinary birthday parties, and funerals of each other. All we needed was a phone call."[19]

Children would always be children. In the next two years, Leoni would enjoy Mario's company playing around the yard or inside the house; wrestling with one another until their heads and knees were bruised and stopping only when an aunt would enter the scene and shout: "*Valientes Filipinos!*" Leoni and Mario had a share of naughtiness teasing their youngest sibling for amusement. Sister Gemma died of illness before she could turn one and Chitang, the youngest was a petulant girl with allergies and fevers when she was young. Sometimes bursting into tears, Chitang would get even with them when Alfredo came to the scene, because he would side with her, being "the only girl". The three siblings, however, would help one another in times of great need. When an earthquake shook Manila, everyone in the house was terribly frightened. Chitang was so nervous that she fainted upstairs. Leoni and Mario, knowing how unsafe it would be to leave her upstairs, carried Chitang, who had grown into a five-foot seven lady, downstairs.[20]

Although culturally the Guerreros were not completely Americanized or pro-American, the material goods they procured for themselves through the U.S.-Philippine free trade betrayed the Americanization of the Philippine economy and every Filipino household, and their dependency on the American market. Indeed, Alfredo and Filomena were better able to look after the material needs of their two boys. They were showered with affection and love from their mother who brought them up "like princes". Filomena would buy them chic clothes: "sailor suits, Fauntleroy blouses, caps, satchels, jackets, play togs". When these did not fit them, they would become hand-me-downs to Chitang. They also had their own tailor, *Mang Roman* who maintained a shop at M.H. del Pilar. Occasionally, *Mang Roman* would come to the house to take their specifications on orders to be made or to deliver ready-made clothes. It would take them many hours to decide on the designs and fittings. They also had a houseboy who did chores for them.[21]

In such an environment, Leoni's early life could not but reflect an interesting mix of the American and the Hispanic. Cranky and easy to anger but still amiable, Leoni was used to "muttering cuss words". Whenever something stupid was said or done, he would blow up — his reaction spiced with *carajo* or *puñeta*. Conscious of his facial and bodily appearance, he would take in yeast, tonics, pills and other American products popularized by advertisements. Unusually tall, lean and with facial features of his mother, he grew up to be extraordinary confident. Mario who looked up to his elder brother was, however, less showy than Leoni, and reserved.[22]

One might find a third strain in the family, neither American nor Hispanic: an appreciation for what was Filipino. Leoni and his brother Mario were English-speakers and could only utter appalling Tagalog but they were sensitive to racial slurs aimed at Filipinos, which got them involved in fist-fights. Such was the milieu they grew up in that acted as a countervailing force against creeping Americanization. Whenever friends and relatives came calling at their home, one of them would sing, deliver a poem or play the piano. Leoni would rush into the living room and recite: "*Moreno pintan a Cristo, Morena la Magdalena, Morenos de los de mi tierra, Viva la gente morena!*" It was a verse honouring the dark-skinned peoples, placing them alongside Christ and Magdalene, which never failed to draw applause.[23]

"MOST SUCCESSFUL CHARM-AND-WIT PRACTITIONER"

Every gathering was a Guerrero affair especially during December when the town fiesta was celebrated with the culminating event, the *Bota Flores*, an offering of flowers to the *Virgen de Guía*, patroness of Ermita. For the three youngsters, however, Christmas Day was a much-awaited event. Every Yuletide season, inside the Guerrero compound, young people, sleepless the night before, would gather after Mass in various groups, then go from house to house of godparents and family friends in the early Christmas morning to ask for an *aguinaldo*.[24]

Leoni whom Chitang described as "the most successful charm-and-wit practitioner in the parish" would head his own group. They would go first to the homes of remote relatives and friends who had been forgotten. They would then visit his godparents, granduncles, and other close relatives where they could also expect to receive Christmas gifts, a duty that is fulfilled once a year. One Christmas morning, Leoni tried to get into the house of his grandparents' neighbours who were an old couple known to be well-off but so austere that even on a special holiday like Christmas, it seemed like nobody lived in the house because the door and the windows were shut. Leoni, bringing along Mario and Chitang, would greet their maid and disarming her with his smile, they would be admitted inside the house. Doña Tentay with a steady scowl on her face upon seeing Leoni would beam and urge the visitors to go upstairs. All seated, Leoni would then call her "Lola Tentay" and kiss the old lady's forehead. She would smile a little and order her maids to bring three glasses of orange juice. Chitang recalled Leoni's diplomatic manoeuvre:

> He would chatter away enthusiastically ... He would praise her earrings, remark on the coolness of her parlor. He would inquire about the gallants of her youth, the men she had condemned ... to a bleak existence by marrying somebody else. I could see by the brightness of her eyes that our *aguinaldos* increased with each artful phrase.[25]

Leoni would also talk about the latest news or even gossips in town: "Did she know that Doña Oñang ordered a new image of the Magdalene from that famous sculptor in Quiapo and that she was presenting it to the parish on Holy Week? Could it possibly have any connection with her libertine of a daughter?" The old lady who could not bear it any longer, perhaps tired, would rise straight to the bedroom while the three would hear the creak of opened wardrobe and drawers. After a silent deliberation in the room, she would come out perspiring, handing Mario and Chitang a two-peso bill each and reserving a large banknote for Leoni. Satisfied from all the fuss he went through, Leoni would kiss her again. The group would thank her and greet her again a Happy Christmas. Then, they would visit their Tío Pepe, a church organist; pass by the house of a cousin who had married a Spaniard; stay long at *Calle* Cortada reciting poems for Don León and Doña Aurora; and finally to an aunt who would hand them cheap editions of Spanish classics. In the end, it was he who made the most out of the Christmas bounty.[26]

Back home, in their mother's bedroom, Filomena would make an inventory of the gifts of cash or in kind, taking away the banknotes for safekeeping because her children were not to spend the money until they have reached the age of twenty-one. Alfredo would enter the room noticing Mario's sullen looks, Chitang's lachrymose face, and Leoni's grin. To appease the two, he would take out from his wallet some bills and all three would now have an equal amount in their respective envelopes. Leoni would fret about some injustice; Alfredo would shrug it off with a big laugh.[27]

Every summer, the whole family would travel to Antipolo to relish the cool breeze up the hill. They would visit the shrine of Our Lady of Peace and Good Voyage and enjoy a picnic at Hinulugang Taktak waterfalls. From such a refreshing experience in Antipolo, they would return to Ermita, the children ready for the coming school year in June.[28]

By the time Chitang was two, Leoni was attending the Ateneo. It would not be long before all three were going to school. Chitang went to Saint Theresa's College, an all-girls school at *Calle* San Marcelino. Mario would join Leoni at the Ateneo de Manila.[29]

Notes

1. Nakpil, *Myself*, pp. 2–3; Nick Joaquin, *Manila, my Manila* (Makati: Bookmark, 1999), p. 171; Robert R. Reed, *Colonial Manila: The Context of Hispanic Urbanism and Process of Morphogenesis* (University of California Press, 1978), p. 63; Ileana Maramag, "An urban history of Manila, 1898–1934" (PhD dissertation, University of the Philippines, 1988), pp. 58–59.
2. Lewis E. Gleeck, Jr., *The American Half-Century (1898–1946)* (Quezon City: New Day Publishers, 1998), pp. 60–61, 107, 204.
3. Nakpil, *Myself*, pp. 3–4; Luning B. Ira with Isagani R. Medina, *Streets of Manila* (Manila: GCF Books, 1977), p. 163; W.M. Guerrero, *Guerreros of Ermita*, p. 5.
4. Maria Luisa T. Camagay, *Kasaysayang panlipunan ng Maynila, 1765–1898* (Manila: The Author, 1992), p. 29; Ira and Medina, *Streets of Manila*, p. 63; Nakpil, *Myself*, pp. 1, 3–4.
5. Cristina E. Torres, "The Americanization of Manila, 1900–1921" (PhD dissertation, University of the Philippines, 2001), pp. 101–5, 236; Nakpil, *Myself*, p. 2; Maramag, "An urban history of Manila", p. 236. See also Cristina E. Torres, *The Americanization of Manila 1898–1921* (Quezon City: University of the Philippines Press, 2010).
6. W.M. Guerrero, *Guerreros of Ermita*, pp. 5, 8–9.
7. Carmen Guerrero Nakpil, *Woman Enough and Other Essays* (Quezon City: Ateneo de Manila University Press, 1999), p. 139; Nakpil, *Myself*, pp. 8, 11–12.
8. Alexander E.W. Salt, *An Introduction to the History of Manila: Notes on the historical origin of the names of the districts, barrios, streets, monuments, etc., of Manila, with some account of the fortifications of the Walled City* (Manila, 1912), p. 275; Carlos Quirino, Introduction to *The First Filipino*, p. xvi; E. Arsenio Manuel, *Dictionary of Philippine Biography* (Quezon City: Filipiniana Publishing, 1955), pp. 213–18. Gemma died barely a year after she was born. A global influenza

pandemic struck Manila and took her life, bringing great grief to the Guerrero family. When Gemma's coffin was interred at La Loma Cemetery, her brother León attempted to toss himself into the pit. There is some dispute about the order of the children's births. Wilfrido Ma. Guerrero believes Gemma was the firstborn; Carmen Guerrero Nakpil gives that distinction to León. See Nakpil, *Myself*, pp. 5, 8, 46–48, and W. Guerrero, *Guerreros of Ermita*, p. 10. Although in Spanish orthography an accent is put over *o* for Leon, Leoni himself was not consistent in his use of the accent on his name. Only in Spain and Latin American countries did the accent appear on his name. The new American dispensation weakened Filipinos' appreciation of their Hispanic heritage and the Spanish language.

9. Nakpil, *Myself*, pp. 7, 8, 11–12, 15.
10. Ibid., p. 12.
11. Ibid., pp. 12–13; Nakpil, *Woman*, p. 139.
12. Ibid., pp. 12–13.
13. Joaquin, *Manila*, p. 217; Florentino Rodao, "Spanish Language in the Philippines: 1900–1940", *Philippine Studies* 45, no. 1 (1997): 95; *Census of the Philippine Islands Taken under the Direction of the Philippine Legislature in the Year 1918*, Vol. 4, part 2 (Manila: Census Office of the Philippine Islands, 1920), pp. 699–700; Pedro Emmanuel Abelarde, *American Tariff Policy towards the Philippines, 1898–1946* (New York: King's Crown Press, 1947), p. 215; Shirley Jenkins, *American Economic Policy towards the Philippines* (Stanford: Stanford University Press, 1954), p. 33.
14. Nakpil, *Myself*, pp. 2, 16–18; W.M. Guerrero, *Guerreros of Ermita*, p. 59.
15. Nakpil, *Woman*, pp. 139, 141; Nakpil, *Whatever: A New Collection of Later Essays, 1987–2001* (Quezon City: Ateneo de Manila University Press, 2002), p. 25; Nakpil, *Myself*, p. 19; L.M. Guerrero, *The First Filipino: A biography of Jose Rizal* (Manila: Guerrero Publishing, 1998), p. vii.
16. Nakpil, *Woman*, pp. 139, 147; Nakpil, *Myself*, pp. 8, 48; Nakpil, *Whatever*, pp. 97, 102.
17. Nakpil, *Myself*, pp. 15–17.
18. Ibid., pp. 12, 25–27; L.M. Guerrero, "My grandfather as I knew him: An intimate glimpse of the life and manners of the greatest Filipino botanist, Leon Ma. Guerrero written by his grandson", *Philippines Free Press* (hereafter cited as *PFP*), 27 April 1935, p. 3.
19. Nakpil, *Woman*, p. 138; W.M. Guerrero, *Guerreros of Ermita*, pp. 5–6.
20. Nakpil, *Myself*, pp. 22, 45, 47; Nakpil, *Woman*, pp. 3, 4.
21. Nakpil, *Myself*, pp. 45, 47–49.
22. Ibid., p. 49.
23. Ibid., p. 23.
24. W.M. Guerrero, *Guerreros of Ermita*, p. 6; Nakpil, *Myself*, p. 147; Nakpil, *Woman*, p. 144.
25. Nakpil, *Woman*, pp. 148–49.
26. Ibid., pp. 149–50.
27. Ibid., p. 150.
28. Ibid., pp. 132–33.
29. Nakpil, *Whatever*, pp. 192, 211.

2

Education under American Jesuits

One of the best schools in pre-war Manila, the Jesuit-run Ateneo, established in 1859 and elevated to a secondary school in 1865, was located in Intramuros, a few minutes ride from home. But Leoni went to Saint Paul Institution at *Calle* Herran (now Pedro Gil Street) for the first two years of grade school. There he learned Basic English from French nuns. As to why his parents sent him to this school — something he himself wondered about all his life — it was because in 1921 Ateneo would only accept boys who had finished their first three primary grades. By 1923 due to requests from its alumni, the preparatory school offered grades from one to seven. In any case, Alfredo's decision for Leoni to study at the Ateneo followed family tradition. His father, brother, and he were Ateneans. His cousins graduated too from Ateneo.[1]

By the time Leoni enrolled in June 1923, it had been three years since the American Jesuits of Maryland-New York Province took over the school from the Spanish Jesuits and introduced an English-based eight-year curriculum: a four-year high school and a four-year college leading to the Bachelor of Arts degree, with provision for drama and theatre as well as sports and athletics, and even military drill. English had become the lingua franca in business and government. Alfredo chose what he thought was best for Leoni. It was at the Ateneo that Leoni's budding Americanization was reinforced by his American teachers, the English-language curriculum, and his exposure to Catholic liturgy.[2]

Almost everyone was a son of an Atenean in Leoni's third grade class where they were taught Christian doctrine in a half-hour class. Each month, he had to approach the sacraments of penance and the Eucharist so that by October 1923, he was admitted to the Sodality of the Virgin Mary. He learned to practise his First Friday devotions; undergo physical exercises every morning under the supervision of the physical director; and join in the games during recess or after class — a routine he would pursue in the coming years.³

Leoni's preparatory years showed a promising academic and extra-curricular aptitude, excelling in English, reading, spelling, arithmetic, geography, writing according to the Palmer system of penmanship, drawing, music, hygiene, good manners and right conduct, and physical science. Graduating with a bronze medal from the preparatory school and second to the highest performer, he entered high school where he had to grapple with the four-year classical Latin programme as well as English literature and composition, Spanish, algebra (in its place were geometry, biology, or physics in the second to fourth year), American history and civics (general history, economics, Philippine history and government), religion, public speaking including debate, and military drill and physical science.⁴

It was during enrolment that Leoni met Horacio de la Costa, a small boy from Mauban, Tayabas (now Quezon). A classmate told him that morning, pointing to a rather shy boy of eleven in a corner of the room: "You see that little boy? He is supposed to be a genius." The two would become close friends later.⁵

Although Leoni and Horacio attended different class sections, their names were frequently listed on the bulletin board and in the school's publication. A third name joined theirs: Jesus A. Paredes Jr. Academic achievers listed in the Roll of Honour were categorized into three levels of *First Honours in Studies*: First Honours for General Average and Two Courses; First Honours for General Average and One Course; and First Honours for One Course. In 1927, Leoni made it to the first, maintaining it till the end of the last quarter. Horacio made it to the third. Jesus made it to the second. The next ranking showed Horacio climbing a notch higher while Jesus tied with Leoni in the first. On the next, Horacio made it to the first and by March, he made to the second. The trio's names were a constant feature on the bulletin board, in the *Ateneo Monthly* and in the *Guidon*. Leoni somehow maintained his academic lead with only a margin of points over Horacio and Jesus. But in his Latin class, his cousin Lorenzo outdid him. Far from being too academic, he was a member of the Ateneo Corps of Cadets and was given cadet commission as second lieutenant in mid-February 1931.⁶

His performance at school inspired his siblings to excel, too. His mother Filomena was proud of him collecting his bunch of medals every school year, keeping them in a red box, and putting them for safekeeping inside an *aparador*. She showed this box once to young Chitang and explained to her why the medals were tied in bundles. The Jesuits had told her that they were tired of putting those medals on Leoni one at a time every year. It was convenient for them to put on Leoni "in one fell swoop".[7]

Of course, it was not all schoolwork for Leoni and his two siblings. At home after doing schoolwork during weekends, Leoni and Mario would learn to play the ukulele. As a hobby they collected programmes of Hollywood movies, keeping them in baskets under their beds. Leoni and Mario were allowed to watch two movies a week. Chitang was forbidden and contented herself with listening to them as they told her about the films. Born an artist, Mario could draw, play the guitar and violin. The three would practise their English at home with Leoni having the decided advantage while Chitang would be the object of laughter for she spoke, as she admitted, "a halting, Dutch-accented English".[8]

By mastering the English language at Ateneo, Leoni had become a consumer of American movies, which was the easiest and most effective way of imitating an American accent, not to mention assimilating values and attitudes extolling America. The school and the mass media were proving to be the channels of Leoni's Americanization. The latter's influence would manifest in Leoni's years at Ateneo, as he pursued journalism and discovered Anglo-American models for his writing.

THE *GUIDON* AND THE MUSE

It was through the *Guidon*, Ateneo's student publication, that Leoni, Horacio, and Jesus — by then the famed trio — cemented their partnership. They were part of its staff members and later its editors. It was in the Ateneo annual, *The Atenean*, however, which broke Leoni's name into print as the class historian for his class during his freshman and sophomore years in high school. The *Guidon* served as the conduit for common interests among the three. A close friendship blossomed among the three that lasted beyond college. First published in June 1929 during the editorship of college senior Manuel C. Colayco, the *Guidon* made Leoni a feature writer in early July 1929. Horacio was appointed one of the five department editors in November. They were promoted as feature editors in early January 1930. Colayco saw their potential; though they were merely junior high school students, they bested college students. From being an associate and news editor Leoni was elected editor-in-chief barely a month before his graduation in March 1931; Horacio was elected his associate editor

— a signal honour to two senior high school students. Encouraged by his achievement in school, Leoni wrote a short story, "Will o' the Wisp", and sent it to the *Graphic*. It would be his first appearance as a writer in a leading national magazine.[9]

In June at the Ateneo, Leoni enrolled for the Bachelor of Arts programme. The course consisted of classes in the principles of poetry and oratory, general literature, Latin, history, mathematics, general chemistry (mechanics taking its place in the sophomore year), debate and military science in the first two years and classes in philosophy, general literature, principles of journalism (philosophy of literature taking its place in the senior year), history (political economy), physics (calculus), astronomy and debate in the third and fourth years. He would excel again in his academic subjects, including in literature, going neck and neck with Horacio and Jesus. In a poetry class of combined sophomores and freshmen under Father Hugh J. McLaughlin, SJ, they studied the works of Virgil, Horace, Cicero and Homer. They next studied the works of Dante, Milton, and Shakespeare. They also went through the works of the English lyricists Shelley, Wordsworth, Keats, Herrick, Tennyson, Coleridge, and Thompson.[10]

Thus did the Americanization of the young Guerrero continue. Fed on a diet of Anglo-American literature, trained by McLaughlin in the fundamentals of writing poetry, and given exercises to polish their craft, Leoni and his friends continued to write and speak in English. So good were they that when they published their works in *Wings* and sent it to Father Connell, the author of *Study of Poetry*, a textbook they had used in class. The Jesuit found time to compliment them. He wrote from the United States to Horacio, "I can say without flattery that I have rarely read a series of freshman compositions in prose or verse as excellent on the whole as yours." He specifically named Leoni, Jesus, and him as having reached the stage of "fertility" in a writer.[11]

No doubt, Leoni's poetic ability came from a tradition in the family. His uncle, Fernando, has published a collection of Spanish poetry. One of Leoni's poems, "Student Days", told of his longing for a carefree past; his peers and he "vainly wish for days when we were happily unwise, and young and free, strangely curious, powerless and glad..." Another of his poems, "I Did Not Know", spoke of flowers, why they came into being but realized in the third stanza that they were meant for his beloved. These two poems were exercises in versification intended to acquaint himself with the muse.

I did not know why God made flowers,
Why He had sprinkled starlets on the land —
I dreamt in dimly-scented bowers,
And did not know what purpose moved His Hand.

Shy violets and lilies slender,
The splendorous burst of orchids as they fade,
Strangely scented, strangely tender,
Why was all this perfumed nation made?

And then, the other day I saw
You in your garden — now I seek no more —
I saw the flower in your hair let low,
And then I knew what God made flowers for.[12]

But, who was this girl whom he loved?

The girl alluded to in the poem was one among several. Members of the opposite sex would call Leoni at home. To dismiss a girl over the telephone whom he did not like, he would instruct the houseboy: "Say I'm out." Overhearing him, Chitang would ask: "Why don't you like her?" "Never throw yourself at a boy," he would say. "And by the way, never write a letter like this one." It was a mushy letter written by another admirer. He would advise her that if she liked a boy that way "write it but don't send it". In any case, he was romancing and dating several girls at the same time. He would talk about his exploits, about a girl whom he liked most, weighing each girl according to his standard to Mario who was doing the same thing.[13]

One breakfast morning, his flirting with the girls came to a hot revelation. Filomena brought out a letter from a Spanish mother complaining of Leoni's unwanted advances to her daughter. Enclosed in it was Leoni's letter to Dolores, a tall and pretty student at Saint Theresa's high school, which she partly read aloud. Out of this hullabaloo, Chitang would badger him to his mortification because of a phrase in the letter she turned into a chant: *Dolor de mis Dolores*. "Like father, like son" soon, Leoni went to the cabarets that his father frequented. In no time, he was caught, and his father, joined by his mother, reprimanded him severely.[14]

While his visits to the cabarets must have stopped, he continued to master English at Ateneo. His facility in writing English was further polished under the tutelage of the American Jesuits. Every day they were given exercises to master its syntax and style by writing essays, their output to be marked by the professor. The professor taught them how to parse a sentence. They were given passages from an English literature textbook to paraphrase. In literature classes, they were asked to read Catholic authors, namely, G.K. Chesterton, Hilaire Belloc and Francis Thompson. Leoni imbibed the wordy style of his favourite Belloc, the British Roman Catholic writer and author who, along with Chesterton, initiated a literary renaissance in Britain.[15]

Yet Leoni did not use English to extol America. In 1933, his entry to an essay writing contest won. Using the church to serve as the metaphor to the Spanish heritage, he keenly argued that "Spain made the Philippines" and even refuted the claim that the Americans came to civilize Filipinos. He believed that it was Spain, which brought civilization. Denying that Catholicism had become irrelevant, he contended that between communism and Catholicism, "only the church can eventually save the world from itself." Thus, while Leoni was becoming proficient in English and appreciative of American culture, he nonetheless maintained his pro-Hispanic, pro-Catholic sentiments, nurtured in his home, though also denying the richness of indigenous culture. While it was true that Spain made the Philippines one nation, it was also true that before colonialism there was an archipelago of many nations in varying degrees of civilization.[16]

THE DEBATER

In a class in general literature again under McLaughlin, barely two months away from the semestral break in January 1932, Leoni was among the seven students selected to participate in a public symposium-contest, dubbed "Quo Vadis? A Seminar on Modern Literature". While Horacio and Jesus delivered on "Free Verse" and on the "Foundations of Modern Tendencies in Literature" respectively, he talked on "Stars of Hope in Modern Literature". That morning, they were dressed in their formal *chaquetillas*. Leoni was the last to speak. Composed, he went to the podium and delivered his piece. "Never was an audience more silent," reported the *Aegis*, "enthralled by the majesty of flowing periods, the glitter of unassailable reasoning, the sharpness of discerning observation". The judges awarded Horacio the Gold Medal for Thought and Literary Excellence and Leoni the Silver Medal for Oratorical Excellence.[17]

Back in high school, Leoni joined the High School Senior Debating Society; several debate meetings of which he served as chairman. At the Annual Semi-Public Prize Debate, his side chose to defend the proposition: "Resolved: that religious instruction in public schools is both necessary and practicable." Horacio's team readied arguments that would prove the proposition untenable. Judges awarded Horacio the medal for the best speaker. Leoni's loss to Horacio did not deter him from pursuing his ambition to be a champion debater. He was rewarded by becoming the president of the college Freshmen Debating Society, then was twice elected as vice-president and finally president in his senior year. During his sophomore year, he enrolled in classes in rhetoric under Father Joseph A. Mulry SJ, to sharpen his skills in oratory and public debate.[18]

Under Mulry, the class was taught the proper ways of speaking and writing clearly. Mulry trained them on how to persuade people effectively either orally or by the written word. He also influenced his "Mulry's boys", as they were called, with his strong Catholic position on social justice that gave a contrary view to secular liberalism and communism in vogue at the time. He even baptized Horacio with the nickname "Skeezix" after the comic strip character. He also gave Francisco Rodrigo the nickname "Soc" after Socrates the year before.[19]

Classes with Mulry were interrupted when a fire razed Ateneo in mid-August 1932. They had to move to Padre Faura Street, to the amenities of San Jose Seminary, which had to be moved to another site. Classes were suspended until November so that Leoni and friends spent the rest of the semester at Padre Faura, their home for the next two years until their graduation.[20]

Towards the end of the second semester in 1933, a public presentation was held called "Democracy, an Exposé on Rhetoric". As one of the five participants, Leoni spoke on the Boholano hero, Francisco Dagohoy. Skeezix, as Horacio was now popularly called, satirized the silly facets of democracy in his speech "The Decay of Democracy". The two won except that Leoni got the silver medal while Skeezix got the gold. The feeling must have been mutual for Leoni when Soc disclosed, "Our only ambition then was to defeat de la Costa in any symposium. He would always be first." This was, of course, in the spirit of friendly competition. Then, one day, in a contest at Saint Scholastica's auditorium, an audience of *colegialas* instead of a panel of judges chose Soc over Skeezix as the best orator but only "by a fluke" as Soc laughingly admitted, after he found out that the girls chose him because he was "cute".[21]

Aside from being freshmen debate club president, Leoni was also a member of the Knight of the Blessed Sacrament Sodality (KBS), promoter of the League of the Sacred Heart (LSH) and member of Alpha Beta fraternity, staff writer for *La Defensa* and class vice president. *La Defensa* was a Catholic weekly publication begun in 1920 as a daily newspaper by the Asociación de la Prensa Catolica, Inc. He maintained for three years his membership of the *Guidon*, the Alpha Beta where he rose from being honourable lictor and right honourable vice consul to consul, KBS and LSH. During his third year, he was a member of the Glee Club, the Ateneo Catholic Instruction League wherein he volunteered to teach youngsters in preparation for their first communion and the Ateneo Players' Guild in which he once served as vice-president. He also headed the Rizal Book Club. He became known as "Rah-jah Guerrero" — a popular member of "The Jumping Jacks" who began cheering for the "blue-and-white" athletes since his high school senior year — and was also once a playing coach to the Bachelor of Arts class basketball team with Skeezix acting as the team manager.[22]

Notes

1. Alegre and Fernandez, *Writer and his Milieu*, p. 85; Nakpil, *Whatever*, p. 192; *Ateneo de Manila Annual Commencement 1920-1921* (Manila: Ateneo, 1921), p. 13. *Ateneo Monthly* (hereafter cited as *AM*), March 1924, no page.
2. For a brief history of the Ateneo, see Jose S. Arcilla, S.J., "Ateneo de Manila: Problems and Policies, 1859-1939" and Raul J. Bonoan, S.J., "Ateneo de Manila: Past and Future", in *The Jesuit Educational Tradition: The Philippine Experience*, edited by Raul J. Bonoan, SJ and James A. O'Donnell, SJ (Budhi Papers no. 9, Ateneo de Manila University, 1988), pp. 29-50; 51-56.
3. *AM* 1, no. 5 (November 1922), no page; *AM Commencement Number* (March 1923): 412; *AM* 2, no. 5 (November 1923): 191; Ateneo de Manila Preparatory School Class of 1924, *Graduates, Awards, Honors* (March 1924), pp. 9-11.
4. *AM Commencement Number* (March 1924): 422; (1925): 504; (1926): 546; (1927): 515; Ateneo de Manila Preparatory School, *Graduates, Awards, Honors* (March 1927), pp. 1, 3, 11, 13. For the curriculum during the preparatory grades and high school, see *AM* (March 1924), no page.
5. Paulynn P. Sicam, "A Man for all Seasons", *Goodman: General Motors Philippines Publication* 2 (April 1977): 11-15.
6. *AM* 6, no. 2 (August 1927): 92; 6, no. 3 (September 1927): 146; 6, no. 5 (November 1927): 369; 6, no. 7 (February 1928): 438; *The Guidon* (hereafter cited as *TG*), 15 November 1929; 10 January, 15 January, 25 June, 9 August, 6 September, 18 October, 17 November 1930; 31 January, 4 March 1931. See also Roberto M. Paterno, "The Young Horacio de la Costa: A Biographical Background 1916-1945", in *Horacio de la Costa: Selected Writings of his Youth 1927-1945*, edited by Roberto M. Paterno (Manila: 2B3C Foundation, 2002), p. xxiv.
7. Nakpil, *Myself*, p. 48.
8. Ibid., Nakpil, *Woman*, p. 139.
9. Leon Ma. Guerrero, "First Year A", *The Atenean* (Manila: Ateneo, 1928), p. 517; "Second Year A", *The Atenean* (Manila: Ateneo, 1929), p. 93; *TG*, 6 July, 1 November 1929; 10 January, 20 March, 6 September 1930; 4 March 1931; Leon Ma. Guerrero,

"Will o' the Wisp: A commencement short story of one who chose to tread on the path of glory", *Graphic*, 18 March 1931, p. 29.
10. "Bachelor of Arts course", *AM* (Commencement, 1926), no page; *TG*, 7 July 1932; 28 October 1933; 31 August 1934; *Wings: A Literary Semi-annual* 1, no. 1 (October Issue), no page.
11. *TG*, 15 July 1932; *Wings: A Literary Semi-annual* 1, no. 2 (March Issue): 21.
12. *Wings: A Literary Semi-annual* 1, no. 2 (March Issue): 21, 69.
13. Nakpil, *Myself*, pp. 49–50.
14. Ibid., pp. 113–15.
15. Alegre and Fernandez, *Writer and his Milieu*, pp. 71, 73, 75; Horacio de la Costa, SJ, *Light Cavalry* (Manila: Catholic Bishops' Conference of the Philippines, 1997), p. 426. See also *TG*, 2 August 1933.
16. Leon Ma. Guerrero, "A Legacy in Stone", *The 1933 Ateneo Aegis* (Manila: Ateneo, 1933), pp. 249–54.
17. *The 1932 Ateneo Aegis* (Manila: Ateneo, 1932), p. 221; *TG*, 23 January 1932; 13 February 1932.
18. *The Ateneo Aegis 1931* (Manila: Ateneo, 1931), p. 98; *TG*, 26 July, 9 August 1930; 4 March 1931; 23 July 1934; *The 1932 Ateneo Aegis* (Manila: Ateneo, 1932), p. 217.
19. Paterno, "Young Horacio de la Costa", p. xxxiv.
20. For a vivid account on the fire of 1932, see de la Costa, *Light Cavalry*, pp. 414–19.
21. Virgilio Canivel, "Exposé of Oratory", *The 1933 Ateneo Aegis* (Manila: Ateneo, 1933), p. 218; *TG*, 22 December 1932; Sicam, "A Man for all Seasons", p. 12.
22. *Wings: A Literary Semi-annual* 1, no. 2 (March Issue): 120; *The 1935 Ateneo Aegis* (Manila: Ateneo, 1935), pp. 34, 160–61; *The 1933 Ateneo Aegis* (Manila: Ateneo, 1933), p. 201; *The Ateneo Aegis Jubilee Number 1859–1934* (Manila: Ateneo, 1934), p. 207; *TG*, 9 August 1930; 25 September 1931; 26 August 1933; Claudio Teehankee, "A Testament of Nationalism and Excellence", in *In Memoriam*, p. 8; Nakpil, *Whatever*, p. 193; Sicam, "A Man for all Seasons", p. 12.

3

The Humorist as Critic, Writer and Actor

Selected editor-in-chief in March 1931, Leoni dominated the journalistic scene at Ateneo and became a champion of Catholicism, another area of contradictions in his formation (modern-American, Catholic-Hispanic). Under previous editors, *Guidon* was an outlet for programmes and activities for Catholic action. Under his management, Leoni believed that Catholic college newspapers such as *Guidon* were necessary to define the position of school authorities like the Ateneo. As editor, he had to beat the deadline for the timely release of the bi-weekly, compelling him and his staff, including Skeezix as associate editor, to work till the wee hours of the day. Believing that four associate editors were enough to fulfil the job, he eliminated the position of news editor but organized the news staff. While constantly on the lookout for innovations and strictly following the schedule, although late releases had to be occasionally put up with, he created a large following because of his witty and funny column.[1]

Initiated prior to his editorship, Leoni's longest-running column "Totoy to Momoy" or "Momoy to Totoy" — patterned as correspondence between two friends — was read by many even beyond Ateneo. Having derived inspiration from American humorist Irvin S. Cobb and English comic author P.G. Wodehouse, Leoni wrote on anything, from plays to carnivals, Christmas to personalities. Outwardly a gossip column, he would occasionally use humour to lampoon various subjects. An American university publication, *The Creightonian*, praised the peerless humour in every letter, followed by recognition from University of the Philippines (UP) Professor Carlos P. Romulo, adviser to the College Editors Guild (CEG), an umbrella organization of leading student publications from different universities in Manila. While funny to some, others, however, were hurt when they were the subject of Leoni's humour.[2]

Annually, Saint Theresa's College would hold a fair to raise funds for the benefit of the Belgian missions. For one to enjoy the fair and at the same time support the missions, one had to buy tickets sold in booths displaying items for sale or offering games like Truth or Consequence. Leoni, a fair-goer, wrote about the tickets thus: "They'll fleece the sheep and they're fleecing them still." An irate *colegiala* confronted Chitang and told her: "Tell your brother he's a real brute!" When she told this to Leoni, he shrugged and laughed it off for he was still the darling of Theresian girls.[3]

In this style of writing Leoni began to get reckless. Thus, another of his literary clashes involved Jose Garcia Villa, a distant relative. Suspended for a year by the UP for publishing obscene poetry in a local magazine, Villa returned to writing verses and had five poems published in the *Philippines Free Press*, the leading bilingual magazine in Spanish and English since 1908, in October 1932. A pompous letter accompanied the poems, deriding the way poetry was being written in the Philippines and claiming that his was something unconventional but nevertheless original. Leoni and Skeezix, poets in their own right, found the poems unacceptable with its novel, unusual structure. In Villa's "How to Tell: Poem for Cecile", syllabication of words were objectionable in modern English such that in the third stanza, loveliness was only left with l while the other letters (oveliness) started on the next line. They decided to address this in a letter to the *Free Press* following another pseudonymous author who parodied Villa's verse. In their letter, they made fun of Villa's disregard for proper English. Three funny verses imitated Villa's style under the heading "etcetera". One was subtitled "prelude".[4]

A Villa fan came to the poet's rescue, citing envy behind such attacks. Leoni and Skeezix made a brilliant riposte, a week after another person sent another letter critical of Villa's poetic effusion. Quoted in full was G.K. Chesterton's poem "To a Modern Poet", whose author, in their opinion, "will not be accused of envying mr villa". Villa kept silent and waited for another year. The *Free Press* out of fair-mindedness published his "Poems for an Unhumble One", naming Leoni in particular along with Vicente M. Hilario, a UP Professor of English. His five poems were preceded by explanations maintaining his rejection of grammar in his poetry for what he called "the higher laws of vision".[5]

Although a new editor-in-chief took the reins in 1932, Leoni as associate editor continued submitting pieces for publication, maintained his old column and opened another bylined column, "Etc...". More serious in tone and more provocative than "Totoy to Momoy", Leoni would attack, pillory and tear to pieces pretentious and presumptuous claims. And a writer from the UP would taste the bitterness of his venom.[6]

Herald writer Salvador P. Lopez wrote in his column about Ateneo de Manila as "the home of lost causes". Anti-Catholic in bias, he believed that in many instances of religious fanaticism, faith had become reason. Like a good knight in defence of his alma mater and faith, Leoni wrote that Ateneo stood for Catholicism as religion, patriotism and cultural education in preparation for life. Leoni maintained that "line of progress goes from reason to faith" because "faith is not a surrender but a conquest", further claiming that the historical foundation of the Church could only lead to the acceptance of faith. Charging Lopez as being obsessed with the "modern spirit of toleration, which more often than not is toleration of error", Leoni called him "a lost cause" for "he is too proud to learn".[7]

"Etc..." became the purveyor of progressive or even radical, at times heretical, ideas. At the height of agrarian problems in the country, Leoni supported the distribution of small lots to farmers out of the haciendas because "we must destroy the problem by creating the farmer." On Filipino literature, he wrote that it "is either Filipino or literature" and that "there are two things needful for the fulfillment of a national literature: a national philosophy and a national tongue" but "the first we are gradually losing and the second we never had." When the issue of divorce was a hot national topic, he believed it to be wrong "because its nature is such that it cannot but be wrong" but betrayed his sympathy to it when he wrote at the end that difficulties could be prevented if the Church would only be "more reasonable" and "relent in extreme cases". While maintaining his two columns, he got involved in another bi-weekly, *Today*, as associate editor.[8]

As editor of the *Guidon*, Leoni rubbed shoulders with other campus editors affiliated with the collegiate guild. Once at a CEG meeting, Leoni confronted the *Collegian* contingent from UP. Armando J. Malay, the *Collegian* editor, had complained that they were not informed about the CEG election at the previous meeting. Malay wrote in his diary, "There was a lengthy debate on when the notice for the elections was sent out. The staff suspected that the elections had been fixed so we couldn't aspire for the presidency." Re-elected CEG president, Ernesto "Ernie" Rodriguez Jr of the *Guidon* told the UP contingent that he was not to be blamed for the delay but the Bureau of Posts. A *Collegian* news editor suggested that in "reparation", the *Collegian* adviser be made the CEG adviser. Leoni, the presiding officer, was among those who objected, resulting in "an uproar". The *Collegian* delegation, except its two staff members, walked out and withdrew its membership from CEG, only to be back the following year with the election of a new editor.[9]

Reading works by popular American writers such as Zane Grey and Stephen Leacock at the library encouraged Leoni to write humorous stories about love and its misadventures for the *Free Press*. His story, "Hello! Miss Information" came out in September 1933. A fan of Rafael Sabatini, the Anglo-Italian writer of popular romantic and piratical adventures, Leoni came up in January 1934 with "Pirates Ahoy!"[10]

During the summer, which in the Philippines meant March to April, of 1934 Leoni began working part-time at the *Free Press*. Using his popular *Guidon* name Totoy, he would pun news stories of the day in "The Times in Rhymes". On its 21 April issue, about Japanese investing money in abaca fields in Bicol, again he revealed his anti-Japanese feelings in the following verse: "Oh, let the Japs get our abaca. | Let them spend their sweat and pelf, | Let the Nippon have more rope | With which to hang himself!" Was his anti-Japan attitude an offshoot of his pro-Americanism? In a debate whether the Philippines should adopt Occidental or Oriental culture, Leoni defended the West by arguing that oriental culture would prove catastrophic to the country. Japan, an oriental culture, had completely occupied Manchuria since 1932; in 1933 and 1934 it was bold enough to offer itself as a possible successor to the Americans in the event of Philippine independence. The Japanese were trying to control internal trade and increased their presence through investments. Threatened by this arrogance, Senate President Manuel L. Quezon, the soon-to-be president of the Commonwealth, asked for more American investments, while Senator Claro M. Recto favoured closer economic collaboration with the United States. Incidentally, the Guerreros employed a Japanese to look after the roses in their roof garden. He turned out to be a spy.[11]

The works of detective fictionist S.S. Van Dine (pseudonym of Willard Huntington Wright) were part of his popular reading fare. At about this time, murder mysteries had become fashionable among high school and college students, with works by Edgar Wallace topping the bill. This opportunity spurred Leoni to write his first detective story, "30,000 Suspects", published in two parts in the *Free Press*.[12]

After several detective short stories, Leoni, tired of two-part stories, tried his hand at writing a murder mystery novelette along with Gilberto Zamora and Jose J. Reyes, writers who got their first break in the *Graphic* like him. Serialized in ten parts, "The Case of the Seven Suspects" ran from early February to mid-April 1935, forcing Leoni to withdraw his participation in the first public defence of scholastic philosophy in the country, the culminating affair in celebration of Ateneo's seventy-fifth founding anniversary.[13]

From reading the European masters in Spanish translation and Rizal in the original, Leoni's literary diet changed. His Ateneo education in the 1930s turned him more "*Sajonista*" — the term Joaquin used for the Americanized Filipino — as he became more acquainted with British and American authors, mainly of pulp fiction, and these in turn influenced his literary inclinations. The 1930s had become the American decade supplanting the preceding decade, the 1920s, which was more European and Hispanic than American.[14]

AMERICAN-ACCENTED KING LEAR RIDING IN A JITNEY

There is yet one more aspect of Leoni's school days that showed the push and pull of Americanization. Ateneo of the late 1920s and early 1930s was no different from Rizal's time. Dramatics played an important part in Jesuit pedagogy with the difference that the plays were staged in English. Students became actors on the stage in a play directed by the Jesuit fathers. Shakespeare was a staple.[15]

Like his cousins, Leoni did theatre acting. His involvement at first was minimal, as a member of the Ateneo Players Guild. During his junior year in high school, he was part of the publicity committee for Edmond Rostand's *L'Aiglon*. He was given a break in January 1930 as Reggie Thornhill in George M. Cohan's *Seven Keys to Baldplate* under the direction of Father Raymond J.H. Kennedy, SJ. It was also during this year when as associate editor for the *Ateneo Aegis*, Leoni wrote a review on dramatics, a section he continued in the following year.[16]

Then, during Leoni's senior year, Mulry challenged their class to stage a play "similar to the medieval European morality plays". The upshot was *The Datu's Jewels*, staged at Ateneo in August 1930. It was a one-act play about the chieftain's missing jewels. It was supposedly stolen by one of the five suspects. The nine-member cast included Leoni who wrote the play. The plot revolved around the resolution of the crime by illustrating pre-Hispanic judicial processes on theft — although Bernad doubts the "anthropological accuracy" of the play's portrayal of the native custom of trial by ordeal. The attempt by Leoni to write about pre-Hispanic custom was laudable. He was trying to Filipinize the usually European- or American-oriented dramas of the school. In September, he played a commoner in the supporting cast of *Julius Caesar* under the direction of the newly arrived Father Anthony V. Keane, SJ.[17]

While others got their debut as versatile theatre actors in previous plays, Leoni had to wait for two more years after the production of Rostand's *Cyrano de Bergerac* in September 1931. He had to divide his time between his editorial work at the *Guidon* and his obligations to the guild. His long wait was over when Father Henry L. Irwin, SJ assumed control over dramatic productions in Ateneo. When Irwin thought of a play to kick off the year 1933, he decided to stage the Shakespearean tragedy *King Lear*. In choosing the cast, he abandoned his predecessors' method of holding general auditions with a jury selecting the actors. Instead, actors had a private audition with him. For this play, Leoni was chosen for the lead role because "he has the advantages of a commanding stature; a deep, resonant voice; a natural attitude for dramatics and an unusual delicacy of interpretation." After several months of gruelling preparation, the cast had a gala performance in October 1933 at the Manila Grand Opera House where all seats were taken. The performance elicited praise from the Manila press. *El Debate* described it as a "titanic play". The press unanimously admired Leoni for his brilliant portrayal. *El Debate* focused its attention on him in Act V, which drew repeated applause from the audience. The *Tribune* cited Act I and the "raving scene" in Act III, the most difficult to execute demanding a lot of rehearsals from him.[18]

His family supported him throughout his years in acting including his last portrayal in the Buskin cast as Richard in *King Henry IV*, and his directorial debut in a play featuring Sherlock Holmes for the All-Frat Fallen Arches Show. Whenever the guild needed props like sofas, rugs, screens, and drapes, Irish-American Father William Jordan, SJ, the Jesuit schoolmaster, would come to their house and Leoni's mother would gladly lend them from their living room. That was the time when plays were held at the *salón de actos* in Intramuros. His family and relatives watched his stardom as King Lear.[19]

It was also about this time that Leoni participated in radio programmes. Americans pioneered the first radio broadcast in 1906 and the first radio news programme in 1920. Two years later, the radio was brought to the Philippines — the first in Asia — and radio stations were established. One of these was KZRM or Radio Manila, set up in 1927. Leoni debuted in 1931, during the first radio debate held in the country, where he would also win the award for best speaker. He next appeared in a Filipino youth programme called *Stage of the World*, participated by mostly Ateneans. The script, written by Leoni, emulated the *March of Time*, an American radio news programme started in March 1931 that theatrically presented news events with sound and music.[20]

His American-sounding accent created a large following. In fact, in his debut portrayal of *King Lear* in 1933, his vocal performance was widely praised: "For more than three hours the public listened to the exquisite verses of Shakespeare *in a pronunciation and intonation rarely heard from Filipino students* [my emphasis]." Years later, before World War II erupted, a colleague in radio, Francisco Trinidad, said that: "For emphasis in announcing, no one can beat Leon Ma. Guerrero. Not even Americans!" That Leoni can even outdo an American speaks a lot about his Americanization.[21]

During his college years, Leoni made friendships that would continue after graduation. It was outside Ateneo that he and his friends would discuss anything under the sun without the guidance of any superior. Great minds met at the Churey's, a coffee shop near Ateneo, where arguments ran without end; it was the lifeblood of the place. They talked about the most mundane to the most profound subject. From basketball games to Robert Montgomery's acting, from a historical discussion of the English Reformation to the political import of the Hare-Hawes Cutting Bill, Leoni propounded his ideas in support of one argument after another.[22]

On the other hand, Leoni would rather reminisce about the long hours spent in *panciterias* drinking liquor in between discussions and afterwards going to Luneta to play football: "Our class had regular sessions in *panciterias* like Antigua and Nueva near Escolta. We drank Sauterne, a horrible sweet white wine, and muscatel. God, I don't know how we would stand such horrible liquor. Then slightly inebriated, we would go to the old Luneta to play football at three in the morning." He did not say that once his intoxicated gang including Skeezix was caught by the Manila police climbing the flagpole in the Luneta. The Ateneo suspended them from their classes. Who its mastermind was they closely guarded but Chitang knew that it was her brother.[23]

Together with Skeezix and Jesse as *summa cum laude*, Leoni emerged top of his class of Batch '35 consisting of other seven Bachelor of Arts graduates. In March 1935, a graduation ceremony was held at the Manila Grand Opera House. On the day of their graduation, Leoni recalled vividly, "We were supposed to wear togas. De la Costa and our other pals, in an early gesture of socialism, decided not to go in our family cars but instead hired a jitney that we rode to go to our graduation, in our togas." For his farewell column to "Etc..." Leoni imagined a conversation among four graduating students in their togas, wondering what would happen next. It might have been the chat inside the jitney: "Santos: 'What begins?' Francia: 'Adventure begins.' Peña: 'Work begins.' Vargas: 'Life begins.' Santos: 'No, gentlemen, the answer is, we don't know what begins.' Francia: 'Well, let's find out.'" And Leoni would find out in the law school and in the *Free Press*.[24]

Notes

1. *TG*, 23 August 1930; 4 March, 25 September 1931.
2. *TG*, 20 July 1929; 25 September 1931; 28 February, 22 March, 29 September 1934; Leon Ma. Guerrero, "Library", *The Ateneo Aegis: A Literary Quarterly*, March 1930, p. 161.
3. Nakpil, *Myself*, pp. 113–14.
4. Jonathan Chua, comp. and ed., *The Critical Villa: Essays in Literary Criticism by Jose Garcia Villa* (Quezon City: Ateneo de Manila University Press, 2002), p. 48; *PFP*, 15 October 1932; *PFP*, 22 and 29 October 1932.
5. *PFP*, 5, 12, 19 November 1932; *PFP*, 17 June 1933. See also Chua, *The Critical Villa*, pp. 254–59.
6. *TG*, 2 August 1933.
7. *TG*, 23 January 1934.
8. *TG*, 23 January, 23 July, 15 October 1934.
9. Marites N. Sison and Yvonne T. Chua, *Armando J. Malay, a Guardian of Memory: The Life and Times of a Filipino Journalist and Activist* (Manila: Anvil, 2002), pp. 55–56; *Philippine Collegian*, 3 August 1934.
10. L.M. Guerrero, "Library", p. 161; Leon Ma. Guerrero, "Hello! Miss Information? A short story", *PFP*, 23 September 1933, pp. 12–13, 51; "Pirates Ahoy! A short story", *PFP*, 13 January 1934, pp. 12, 13, 45.
11. Leon Ma. Guerrero, "The Times in Rhymes by Totoy", *PFP*, 21 April 1934, p. 28; *TG*, 15 October 1934; Gleeck, *American Half-Century*, pp. 361–62; 370–71; Nakpil, *Myself*, p. 12.
12. L.M. Guerrero, "Library", p. 161; "They like thrillers" *PFP*, 10 September 1932, p. 16; Leon Ma. Guerrero, "30,000 Suspects: A Short Story" part I, *PFP*, 7 July 1934, pp. 12, 13, 49; part II, *PFP*, 14 July 1934, pp. 12, 13, 48.
13. *TG*, 18 February 1935; A.E. Litiatco, "Giving beginners a break", *Graphic*, 1 February 1934, p. 11; Leon Ma. Guerrero Jr., Gilberto Zamora and Jose J. Reyes, "The Case of the Seven Suspects"; Chapter I, *PFP*, 9 February 1935, pp. 16, 17, 48, 49; Chapter II, *PFP*, 16 February 1935, pp. 16, 17, 48, 49; Chapter III, *PFP*, 23 February 1935, pp. 16, 17, 43, 44; Chapter IV, *PFP*, 2 March 1935, pp. 16, 17, 43, 44; Chapter V, *PFP*, 9 March 1935, pp. 16, 17, 44; Chapter VI, *PFP*, 16 March 1935, pp. 16, 17, 48; Chapter VII, *PFP*, 23 March 1935, pp. 16, 17, 44; Chapter VIII, *PFP*, 30 March 1935, pp. 16, 42, 43, 44; Chapter IX, *PFP*, 6 April 1935, pp. 16, 17, 44; Chapter X, *PFP*, 13 April 1935, pp. 16, 17, 42, 43, 44.
14. Nick Joaquin, "Pop Culture: The American Years", *Filipino Heritage*, Vol. 10, edited by Alfredo Roces (Manila: Lahing Pilipino, 1978), p. 2273; Nick Joaquin, "First 50 Years Were the 'Most!'", *PFP*, 30 August 1958, pp. 50, 58.

15. Miguel A. Bernad, *Dramatics at the Ateneo: A History of Three Decades 1921–1952* (Manila: Ateneo Alumni Association, 1977), pp. vi, 3, 8. See also *TG*, 2 August, 30 September, 17 October 1933.
16. Bernad, *Dramatics*, pp. 44, 51, 54, 229–31; *TG*, 12 July, 9 August 1930; L.M. Guerrero, "Dramatics", *The Ateneo Aegis: A Literary Quarterly*, March 1930, pp. 167–69; L.M. Guerrero, "Dramatics", *The Ateneo Aegis: Commencement*, March 1931, pp. 99–100.
17. Bernad, *Dramatics*, p. 51.
18. Ibid., pp. 59, 78, 80, 84–85, 233.
19. *TG*, 23 January, 30 November 1934; Alegre & Fernandez, *Writer and his Milieu*, p. 72; Nakpil, *Whatever*, p. 192.
20. Elizabeth L. Enriquez, "Appropriation of Colonial Broadcasting: A History of Early Radio in the Philippines, 1922–1946" (PhD dissertation, University of the Philippines, 2005), pp. 57, 67; del Rio, "Guerrero in Radio: Once a Newspaperman, he finds scripts and magazine stuff equally stimulating to write", *Graphic* (26 December 1940), pp. 58–59.
21. Simuon Almario, "Radio Gossip", *Graphic*, 26 December 1940, p. 58.
22. De la Costa, *Light Cavalry*, pp. 420, 424.
23. Sicam, "A Man for all Seasons", p. 12; Nakpil, *Myself*, p. 105.
24. Ibid., p. 13; *TG*, 9 March 1935.

4

Juggling Law and Journalism on the Eve of War

In the summer of 1935, Leoni decided to work as a staff member of the *Free Press*. His work was interrupted in April when his grandfather died. As a tribute to Don León, he wrote a personal essay published in the *Free Press*. In the necrological rites held three months later, he represented the family and expressed gratitude for the honour accorded to his grandfather. A scholarship opportunity shaped in part his decision to take up law at Philippine Law School (PLS) in June at *Calle* Bustillos in Sampaloc — he would be a full scholar. He was not the first in the family to take up law — two of his uncles, Fernando María and Cesar María, were lawyers. That he had become enamoured of the legal profession was shown by a short story, "An Enemy of Caesar", he wrote in April.[1]

Before classes started in June, he went to Japan as a tourist and came out with several articles about his trip, which happened after the Sakdal uprising in early May. He reported on how the Japanese treated Benigno Ramos, the exiled leader of the Sakdals, whom many Japanese considered as "the great liberator" of the Philippines. One article told about their stay in Japan: the first week was spent in a hotel that was no different in Manila and the second week in Fukidecho where he and his companions were able to experience Japanese hospitality, taste sashimi, sleep on the floor and take a shower in a public bath. Another article warned readers about a travel racket to Japan run by a crook who would make a big profit out of the credulous tourist.[2]

Having enrolled in night classes, Leoni worked during the day in the *Free Press* with offices at *Avenida* Rizal in Santa Cruz. The editorial office occupied half of the third floor that had at its centre its founder and publisher Robert McColluch Dick's desk. Behind it was the associate editor's and behind each post sat the staff writers. Behind one of these desks was Leoni with his foot up on his chair and a pipe in his mouth. F. Theo Rogers, a Bostonian of Irish descent, acted as the boss when Dick went abroad. Frederic S. Marquardt was the associate editor and the rest of his colleagues were D.L. Francisco, Juan Collas, Leon O. Ty, Filemon Tutay and Teodoro M. Locsin.[3]

Leoni also wrote about international affairs, especially on the latest developments in the war in Europe and in East Asia. He brought to the fore the imminent threat of invasion of Abyssinia by Il Duce Mussolini who wanted to exploit the land's natural and mineral resources. Because of perceived inadequacy of the League of Nations in defusing the problem, he followed it up with a provocative article on the league, describing it as mere pawn of the great powers because "the league is united and interferes only" when their interests "are at stake".[4]

The Chinese in the Philippines caught his attention. He presented them in a balanced feature article beginning with their pre-colonial contacts with Filipinos, the Spanish persecutions they had to suffer and the revolts they initiated, to their presence in every business enterprise in the country. Since he was a basketball fan, he also covered the National Collegiate Athletic Association (NCAA) rooting for the Ateneo Blue Eagles although the crown went to San Beda. He also reported the flight of the Pan-American clipper from the West Coast to the Philippines along the galleon route, which cut short travel time. In between these feature essays, he would write short stories.[5]

At the law school, Leoni had an Atenean friend, Elpidiforo "Elpi" Cuna whom he called "colonel" during their military drills the previous year. Elpi shared with him the pleasures and ordeal of law studies. A mere freshie, Leoni was elected vice-president of the law school's student society. He represented his school in several national and international debate and oratorical tournaments where he was awarded best speaker or the gold medal. One prize-winning oratorical piece he delivered attacked the cacique as being the cause of agrarian discontent in the countryside because of his "dictatorship of greed". Being active in extra-curricular activities did not result in low grades because he also excelled academically by garnering the highest grade average in the entire school. In between classes, he would frequent the El Porvenir Restaurant in Intramuros, to eat his *merienda* of *bibingka* and hot chocolate while reading his law books and listening to the record *Song of India* amidst the hustle and bustle of fellow law students who were also working for their studies. He became the editor of *The Barrister*, the law school's monthly magazine; improved its content by featuring articles written by Supreme Court justices and government officials, murder and crime stories for its literary side and controversial legal cases; and adopted the motto "legal side of the news" that two months after, the magazine got an award from the CEG. On the side, Gaston-Roces Publication Company enlisted him as editor for *Promenade* patterned after the American magazine *Sports Spotlight*. His short stories graced its first issue.[6]

SUPPORTING QUEZON'S SOCIAL JUSTICE PROGRAMME

Meanwhile, the coming Commonwealth national elections in September 1935 lured Leoni to participate in youth politics, at utter odds to his own position in February 1934 as revealed in his *Guidon* column "Etc...", when he found youth organizations such as The Young Philippines and New Youth as "too much youth and not much movement". He enlisted as a member of the National Committee on Organization of Junior Coalitionists, which became the Junior Coalition League. The league was an offshoot of the merging in June 1935 of Senate President Quezon's Partido Nacionalista Democrata and Senator Sergio Osmeña's Partido Nacionalista Pro-Independencia in their effort to win the youth for the elections. Leoni showed his pro-Quezon sympathies by speaking for the coalition in one of their youth rallies. During his last two years at Ateneo, he was one of the rabid opponents of the Hare-Hawes-Cutting Bill in a debate, believing that it was a threat to Philippine sovereignty. Shortly after these youth engagements, he was invited to Malacañang a number of times because President-elect Quezon wanted to cultivate relations with student leaders.[7]

Leoni's pro-Quezon stance, hence pro-government convictions, was reflected in his support for the Allied Youth, which replaced the defunct Filipino Youth. He delivered pep talks and possibly contributed to the substance of the group's principles. One of these was "to enhance social justice" clearly in accord with President Quezon's Social Justice Programme. More explicit in his acclamation for the president was a cheerful, almost flattering assessment of the Commonwealth's first three months in which he said that the achievements made were "enough, it might almost be said, to serve the full six years of his [Quezon's] presidential term."[8]

Year after year, Leoni attended the Ateneo alumni homecoming. It was an annual tradition facilitating his regular encounter with fellow Ateneans. The annual homecoming was also because of his active membership in the Junior Alumni Association. The Jesuit fathers also made it a point to communicate with their former students. During one of these meetings Father Mulry reported on the danger of a Communist revolution in Central Luzon where severe land tenure problems could be found. He discussed his plan for a social justice crusade in line with President Quezon's programme to be carried out with the help of the alumni like Leoni. One direct outcome was the creation of Bellarmine Guild, later changed to Chesterton Evidence Guild in 1939, that aimed to provide dialogues on sensitive issues like divorce, communism and Masonry, the promotion of social justice and religious instruction in schools.[9]

Supporting social justice did not stop Leoni from engaging in theatre. He played the role of Dr Wells in Avery Hopwood's *The Bat*, a mystery thriller adapted from the novel by Mary Roberts Rinehart produced for the inauguration of the Ateneo auditorium in February 1936. It was attended by top public figures in the country, including President Quezon.[10]

AGAIN A MURDER MYSTERY NOVELETTE, THEN PROFILES

Getting inspiration from *Rackety Rax*, a book made into a film in 1932 about a college football racket, Leoni wrote *His Dishonor, the Mayor*, which satirized the excesses of the office turned into fiefdom. Published in six parts, it was collated into an illustrated book in 1936. The novel was followed throughout the islands with less than 3,000 entries submitted to the guessing game for the correct heading for each of the six chapters of the novel. Fan mail arrived at the office congratulating the author and asking for an autograph for the copy of the novel they ordered. One reader had noticed the illustrations of the news reporter as having the physiognomy of the author. Another suggested that the novel be brought to the screen with the author playing the role of the news reporter. In the coming Christmas, Leoni received gifts from readers and as Totoy he wrote a set of funny letters regarding them.[11]

In late January 1936, he interviewed at the state university an Irish priest who accused the UP faculty of anti-Catholicism as regards the Rizal retraction. The retraction controversy was about whether Rizal signed or not a document retracting or repudiating all his anti-Catholic writings in order to return to the bosom of Roman Catholic Church. Writing short stories on the side, Leoni's fascination with international affairs was heightened by what was happening in Europe, particularly Franco's Spain, and China.[12]

In the first two quarters of 1937, Leoni continued writing about topics he loved most from soccer, the 1937 Eucharistic Congress in Manila, the

Botel-Tobago people to his abiding interest in international affairs — from Nazi Germany, the Spanish Civil War, to the undeclared Koumintang war against the Japanese. Towards the middle of the year, he shifted to writing profiles of prominent figures in government with Executive Secretary to the President Jorge B. Vargas inaugurating the first in the series, followed by Vice President Sergio Osmeña, National Assembly Speaker Gil Montilla, and Director of the National Information Board Mauro Mendez.[13]

On the celebration of Spain's *día de la raza* in the second week of October, he wrote a fitting article on Spain's legacy in the Philippines, describing it as "more enduring than bronze" the Philippines' inheritance of the Catholic religion which made the country "more Spanish than American" in culture. He reported on the efforts of sixty-one assemblymen in their memorandum to the Department of Public Instruction endorsing religious instruction in the islands. Loyal to the Church and defender of the faith, he put an end to the bigotry and wiped away the doubts surrounding the Friday devotions in Quaipo. He chronicled the rise and decline of the Manila carnival in February 1938. Since he was taking up law, he narrated the stages in the prosecution and settlement of a traffic violation, exposed the emasculated power of the Court of Industrial Relations in dealing with capital and labour and dealt with the regulation of public utilities by the government.[14]

By March 1938, he would be absent from his writing duties to prepare his wedding to Anita Corominas.

A MISHAP BEFORE MARRIAGE

The playboy in Leoni had come to pass when he met Anita Corominas, a thespian, during her portrayal of *Ben Hur* at Saint Theresa. The infatuation began when he saw her play the Moorish lead role in *Magda or Mohammedan Revenge*, writing deliriously — even naming her — in the *Guidon*. A class valedictorian, Anita or Annie had a degree in mathematics. She went back to Cebu after her graduation, making communication through letters or by telephone a necessity. As early as September 1935, he was rumoured to be getting married to Annie, which he denied. But pressure from friends grew as one by one were afflicted by "marriage fever". He had to go to Cebu.[15]

Opportunity knocked at his doorstep when the Cebu Carnival, through the pretty reigning Miss Visayas, Lily de Leon, invited Mario to be her escort. Leoni went with Mario to Cebu. He was able to see Anita, but not without a mishap. No word from them came to Ermita until a call was received from General Guillermo B. Francisco, head of the Philippine Constabulary.

The general, Leoni's uncle, got a distress call from them forcing him to prepare their rescue by dispatching a Coast Guard cutter. Leoni was sent to Cebu to cover the carnival. On the night that the *Free Press* article came out, he was accosted in a restaurant by one of the Osmeña brothers and someone attacked him. They were brought to the police station and released the following morning. In the same restaurant, he approached a group of Cebuanos but he was again attacked; in the police station, he decided to drop the charges. The Cebuanos were offended because he had written that Cebuanos were liberal in their private morals, had few marriages but many children with a convenient system called "*puyo-puyo*" and that even the natives would bet that one out of every five woman he would see would be pregnant. Leoni retracted some of what he wrote in the said article. It was also rumoured that one of the Osmeña brothers resented Leoni's brother Mario who was said to be courting Miss de Leon, so Mario was urged not to attend the Miss Visayas' night to avoid greater public disturbance.[16]

After the fracas, Leoni proposed marriage to Anita. Alfredo had to come to Cebu to ask for the hand of the bride. Preparations went into full swing. Invitations were sent out and arrangements made for the wedding in Ermita Church and the reception at the Manila Hotel. Suddenly, a message from the Corominas family came cancelling the wedding. Don Jose Corominas, a Spanish migrant and wealthy industrialist, had received reports putting the Guerreros, especially the father and sons, in bad light. They were said to be philanderers. Nonplussed, Alfredo who had ordered the construction of another bedroom in the house being built on Donada Street in Pasay meant as a wedding gift, casually explained that the room would be rented out.[17]

Then in late March 1938, the wedding — a well-covered event in the society pages — was finally held on a Thursday morning at the Ermita Church with Leoni's uncle, Pangasinan Bishop Cesar Ma. Guerrero the officiating priest. Lamberto "Bert" Avellana was one of the veil sponsors while Alberto Z. Romualdez was the best man. Dressed in Western gown, Annie was stunningly pretty beside a tall man who barely an hour ago had been delivered from a stag party. The reception was held at the Manila Hotel at its Wintergarden, the most exquisite function room. The newlywed couple went to Bali, Indonesia for their honeymoon.[18]

The couple passed through Celebes in the town of Makassar before proceeding to Bali. Leoni felt that Makassar was like any Spanish town in the Philippines. In Java, they took a ride on the Java Express from Sourabaya down to the seaport where they were ferried by boat to Bali; throughout the trip they managed to see temple upon temple in the paddy fields. They bought Balinese clothes, enjoyed Balinese music and dance, and the scenery, interrupted only by his need to have an injection for which crude methods of the doctor shocked him. From Bali, they went back to Sourabaya and travelled to Djokjakarta and saw by chance the sultan alighting from his vehicle from the car they were riding in, and the "magnificent" Borobudur.[19]

MORE PENETRATING PROFILES, CURRENT EVENTS ANALYSES

Back from Bali, Leoni took his pen to write about a member of the National Assembly: Pedro Hernaez y Conlu of Negros, followed by another assemblyman, Camilo Osias of La Union, Nacionalista Party campaign manager Benigno Aquino, retired senator Juan Sumulong, Jose Yulo, the justice secretary, and attorney Claro M. Recto.[20]

By mid-1938, Leoni was dipping into current national issues of the day such as the plight of the coconut industry. Once in a while he would digress to take up issues connected to his legal studies such as the case of a consented abortion that resulted in a homicide which took two years for the wheel of justice to turn, remaining unsolved and nearly "forgotten in a file". For Christmas 1938, he gave an account on the early Christians in Bali. This and an earlier essay demystifying the Quaipo devotions earned him second and third prizes respectively in March 1939 for the best essays awarded by the Women Writers Club, and eventually the first prize for his essay on infant mortality in the Philippines, awarded by the Philippine General Hospital in the first national baby beauty and health writing contest held in July. With the war raging in Europe in April, Leoni was satirical and humorous in his account of what he called "Easter fashion", commenting on the new style of European dress and attires suited to the trenches and barricades.[21]

To look into the tenancy problem in Central Luzon, he was sent to Bulacan in May 1939 to have a first-hand account of the situation in the Buenavista Estate, a huge tract of land owned by the Catholic Church, particularly the San Juan de Dios Hospital that was leased to the government for the latter to manage into a cooperative corporation. Back in Manila, he covered the arrival of a vaudeville troupe, wrote about his "forgotten hero", Apolinario Mabini, who "did something much more difficult; he lived for his country"; reported on the passage of the eight-hour labour law; publicized the reproduction into film of the *Florante at Laura*; explored the expansion of the National Development Company into textile mills; questioned the priorities of the Philippine tobacco industry; reported on the game between Ateneo's Blue Eagles and La Salle's Green Archers; interviewed Pura Villanueva-Kalaw on the anniversary of the women's suffrage movement; subtly ridiculed the proposal to postpone independence as "a lot of opium"; gave an account on the theory that the real Hitler was already dead and the present Hitler was a fake; announced the screen test for pretty faces by a Filipino film outfit; profiled a prostitute, a victim of white slavery; gave an account of the Atenean farming adventure in Mindanao; and wrote a Christmas story.[22]

A CHRISTMAS STORY AND SHOWBIZ LIVES

"Still Small Voice" would be the last short story that Leoni would write. The story was set on Christmas Eve in 1939 when a mysterious station began to broadcast in all radio frequencies all over the world a message of peace, causing consternation among warring nations: Britain, France, and Poland were at war with Germany. In Germany, an order was issued to put a stop to the programme and an advisory from a Nazi official was broadcast telling the German people to stop listening to the evil propaganda coming from "Comm — those democratic swine of the freedom movement". In London, members of parliament accused British Prime Minister Neville Chamberlain of treachery and cowardice while the speaker resolved that the war would be pursued, earning him thunderous applause. In Tokyo, a rebellion broke out; regiments professed loyalty to the emperor; and an elder statesman, mistakenly accused of masterminding the broadcast, was shot to death. In the United States, in an apartment, radios were turned off by people sick and tired of listening to commentaries on the war, tuning in to music channels instead. Shortly, the mystery station went off and "they never did solve the secret of that Christmas appeal for peace." Believing that it was British propaganda, the Germans claimed they traced its source to Bethlehem and that the speaker had a Jewish accent. But the British exclaimed: "Why it was Goebbels — Sure, we know it was Goebbels all the time."[23]

The war continued in Europe but the following year in 1940, Leoni started a new series on the lives of Philippine movie stars, writing "down-to-earth, frank" portraits of show business personalities unlike the common practice of glamourizing their lives. He set it off with the story of Rogelio de la Rosa, followed by Rosa del Rosario, Ely Ramos, Fernando Poe, Rosario Moreno, sisters Mila del Sol and Gloria Imperial, Corazon Noble and Josefino Cenizal. The series was patronized so that

Teddy Locsin could continue writing about Filipino movie stars after Leoni left the *Free Press*.[24]

In between these close-ups, Leoni would write about some hilarious incidents or some serious happenings in the countryside. He went to Pampanga to report on Pasudeco mills strike, followed up the government's response to the problem focusing on the role of the new Secretary of Labour Jose Avelino. He wrote about a land grant, the family history of the Ylagans, the Philippine Supreme Court's decision to abide by a legal precedent in granting citizenship to a Chinese national, and a profile on Maria Aurora Quezon.[25]

Those years Leoni worked with this bilingual weekly could never deny the influence of his editor Robert M. Dick, a lanky American Scotsman, in his spoken and written English as he himself admitted, for Dick was "a stickler for correct spelling and punctuation". But, more importantly, as the *Free Press* was known for its fairness and its pro-Filipino stand on all issues unlike the pro-American *Bulletin*, earning it a name as the "Bible of Filipinos", he broadened his grasp of Philippine society and strengthened his pro-Filipino convictions with a little touch of pro-Americanism, praising America for the material comforts. A staff member for two years before becoming its literary editor, he earned as much as PHP600 a month when others were only making PHP60–100. Once, *Herald* publisher Carlos P. Romulo tried to hire him but Dick raised his salary by a hundred pesos which made him stay on with the *Free Press*. As literary editor, he once rejected a play written by his playwright cousin, Freddie.[26]

As soon as he became the editor of the magazine, he introduced innovations in style and content; thus, capturing a larger market over its rival *Graphic*. Knowing that *Graphic* was strong in highbrow fiction, he transformed the fiction scene at the *Free Press* by breaking free from the traditional O. Henry mould characterized by a surprise or a sudden twist at the end, towards Collier's style, which was concise, straightforward and readable. Another of his innovations was the weekly's layout.[27]

RADIO IN THE SERVICE OF SOCIAL JUSTICE

Radio was the other arena that Leoni conquered this time with his voice. He was a senior high school student when his voice went on air in the first radio debate in the islands over KZRM, getting him an award for the best speaker. "It was rather prophetic that I should win the award over the air," he said in 1940, because three years earlier he commenced working as a radio speaker for "Mummers of the Air", an exclusive Ateneo alumni production aired over KZRM every Sunday night. Then, over KZIB, using the pseudonym Ignacio Javier, the combined names of two greatest Jesuits, he inaugurated the first and only regular commentary on local news. Sometime in 1938, the Jesuit-directed Bellarmine Guild, later known as the Chesterton Evidence Guild, launched the "Catholic Hour" and recruited him to deliver dramatic dialogues every Sunday night. Also called *Commonweal Hour*, the radio programmes captured the imagination of people from all walks of life. Those were the Catholic answers and beliefs that Leoni also held, to the most pressing concerns confronting the nation.[28]

Again radio work did not mean he could not engage once in a while in theatre. When Bert Avellana organized his Barangay Theater Guild in March 1939, Leoni became a charter member and wrote a backstage story of the guild's first public performance at the Manila Grand Opera House in late April. A reformatted "Catholic Hour" called *Commonweal Service* greeted the airlanes over KZRM and KZRF in September. He performed the role of a Catholic priest in *Storm over Nuevaluz*, a radio drama about the evils of communism written by Skeezix, now an Ateneo faculty member. Father Mulry's vision of a social justice crusade came to fruition in the radio segment *Court of Social Justice*, a part of the reformat, moderated by Leoni. It was during this time that he wrote the radio plays — *The Usurer, Unite, Huelga, The Two Brothers* and *No, Mr Russell* — which were subsequently published by the guild in 1940 and dramatized in the programme.[29]

Tackling real cases, Leoni would dramatize them and point out "doctrines of social justice in action" and applications of papal encyclicals on labour to local conditions. Short scenes from Shakespearean plays like *Julius Caesar* in which he played Brutus, occasionally disrupted the daily routine. Outside the "Catholic Hour", he moderated for the *Town Meeting of the Air* over KZRM, tackling social issues of the day.[30]

He had turned into a famous radio personality shuttling back and forth from KZRH's Heacock Building in Escolta to KZRM's Insular Life Building along Plaza Cervantes in Binondo. His influence was not only felt in print but also on the airwaves. That way, he passed on to his readers and listeners his Catholic persuasion that the answer to communism was Quezon's social justice.[31]

A forerunner of "proletarian literature", he saw literature as a vehicle for social change. Thus, when a debate jolted the literary scene in 1937 in what is now known as the "Villa-Lopez controversy" which dragged on for the next two years, he shrugged off the issue as old hat. Jose Garcia Villa argued that art must be above and outside politics. Salvador Lopez, on the other hand, stressed the role of a writer in responding to the needs of society.

Leoni's name was drawn into the debate when Arturo Rotor, a partisan of Lopez, vilified Filipino writers because he believed they were unable to connect with the aspirations of the people. A.E. Litiatco accused the other camp of imposing a "dictatorship in literature" and cited Leoni, his verses in particular, as one among Filipino writers who were socially conscious. Weekly magazines such as *Graphic*, *Vanguard*, the *Literary Apprentice*, the *Leader* and the *National Review* became the venues for writers of either camp to air their stand but not the *Free Press*. Leoni had been practising what Lopez was preaching so as literary editor he did not bother to get involved in the debate.[32]

The Villa-Lopez debate was borne out of the political and economic conditions that Filipino writers found themselves in the mid and late thirties when peasants in the feudal Central Luzon and Tagalog region protested and revolted against an iniquitous land tenure system. Quezon instigated his social justice programme to solve agrarian problems in those areas. As propagandist for the radio programme under the Chesterton Evidence Guild, Leoni composed radio plays conforming to Quezon's vision of a just society where the government rescues the plight of the common man. Thus his literary production during this period would without doubt place him on the side of Lopez.[33]

ATENEO MEETINGS, THE GANG AND LEGAL PRACTICE

Leoni, sometimes with Annie, never missed monthly alumni meetings, the Mass and the communion, and the NCAA cage fights. Although busy with work, he had time to send a humorous letter to the *Guidon* and suggest ways to improve the paper and means to involve the alumni as well as his provocative thoughts on *Hamlet*. Upon learning that a staff member by the nom de plume Nostradamus, MD began writing in the style of "Totoy to Momoy", he sent a short and comic notice of congratulations. When the Ateneo Alumni Association (AAA) had projects, he was there to support, usually as a member of the publicity committee. One of these was the grand alumni bay cruise whose proceeds would go towards the construction of a swimming pool and natatorium. It was a night of fun with guests like Attorney, now Associate Justice, Recto, Judge Cesar Bengzon and a host of others. Again, in December 1939, he joined the publicity committee for the grand alumni homecoming. His attendance at these alumni meetings and gatherings paved the way for meeting important people both in government and in business. A few weeks before, he passed the bar placing thirteenth after graduating with highest honours in March. Although he had only a month's time to review after Dick allowed him a leave of absence, he got a grade of 100 per cent in international law.[34]

Pressures from work at the *Free Press* and then his legal practice did not diminish his hanging out with his friends. He was loyal to his gang of Ateneans. His oratorios were performed in a variety show he supported along with other Ateneo alumni. He sponsored a stag party for Bert Avellana on his marriage to Daisy Hontiveros. But the sudden death of his law school friend, Elpi Cuna, saddened him and Annie. He was in a state of disbelief when he heard the news that Elpi died at a young age leaving behind a wife and a son. Elpi was therefore missed in a number of gatherings. Leoni and Annie met old friends in Soc Rodrigo's farm in Bulacan. They would also host the gang at their house in Pasay. At all these meetings, the gang's confidant, Father Mulry whom they nicknamed "Pitong" was present.[35]

Now an attorney, Leoni was appointed by President Quezon as secretary at the Supreme Court, then transferred to the Manila City Fiscal's Office as assistant city fiscal and finally made his way in a very short time to the Office of the Solicitor General in Intramuros. But his decision to enter the government bureaucracy was not easy. Leoni loved the newsman's bohemian way of life. Dick even went out of his way to persuade his mother to allow him to continue working with the *Free Press* so that eventually he would become the heir as owner-publisher. Filomena who "wanted to keep her flock away from the blandishments of newspaper work" had her way. Out of filial duty, he chose to pursue a legal career in Intramuros, after having grown up in Ermita and worked in Santa Cruz, that would lead him to still unknown destinations, bringing along his pen — both his asset and his liability.[36]

Thus, here was Guerrero, young at 25, Americanized as the rest of his generation, so pro-American. Yet, he maintained his Hispanic leanings, hence pro-Filipino sentiments, and displayed his anti-Japanese sympathies. But it will not take time for this to change.

Notes
1. Sicam, "A Man for all Seasons", p. 13; I.T.R., "Atty. Leon Ma. Guerrero in The Bench and Bar in News", *Lawyers Journal*, 21 December 1949, p. 667; L.M. Guerrero, Jr., "My Grandfather", p. 3; *TG*, 15 July 1935; Leon Ma. Guerrero, "An Enemy of Caesar", *PFP*, 20 April 1935, pp. 12, 13, 52.
2. Leon Ma. Guerrero, "How Japan looks at Ramos", *PFP*, 1 June 1935, pp. 4, 5; "Life a la Tokyo", *PFP*, 8 June 1935, pp. 2, 3, 46; "The travel racket", *PFP*, 22 June 1935, pp. 2, 3, 11.

3. Nick Joaquin, "708 Avenida Rizal", in *Joseph Estrada and Other Sketches* (Manila: National Bookstore, 1977), pp. 216–19.
4. Leon Ma. Guerrero, "Mussolini Goes Lion-hunting", *PFP*, 20 July 1935, pp. 2, 3, 33; "What can we expect from the League of Nations?", *PFP*, 28 September 1935, pp. 2, 34, 35.
5. Leon Ma. Guerrero, "China's Contribution to the Philippines", *PFP*, 12 October 1935, pp. 45–47; "San Beda Cops Collegiate Title", *PFP*, 19 October 1935, pp. 38, 60; "Along the galleon route", *PFP*, 30 November 1935, pp. 8, 24.
6. *TG*, 30 July, 16 August, 21 October, 16 November, 20 December 1935; *PH*, 12 November 1935; *TG*, 30 June, 15 July, 30 July, 15 August, 17 October 1936; 30 June, 30 July, 16 August 1937; *Times Journal* (hereafter cited as *TJ*), 27 June 1982. For a sample of his winning oratorical piece, see Leon Ma. Guerrero, "The Dictatorship of Greed", *Filipiniana Reference Shelf* (Manila, 1940), pp. 7–9, 19.
7. *TG*, 2 August 1933; 28 February 1934; 16 August 1935; Nakpil, *Myself*, p. 123.
8. *TG*, 6 October 1938; Leon Ma. Guerrero, "Setting the national pace", *PFP*, 15 February 1936, p. 2.
9. *TG*, 15 July 1937; 10 October 1940; *Catholic Hour Pamphlets, 1939–40* (Manila: Chesterton Evidence Guild, 1940). See also Victor B. Ibabao, SJ, "Aspects of Catholic social action in the Philippines prior to World War II: The contributions of Father Joseph A. Mulry, the Jesuits, and the Ateneo alumni", MA thesis, Ateneo de Manila University, 1986.
10. Bernad, *Dramatics at Ateneo de Manila*, p. 106; *TG*, 21 January and 25 February 1936.
11. E.A. Cruz, "Leon Ma. Guerrero — the writer", *TJ*, 26 June 1982; L.M. Guerrero, "His Dishonor, the Mayor" Chapter I, *PFP*, 14 December 1935, pp. 20–22; Chapter II, *PFP*, 21 December 1935, pp. 18, 19, 24; Chapter III, *PFP*, 28 December 1935, pp. 16, 17, 48; Chapter IV, *PFP*, 4 January 1936; Chapter V, *PFP*, 11 January 1936; Chapter VI, *PFP*, 18 January 1936; "His honor, the author", *PFP*, 15 February 1936, p. 10; Leon Ma. Guerrero, "Thanks for the present by Totoy", *PFP*, 14 December 1935, p. 12. The last three issues of the novelette are not available in the microfilm; thus the dates are approximations and the pages are missing. See also L.M. Guerrero, *His Dishonor, the Mayor* (Manila: Philippines Free Press, 1936).
12. Leon Ma. Guerrero, "The guardian angel of the UP", *PFP*, 1 February 1936, pp. 6, 7, 60; "Bullets after ballots in Spain", *PFP*, 1 August 1936, pp. 8, 38; "United We Fight", *PFP*, 17 October 1936, p. 8.
13. Leon Ma. Guerrero, "The Siamese inquisition as told by Arsenio Lacson", *PFP*, 23 January 1937, pp. 2, 34, 38; "The inconstant people", *PFP*, 30 January 1937, pp. 2, 3, 32, 33; "Found: The lost horizon", *PFP*, 12 June 1937, pp. 2, 3, 32; "The battle of the gods", *PFP*, 19 June 1937, pp. 8, 34, 35; "Midnight in Spain", *PFP*, 17 July 1937, pp. 8, 35; "Yellow fever", *PFP*, 24 July 1937, pp. 2, 28; "Shanghai encore", *PFP*, 21 August 1937, pp. 8, 41; "The phantom president", *PFP*, 7 August 1937, pp. 8, 40; "The Forgotten President", *PFP*, 28 August 1937, pp. 10, 35, 36; "The silent

speaker", *PFP*, 11 September 1937, pp. 24, 40; "Apostle of Malacañang", *PFP*, 18 September 1937, pp. 10-11.

14. Leon Ma. Guerrero, "More enduring than bronze", *PFP*, 9 October 1937, p. 10; "The private life of a bill", *PFP*, 16 October 1937, pp. 10, 11, 42; "The fourth r", *PFP*, 27 November 1937, pp. 10, 11, 34-H; "Conversation with the devil", *PFP*, 8 January 1938; "The merry go-round broke down", *PFP*, 12 February 1938, pp. 2-3; "Ninth endorsement", *PFP*, 12 February 1938, pp. 24-25; "Solomon without a sword", *PFP*, 19 February 1938, pp. 12, 42-45; "Everybody's money", *PFP*, March 1938 (?), date and page number cannot be determined from the copy at the National Library of the Philippines.

15. *Manila Chronicle* (hereafter cited as *MC*), 22 March 1965 and 9 June 1966; *TG*, 29 November 1933; 30 September 1935; Nakpil, *Myself*, pp. 134-35.

16. Nakpil, *Myself*, p. 135; "Cebu incident clarified", *PFP*, 16 May 1936, p. 37; Leon Ma. Guerrero, "Cebu goes round and round", *PFP*, 9 May 1936, pp. 10-11, 36-37; "Cebu — Correction", *PFP*, 16 May 1936, p. 7.

17. Nakpil, *Myself*, p. 136; Leon Ma. Guerrero, "3 wives", *Promenade*, January 1938, pp. 18, 19, 52.

18. *TG*, 15 March 1938; Nakpil, *Myself*, p. 137.

19. Leon Ma. Guerrero, "Synonym in Celebes", *PFP*, 23 April 1938, pp. 8, 46, 48; "Java Express", *PFP*, 7 May 1938, pp. 12, 13, 60-61; "Bali-hoo", *PFP*, 14 May 1938, pp. 2, 3, 42; "Bali Faces", *PFP*, 21 May 1938, pp. 6, 7, 47.

20. Leon Ma. Guerrero, "Left-hand man", *PFP*, 14 May 1938, pp. 16, 44-45; "No, no, a thousand times no!", *PFP*, 4 June 1938, pp. 16, 43; "Life of the party", *PFP*, 30 July 1938, pp. 4-5, 50; "Dreamer, not demagogue", *PFP*, 17 September 1938; "The Old-Fashioned Virtues", *PFP*, 24 September 1938, p. 4; "The miraculous lawyer", *PFP*, 8 October 1938, pp. 2, 3, 45-46.

21. Leon Ma. Guerrero, "Forgotten story", *PFP*, 13 August 1938, pp. 2-3; "Early Christians in Bali", *PFP*, 31 December 1938; *TG*, 7 March, 15 July 1939; "Easter fashions", *PFP*, 1 April 1939, pp. 8, 44.

22. Leon Ma. Guerrero, "A smile for Manila", *PFP*, 10 June 1939, pp. 2, 3; "Mabini: Forgotten hero", *PFP*, 17 June 1939, pp. 28-31; "Labor-saving time", *PFP*, 24 June 1939, pp. 6-7; "Most Celebrated Filipino Love Story", *PFP*, 15 July 1939, pp. 2-3; "Weaving a future", *PFP*, 29 July 1939, pp. 2-3, 51; "The valley of a million smokes", *PFP*, 23 September 1939, pp. 56, 58; "All for sportsmanship!", *PFP*, 28 October 1939, pp. 41-43; "Woman suffrage comes of age", *PFP*, 4 November 1939, pp. 6-7; "The year of second thoughts", *PFP*, 11 November 1939, p. 6; "Hitler faces death", *PFP*, 18 November 1939, pp. 3, 39-40; "Screen test for the 'colegiala'", *PFP*, 25 November 1939, pp. 4-5; "Case history", *PFP*, 2 December 1939, pp. 6-8; "Initiation in Mindanao", *PFP*, 16 December 1939, pp. 10-11.

23. Leon Ma. Guerrero, "Still small voice", *PFP*, 9 December 1939, p. 8.

24. Cruz, "Leon Ma. Guerrero — the writer", p. 3; Leon Ma. Guerrero, "First Pampanga menace", *PFP*, 13 January 1940, pp. 3, 40; "She grew up with the movies", *PFP*,

20 January 1940, pp. 6–7; "Chip on his shoulder", *PFP*, 27 January 1940, pp. 16–17; "The lone ranger", *PFP*, 3 February 1940, p. 3; "The housekeeper's daughter", *PFP*, 10 February 1940, pp. 16–17; "The dead end kids", *PFP*, 17 February 1940, pp. 6–7; "If she were a song ...", *PFP*, 9 March 1940, pp. 6–7; "The Magnificent Brute", *PFP*, 16 March 1940, pp. 6–7.

25. Leon Ma. Guerrero, "The terrific and tear-jerking tale of the toothpick containers by Totoy", 13 January 1940, p. 52; "Peace! Peace! ... But there is no peace!", 20 January 1940, pp. 3–5, 40; "Pampanga peacemaker", 27 January 1940, pp. 4–5; "But the living do not rest in peace", 10 February 1940, pp. 3, 4, 40; "Citizens by judicial decision", 24 February 1940, pp. 6–8; "The royal family", 24 February 1940, p. 2; "The great man's daughter", *PFP*, 2 March 1940, pp. 2–3.

26. "Authors' Vignettes" in *Philippine Prose and Poetry Volume Three* (Revised edition) (Manila: Bureau of Printing, 1961), p. 335; Frederic S. Marquardt, *Before Bataan and After: A Personalized History of Our Philippine Experiment* (New York: The Bobbs-Merrill, Co., 1943), p. 72; Michael P. Onorato, *Frederic S. Marquardt: Philippine Memories* (Fullerton: Oral History Programme, California State University, 1986), pp. 3, 14, 15; Leon Ma. Guerrero, "The Times in Rhymes", *PFP*, 20 August 1938, p. 45; Alegre and Fernandez, *Writer and his Milieu*, p. 74; W.M. Guerrero, *Guerreros of Ermita*, p. 127.

27. Cruz, "Leon Ma. Guerrero — the writer", p. 3.

28. *The Ateneo Aegis* (Manila: Ateneo, 1932), p. 262; Del Rio, "Guerrero in Radio", pp. 58–59; *TG*, 30 July 1937; 16 September 1938; 7 March; 19 September; 6 November 1939; 28 June; 30 July 1940; 10 October 1940; De la Costa, *Light Cavalry*, p. 593.

29. Leon Ma. Guerrero, "Curtain up!", *PFP*, 29 April 1939, pp. 10–11; *TG*, 19 September; 6 November 1939; Paterno, "The Young Horacio de la Costa", pp. l, liii, lv; Leon Ma. Guerrero, *Catholic Hour Pamphlets, 1940–1941: The Usurer* (Manila: Chesterton Evidence Guild, 1941), pp. 3–16; Leon Ma. Guerrero, *Catholic Hour Pamphlets, 1940–1941: Unite* (Manila: Chesterton Evidence Guild, 1941), pp. 17–40; Leon Ma. Guerrero, *Catholic Hour Pamphlets, 1940–1941: Huelga!* (Manila: Chesterton Evidence Guild, 1941), pp. 3–18; Leon Ma. Guerrero, *Catholic Hour Pamphlets, 1940–1941: The Two Brothers* (Manila: Chesterton Evidence Guild, 1941), pp. 19–32. See also *TG*, 30 August 1941. Leon Ma. Guerrero, *Catholic Hour Pamphlets, 1940–1941: No, Mr Russell* (Manila: Chesterton Evidence Guild, 1941), pp. 19–28.

30. *TG*, 28 June, 30 July 1940; De la Costa, *Light Cavalry*, p. 595; Sylvia Mendez Ventura, *Mauro Mendez: From Journalism to Diplomacy* (Quezon City: University of the Philippines Press, 1978), pp. 79–80.

31. Nakpil, *Myself*, p. 126.

32. Abdul Majid, *The Filipino Novel in English: A Critical History* (UP, 1970), pp. 40–41; Cruz, "Leon Ma. Guerrero — the writer", p. 3; Chua, *The Critical Villa*, pp. 181–82; A.E. Litiatco, "Dictatorship in Literature", in Manuel Arguilla, et al., *Literature Under the Commonwealth* (Manila: Alberto S. Florentino, 1973), p. 37. For bibliographical references to this debate, see Chua, *The Critical Villa*,

pp. 181–82. Litiatco referred to Guerrero's Goriong Gutum but in fact it was "Gabriel Gutum". See Guerrero's "Times in Rhymes", *PFP*, 16 January 1937, p. 45.

33. Teodoro A. Agoncillo and Milagros C. Guerrero, *History of the Filipino People* (Quezon City: Malaya Books, 1970), pp. 416–20. See Guerrero's radio plays in *Catholic Hour Pamphlets, 1939–1940* (Manila: Chesterton Evidence Guild, 1940) and *Catholic Hour Pamphlets, 1940–1941* (Manila: Chesterton Evidence Guild, 1941).

34. *TG*, 28 June 1935; 13 August, 30 October 1937; 15 July, 30 July, 17 August, 31 August, 6 October 1938; 6 November, 29 November, Christmas Issue 1939; 28 June 1940; 24 August 1940; I.T.R., "Atty. Leon Ma. Guerrero", p. 667.

35. *TG*, 15 March, 30 June, 18 November, Christmas Edition 1938; 31 January, 15 February, 29 November 1939; 17 July 1940. The gang consisted of Mr and Mrs Henry Quema, Soc Rodrigo, Jesse Paredes, Rod Sarenas, Leoni Guerrero, Pete Gallardo, Dr and Mrs R.G. Avellana, Vic Baltazar, Manny de Leon, Teddy Fernando, Charlie Nivera, Dodi Diaz, Gaudy Besa, Alberting Romualdez, Jose Coruna, and Plinio Gaston.

36. I.T.R., "Atty. Leon Ma. Guerrero", p. 667; *TG*, 28 June and 9 September 1940; Nakpil, *Whatever*, p. 29; Nakpil, *Myself*, p. 133.

II

To Tokyo and Back: The Making of a Diplomat

I shall see them as I have always seen them
A ragged processsional of gaunt, grim and ghostly men.
Marching from a field that slept;
No longer underneath their stars and stripes,
But under the blood-red banners
Of an alien conqueror that had come
Like shadows in the night...

Maximo V. Soliven, *The Men of Bataan*

"The enemies can kill all of us, their bombs may destroy, but they cannot kill the ideal, the aspiration and the longings of the one billion peoples of this part of the world to be free, to be left alone so that Asia may be for the Asiatics and my Philippines may be for the Filipinos..."

President Jose P. Laurel,
Speech before Japanese imperial officials, 1945

"We are committed to the cause and the international program of the United States of America ... Our safest course ... is in the glistening wake of America whose sure advance with mighty prow breaks for smaller craft the waves of fear."

President Manuel A. Roxas,
Independence Day Address, 1946

5

The Assistant Solicitor

At Arzobispo Street in Intramuros, Leon Ma. Guerrero started to work as assistant solicitor in the Office of the Solicitor General in the last quarter of 1940. Solicitor General Roman Ozaeta entrusted to him the preparation of the brief on the appeal case of Ferdinand E. Marcos, a brilliant Ilocano law student accused of murdering Julio Nalundasan, the electoral opponent of his father.[1]

In December 1938 Guerrero, then a senior law student, had read from the headlines that a fellow law student by the name of Marcos was arrested. Vicente J. Francisco, a leading trial lawyer, handled the case that implicated not only Marcos but also his father Mariano, his uncle Pio, both lawyers, and Quirino Lizardo as accomplices. Delaying tactics were employed by the defendants so that Marcos could take the bar exam in August. Marcos took the bar that Guerrero took in four successive Saturdays. In the first week of September, the four accused went on trial and finally in late November, Judge Roman Cruz of Laoag declared Marcos and Lizardo guilty of murder but absolved the father and the uncle. Marcos, however, topped the bar; he applied for provisional liberty on bail to appeal his case before the Supreme Court but the motion was denied until President Quezon informed Cruz that he was amenable to it. Marcos insisted on winning his appeal before the magistrates of the highest court. In less than a year, he prepared his brief proving his innocence of the crime. Thus, Marcos the appellant and Guerrero the prosecutor met for the oral arguments on the appeal as scheduled by the Supreme Court on 12 October 1940.[2]

A precedent in Philippine legal history, it was the first time that a twenty-three-year-old convicted murderer would argue his case before the high bench. That Saturday, at the *Ayuntamiento*, members of the Manila bar, conspicuous in their black togas, packed the court hall. Outside, a throng of spectators, mostly law students, cheered for Marcos who wore a white suit and white shoes. Members of the diplomatic corps and a representative from the Office of the American High Commissioner were present.[3]

Guerrero felt the burden on his shoulders. He would argue his case not only in front of the justices of the High Court but also before the public. That night at home, he was edgy, reading, committing to memory the arguments that could either unmake the appellant or himself. Winning the case was secondary to proving the soundness of his arguments before the court. His mother, knowing the case was "*cause célèbre*" pitting two brilliant young men from Ateneo and UP, was "silent but, as usual, prayerful". One day, a visitor in *terno* who turned out to be Mrs Marcos, mother of the appellant, came to the house and talked to her in private.[4]

Informed about the visit or not, Guerrero woke up early, ate his breakfast, kissed and said goodbye to his wife Annie and drove his car straight to the *Ayuntamiento*. All seats in the hall were occupied. Everyone kept silent as the justices entered. The presiding justice, Jose P. Laurel, seated at the centre of the platform, called on the appellant to state his case. Guerrero listened intently. Without questions from the justices to the appellant, Guerrero stood up and asserted the culpability of the appellant and Lizardo in favour of reaffirming the judgment of the Lower Court. But a justice asked him if the accomplice turned state witness, Calixto Aguinaldo, was an accessory to the crime. He said yes. If he was, asked another, then his testimony came from a polluted source. Guerrero argued that the legal angle had been weighed and the Department of Investigation and the constabulary gave credence to it after months of research. When the justices seemed dissatisfied with his reply, he knew he had lost his case. In two weeks, his intuition was confirmed when he heard the decision penned by Justice Laurel acquitting Marcos and Lizardo, finding Aguinaldo's testimony incredible and absurd and the prosecution's evidence indefensible. After this infamous case, Guerrero was entrusted to work on the Pasudeco massacre and the Camasura swindles among others. Obviously, the case did not affect his career. He had become a sought-after speaker gracing the Rotary Philippines' meeting in January 1941, Ateneo High School's commencement in March, and the Junior House of Representatives in July.[5]

A QUEZON LOYALIST

Like his father, Guerrero was a loyalist of President Quezon though his mother favoured Vice President Osmeña. His fierce loyalty stemmed from his work as Quezon's speechwriter in a team consisting of Hernando Abaya and Filemon Poblador and headed by the "superghost", Justice Jose Abad Santos. When he was asked by the Chesterton Evidence Guild to write a script on the fifth anniversary of the Commonwealth, he produced "March of Time", extolling the achievements of the Commonwealth particularly the successes of Quezon's social justice programme. As solicitor, he defended proposals to amend the Constitution to give way to a four-year presidency subject to re-election as against a fixed six-year term, and the restoration of a senate in a bicameral congress, amendments that were approved in a national plebiscite in June 1940.[6]

An article he wrote for the *Free Press* on the re-election amendment circulating in the press in 1939 showed where his sympathies lay. It was a debate between a Mr Pro and Mr Con. Arguing that democracy in the Philippines was nothing but mere appearances, Mr Pro said: "... Why shouldn't the Philippines develop its native brand of democracy, with one party in power, a commanding executive for unlimited re-election, appointive local officials and so on down the line. You must admit that that is the kind of government our people seem to want..." Mr Con objected: "You forget our tradition of freedom, the spirit of revolution!" to which Mr Pro reacted stridently: "We never had a tradition of personal freedom. We have, on the contrary, a tradition even an aptitude and an inclination for the rule of bosses and caciques." As regards Quezon, Mr Pro spoke highly of the man as "the only one who can give us national unity, unity between classes, regions, political factions. Take him away and you'll have all the big-shots, not to mention labor and capital at one another's throat. So why not keep Quezon as long as we can? Why not amend the constitution to allow it?"[7]

Quezon was foisting his "partyless democracy" when Guerrero was handling the Marcos case and teaching law at the Ateneo. Despite the growing accusations of dictatorship, the president believed that parties were unnecessary in a democracy, calling for their suspension. After resigning from the *Free Press*, Guerrero applied for a teaching job at the Ateneo College of Law and Dean Manuel Lim took him in. He was made moderator of the Bellarmine Club whose members, all barristers, met regularly once a week and took part in radio broadcasts for the *Commonweal Service*.

Guerrero participated in a mock trial on the abolition of political parties in the Philippines on a play he wrote entitled *Partyless Democracy* aired over KZRM. As the government counsel, he argued for the possibility of a partyless democracy in support of Quezon. Though it was a mock trial, his position betrayed his loyalty to Quezon although as the author, he also represented the voice of the opposition through the character "Antonio Prospero" who said that "due to the overwhelming control of the Nacionalista Party we have been having, in fact, if not in theory, a no party-government for the past decade." Again in a drama aired over KZRM sponsored by the club, he presented the advantages and the incongruities of the National Defence System. In another drama tackling whether compulsory military training was a violation of personal liberty, the prosecution attorney argued for the negative. They were timely presented to the listening public because the possibility that war would escalate in the Far East was not far-fetched considering that Japan had invaded China.[8]

In those critical times, Guerrero believed that a strong leader was needed. He saw in Quezon the necessary leadership to oversee a country in transition. When de la Costa's *Salazar* was to be broadcast over KZRM, Guerrero played Antonio de Oliveiro Salazar, in a plot revolving around his role in the rise of the corporative state in Portugal. Annie participated as the sister of Salazar. This and the earlier *Partyless Democracy* generated a half-year controversy with A.V.H. Hartendorp, editor of the *Philippine Magazine*. Hartendorp charged the people behind the broadcast of supporting Fascism that was at its height in Europe and called them "anti-democratic, anti-American and anti-Commonwealth". The Chesterton Evidence Guild was, to outsiders, a clerico-fascist organization in favour of Hitler, Franco, and Salazar. They retorted to Hartendorp in a broadcast, while the secretary of public instruction suspended the magazine as required reading for public high school seniors. The Civil Liberties Union (CLU) sent a resolution arguing for the lifting of the ban. Guerrero along with other loyal Chestertonians sent a memorandum to the CLU asking them to reconsider their position because, though the controversy was political, Hartendorp had violated the state's absolute neutrality, the principle on which the public school system rested. Whether Guerrero supported fascism or had just expressed support to the Jesuits was uncertain but he approved of Quezon's authoritarian tendency, a quality he believed was imperative in an impending war.[9]

It was August 1941 when he wrote a script for the *Commonweal Service* about a man struggling against tuberculosis. It was timely because Quezon would celebrate his birthday in two days. The president who was suffering from tuberculosis, was listening to the radio and wired KZRM to congratulate them on the programme. Guerrero must have been pleased that the character Damaso whom he created touched the ailing president.[10]

In the coming November elections, Guerrero campaigned for Quezon. A member of the Allied Youth, he supported the move to affiliate the organization with Nacionalista Party as a counter to the UP students-led Young Philippines party, a member of the opposition coalition known as Allied Minorities. From October to November members were scheduled every Monday to speak and campaign for the party on KZRH. Guerrero was scheduled on the first Monday of November and had the chance to campaign for the Nacionalista Party with the president himself. The re-electionists Quezon and Osmeña won as well as the majority of the party candidates. The Atenean campaign paid off but the winners could not savour their victories, for the war in the Pacific loomed over the islands.[11]

Notes

1. Quirino, "Introduction", in *The First Filipino*, p. xvii; Teehankee, "A Testament…", p. 8; I.T.R., "Atty. Leon Ma. Guerrero", p. 665; Miguel R. Cornejo, *Cornejo's Commonwealth Directory of the Philippines* (Manila, 1939), pp. A-18, A-44.
2. Hartzell Spence, *For Every Tear a Victory: The Story of Ferdinand E. Marcos* (New York: McGraw Hill Book Co., 1964), pp. 47, 50, 52, 101, 103, 104, 109–12; I.T.R., "Atty. Leon Ma. Guerrero", p. 667. Spence's account is obviously biased; the biography was commissioned in anticipation of the 1965 Philippine presidential elections.
3. Spence, *For Every Tear a Victory*, p. 112.
4. Nakpil, *Myself*, p. 134.
5. *People v. Marcos, et al.*, 70 Phil. 468 (1940); "News of the week: Not guilty", *PFP*, 26 October 1940, p. 59; "Front page faces: He saved himself", *PFP*, 2 November 1940, p. 24; Spence, *For Every Tear a Victory*, pp. 113, 114 and 117; I.T.R., "Atty. Leon Ma. Guerrero", p. 665; *Priscilla y Samar v. People*, 71 Phil. 200 (1940); *TG*, 31 January, 12 March, 12 July 1941.
6. *TG*, 27 November 1940; Nakpil, *Myself*, p. 122; Hernando J. Abaya, *The Making of a Subversive — A Memoir* (Quezon City: New Publishers, 1984), p. 44; L. Ma. Guerrero, "Why I'll vote yes", *PFP*, 15 June 1940, p. 2.
7. Leon Ma. Guerrero, "Reelection for Quezon? As his enemies see it!", *PFP*, 6 May 1939, pp. 2–3.
8. Leon Ma. Guerrero, *Partyless Democracy* (Manila: Chesterton Evidence Guild, 1941); Joseph R. Hayden, *The Philippines: A Study in National Development* (New York: The Macmillan Company, 1955), p. 450; *TG*, 4 and 24 September 1940; 12 July 1941; *Aegis* (Ateneo de Manila, 1940), p. 24.
9. Paterno, "The Young Horacio de la Costa", p. lv; Rosalinda P. Ofreneo, *Renato*

Constantino, p. 35; *TG*, 9 September 1940; Federico Mangahas, "Let's Look to Portugal", *Philippines Herald* (hereafter cited as *PH*), 2 October 1940 as published in *Maybe, Incidentally: The satire of Federico Mangahas*, essays selected and edited by Ruby K. Mangahas (Quezon City: University of the Philippines Press, 1998), p. 433; Hernando Abaya, *The CLU Story: 50 Years of Struggle for Civil Liberties* (Quezon City: New Day, 1987), pp. 27-28. See also "Hartendorp vs. the Ateneo", *PFP*, 1 February 1941, p. 37.
10. *TG*, 30 August 1941.
11. *TG*, 8 November 1941; Ricardo T. Jose, "Manuel L. Quezon and the Commonwealth, 1935-1944", in *Philippine Presidents: 100 Years*, edited by Rosario Mendoza Cortes, (Quezon City: New Day Publishers & Philippine Historical Association, 1999), p. 126.

6

From Intelligence Officer in Bataan to the Return of Ignacio Javier

Guerrero did not believe that Japan would attack the Philippines because it would mean engaging the United States. Still, the radio commentator known as Ignacio Javier was critical of Japanese aggression starting in Manchuria in 1931, China in 1937 and northern Indochina in 1940. After Pearl Harbour was attacked on 8 December 1941, he was even more relentless in his denunciation of the Japanese along with Salvador "SP" Lopez, a fellow newsman. They belonged to a group of broadcast and print journalists who saw Japan as a threat; they would be loosely called "Japanophobes" along with others of similar persuasion.[1]

His career as a solicitor was cut short the next day after the Pearl Harbour bombing and the almost simultaneous bombings on Clark Field, Baguio and Davao, putting employees of the courts and other offices in the bureaucracy in a state of panic. A few days before Manila fell however, he was still broadcasting over the air. Then, upon the advice of the Jesuit Superior, Father John F. Hurley, SJ, who told them that "the Japs will make mince meat of the two of you if they find you here" and the Jesuits' help in securing a transport through the assistance of Mr Chick Parsons, he and Lopez fled from the burning city by clinging to the deck of a Luzon Stevedoring barge with anti-aircraft guns. It was the night of New Year's Day. The barge kept on circling the bay throughout the night until it brought them to Bataan. Americans arrested them for they suspected them to be Japanese spies. Fortunately Major Carlos P. Romulo of the United States Army Forces in the Far East (USAFFE) Public Relations in a visit to Bataan recognized the two familiar faces from his *Herald* days and got them released and commissioned. Since the Americans needed only one Filipino propaganda officer in Corregidor, Lopez who had a boil went with Romulo while Guerrero stayed in Bataan.[2]

FROM MIS TO THE VOICE OF FREEDOM

In Bataan, Guerrero was assigned to the Military Intelligence Service (MIS) unit with the rank of first lieutenant under Brigadier General Simeon de Jesus. He did not know that in Manila the Japanese, upon their arrival in January, were looking for him and Romulo for immediate execution. It was at a summer training camp for army cadres before the war when he could complain about mosquitoes and bedbugs as well as the poor accommodation. He had to overcome his shyness in using big common-room bathrooms and toilets. At the camp in the thick of the action, he was told to edit a daily news bulletin, *See You in Manila* (*SYIM*), along with Captain Fred Ruiz Castro, and Lieutenant Felipe Buencamino III who graciously shared his tent with him. More than being a mere acquaintance and fellow Atenean, Buencamino, who had taken up law the previous summer, had complained in the *Free Press* about legal language and its technicalities being too difficult for non-lawyers, to which as solicitor Guerrero had diffidently replied but received another rejoinder from Buencamino.[3]

Always thinking of Annie, Guerrero killed time by smoking papaya leaves to compensate for the lack of Chesterfields and Camels; joining in discussions on prostitution and the expected reinforcement convoy, which never came; engaging in pranks with his two buddies like stealing canned sardines from their superiors; taking turns to visit a pretty Pampangueña in the evacuee camp; and drinking whisky, again with his two friends. He wrote in late January 1942 for the *Voice of Freedom* a script on Erlinda, a dead girl abused and found by a patrol team with a handkerchief bearing that name made into a battle cry: "Remember Erlinda!" He was overjoyed to receive a note and a knitted sweater from Annie. It was February when he thought of writing a work of fiction on Bataan. Then, he fell ill. In between spells of dysentery and malaria, he wrote drama scripts and edited *SYIM*. He also stood as counsel for some of the accused in the court martials to determine the persons responsible for the Japanese breakthrough in the western sector that threatened Bataan and nearly precipitated the fall of the Rock.[4]

In early April, he was so ill that he feared he would die. Having learned of his condition, Romulo decided to let him go to Corregidor. Reaching the shore, he tottered his way into the arms of his classmate, Manuel "Manny" de Leon. After recuperating from his illness in the hospital tunnel, he joined the *Voice of Freedom*. He was happy to see Lopez and Romulo in a four-metre cubicle adjacent to General Douglas MacArthur's headquarters inside Malinta tunnel, where the *Voice* was based. Manned by five other personnel, the studio was cramped with a typewriter, a microphone and an electric fan on a worktable, a communications receiver on a smaller table, a single record turntable, and three wicker stools.[5]

Inaugurated in January to serve as a channel of optimism by putting on air messages of hope for the Filipino civilian population and the armed forces, the *Voice* would transmit news summaries daily from radio reports all over the world printed in *The International News Summary*. The broadcasts were made in the morning, noon and night. Guerrero wrote, typed his own scripts, and took part in these broadcasts. He knew that in no time Bataan would fall. On 3 April, the Japanese launched their great offensive, breaching 6 April the line that General Vicente Lim's 41st Division valiantly defended.[6]

The battle-weary Filipino-American forces continued to fight on amidst hunger, disease and the ceaseless salvo of bullets and deafening hail of bombs from the enemy that forced them to surrender on 9 April. It was in mid-February — less than two months away from the clutches of the enemy — when Quezon and Osmeña and their families were spirited away to Australia and from there, they took a ship to San Francisco where Quezon established a government-in-exile. Guerrero could have joined the presidential plane but he turned down the offer of a seat because he was thinking of Annie.[7]

Everyone knew that it would be a matter of hours before the surrender of Bataan was inevitable. The difficult part was letting the world know of the fall because it would discourage the Allied forces. At the studio, the staff were undecided whether to announce the fall at 8:00 p.m. It was 5:00 p.m. Lopez said glumly: "I have no heart to write" while the others seemed lost, misty-eyed as they sat listening to him. He looked at Guerrero: "Leoni, why don't you write it?" Also feeling terrible, he politely declined. Lopez had no choice. Having put a sheet of paper in the typewriter, while he began tapping the keys, he asked: "What is there to say? How does one describe the savor of defeat? What can one say except that this is only the end of battle but not of the war?" After about half an hour, he finished the script, submitted it to Captain Kenneth Sauer who replaced Romulo. Romulo had fled in a repaired plane he boarded in Bataan. At 8:00 p.m., Norman Reyes read the piece over the air. In Ermita, the Guerrero family listened to the radio they managed to keep away from Japanese confiscation. They huddled around the radio as they listened to what seemed to Chitang was Leoni's voice announcing the fall.[8]

THE FALL OF CORREGIDOR

Guerrero was spared the horrors that Buencamino and Castro went through; the latter two had survived the ordeal of the Death March, the brutal movement, mostly by walking, of Filipino and American Prisoners of War (POWs) from Mariveles, Bataan to Capas, Tarlac. When Bataan fell and surrendered to the Japanese forces, Guerrero and his colleagues continued manning the radio station. He took charge of the broadcasts to keep the morale of the people high in a month of siege and bombardment. Sometimes, the *Voice* missed a broadcast and Lopez would alternate with him as the announcer. Thus, on 29 April, he did not take part in the broadcast.[9]

Every night amid the pall of gloom engulfing the archipelago and beyond, Guerrero or anyone from the *Voice* would broadcast on air: "Corregidor still stands!" providing a flicker of hope to millions of people in the countryside and in the world. Although the broadcasts were helpful in keeping the hopes of the people high, one American officer found them disgusting.[10]

In the twilight of the surrender, Guerrero witnessed the demoralization that set in among his comrades while the Japanese bombarded the fortress day and night.

> The battery crews began to mock and curse the well-groomed officers and men who through no fault of their own enjoyed the inestimable privilege of doing their duty inside the Malinta tunnel. Subordinates began to entertain unjustified suspicions of the courage of superiors who, in strict accordance with military ritual, could command their inferiors to expose themselves while they themselves remained under the shelter. Citations, medals, decorations, silver stars and purple hearts were scattered generously. But this largesse could hardly disguise the inherent aristocracy of the army, which became even more hateful in the distorted light of the evening of defeat.[11]

The Japanese forces showered Corregidor unrelentingly with hails of bombs, forcing Lieutenant General Jonathan "Skinny" Wainwright, commander of the United States Forces in the Philippines (USFIP), formerly the USAFFE, to surrender on the morning of 6 May. The night before, the Japanese, despite being under heavy fire from the colossal U.S. Army 12-inch guns, managed to land on Corregidor which was being gallantly defended by the American soldiers. But the superior number of enemy forces rather than valour was the crucial factor that decided the victor. Wainwright eventually ordered his men to disarm and destroy everything that would be useful to the enemy — documents, arms, ammunition, and the radio equipment after the surrender was broadcast at 10:30 a.m. The broadcast went on air in Japanese but it went unheeded as the Japanese continued shelling the island. The message was repeated at 11:15 a.m. but the enemy sustained their ferocious assault. At noon, Wainwright ordered the American flag to be lowered from the flagpole and to raise a white flag. When the bombardments slackened, Wainwright decided to meet the Japanese.[12]

While negotiations were taking place at Denver Hill, all USFIP units were ordered to march out of the tunnel with their hands behind the back of their heads. Moments past the surrender, Guerrero, Ruiz and his friend managed to sneak out and went into the Marine tunnel to forage for canned goods as they were starving. Ruiz and his companion found a pile of canned peaches on top of a huge heap of worthless peso notes and Guerrero found a can of tomato juice. There were rumours that they would be massacred, as guns continued to be fired on Carabao Island. They did not know that the Japanese were pressuring Wainwright to surrender all USFIP forces, not only those in Corregidor. After talking to General Masaharu Honma who was adamant on this condition, Wainwright was forced to accept the demand upon seeing additional Japanese forces landing on the island. On 7 May, at the KZRH studio in Manila, he ordered other USFIP commanding officers to surrender. Thus, the more than 10,000 USFIP POWs including Guerrero were saved momentarily from sure death.[13]

POW TO CAPAS

There was a lull between the formal surrender and the occupation of the island before the Japanese could take full control of the prisoners on 8 May when most of them were detained in an enclosure on Bottomside. They were ordered to move around Malinta Hill and temporarily assembled on 10 May at the two ruined seaplane hangars located along the coast of San Jose Bay. They had to stay there for fourteen days without adequate food and water. Sanitation became a severe problem because there were no toilets. On the night of the 24th, awakened from their sleep to get ready for the trip to Manila, they cooked rice and made them into little balls. The next morning, they were ordered to board three ships and the following day at 11:00 a.m., the ships docked at Pier 7 in South Harbour. Farther south, another ship unloaded the Americans who were segregated from the Filipinos; they waded to the shore. Filipino POWs, mostly weakened by dysentery, were lined up by height and so Guerrero was in front. The Japanese ordered them to march from the port by way of Padre Burgos, crossing the Pasig River until Azcarraga Street (now Recto Avenue) and from there straight to Bilibid Prison.[14]

Walking along with other POWs, Guerrero feared that his family might not recognize him. He had his hair clipped short and skin sun-burnt. The thump of shoes as they marched along the road mixed with the chorus of cries from the crowd in the streets. Passing by the legislative building he saw Marina Vargas, wife of Jorge Vargas, chair of the Executive Commission, with her eyes alert, and he thought she was looking for her son. Beside her, he was consoled to see Chitang and Mario feeling sorry to see him emaciated and tired from the war. Occasionally, he would see an open truck teeming with Japanese soldiers manning machine guns on patrol. He saw Japanese soldiers posted along the route to control the crowd. As they advanced through Azcarraga, he saw again his siblings sprinting down the street. At Bilibid Prison, he saw cells teeming with prisoners. At past 9:00 p.m. in the evening, he received his ration of salt-sprinkled rice balls after the leader of his group was given a five-gallon tin can with rice. Though insipid, he welcomed the hot rice to his starving stomach. Staying only for a few days, they marched again to the railroad station for a journey up north in Capas, Tarlac. Early that morning, they were given a ball of rice and some were lucky to receive two bulbs of green onion while another ball of rice was distributed for the midday meal.[15]

Getting off the trains, Guerrero along with fellow prisoners was herded in groups inside Camp O'Donnell. He was separated from the crew of the *Voice of Freedom*. Lopez escaped three days before the fall of Corregidor aboard a PBY navy plane destined for Australia but the plane met with an accident at Lake Lanao. Lopez and two others were left in Mindanao joining the staff of General Manuel Roxas in Malaybalay, Bukidnon. The other four members — Ted Wallace, Norman Reyes, Chuck Boyle and Francisco "Doro" Isidoro — were imprisoned at Fort Santiago. They were told to get off the ships ahead of their fellow prisoners. First they were imprisoned at the British Club at San Marcelino Street and after a week, they were taken to the KZRM studio and on the 30th, they were taken to Fort Santiago. Each of them was grilled about the whereabouts of Quezon, Romulo, Ignacio Javier and the *Voice of Freedom*. Ignacio Javier was of course Guerrero. They never squealed on him to the Japanese. All survived the war except Boyle who died of dysentery.[16]

Guerrero was among the 3,000 Filipino POWs who arrived at Camp O'Donnell in Capas, Tarlac in late May. A Filipino POW who had been at the camp a month earlier observed that the new arrivals were in better shape than they were with their laundry bags containing canned goods, underwear and sulfa pills. At the camp, Guerrero was elected chief cook of his group to his surprise. He realized years later that it was "a tribute, no doubt, to my small appetite and rather dubious chances of survival". For more than a month, he carried on with a bare minimum of food and water to survive. News of their release was thwarted when they were transferred again to Bilibid where Guerrero awaited his freedom. When he left the camp, he gave his mosquito bar to his friend Ruiz. At Bilibid, he met Doro Isidoro.[17]

OUT OF BILIBID: WRITING FOR VARGAS AND THE HODOBU

Guerrero's release from Bilibid sometime in July 1942 was made possible through the intercession of Jorge Vargas when his mother and Chitang went to Mandaluyong and beseeched the chairman of the Philippine Executive Commission to look into his situation. Vargas, Guerrero's former boss when he was writing speeches for Quezon, took him in as technical assistant to prepare speeches and act as secretary. Guerrero knew Vargas back in 1936 when he was brought along by Dick to become one of the charter members of the Philippine Book Guild. Vargas along with Recto, Romulo and Lopez were also charter signatories. The meeting was followed a year later by a feature article on Vargas for the *Free Press*. Annie was relieved to know that her husband, away for more than six months, was finally free but had to report every now and then to Fort Santiago.[18]

From July until early October, Guerrero wrote speeches for Vargas but in mid-October he was recruited to the Hodobu, the Department of Information, formerly called the Sendenbu or the Propaganda Corps. He was forced to work with them because the Japanese threatened him about Annie; they kept on harassing her. Upon his advice, Annie went into hiding in the house of the Cruzes in Paco, where in August Chitang resided since her marriage to Ismael Cruz, the grandson of Maria Rizal. At about this time, his uncle, Cesar Ma. Guerrero, the auxiliary bishop of Manila, began collaborating with the Japanese to protect the interest of the Catholic Church and to carry on the Burgos-initiated Filipinization of the Catholic Church's hierarchy.[19]

Beginning 12 October, Guerrero, again as Ignacio Javier, went on the air to anchor the programme *The Philippines Today* every night at 8:45 p.m. at KZRH radio station on the top floor of the Heacock Building in Escolta. The *Tribune* carrying the news of his upcoming programme described it as an analysis of news from home and abroad, focusing on the Filipino role in building the Greater East Asia Co-Prosperity Sphere. In his first broadcast, Guerrero put in perspective his co-optation to the Japanese. The war disillusioned him about America's promise to defend the Philippines due to the convoy that never arrived. He argued further that the present was an opportunity for Filipinos to acquaint themselves with the East, with the Japanese as their "elder brothers". Whether he was sincere or not, a Dominican rector who was listening to him that night noted in his diary that rumours had it that he was "faced with a choice between talking pro-Japanese or facing a firing squad".[20]

At KZRH he met Filipino personnel recruited for propaganda purposes. Some were friends and acquaintances before the war — Vero Perfecto, pre-war station manager of KZND and a USAFFE comrade in Bataan, Simon Almario, and Marcelo Victoriano. Pilar Lopez-Concepcion served as his secretary and stenographer. Besides getting his salary from the Department of Information under the Japanese Army, he was given rations of rice and sugar, rare commodities during those days.[21]

Propagandist at night, Guerrero continued to be secretary to Vargas during the day writing drafts of speeches and statements to be typed by his secretary at the studio. However, because he was doing well at KZRH, by mid-January 1943, Vargas received a memorandum saying that the Department of Army wanted to retain him and that he [Vargas] may "get other men in place of Mr Guerrero in case... [he] need[s] a full-time assistant". Guerrero's article on Rizal in the context of the Japanese Occupation saw the objectives of *La Liga Filipina* parallel with the *Kapisanan sa Paglilingkod sa Bagong Pilipinas* (KALIBAPI) and the neighbourhood associations being set up in the entire country. His reminiscences on the last days of Corregidor and its fall were published in the Japanese-sanctioned *Philippine Review*, with readers congratulating him for their "sweeping truthful frankness". His broadcast on the Philippines and Burma (Myanmar), at a time when these two countries were promised independence, was a perceptive comparison between the two countries that demonstrated his abiding interest in international affairs, such that it was printed out of popular demand.[22]

Three transcripts of his broadcasts were preserved and all smacked of his anti-Americanism and expression of support for Japan. One broadcast showed his pragmatism in economic terms. Because the Philippines, he said, was made dependent on the American market, Filipinos should take advantage of this opportunity by becoming receptive to Japan and by extension to other Asian countries. His apparent pro-Japanese stand in his broadcasts earned him enemies. Guerrillas in Panay regarded Ignacio Javier as their favourite radio voice before the fall of Corregidor but "our love for him [Ignacio Javier] came to be replaced by [sic] hatred."[23]

In truth, Guerrero detested the Japanese military so that whenever possible he tried to avoid talking to them. He loathed his job completely but since he had no choice, he had to continue with all his scripts checked by the Japanese to see if they tallied with official communiqués from DOMEI news agency. He evaded Japanese censorship by slipping in actual facts to inform the public. A guerrilla who had a balanced assessment of the programme heard him telling about the exploits of Yamamoto, Yamashita, and Honma because "he had no choice in the matter" but also detected the leaks about engagements he incorporated into the broadcasts. Several times, he was reprimanded by the head of the Hodobu and was nearly arrested by the Japanese military. He refused to accede to the urging of his uncle the bishop to express a definite stand on the side of the Japanese, and, as a consequence, broke relations with the latter during the remainder of the Japanese Occupation.[24]

The war completely changed his attitude towards America. He held the pre-war belief that professing loyalty to America was the same as pledging allegiance to the Philippines. But this double allegiance had turned out to be illusory. In his conversations with Chitang, he revealed later: "I became anti-American in Bataan and Corregidor. We ate raw onions and bad rice, while they had steak at the table. We wore coconut helmets, the Americans wore regulation steel." From then on, a nationalist sentiment in Guerrero was born from the crucible of the war, neither in favour of the Japanese nor against the Americans but pro-Filipino. Serving the Japanese who were promoting Filipino culture made him realize and value his own nationality.[25]

Notes

1. Nakpil, *Myself*, p. 126; A.V.H. Hartendorp, *The Japanese Occupation of the Philippines*, vol. 1 (Manila: Bookmark, 1967), p. 313. Salvador P. Lopez, "The Laughter of Leoni", *TJ*, 23 June 1982, p. 4.
2. Ibid.; Carlos P. Romulo and Beth Day Romulo, *The Philippine Presidents* (Quezon City: New Day Publishers, 1988), p. 28; Leon Ma. Guerrero, "Past and Present", *MC*, 30 January 1954, p. 4; Leon Ma. Guerrero, "Corregidor Revisited: Posting on Rock was a blessing", *Manila Times* (hereafter cited as *MT*), 8 May 1972, pp. 1, 6. Felipe Buencamino III, *Memoirs and Diaries of Felipe Buencamino III, 1941–1944* (Makati City: Copycat, 2003), p. 2.
3. Buencamino, *Memoirs*, p. 32; I.T.R., "Atty. Leon Ma. Guerrero", p. 665; Beth Day, *The Manila Hotel: The Heart and Memory of a City* (Manila, 1986), pp. 112–13; Leon Ma. Guerrero, "Rich boy joins the army as told to Leon Ma. Guerrero", *PFP*, 29 April 1939, pp. 4–5; Felipe Buencamino III, "The law and the non-lawyer", *PFP*, 26 April 1941, pp. 16–17, 19; Leon Ma. Guerrero, "The language of the law", *PFP*, 10 May 1941, pp. 16–17; Felipe Buencamino III, "Let's get rid of lawyers and lawyer-judges", *PFP*, 21 June 1941, pp. 16–17, 19.
4. Buencamino, *Memoirs*, pp. 36, 41–45, 49, 54, 73, 85, 110.
5. Guerrero, "Posting on Rock was a blessing", pp. 1, 6; Fidel L. Ongpauco, *They*

Refused to Die: True Stories about World War II Heroes in the Philippines 1941–1945 (Canada: Levesque Publications, 1982), p. 111; Norman Reyes, *Child of Two Worlds: An Autobiography of a Filipino-American or Vice Versa* (Manila: Anvil, 1995), p. 276. The personnel was composed of Romulo, Major Wallace Ince, the pre-war manager of the Manila radio station KZRM, whose name on air was Ted Wallace and Romulo's right-hand man; Major SP Lopez, who wrote English scripts for the broadcast; First Lieutenant Francisco "Doro" Isidoro, the Rock's coast artillery commander, the Tagalog scriptwriter and translator in Tagalog; Technical Sergeant Charles "Chuck" Boyle; Norman Reyes, a former KZRM announcer; Guerrero who did the broadcasts and also wrote English scripts; and an anonymous American enlisted man who served as the studio's technician.

6. Teodoro A. Agoncillo, *The Fateful Years: Japan's Adventure in the Philippines, 1941–45*, vol. 1 (Quezon City: UP Press, 2001), pp. 279–81; Ongpauco, *They Refused to Die*, pp. 112–13.
7. Romulo, *The Philippine Presidents*, pp. 32–36; "Young Asian with Ideas", *Saturday Mirror Magazine* (hereafter cited as *SMM*), 20 February 1954, p. 12.
8. Ongpauco, *They Refused to Die*, pp. 112, 119–20; Nakpil, *Whatever*, p. 196.
9. Benito J. Legarda, Jr, *Occupation '42* (Manila: DLSU Press, 2003), p. 74.
10. Richard C. Mallonee, *Bataan Diary*, II, p. 63 as quoted in Louis Morton, *The Fall of the Philippines* (Washington, D.C.: Center of Military History, United States Army, 1989), p. 385.
11. Leon Ma. Guerrero, "The Last Days of Corregidor", *Philippine Review* (May 1943), pp. 9–12.
12. Ongpauco, *They Refused to Die*, p. 113; Agoncillo, *Fateful Years*, 1, pp. 287–88.
13. Leon Ma. Guerrero, "Corregidor Revisited: Wainwright's bravest act", *MT*, 7 May 1972, pp. 1, 6; Agoncillo, *Fateful Years*, 1, pp. 291–94.
14. Leon Ma. Guerrero, "Corregidor Revisited: The day Manila wept", *MT*, 9 May 1972, pp. 1, 6; Combat History Division G-1 Section, Headquarters AFWESPAC, *Triumph in the Philippines*, Celedonio A. Ancheta, ed. (Manila: National Bookstore, 1977), pp. 169–70.
15. Guerrero, "The day Manila wept", pp. 1, 6; AFWESPAC, *Triumph in the Philippines*, pp. 170–71.
16. Ongpauco, *They Refused to Die*, pp. 114–17.
17. Ibid., p. 117; Guerrero, "Wainwright's bravest act", pp. 1, 6; Mariano Villarin, *We Remember Bataan and Corregidor: The Story of the American and Filipino Defenders of Bataan and Corregidor and Their Captivity* (Baltimore: Gateway Press, Inc. 1990), p. 158.
18. "Leon Ma. Guerrero" in Leon Ma. Guerrero, Box No. 140, Folder No. 4 Case No.__, *People's Court Papers*, University of the Philippines Main Library (hereafter cited as *LMGPCP*); Abaya, *The Making of a Subversive*, p. 44; Nakpil, *Myself*, pp. 175–76; Manuel E. Arguilla, *How my brother Leon brought home a wife, and other stories* (Philippine Book Guild, 1940), p. 247; Guerrero, "The phantom president", *PFP*, 7 August 1937, pp. 8, 40; Father James B. Reuter, S.J., interview by author,

13 May 2006, Manila; Carmen Guerrero Nakpil, interview by author, 27 April 2008, Manila, telephone.
19. Carmen Guerrero Nakpil, interview by author, 27 April 2008, Manila, telephone; "Young Asian", p. 12; Nakpil, *Myself*, p. 177; Alfredo Parpan, "A Study of Church and State Relations during the Japanese Occupation: The Jesuits in the Philippines 1942–1945" (MA thesis, University of the Philippines, 1979), p. 78; David J. Steinberg, *Philippine Collaboration in World War II* (University of Michigan Press, 1967), p. 52; Jose Burgos, a martyred priest who died on the garrotte during the 1872 Cavite Mutiny along with Fr. Mariano Gomez and Fr. Jacinto Zamora, the triumvirate forming the Gomburza, was a leading figure in the secularization of the Philippine Catholic Church, which was the movement for the transfer of parishes from the regular clergy to the seculars.
20. *Tribune*, 11 and 12 October 1942; Ignacio Javier, "Not as Enemies but as Elder Brothers", *Sunday Tribune Magazine*, 18 October 1942, pp. 2, 6; Juan Labrador, *A Diary of the Japanese Occupation* (Manila: Santo Tomas University Press, 1989), p. 136.
21. Enriquez, "Appropriation of Colonial Broadcasting", p. 183; "Memorandum for SP Gatmaitan, 22 January 1946", in *LMGPCP*. See also Elizabeth L. Enriquez, *Appropriation of Colonial Broadcasting: A History of Early Radio in the Philippines, 1922–1946* (Quezon City: University of the Philippines Press, 2008).
22. Armando J. Malay, *Occupied Philippines: The Role of Jorge B. Vargas during the Japanese Occupation* (Manila: Filipiniana Book Guild, 1967), pp. 81–82; Leon Ma. Guerrero, "Rizal and the New Order", *Voice of the New Philippines: A Collection of Lectures on Current Topics* 2 (February 1943), p. 45; "The Last Days of Corregidor", *Philippine Review* (May 1943), pp. 9–12; "The Fall of Corregidor", *Philippine Review* (July 1943), pp. 7–15; *Philippine Review* (August 1943), p. 60; "The Philippines and Burma: A Parallel", *Philippine Review* (September 1943), pp. 46–50, 59, 65.
23. Ignacio Javier, "The Philippines Today: Independence for the Philippines", Scrapbook, Executive Commission 7 (December 1942–January 1943), 145: 3–4 in *Jorge Vargas Papers*, Jorge Vargas Museum and Filipiniana Research Center, University of the Philippines Diliman.
24. "Memorandum for SP Gatmaitan", in *LMGPCP*; Jose M. Hernandez, "USAFFE Record Will Stand Scrutiny of Entire World, Writer Asserts", *Evening News* (hereafter cited as *EN*), 15 May 1947; Nick Joaquin, "The Mysterious Guerrero Bishop" in *Nora Aunor and other Profiles* (Quezon City: National Book Store, 1977), p. 75.
25. *Malaya*, 13 April 2005. For valuing his culture, see his "Rizal and the New Order", pp. 43–46.

7

Second, then First Secretary

When the Japanese-sponsored Philippine Republic was inaugurated on 14 October 1943 with Jose P. Laurel as president, Guerrero thought he was no longer a prisoner but a free man, a citizen of an "independent" nation. Resigning from his work in the Hodobu, he waited until December when he was appointed Second Secretary to the Philippine Embassy in Tokyo to be headed by Vargas, now the ambassador whose superior was Minister of Foreign Affairs Claro M. Recto. In the second week of February 1944, leaving behind Annie, he accompanied Vargas, his son and daughter Roberto and Teresita, his private secretary Feniquito, Francisco Lavides the counsellor, and Faustino Sy-Changco, also second secretary, in a trip to Tokyo. At Nielson Airport, President Laurel, Japanese Ambassador to the Philippines Shozo Murata, Speaker Benigno S. Aquino, Chief Justice Jose Yulo, General Shigenori Kuroda and Japanese Navy and Army commanders were there to send them off. Before heading for Haneda Airport in Tokyo, they spent two days and two nights in Formosa (now Taiwan). On 14 February, the party arrived in Tokyo where they met representatives from the Japanese Foreign Office. Their arrival was welcomed in the press because they would complete the five-member nations of the Greater East Asia Co-Prosperity Sphere for greater cooperation among them and Japan. Ambassadors of China, Manchukuo, Thailand, and Burma were in Tokyo ahead of Vargas and his party.[1]

They stayed for two weeks at the Imperial Hotel near the Emperor's Palace because the purchase of a building that would become the chancery of the Philippine Embassy was under negotiation. Guerrero met Leocadio de Asis, one of the ten Filipino police officers sent to study in Japan in one of the latter's visit to the hotel. Purchased at a million pesos, the Yasuda mansion atop the Kudan Hill was not ready for occupation because its heating system was clogged from disuse. The cold of February was intolerable to Vargas so that they stayed in the hotel. By mid-March, the embassy staff left the hotel and moved to the mansion with a wide lawn apt for parties, located at 18-1 Fujimi-cho, 1-chome, Kajomachiku, a walk away from the Japanese Foreign Ministry's office building.[2]

Since the embassy building had only three bedrooms in the upper floor reserved for Vargas, his teenage daughter and three sons, Guerrero had to find his own quarters elsewhere. The butler's pantry became the counsellor's office; the cloak-room became the Japanese adviser's while the high-ceilinged atelier served as the chancery where Guerrero and his colleagues prepared notes verbale, visas, telegrams, requests for rations and other diplomatic forms.[3]

Prior to the embassy's set up, Filipinos in Japan had become targets of suspicion as spies, particularly those who had Japanese wives or paramours. The embassy could now attend to the welfare of Filipinos who were looked upon as subjects of an enemy country, the United States. *Pensionados* were received in the embassy for whatever they needed. Although no appropriation was allotted from Manila, the embassy got Filipinos out of jail and extended some relief. It also employed three boxers famous throughout Japan (Joe Eagle, Loreto "Baby" Gustilo and Emmanuel Valdes). Stranded students who had facility in Nihongo (the Japanese language) like Teodoro Rodriguez were taken in as interpreters. One of the police officers or "constaboys" as they were called, Alfonso Sirilan was given a job as embassy assistant.[4]

The glamour of life at the embassy that Guerrero was accustomed to back in pre-war Manila began on 19 March when Ambassador Vargas hosted a tea party for the twenty-seven Filipino *pensionados* including de Asis. An impromptu programme was held in which Vargas exhorted the grantees to persevere in their studies and generously welcomed them any time to the services of the embassy. Guerrero attended the needs of the visitors and even talked to the few Japanese who were present in the party. The following week Guerrero celebrated his birthday at the embassy. Joining him were six *pensionados* and the embassy staff who enjoyed eating cake at the simple celebration. By 31 March, Guerrero celebrated his sixth wedding anniversary alone because Annie was left in the Philippines. Since it was also "Viernes de Dolores" or Friday of the Seven Sorrows of the Virgin Mary, he went to Mass at the German Jesuits-run Sophia University's chapel; along with Teresita Vargas and Sy-Changco. They met de Asis. The next day, de Asis visited the embassy where he had a nice chat again with the three and a staff member took their pictures.⁵

The ambassador went home to the Philippines in late May but he instructed his staff to report on their activities while he was away. It was in June when, aside from paperwork preoccupying them during the earlier months, Guerrero and his colleagues prepared for parties. On the first day, they received high-ranking officials from the Daitoa Ministry. Four *pensionados* entertained the guests with one playing the piano and later guitar while the others sang Japanese and Filipino songs. The guests also performed. When the guests left, Guerrero joined in the singing of "*Chitchirichit alibangbang*" and "*Tayo na sa Antipolo*" that extended the party till 9:00 p.m. On the fourth day, Filipinos residing in Tokyo and Yokohama, even those with assumed Japanese names, met at the embassy to agree on the establishment of a Filipino association in Japan, the Kapisanan ng mga Pilipino sa Nippon (KAPINI). Guerrero assisted Counsellor Lavides who presided over the gathering. It was indeed a Filipino affair because at lunchtime everyone enjoyed *lechon* and *dinuguan*. On the 19th, a simple but memorable programme was held in commemoration of Jose Rizal's birthday. Guerrero entertained Filipinos living in Tokyo and Yokohama and representatives of the Daitoa and Army ministries; heard someone deliver an English translation of *Mi Ultimo Adios*, Rizal's farewell poem, and participated in the unveiling of an oil portrait of Rizal by a Japanese painter.⁶

EYES AND EARS WITHIN THE WALLS

Usually programmes and parties were held not only in the hall and in the lawn but in other sections of the mansion including the gold-and-brown living room, the Spanish dining room and the Japanese coffee room, where official guests, ambassadors, generals, ministers and their ladies could come, stay, and leave. It was here that Guerrero heard Horiguchi, Laurel's financial adviser, mention his plans "to sponge up inflation in the Philippines with a trunkful of pearls" or about his stories "of ragged Filipinos ringing the faucets near the Rizal Memorial Stadium where the Japanese garrison washed their mess-tins, and bidding fantastic sums for the grains of rice that were left over". It was also here where he witnessed the squabble between Siamese and Burmese counsellors over the smuggling perpetrated by the former's compatriots that prompted the latter to say: "We in Burma are not even indigent. We are just trying to get up to the zero level." Here, beside the hearth, the Chinese ambassador muttered unhappily about peace. Here also the German ambassador sighed over Japan's suspicious attitude and ineptitude. And the intoxicated General Shigenori Kuroda, former commanding general of the Japanese Army in the Philippines, was heard to have said unkindly about Yamashita: "Yamashita was not so bright. I know. He was my classmate. Well, who's sorry now?"[7]

It was within the walls of the mansion that Guerrero, promoted to first secretary of the embassy, cultivated acquaintances among the diplomatic corps of different countries and thus got acquainted with the intricacies of international power relations. "It is a testimonial to the unique character of the Filipino culture," he would note, "no less than to the diplomatic talent of Jorge B. Vargas, that the Philippine Embassy in Tokyo had, from its establishment, quickly become the logical bridge between the Latin and Nordic, Occidental and Oriental." "There was perhaps no significant diplomatic activity possible in Tokyo at that time," he recalled, "outside of the subtle and intricate game with the Soviet Union; the political struggle had long ago plunged into that sanguinary and decisive continuation defined by Clausewitz as war, and the agile intelligence of the bargainer had long ago been caught under the armored tread of brute force." Nonetheless, he managed to know "the truth about other countries and lie about [his] own … for whatever it might be worth to the Foreign Office in Manila…".[8]

These mere acquaintances had developed into close friendships. A Bulgar whom he used to talk with argued that the Soviet Union's destiny could be found in Asia and not in Europe. There was this passionate Finn who in between toasts of liquor would boast that his race was kin to the Japanese and when his country surrendered to the Allied forces, he said with bitterness that "all cooperation in the Axis you could put in a small handbag". Another was a Thai prince deported back to his country at the Japanese Government's instigation because of his secret dealings with Soviet diplomats. There was the Chinese who told him with much exasperation:

> You know we are all playing the same game. We don't like the Japanese but what can we do? This way, China cannot lose. If the Americans win, then Chiang Kai-shek wins. If the Japanese win, then Wang Ching-wei wins. But of course we cannot tell the people this so they do not understand. They are very unhappy. They have nothing to eat. If they plant rice, then the guerrillas come and say, you give us one-half. Then the Japanese come and say, you give us one-half. So the farmers do not plant. The people do not eat. This war is foolishness.

He was also privy to the secret of an Italian attaché, exiled because his wife was Mussolini's mistress; about a French count, married to a Hungarian blonde who had his leg smashed by a driver's crowbar in Tokyo and a German secretary addicted to collecting nudes.[9]

Indeed, according to Guerrero, Vargas "does not suffer by comparison" with other envoys. The Manchu ambassador, dean of the corps, and a millionaire, did not know how to speak in any other language except Chinese and had to be always surrounded by interpreters while the Nanking envoy was "as typical as old China as a pair of comfortable and unobtrusive padded slippers". The Turkish and French ambassadors arrived late in Tokyo but on time for them to personally sever relations with the Japanese Government. Meanwhile, the schizophrenic minister of Romania was recalled for he imagined himself to be the mother of Jesus. The Danish envoy, "an indefatigable golfer", befriended Eddie, Vargas' son, when he learned that the latter was a champion back home. The Thai and the Burmese ambassadors, both learned men, had difficulty expressing themselves that they became the objects of jokes as the "three famous stutterers in Tokyo" along with the German ambassador, Stahmer. A former director of the Thai national museum, the Thai envoy brought a Thai cultural dance troupe to Tokyo. Then there was the story about the Burmese and the Thai envoys circulating in the diplomatic community. Apparently when the Thai envoy invited the Burmese ambassador to a musical play he composed, the latter became nauseous during the presentation of Siam's victory over Burma in their long history of wars.[10]

However, Filipinos like Guerrero built the most friendly relations with the Burmese "not only because of the parallelism between our countries but also because their education and ideals made them personally most sympathetic". Dr Thein Maung, head of the Burmese mission, "a physician by training but a newspaper publisher and politician by profession" invited him to "several intimate meals and discussions". He noticed the outward manifestations of their nationalism by what they wore even in winter — those native *longyis* made of silk; by their inability to dance modern dances; by their loyalty to their native tongue for they spoke English only to those who did not understand their language but "how desperately they had believed in Japan's generosity and how cruelly they had been deceived!" He also had intense discussions with a Burmese military attaché "on who was more understanding and generous and democratic, the Americans or the British."[11]

LIVING IN TENSE TOKYO

Annie flew unexpectedly to Japan in late September 1944 after many months of being away from Guerrero who had missed her so much. He could have joined her because Recto had approved his application for a fifteen-day furlough, but Annie conveyed to him Recto's advice on postponing the trip, in addition to the recent war developments, so that he decided to cancel his plan. Just two days before she arrived, the Americans bombed Manila. Upon her arrival, President Laurel had declared a state of war against the United States and Great Britain. It was just a month ago when American forces had conducted their air attacks destroying the Sasa naval airdrome in Mindanao and other strategic military installations. She told Guerrero the latest news about the war in the Philippines and his family in Ermita. People had kept their faith in the return of General MacArthur and the Americans. Guerrero and Annie knew that the Japanese war machine had been sapped of its power and the United States had inch-by-inch successfully gained territories such as Saipan and Guam. On 20 October 1944, American forces landed on Palo, Leyte. MacArthur had returned. This led to the greatest naval battle which resulted in Japan's ignominious defeat.[12]

This was the situation when Guerrero had to leave Annie in Tokyo because Vargas brought him along on an inspection trip to Manchukuo along with a Japanese interpreter. Feted by the Manchukuo Government, Vargas at a banquet after hearing that Japanese forces had sunk 500 American ships in Leyte, extolled the Greater East Asia Co-Prosperity Sphere in a speech crafted by Guerrero. However, during the interview, Guerrero overheard a newsman asking Vargas his opinion about the report and quipping, "Surely, we are winning the war!" to which the ambassador retorted with veiled sarcasm: "I don't know. Of course, that might be true. But I have one question in my mind: If the Japanese Imperial Navy had sunk 500 enemy vessels in Leyte Gulf, how is it possible for the Americans to keep on advancing north?" The newsmen were stunned and Vargas never bothered to elaborate. Soon after, Vargas and his party went on another trip, this time, to Mukden and Harbin where they were brought to war factories mass-producing hundreds of tanks, planes and other military hardware but now in lesser capacity than before.[13]

The trip opened Guerrero's eyes to the near possibility of Japan's defeat. It occurred to him that since he was still writing speeches for Vargas, he would craft those speeches with this in mind. Vargas also instructed him to write speeches with double meanings that only a discerning ear could understand where their sympathies lay. So, when Guerrero wrote the speech titled "One Fate — One Destiny" delivered by Vargas at a rally held in Hibiya Park sponsored by the Asia Development Headquarters of the Imperial Rule Assistance Association in early February 1945, he made the Japanese believe that they could still turn the tide of battle in the Philippines by admonishing them to send the Japanese forces under General Yamashita "the planes, tanks, ships, guns and ammunition that they need, and they will stop the Americans". Yet, could they produce planes, tanks, guns and ammunition when every day Japanese war factories were being bombed by American aircraft? He knew the futility of the high hopes that the speech could raise: "But where shall these planes, ships, these guns and ammunition come from? They must come from us in the homefronts, and come with speed, with swift and ever-increasing volume, if they are to produce sure victory for our side and crushing defeat for the enemy." It was like him and Vargas saying that the Japanese were doomed![14]

In Ermita, in November 1944, an American bomb was accidentally dropped at the Guerrero residential compound, causing the death of Guerrero's aunts Felisa and Dolores, while his cousin Dr Luis Ma. Jr died from brain injury from falling debris in the bomb shelter. Luckily his brother Mario and cousin Enrico Mossessgeld who were staying in the basement of their grandfather's house were buried but safe and alive under the rubble.[15]

Guerrero disclosed his sadness about the misfortune in a letter to Lopez who was working now as the press and publications officer at the Ministry of Foreign Affairs. Lopez wrote back in late November sending his sympathies. He continued: "For one so far away like yourself, it must be painful to think that the war which now engulfs us has actually struck a blow so close to home." Aside from venting his fears about the ongoing war, Guerrero informed Lopez about news in Tokyo and sent news clippings from *The Nippon Times* that Lopez admitted: "I myself read them greedily, of course, for the famine here is not confined to the things of the body, as you very well know." He added that: "[t]he Minister highly appreciates your sending the clippings from *The Times*." Lopez had decided to stay on at the Ministry of Foreign Affairs although two-thirds of its personnel, officials or otherwise, had been laid off. He shared candid stories about their daily struggles for self-preservation. He related about his Japanese friends who had just come back from a visit to their country, telling him that "conditions in Japan continued to be fairly normal. The ration system functions like clockwork, they say." The report was probably true to a certain extent but it was also a conscious effort of his friends to ignore the present nervous realities that Japan was facing in the light of Japanese reverses in the ongoing war as opposed to the advances made by the Allied forces in late 1944 that Guerrero was aware of.[16]

The appointment of Teodoro E. Evangelista as vice-minister replacing Emilio Abello encouraged Guerrero to send a short letter of congratulations, revealing the difficult feelings he felt in serving the country in those challenging times: "I believe as I have shown by my own acts that we cannot be censured to serve the country and the people to the best of our ability under circumstances where the easier part of patriotism would be merely to stand aside and criticize or condemn." In a letter crafted by Lopez, Evangelista sympathized with what Guerrero felt:

> I share your generous sentiments regarding the motive that impels those of us who have elected to remain in the service of our people during these critical days. It were childish, indeed, to continue in the service for reasons of personal gain or glory at a time when power and position impose a responsibility out of all proportion to the rewards they confer. That is why I consider it sufficient recompense to be able to feel in oneself a sense of gratification in being able to do something, however, little, for our country and our people in this most trying period of our history.[17]

In 1944, food was becoming scarce in Tokyo. People lined up in the streets for their daily rations. The government limited transportation in the city as petrol was restricted for use by the military. Everyone was anxious when the war would end. By 1945, the uneasiness in Tokyo must have intensified as the American forces started its campaign against Japan. Life in Tokyo for the Filipinos, especially the embassy staff, was getting dangerous and difficult. Air raids were frequent since March. Thus, Guerrero and Annie went back to the embassy building and contented themselves in the "Japanese rooms in the back of the ground floor". In one instance, on 26 May, a fire almost razed the embassy after a disastrous raid. Every time a siren wailed, the staff would go down the basement that was stocked with provisions. They would stay there until the dull thuds of explosion were gone. Although incendiary bombs pierced in several places the roof of the mansion, ruining the garden, the embassy as well as the British ambassador's office were kept intact amidst the devastation that destroyed "every diplomatic establishment in Tokyo".[18]

Resentment against foreigners including Filipinos had begun to build up in Japan. They had become targets of vicious Japanese hate campaigns and harassment so different from the reception of a musical comedy held in January 1945 that drummed up Japanese support for the defence of the Philippines. Guerrero, who had taught himself Nihongo, overheard one day a curious young boy posing irreverent questions to his mother: "*Okasan*, why does that foreigner have better clothes than father? Are not the Japanese the richest and strongest in the world?" Guerrero might have feared for his life and Annie's when he received a news clipping from a Finn who came across it while looking at their legation's files. It was a story about the 1923 earthquake in Tokyo and the racial outburst of the Japanese who blamed the calamity on the foreigners. They ran after a thousand Koreans and those who were caught were clubbed and stoned. Guerrero's own colleague in the embassy did not escape suspicion from the neighbourhood authorities wary about the tapping sounds in the evenings when in fact he was only typing his translation of Kathleen Norris' novel *Mother*. Guerrero, too, was subjected to mild military harassment. A Japanese acquaintance was arrested because he was allegedly providing Guerrero "malicious rumours" and classified maps that were actually "merely reproductions of outdated coast and geodetic survey maps for public distribution". Summoned only after he waived his diplomatic immunity before a navy court martial officer, Guerrero refuted the allegations, which led to the release of his acquaintance upon paying a fine.[19]

As life in Tokyo was becoming tense after the intense air raid of 10 March, the embassy become the refuge of Filipinos caught in difficult circumstances of the war. On one occasion, three Filipinos (Diony de Leon, Jose Desiderio and Mama Sinsuat) disgruntled with their work at the Yokohama Police Academy, ran away by climbing over the academy's walls and sought protection in the embassy. Ambassador Vargas managed to persuade them to return to the academy. On their return, "the Japanese police lined them up against the wall and practiced samurai sword thrusts with the blades directly above their heads. They had the fright of their lives." On another occasion, a Filipino *pensionado*, Jose de Ungria, was arrested and held in custody by the military for trying to escape to Russia. After getting approval for his reassignment to a fishing school in Hokkaido, he ran away and managed to cross the border but to his chagrin, it turned out to be a military area. He was caught in a town away from Sakhalin and beaten up, losing a couple of teeth. Ambassador Vargas, upon learning this, sent Guerrero to negotiate with Japanese authorities for the student's release. He succeeded only on the pretext that Ungria was "out of his mind with homesickness".[20]

In the middle of these things, Guerrero received the distressing news that his brother-in-law, Toto Cruz, was nabbed from their home and executed by the Japanese, leaving behind Chitang and a two-year-old daughter, Gemma Teresa. His cousin, Dr Tristan, was killed in a street skirmish when Ermita became the battleground between the attacking Americans and retreating Japanese.[21]

Guerrero had an inkling of the changing tide that was coming. On Quezon's death in August 1944, Osmeña assumed the presidency and ordered the creation of a board that would investigate charges of disloyalty to the Commonwealth and the United States. Laurel continued to hold the reins of government but he and his cohorts would have to face the painful reality of siding with the enemy. They had to surrender to the "legitimate" government.[22]

WAITING FOR AND JOINING THE LAUREL PARTY

Soon, the embassy received a cable about a trip Laurel and his companions would be taking from Tuguegarao to Tokyo. The group suffered the exigencies of travel in a time of war. The embassy got hold of the information that they boarded the *Awa Maru* in Formosa but the embassy lost contact with the vessel, causing much concern. In fact, Laurel and his companions, like forsaken and forgotten refugees, had to wait for more than two months at Sozan in Formosa before Tokyo would order their evacuation. Guerrero and his colleagues were relieved when they learned that Laurel's group had not taken the *Awa Maru* because it had been sunk. Finally on 27 June 1945, Guerrero saw them at the Shimbashi station getting off from the train that carried them from Nara to Tokyo.[23]

The trip was not over. Guerrero went with them to the Imperial Hotel, which stood deserted and stripped of its former splendour. They were billeted in suite no. 202 where inside and outside, Japanese were posted to watch over them. Guerrero was privy to the attempts of the Japanese to pressure Laurel. The Japanese tried to draw a public statement in support of Japan but Laurel frustrated their efforts. The first night was a long night since Guerrero and the embassy staff were eager to know what forced them to leave the Philippines. And so, Guerrero listened to Laurel attentively, the story that he would later recount. After Laurel and his companions had met with the Japanese emperor the following morning, Foreign Minister Togo hosted a state dinner for them at the Imperial Hotel. It was here where Guerrero heard Laurel deliver the statement the Japanese were waiting for and that rang clear to Guerrero in 1954:

> The enemies can kill all of us, their bombs may destroy, but they cannot kill the ideal, the aspiration and the longings of the one billion peoples of this part of the world to be free, to be left alone so that Asia may be for the Asiatics and my Philippines may be for the Filipinos...".

In another speech, this time in a villa, he listened to Laurel speak of a yearning to go home, evoking tears from him and the other Filipinos. He parted with Laurel and his companions because they were headed to Nara.[24]

In Nara, Laurel continued to assume the leadership among the Filipinos. He wanted to gather the Filipinos there, numbering sixty, in one place "in order to meet future emergencies with a united front". Informed of the plan, Vargas mobilized the embassy to communicate this concern to the proper authorities. Since no response from the Foreign Office was forthcoming, Guerrero and his colleagues took the initiative of disseminating the plan to the Filipinos especially the *pensionados*. The students came to Tokyo and Nara in small groups. But a turn of events prevented Laurel from pursuing the plan because on 6 August, the atomic bomb was dropped on Hiroshima, then on Nagasaki on 9 August, forcing the Japanese emperor to surrender Japan on 15 August. Shortly after, Laurel declared the formal end to the Japanese-sponsored Philippine Government.[25]

In all these developments Guerrero was in the diplomatic evacuation centre in the mountains of Hakone visiting Annie who had been there days before. He had heard the news about the bomb over the radio sent by his best friend in Japan, Colonel Aung Than, the Burmese military attaché in Tokyo. His trip had become more than a visit for he renewed ties with his friends in the diplomatic community. In the last week of August, Guerrero accompanied the embassy staff and Vargas to their extension office on the second floor of the Imperial Hotel. On 30 August, Guerrero, while having a good time in the dining room of the hotel, met David "Dave" Boguslav, correspondent for *The Times* and the *Chicago Sun*. He had a long conversation with Dave who was with other press people. After the talk, Guerrero joined them in a ride to the embassy where they met Vargas. He met Dave again when Dave came back to the hotel in the same week.[26]

APPLYING FOR REPATRIATION

Beginning September, Guerrero stayed in the mountains of Hakone with Annie. The Americans had arrived in Japan but he had little idea what would happen next. When he learned of Vargas and Laurel's arrest and imprisonment, he feared he might be subjected to the same treatment. Days passed and he did not suffer from any indiscriminate searches, seizure and interrogation. He wanted to visit Vargas, Laurel, Camilo Osias and Benigno S. Aquino in Sugamo Prison but only family members were allowed. To maintain his contact with his superiors, he sent them Manila newspapers, presumably sent to him by his friends back home. He sent letters telling them about the collaboration trial of Teofilo Sison, Minister of Justice in the Japanese-sponsored Philippine Republic, who was the first high official to be indicted, and about Manuel Roxas' campaign for political leadership, and the elections that followed. Vargas wrote him three letters while Laurel sent him a short note. Vargas was considering him to be one of his defence counsels. In December, Guerrero arranged for a trip home with his wife but was flatly told that transportation was very limited and he had to wait for the people in Sugamo. In the summer of 1946, he applied for repatriation but again it was rejected. Nevertheless the life in the mountains and by the seashore fascinated Guerrero and Annie who had no choice but to stay there until July:

> Life in the mountains of Hakone and afterward by the seashore at Atami had been pleasant. We had renewed many old friendships and made new ones among the diplomats there with the New Yorker married to an Italian painter who had satisfied a boyhood book-love of Japan by becoming secretary-interpreter; with the Manila beauty (Angela Camahort) whose husband had been caught by the war in Japan, called to the colors, and drafted to the embassy; with the oddly-paired Germans who had escaped from a British concentration camp in India by passing themselves off as English officers and had barely convinced the kempei-tai they were not spies sent across the lines in Burma.[27]

At last, repatriation came. Guerrero was chatting with Romulo at the Tokyo correspondents' club when three Americans came looking for the general. He learned that they were going home, prompting him to return immediately to Atami. Annie, informed about the good news, started to pack their things. A party that night was held in celebration of Philippine independence. It must have been both exhilarating and melancholic for Guerrero and Annie to observe the celebration of independence for the first time outside the country. Nonetheless, they went for a dance on a night that would be their last in Atami. The following day, they travelled to Tokyo where they stayed in the air transport command hostel. There, they had another round of farewell party with fellow Filipinos. They waited for more than two weeks until 23 July when they finally departed for home.[28]

That morning, they woke up before 7:00 a.m. when an American officer called them for a drive to the airfield. At the airfield, they were excited running to meet the people from Sugamo whom they had not seen for ten months. After putting their baggage inside a reconverted B-17, they climbed into the fuselage with Laurel and Aquino seated in the rear compartment while Vargas and Osias took the front compartment ready for the take-off. Up above, as they were informed that the bomber had arrived in Philippine airspace, they saw Manila below completely devastated. Upon seeing the horrors of war inflicted on his city, sadness engulfed Guerrero: "But Manila was not dead; or what was dead of it, was not yet buried so that the returning native must endure the horror of recognizing with a start the gaunt scarred face he remembered as once lovely." A group of soldiers, photographers, and reporters were waiting at the airport as the plane landed. Upon their exit from the bomber, they would face a new life. Laurel, Vargas, Aquino, and Osias would face trial in the People's Court.[29]

Notes
1. Hartendorp, *The Japanese Occupation of the Philippines*, I, p. 92; Leon Ma. Guerrero, "Tokyo Diary", *Manila Envelope* 2 (May 2006), p. 24; Ricardo T. Jose, "Test of Wills: Diplomacy between Japan and the Laurel Government", in *Philippines-Japan Relations*, edited by Setsuho Ikehata and Lydia N. Yu-Jose (Quezon City: Ateneo de Manila University Press, 2003), pp. 200–1, 217 n59; Malay, *Occupied Philippines*, pp. 128–29.
2. Ibid., pp. 129–30. A.V. H. Hartendorp, *The Japanese Occupation of the Philippines*, I, p. 92; Leon Ma. Guerrero, *Twilight in Tokyo: The Inside Story of Laurel during the Last Days of Imperial Japan* (Manila: Manila Times Publishing Company, 1946), p. 101; Leocadio de Asis, *From Bataan to Tokyo: Diary of a Filipino Student in Wartime Japan 1943–1944* (Center for East Asian Studies, University of Kansas, 1979), p. 118.
3. Guerrero, *Twilight in Tokyo*, p. 102.
4. Ibid.; Lydia N. Yu-Jose, *Filipinos in Japan and Okinawa 1880s–1972* (Research Institute for the Languages and Cultures of Asia and Africa, Tokyo University of Foreign Studies, 2002), p. 97.
5. De Asis, *From Bataan to Tokyo*, pp. 121, 125, 127, 129–30.
6. Ibid., pp. 153–54; Guerrero, *Twilight in Tokyo*, p. 102; Yu-Jose, *Filipinos in Japan and Okinawa*, p. 101; De Asis, *From Bataan to Tokyo*, pp. 158–59; Malay, *Occupied Philippines*, p. 131.
7. Guerrero, *Twilight in Tokyo*, p. 103.
8. Ibid., p. 104; Jorge B. Vargas to Claro M. Recto, 13 July 1944, *Japanese Occupation Papers*, University of the Philippines Main Library.
9. Guerrero, *Twilight in Tokyo*, p. 104.
10. Ibid., pp. 104–5.
11. Ibid., pp. 105–6.
12. Malay, *Occupied Philippines*, p. 205; Leon Ma. Guerrero to Claro M. Recto, 30 August 1944, *Japanese Occupation Papers*, University of the Philippines Main Library.
13. Alfredo Saulo, *"Let George do It": A Biography of Jorge B. Vargas* (Quezon City: University of the Philippines Press, 1990), p. 162.
14. Malay, *Occupied Philippines*, pp. 130, 132–33; Saulo, *"Let George do It"*, pp. 171–72, 224.

15. W.M. Guerrero, *Guerreros of Ermita*, p. 65.
16. Salvador P. Lopez to Leon Ma. Guerrero Jr, *Historical Bulletin* 11, no. 3 (September 1967): 340–43.
17. Quoted in Abaya, *The Making of a Subversive*, pp. 57–58.
18. Malay, *Occupied Philippines*, p. 132; Guerrero, *Twilight in Tokyo*, p. 103.
19. Guerrero, *Twilight in Tokyo*, pp. 87–88.
20. Ibid., p. 89; Villarin, *We Remember Bataan and Corregidor*, pp. 238–39.
21. Nakpil, *Whatever*, p. 199.
22. Steinberg, *Philippine Collaboration*, p. 140.
23. Guerrero, *Twilight in Tokyo*, pp. 74–86 passim. The Laurel party consisted of Dr and Mrs Jose P. Laurel, their three daughters (Natividad, Rose and Potenciana), their sons Mariano, Jose Jr (Pepito), Salvador (Doy) and Arsenio (Dodjie), Mrs Betty Laurel and her two children, Benigno S. Aquino, General Mateo Capinpin and Mr and Mrs Camilo Osias.
24. Guerrero, *Twilight in Tokyo*, pp. 72–86, 89, 90–93.
25. Ibid., pp. 93–96.
26. Ibid., pp. 95, 98, 100.
27. Ibid., pp. 109–10; Jorge Vargas, "Sugamo Diary", in *The Burden of Proof: The Vargas-Laurel Collaboration Case* by Teodoro A. Agoncillo (U.P.-Jorge B. Vargas Filipiniana Research Center, 1984), pp. 271, 295, 298, 315, 325.
28. Guerrero, *Twilight in Tokyo*, p. 110.
29. Ibid., pp. 110–11.

8

At the Home Office: The Diplomat as Historian

In the newly created Department of Foreign Affairs that held offices first at Malacañang Annex then moved to Arlegui Street in Manila, Guerrero applied in August 1946 for a post and was accepted, becoming the assistant chief of division, Division of European and African Affairs under Dr Jacinto C. Borja. Under the Office of Political and Economic Affairs, the division was responsible for the crafting of governmental policy in its conduct of relations with states of Europe and Africa. As assistant chief, he assisted Borja in developing basic country and area studies to guide Philippine foreign policy in those countries. He consulted various offices and agencies of the government in the formulation of policy; provided information to these offices to guide them in the conduct of their activities that impinge on Philippine policy towards other countries, and other tasks. He also worked with Teodoro "Doring" Evangelista, still his superior, who held office at the Office of the Counsellor on Political and Cultural Affairs. The wartime ministry became the nucleus of the new department.[1]

Guerrero was also taken in as confidential secretary to Vice President, and also Secretary of Foreign Affairs Elpidio Quirino. He wrote memos, letters, speeches and would perform other tasks ordered by Quirino such as taking down notes in meetings presided by his boss. Then, he was promoted to Chief of Protocol. By virtue of the reorganization implemented in January 1947, the Division of Protocol was placed under the office of Undersecretary Bernabe Africa. As head of the division, Guerrero was responsible for arranging the presentation of ambassadors and ministers accredited to the government. He corresponded with foreign governments on their acceptability and the acceptability to foreign governments of Filipino counterparts. He arranged national and international events here and abroad in which the Philippines participated; made arrangements for the visit of Philippine officials and organizations abroad; arranged for the entry of American forces and their supplies in accordance with treaties; prepared letters of credence, commissions, exequaturs, certificates of recognitions, and other correspondences regarding the exchange of diplomatic and consular representatives and the opening and closing of diplomatic and consular offices; and maintained a record of all officers and staff of foreign governments in the Philippines and published it into a list annually.[2]

It was at this point that he had a first-hand understanding of and participation in the ongoing negotiations between the Philippines and the United States that would largely define Philippine-American relations. The Philippines' safest course, in President Manuel Roxas' view during his Independence Day address, after the devastation caused by the war, was "in the glistening wake of America". By enunciating closer Philippine-American ties, the Philippines was inevitably drawn into the side of the United States, becoming entangled in the Cold War between two superpowers, the United States and USSR. One of the first treaties signed between the Philippines and the United States was the military agreement, the signing of which Guerrero had the opportunity to witness in Malacañang in March. He was also present during the negotiations on the treaty of amity between the Philippines and an anti-communist ally, the Republic of China held in Manila and one in Baguio that was signed between Quirino and Minister Chen Chih-Ping in February and ratified by the Senate in May.[3]

IN DEFENCE OF LAUREL: TWILIGHT IN TOKYO

But the trials of Laurel and Vargas in the People's Court disturbed Guerrero. To him, it was a curious phenomenon — he called it a war neurosis — that since his return to Manila, everyone was supposed to either side with or be against Laurel. One night he wrote the first part of the serial he titled *Twilight in Tokyo*, submitted it to the *Manila Times* and on the first day many people bought a copy. He continued to submit his pieces every day and the response was enthusiastic. The serial was a best-seller so that the publisher collected the fourteen articles into one volume with a translation in Tagalog by October 1946. The serial evoked responses from readers as well as protagonists in the story to clarify unclear points in the narrative. In answer to his question raised in the fourth article whether the guerrillas knew who they were attacking when the Laurel convoy was on its way to Tuguegarao, Captain Duque, PA, also a friend of his, called at Sampaloc a day after the article was published. Duque of the Volckmann's guerrilla group told him that they knew. The mission of the attack was to capture the Laurel party alive but they were prevented from doing so because of the Japanese heavy counter-attack, so they withdrew. Dave Boguslav, to whom Guerrero attributed the term "first Yank into Tokyo", rectified the notion, writing that he "was one of the first four". Ben Osias, son of Dr Osias and one of the *pensionados*, provided a glimpse of life after the Laurels and Osiases took residence in the embassy.[4]

The serial turned out to be a testimony of Guerrero's lucid memory and superb historical plot that an intelligent reader might think that it was penned back in Tokyo or in the mountains of Hakone. The descriptions of places, personalities and events were written with a clarity of detail only a journalist and writer could have done. It was possible that he had taken some notes while in Tokyo. That he did some more interviews back home to supplement the data he got from the Laurel group when they arrived at the Imperial Hotel or in the bomber plane on their way to Manila was also possible. Guerrero quoted the letters of Vargas to Pedro Lopez, the letter of Laurel to Yamashita and other important documents in the serial. It was unknown whether he wrote the story on his own volition but the range of sources that were consulted indicated that Laurel and Vargas supported the undertaking, which had put them in a good light while they were being prosecuted in the People's Court. As to the impact of the serial during their trial and prosecution, it could not be ascertained but Guerrero's motive of influencing public opinion might have been achieved to some extent.[5]

WRITING A FILIPINO HISTORY OF BATAAN: THE PASSION AND DEATH OF THE USAFFE

The success of the serial motivated Guerrero to write another the following year. It was the fulfilment of a plan conceived even in his days in Bataan when he planned to write a work of fiction. It evolved into non-fiction with the title, *The Passion and Death of the USAFFE*. But he was motivated by another reason: he was discontented and disappointed with books on the war, one of which he had just reviewed, so that Filipinos "looking for a history of the liberation of his country that will give him a clear idea of how it happened, will have to seek it elsewhere", such as in his narrative of the war. Its publication was opportune for he timed its first instalment out of sixteen, on 9 April — the fall of Bataan, which fell on a Lenten season.[6]

"Bataan", asserted Guerrero, "was a Filipino fight. That is as good a point as any at which to start any history of Bataan. For it is a point that seems to have escaped most of those who have written books about it; apparently it was never heard of in Hollywood." He was quick to point out that his assertion did not in any way undervalue the contribution of the Americans in terms of strategy, logistics and supplies, and command, but the men on the line were mostly Filipinos, about 50,000 to 60,000 compared to 10,000 Americans who were mostly reserve officers. After five years, he believed, it was now possible to write it with little misinterpretation as against a history that was written too soon that it could be seen as mere propaganda, or if it was too long after the event, it might be deemed as hearsay. It was a revisionist history for he debunked the myths clouding Filipinos' interpretation of Bataan. First, it was never an American fight. Second, the notion that the USAFFE fought "against overwhelming odds" or "in the face of overwhelming numerical superiority" was not true as he cited Japanese testimonies in General Honma's public trial that there were around 50,000 Japanese when they laid siege to Bataan. Third and last, Bataan did not save Australia contrary to popular belief. Australia "was saved by the American naval victory in the Coral Sea". The last two positions would earn him prejudiced reactions, insults and intrigues from the very organization he wrote about.[7]

Some veterans of Bataan and Corregidor resented the articles, calling for raps against Guerrero and the publisher. One open letter to Solicitor General Lorenzo Tañada of the People's Court asked why Guerrero was not indicted in court, citing his radio propaganda work for the Japanese. Rodolfo Palma, an ex-USAFFE captain, decried the serial as desecrating the memories of dead comrades and hurled *ad hominem* attacks at the author. He was firm in his belief that Bataan saved Australia and was critical of Guerrero's use of Japanese accounts.[8]

In reaction, Guerrero was firm in his convictions that his point was "Bataan was a fight by and for Filipinos." "I cannot agree with Capt Palma," he wrote, "that Bataan's dead are more honored by saving Australia than by defending the Philippines." He defended his use of Japanese accounts:

> I have used them and will continue to use them whenever they are pertinent because they constitute historical material, which so far as I know has never before been available to the general public and should thus be of interest to the impartial reader. I believe that a real history of Bataan can be written only if the historian is ready to examine and evaluate information from all possible sources without patriotic prejudice.

As regards the attacks made against him, he claimed:

> While my services on Bataan were probably negligible, I should like to state, for the record, that I was assigned to the Military Intelligence under Brig. Gen. Simeon de Jesus and was therefore in a position, not open to all, to gather and evaluate information from all sectors in Bataan... I did not come under the Japanese voluntarily. The Office of Special Prosecutors is a better judge of that than Capt. Palma and I am not aware that any indictment has been filed in the People's Court.[9]

After Palma's attacks, the USAFFE veterans appointed Jose M. Hernandez, a former USAFFE major, to present their views on the issues provoked by the serial. The arguments by Hernandez were no different from Palma's. Hernandez tried to refute Guerrero's arguments by citing USAFFE sources that the USAFFE was really outnumbered; that Bataan saved Australia; that the use of Japanese sources was an evidence of Guerrero's bias against them; and that Guerrero's account could not be relied on because Guerrero's credibility was questionable.[10]

Guerrero in response cited contradictions in Hernandez's articles; he maintained his stand on the primary points and concluded that they did not disagree on many points as a matter of fact. As to his use of Japanese sources, he asked Hernandez on who would be more reliable in assessing Japanese strength — American or Japanese. "If I wrote the *Passion*," Guerrero explained, "it was in the humble desire to give the USAFFE and our country their just share in the glory of Bataan and the martyrdom that followed, a share that, it seemed to me, had been grossly belittled in the foreign accounts of the campaign." Palma and Hernandez were only two of the many veterans outraged by Guerrero's serial. They found in the *Philippine Liberty News* the opportunity to voice out their disagreements with him and his work, attacks that were mainly personal without noting the main thesis. As for the reply of the Solicitor General's Office to the question why Guerrero was never indicted in court for collaboration, Tañada wrote that there was insufficient information to file a case against Guerrero. In fact, the office did investigate Guerrero but found the two-witnesses rule in the indictment not applicable since the two who testified exonerated Guerrero from any collaboration charges.[11]

There were unfounded fears that the serial might hurt the interests of the veterans and that it jeopardized Philippine-American relations. Congress, in reaction to his articles, suppressed his post in the Department of Foreign Affairs as chief of protocol, forcing him to resign in May. His resignation from the department, contrary to the advice of his superior, Vice President Quirino, would be the start of his career for six years outside the Foreign Service.[12]

The war years opened his eyes to the grim reality of Philippine-U.S. relations in that America was not forthcoming in repaying Filipino loyalty, completely shattering whatever illusions he had on pro-Americanism as a corollary of Filipino nationalism. Filipino nationalism, to him now, would mean being independent of the United States, finding a cure to the Filipinos' excessive pro-Americanism by looking East, towards Japan and other Asian countries. The irony of it all was that he was at least instrumental in the crafting of agreements that placed the Philippines heavily dependent on the United States.

Notes

1. *Official Directory of the Republic of the Philippines* (hereafter cited as *OD*) *1946* (Manila: Bureau of Printing, 1946), pp. 9–10; *OD 1947*, p. 15; Office of Public Information, Malacañang, *Republic of the Philippines Government Manual 1950* (Manila: Bureau of Printing, 1950), pp. 175–76, 179.
2. "Notes on the authors", in *The Voice of the Veteran: An Anthology of the Best in Song and Story by the Defenders of Freedom*, edited by Manuel E. Buenafe (Republic Promotion, 1946), p. 88; *Government Manual 1950*, pp. 177–78.
3. Honesto T. Vitug, *I Shot the Presidents* (V.G. Puyat, 1989), p. 62; Shi-ching Hsiao, *Chinese-Philippine Diplomatic Relations, 1946–1975* (Manila: Bookman, 1975), pp. 14–21.
4. L.M. Guerrero, *Twilight in Tokyo*, pp. 71, 89, 98–100.
5. Ibid., pp. 71–111.
6. *Philippine Review* (May 1943), p. 2 and (August 1943), p. 60; Leon Ma. Guerrero, "Review of *Children of Yesterday* by Jan Valtin", *Pacific Affairs* 20, no. 1 (March 1947): 88; Leon Ma. Guerrero, "The Passion and Death of the USAFFE", *EN*, 9 April 1947, pp. 1, 2.
7. Guerrero, "The Passion and Death of the USAFFE", *EN*, 9 April 1947, pp. 1, 2; 10 April 1947, pp. 1, 2, 10; 14 April 1947, pp. 1, 3, 13; 16 April 1947, pp. 1, 2; 17 April 1947, pp. 2, 15, 16; 18 April 1947, p. 9; 21 April 1947, p. 8; 22 April 1947, pp. 9, 10; 23 April 1947, p. 7; 24 April 1947, p. 12; 26 April 1947, pp. 13, 14; 28 April 1947, p. 4; 29 April 1947, p. 9; 30 April 1947, pp. 10, 13; 1 May 1947, pp. 6, 10; 2 May 1947, pp. 11, 14; 3 May 1947, pp. 14, 15.
8. Tomas Santiago, "Open letter to Solicitor General Lorenzo Tañada, *Philippine Liberty News* (hereafter cited as *PLN*), 1 May 1947, p. 6; Rodolfo Palma, "Ex-USAFFE Captain says Guerrero Opus a Desecration of Dead Heroes", *EN*, 11 April 1947. I tried to access the *Evening News* and other publications in the collection of the National Library of the Philippines to get the page numbers but unfortunately the serials section is in a state of disarray at the moment.

9. "Author says his point was: Bataan was a fight by and for Filipinos", *EN*, 14 April 1947, p. 6.
10. Jose M. Hernandez, "Passion and Death of the USAFFE Full of Errors, Spokesman Maintains", *EN*, 13 May 1947; "USAFFE Record will stand scrutiny of entire world, writer asserts", *EN*, 15 May 1947.
11. "Guerrero rebuts critics on 'Passion'", *EN*, 16 May 1947, p. 13; 'Memorandum for SP Gatmaitan, 22 January 1946' in Leon Ma Guerrero, Box No. 140, Folder No. 4 Case No._, *People's Court Papers*, University of the Philippines Main Library. See *PLN* for the series of attacks with editor's slant against Guerrero. Guerrero was given chance to answer back his critics in "Guerrero answers critics", *PLN*, 1 May 1947, p. 7 and "Again, Guerrero", *PLN*, 3 May 1947, p. 7.
12. *EN*, 16 May and 18 July 1947.

III

Going In, then Out of the Political Jungle: Padre Burgos to Arlegui

"[T]he main political parties, the *Nacionalista* and the Liberals degenerated into opportunistic coalitions of power groups maneuvering for advantage in the scramble for spoils."

Leon Ma. Guerrero, *Today Began Yesterday*

"Our foreign policy was conducted from the very beginning, and is being pursued on the erroneous assumption of an identity of American and Filipino interests, or more correctly of the desirability, and even necessity of subordinating our interests to those of America … It is folly to expect that any other nation will even sacrifice its welfare and security to pure idealism or to pure sentimental attachments. As Filipinos, we must look out for ourselves because no one else will. That is the very essence of our independence."

Senator Claro M. Recto, *UP Commencement Address*, April 1951

9

The Legal Counsel, Professor and Translator

The Legislative Building at the corner of Taft Avenue and Burgos Street was an imposing architectural edifice destroyed during the war. That first day of September 1947, Guerrero rode his car from Lipa Street in Sampaloc to apply for a job as legal adviser, not in Padre Burgos Street but in the Manila City Hall, the temporary office of the Philippine Senate until it moved three years later to the rebuilt and refurbished complex. Having given up his work as first assistant attorney at Gibbs, Gibbs, Chuidian and Quasha law firm, the job he had after he resigned from the Department of Foreign Affairs, he filled up a form stating his name, birth, and the usual personal matters, but there were quite unusual questions which he answered nonetheless. "Are you an habitual gambler of card, cockfighting, etc?" He wrote down "No." "Are you addicted to any drug or intoxicating liquor?" "No." "Are you punctual in the payment of your debts?" "Yes." "Are you related (by blood or by law) to anybody now working in the Senate?" He wrote "Yes." His second cousin, Efrain Ma. Guerrero, was working in the Senate. On space allotted for references, he only wrote Antonio Zacarias. On that same day, he was sworn in as legal adviser by Zacarias, the Secretary of the Senate.[1]

From the executive branch of government, he would now be working at the legislative branch. As legal adviser, he would advise the secretary on legal matters particularly on bills and resolutions affecting the office and the entire Senate without having to be insulated from politics. Working full-time at the Senate allowed him to go to Albert, Reyes, Guerrero, Roces law offices for his private legal practice. It was in November when the senatorial elections were held. Guerrero saw Laurel's re-emergence into the political scene when the latter decided to run for senator under the Nacionalista Party. President Roxas, however, persuaded him to get out of the opposition. Roxas did try hard to convince Laurel from participating in the elections until after the issuance of amnesty in late January 1948. Laurel decided not to run while Osias went on with his senatorial ambition. The senatorial elections, "the first of graft-ridden elections that were to mark Philippine post-war politics", were a clear victory for the Liberals who won the seven seats with only one coming from the opposition, Osias.[2]

The first quarter of the new year greeted the country with the sudden death of President Roxas in April; Vice President Quirino assumed the presidency. A host of scandals came out in the early months of the Quirino administration — cases of graft and corruption that were tolerated, hidden and accumulated in the later part of the Roxas administration. Surplus property, streptomycin, NACOCO, PRATRA and other scandals rocked the new administration and inside the Senate halls, a political squabble fuelled by intrigues was about to ensue, drawing the interest of Guerrero who was made legislative counsel in mid-February earning him an increase in salary although the line of work was the same.[3]

Guerrero observed how petty political quarrels blackened Senate politics in the way Senator Vicente J. Francisco conducted his political antics with Senate President Jose Avelino. Francisco accused Avelino of plotting to evict him as chair of the Senate Code Committee, dragging the president into the controversy. Amid this political circus, Avelino appointed Guerrero secretary to the delegations of the Senate to two expense-paid gatherings in Italy — the International Parliamentary Union Conference and the International Meeting of Parliamentary Representatives and Exports for the Development of International Trade. His first time going to Europe, Guerrero attended the conference in Rome on 6–11 September, taking down notes for he was required to submit a "report on his activities". He did the same thing when he attended the second meeting in Genoa, staying there from 14 September until he went home together with the delegation four days later.[4]

Coming back from Europe, Guerrero learned of another controversy following the Avelino-Francisco ruckus that undermined the integrity of the Senate. In the hall he heard Senator Fernando Lopez demanding the investigation of the immigration commissioner who implicated Lopez in the immigration quota allocation graft scheme in the bureau. The investigation lasting for six months coincided with the explosion of another controversy in the first quarter of 1949 that had repercussions in the nation's political climate. Avelino was ousted from the Senate presidency in a series of political squabbles, ending his more-than-three-year reign.[5]

The Liberal Party set a caucus in mid-January 1949 to straighten out differences that threatened a split within the party. The caucus proved to be Avelino's undoing, contrary to what he told to the press that he would fight Quirino on the issue of party loyalty. Avelino's two-hour harangue at the *bahay kubo* adjoining the palace was reproduced in the press, provoking the indignation of the people by its blatant endorsement of corruption.[6]

As he tried to recall his years in that First Congress, Guerrero in 1975 interpreted the foregoing in a different light, placing it in the context of the Japanese Occupation:

> The bare need for survival under a ruthless enemy had bred a cult of violence, a neurotic avidity for riches and the unspoken but nonetheless overwhelming conviction that might made right. "We are not angels," a senate president told his party caucus when he was accused of the irregular disposal of U.S. surplus properties to build up campaign funds. "What are we in power for?"

Indeed, Avelino, the Senate president unnamed in Guerrero's recollection, was incriminated in the surplus property scandal but it was not clear whether it was "to build up campaign funds". Guerrero's intimate knowledge of his superior's ambition to become president and the intrigues in the Senate made his conclusion plausible.[7]

The factionalism in the Senate led to the unseating of Avelino who cried foul and plotted his return and the ouster of the Senate under Mariano Jesus Cuenco. Guerrero's position was caught in the political storm. Senate President Pro Tempore Melecio Arranz reasoned in a letter to Guerrero that the Senate incurred an overdraft of approximately PHP115,000 and that there was no fund available to support Guerrero's temporary post. Arranz, however, added that he could apply for a leave of absence so that he "will be paid after the necessary requirements are complied with". In reality, his position was subject to the whims of the Senate president. The notice of termination was quite unexpected because he was given time to clear all obligations in just four days. He was cleared of money, property, accounts receivables and advances except his book loan responsibility. The chief librarian listed a number of unreturned books, almost all of which had to do with law, he was still using in his teaching and research at Far Eastern University (FEU) and at Francisco Law School. His services as the legislative counsel was extended by more than two months, or adding the leave, to at least four months, enabling him to sit and watch the suspension of Avelino.[8]

The Avelino case was really partisan politics dividing the Liberal Party and the nation. The post-war politics before 1974 was characterized by a two-party system in which the bicameral legislature, particularly the Philippine Senate as the upper house, served as the training ground for possible contenders to the Philippine presidency. In this rather strange case, with Avelino exercising an influence equal to the party leader as Senate president, the Liberal Party was split in two. It was a showdown between the Avelinistas, supporters of Avelino in the Liberal Party, and Quirinistas, partisans of President Quirino, also the party leader, in the same majority party in the Senate vying for power with the Nacionalistas as the minority party acting as fiscalizer of the administration party, which exploited the split to their advantage. Avelino's conviction did not end the political squabble between Avelino and Quirino. With one less member, incidentally the leader, from the Avelinistas, the Senate composition was tilted in favour of the Quirinistas but Avelino, though he was ousted, was far from being powerless.[9]

TEACHING AND RESEARCHING LAW

Although he watched with both interest and annoyance the squabbles in the Senate, Guerrero had to find other ways of releasing his energy productively. That, he found in teaching, at the FEU Institute of Law whose dean was Mariano A. Albert, one of his law partners. Guerrero belonged to the faculty roster teaching public international law, pleadings and brief-making, and thesis. Among the twenty-one faculty members were familiar colleagues such as Francisco Lavides whose expertise was remedial law, and constitutional law professor Jose P. Laurel. At one time, he was invited to the Beta Sigma Lambda party held at Starlit Deck Avenue Hotel. The Beta Sigma Lambda was an exclusive FEU law fraternity. As a member of the law faculty, he was honoured to be invited together with Annie on a night of dancing and cocktails. He used to go to class in a suit and he would be seen smoking a cigarette or a saddle-bit Peterson pipe in his room or while chatting with fellow professors. As professor in the senior law class of 1948, a class that was interrupted by the war, he was part and parcel of the education of the thirty-five students who finally graduated that year.[10]

From FEU, he would go on to Francisco Law School where he was assigned a variety of subjects: international law, constitutional law, political law bar review, jurisprudence, and brief-making and forensic literature. While teaching at Francisco Law School, he assisted Senator Vicente J. Francisco, his dean, in the writing of the book *Legal Thesis Writing and Forensic Literature*. Francisco noted the lack of a manual on a subject regarded as trifling by many law students and professors. Guerrero edited the text of Part One consisting of ten chapters that dealt with thesis writing by "adapting it to the needs of the local curriculum".[11]

He also did research for a text on international law. In a letter to Lopez, now assistant to Ambassador Carlos P. Romulo, Permanent Philippine Representative to the United Nations, he asked if Lopez could extend help with the research because he wanted to emphasize Philippine policy and interpretation with respect to international law. "Since Ambassador Romulo and your office are undoubtedly the most active", and to convince Lopez all the more, he added, "and I should like to add authoritative spokesmen of our foreign policy, I should very much like to have as complete a set as possible of the various statements, debates, attitudes, etc., which you have taken in the United Nations." Not only a set but he asked if it "will be possible to get something like this from extra [documents] in your files or [some] files of the UN."[12]

Actually, Guerrero had already mentioned this project to Romulo when the latter was back in Manila. Romulo told him to remind him perhaps by letter or telegraph so that he could send the material to him from New York. Guerrero did not want to bother the busy ambassador and he said to Lopez: "I am therefore presuming on your goodwill" to try and send the message to Romulo. If Lopez lacked the time, he suggested somebody to take care of it because: "I am very much interested in the matter and I will really appreciate anything you can do." If it was time to ask for a favour, it was also time for news to a friend away from home: "As you may have heard, things are rather a mess here in Manila. The whole political situation is in confusion and you are well out of it, there in New York. I am sorry your proposed increases got caught in the crosscurrents in the House. There is still a chance they may be restored in the conference committee." "I hope to see you soon. In the meantime, have a good time." He sent his regards to Mary, wife of Lopez but to Romulo, he had a parting shot: "Tell him we are all waiting for 1953." As early as May 1949, Guerrero was party to the secret presidential ambitions of the ambassador. Still he added a postscript with a cryptic remark: "You had better write me at home, 1629 Donada, Rizal City (Pasay) since nobody knows what is going to happen next." The "mess" that Guerrero mentioned in his letter referred no doubt to the political debacle in the

Senate in the early part of this year that continued without let-up until the November elections.[13]

THE LEGAL COUNSEL IN ACTION

Having been instrumental in the reorganization of his office, Guerrero applied for and was appointed legal counsel and chief of division in July 1949. He headed an office separate now from the office of the Secretary of the Senate. Again, he would observe the gratuitous display of factionalism in the Senate. The Avelinistas in the Senate, after learning about the informal alliance between Quirinistas and the Nacionalistas to carry out the legislative programme of the administration, resigned en masse from their committee chairmanships and memberships. They agitated for the repeal of the emergency powers vested on the president since 1941. The opposition senators supported this move. Senator Ramon Diokno in a Senate speech accused Quirino of "seeking to insure his election by the use of these powers" and even expressed in public that the president "desires to push through certain measures involving enormous appropriations of public funds which are mainly intended to help him in the polls."[14]

It was at this juncture that Guerrero, the legal counsel, filed a suit together with Attorney Claro M. Recto along with other petitioners with their respective cases to challenge the continued exercise of emergency powers by President Quirino. To have sufficient interest to challenge the legality of Executive Order No. 192 restricting the export of certain products from the Philippines, Guerrero had to assume the personality of a shoe exporter to seek a writ of mandamus to compel the administrator of Sugar Quota office and the Commissioner of Customs to issue him a permit licence to export. All the petitioners rested their cases on the proposition that the Emergency Powers Act (Commonwealth Act No. 671) had ceased to have any effect. The Supreme Court declared null and void all the executive orders, including Nos. 225 and 226 that could channel funds for electioneering purposes of the incumbent.[15]

The involvement of Guerrero in this case was dictated by the nature of his job. As legal counsel attached to the Legislative Reference Division, he "... when requested, renders legal assistance, prepares opinions for draft bills and resolutions and provides materials on legislative matters for the President, the different Committees and Commissions and the members of the Senate." The division also "reviews bills and resolutions submitted to it for study before they are presented for the consideration of the Senate." The office had a library with a chief librarian to maintain it and procure library materials available for request in a reading room for the members and technical staff of the Senate.[16]

Guerrero was caught between two warring factions in the Senate, the Avelinistas and the Quirinistas and pressured by a third party, the Nacionalistas. It was a delicate balancing act for him to work with senators whose motives were politicking rather than legislating. "[T]he main political parties," Guerrero acutely observed, "the Nacionalista and the Liberals degenerated into opportunistic coalitions of power groups maneuvering for advantage in the scramble for spoils." The Nacionalista legislators in both houses were agitating for amendments to the electoral code by abolishing bloc-voting, giving election inspectors to the Avelinistas and increasing the powers of the election commission. Quirino sensing his pet bills were getting derailed in the Senate called both wings of the party to a meeting. Back in the Senate, the reconciled Liberals agreed to pursue the president's legislative agenda but were met with opposition because the Nacionalistas resigned from their committee chairmanships. They also planned to lift the suspension of Avelino to break up the ranks of the Liberals by calling for a resolution by voting to this effect but Acting Senate President Cuenco adjourned the session to frustrate the plan. Avelino, after having been suspended, carried out his campaign for the presidency in a three-cornered contest with Quirino running as the Liberal Party standard bearer under his wing while Jose P. Laurel got the Nacionalista nomination.[17]

In mid-October 1949, prior to the presidential elections after getting reappointed as legal adviser, Guerrero was involved in the election inspector case with Senator Francisco. Since Francisco became the running mate of Avelino in the other wing of the Liberal Party, the case was very crucial for Francisco and Guerrero asked for representations of the Avelino wing in the board of inspectors in the coming elections and in the counting. The verdict on the case favoured the petitioner. Francisco, whom Avelino subjected to political intrigues, later took the unenviable position of defending Avelino. "It was obvious to everyone," Guerrero wrote about his dean, "that Senator Francisco had every reason to side against Senate President Avelino and it caused extreme surprise therefore when he did exactly the opposite." "His conviction, however, that Mr Avelino was innocent" he added, "was unchanged throughout the various political maneuvers and the heated election campaign that followed...". He was aware: "that Senator Francisco played a decisive role in the constitutional crisis that preceded the proclamation of the election results. It was largely through his infinite tact and ready resourcefulness that the delicate task of rapprochement between the two rival wings of the majority party was consummated."[18]

The "constitutional crisis" Guerrero referred to and had some personal knowledge of was plotted by the defeated presidential candidates, particularly Avelino and Laurel, in the elections that he described as "an international scandal" due to fraud and terrorism. There were nightly meetings in late November in the house of Avelino, planning on how to prevent Quirino from being proclaimed by Congress on 13 December. They did not foresee a glitch in the plan till 5 December when Arranz issued a manifesto challenging the leadership of Cuenco. Arranz claimed that it should be he instead of Cuenco who should call the joint session of Congress, for the rules of the Senate did not recognize a Senate president in an acting capacity. He claimed that it was he, as the Senate president *pro tempore* based on Senate rules, who should take over the duties left by Avelino. Two days later, he resigned from the Quirinista Liberal Party. Without a presidential proclamation and a vice president, Arranz would become the president overnight. The plot was thus revealed to the administration and to frustrate the plot, party heavyweights including outgoing Senator Francisco went to Avelino to request him to desist from participating in Arranz's plot. The Liberal Party leadership promised Avelino his restoration as senator. A meeting in the palace on the eve of the proclamation of winning candidates reconciled the two camps into one cohesive majority party. Thus, Quirino and Lopez were proclaimed president and vice president respectively while Avelino was back in the Senate.[19]

Working behind the scenes, Guerrero as the legal counsel had to play neutral. His office catered to both the Liberal Party, either Avelinista or Quirinista, and the Nacionalista Party. If a senator needed advice on parliamentary procedures or the passage of a bill or the filing of a mandamus, he had to abide by these requests. In order to avoid the accusation that he was playing favourite with one party, he deemed it necessary to be circumspect in issuing statements that will give away his political leaning.

THE TRANSLATOR

To distract him from his political and legal chores, Guerrero resumed his humorous but "nasty" pieces in the guise of letters under assumed names. One of the victims was Arsenio Lacson, a fellow journalist, who was working for the *Star Reporter*, known for his unsavoury mouth for his frankness that earned the ire of President Roxas who suspended him from the airwaves. Under the assumed name, Luis Garces, Guerrero described Lacson and his colleague "unmitigated scoundrels" and maligned their daily as "a yellow sheet run by yellow newspapermen". Not to be intimidated, Lacson wrote in his column that he does not give a damn to Luis Garces or Jose Robles, another alias used by Guerrero: "A guy who would snipe behind the ambush of an assumed name wouldn't have the guts to face a blind, paralyzed rabbit. He has sunk so low that he can, with a top hat on, walk on tip-toe under a worm." Guerrero, who was not onion-skinned, must have laughed his head off upon reading it.[20]

Renewed in January 1950 as legal counsel and chief of division, Guerrero attended the new session headed by Cuenco. Quintin Paredes was voted Senate President Pro-tempore. Aside from Paredes, there were other new faces in the Senate but old in the game of politics. In the Second Congress, Guerrero would behold as an insider "the game of the musical chairs" in the Senate. The first year of the Second Congress was marked with the pre-eminence of five new senators, Justiniano Montano, Lorenzo Sumulong, Tomas Cabili, Esteban Abada and Macario Peralta, dubbed by the press as the "Young Turks". Their clout as an independent group earning them the title "Little Senate" made the reunited Liberal Party and Nacionalista senators hostage to their votes. Avelino with Arranz sought to join forces with Nacionalistas. Back in the Senate in December after winning his seat, Eulogio Rodriguez of the opposition party joined the alliance known as the Democratic group, which spelled doom for the "Young Turks". Guerrero would observe the leverage played by the Democratic group in the Senate. He did not find it surprising since the Senate consisted of power blocs of individual senators apart from the majority and minority parties. Without their prior approval to any of his decisions, Cuenco was a lame-duck Senate president. He could not release funds nor make an appointment without the group's assent. There was a committee of three consisting of Avelino, Arranz and Pablo Angeles David monitoring and policing his actions. In that position of power, Avelino began aspiring for the Senate presidency only to be thwarted by a vigilant Cuenco who was informed about the plot.[21]

A diversion to Guerrero's Senate duties was a commissioned translation. In April he got into translating Rizal's childhood memoirs, the *Memorias de Un Estudiante de Manila*, serialized in June for the *Manila Times*. He collected the instalments, Rizal's seven early poems and also two of his plays and published them as *The Young Rizal*. His involvement in the translation, however, was accidental. A Tomas Barretto approached him to translate the manuscript. Barretto's uncle, Alberto Barretto funded the publication. Both held the copyright of the Spanish edition, with Tomas Barretto the editor of the Spanish text.[22]

Guerrero translated the memoirs in two successive days, Holy Thursday and Good Friday. The other translations were done when he was free. Its publication in book form was delayed for about a year for he undertook research to make annotations, which irritated him but he understood that they were necessary for his generation was separated from Rizal "by half a century of fundamental changes". He had to read and explain in the notes the educational contests between Carthaginian and Roman empires as experienced by the young Jose, the Greek and Latin mythologies among others. He collaborated with his friend, Skeezix, now Father de la Costa, in translating a number of Rizal's poems which required him to read Jaime de Veyra's anthology of Rizal's poems and also Charles Derbyshire's translation of "Mi Retiro". He thought that Derbyshire's should be rewritten entirely. "[T]ranslating poetry", he wrote to Skeezix "is a dull and exacting business...".[23]

In the course of his translation, he realized that translation work was not easy; and it was perilous. Quoting the Italian proverb that "translators are traducers", translators in their clumsiness and infidelity, he believed, "expose their classic original to shame and contempt". To him, "translation is only a higher form of plagiarism; only the writer who cannot create, translates." Although a laborious enterprise, translation "is often a necessary evil" and more so "a patriotic duty" in the case of Rizal and his contemporaries. Through translation, Guerrero thought that he was liberating Rizal from "the tragedy of unreadability" since Spanish had "fallen into general disuse".[24]

Released the following year in 1951, and getting him a knighthood from the Knights of Rizal in December, Claro M. Recto, his superior in the law office, graced the opening pages of his book with an introduction. Recto, whom Guerrero also considered his mentor, pointed out the importance of going back to the original texts to know Rizal better instead of relying on biographies assuring the readers of the competence of the translator. The language barrier hindering the old and the present generation had been hurdled by the translation and that "no other Filipino can do it better than Guerrero", said Recto. Referring to the translator's honesty and fidelity to the original text, he stated: "I can vouch for the fact that during our long-standing association he has done me, to my satisfaction, the same service he now renders to Rizal." It was an expression of confidence in Guerrero who served as assistant attorney and later associate attorney in Recto Law Offices.[25]

Notes

1. "Application Form", "Oath of Office as of 1 September 1947", "Certificate of Appointment as of 1 September 1947", in Leon Ma. Guerrero File, Personnel Files 201 (hereafter cited as *LMGFPF*), National Archives of the Philippines.
2. "Application Form" in *LMGFPF*; "Leon Ma. Guerrero", in *Biographic Register* (Manila: Bureau of Printing, 1970), pp. 37–38; Lewis E. Gleeck Jr, *The Third Philippine Republic* (Quezon City: New Day Publishers, 1993), pp. 73–75; Ronald Edgerton, "The Politics of Reconstruction in the Philippines" (PhD dissertation, University of Michigan, 1975), pp. 369, 374.
3. "Certificate of Appointment as of 10 February 1948", in *LMGFPF*. For a brief discussion on the nature of these scandals, see Gleeck, *The Third Philippine Republic*, pp. 85–87.
4. On the political squables in the Senate, see Elpidio Quirino, *The Memoirs of Elpidio Quirino* (Manila: National Historical Institute, 1990), pp. 41–42; "Appointment as Secretary to the Conferences", in *LMGFPF*. According to Guerrero himself, he wrote "Report from Europe" and I suspect that this report was the same report he wrote for the two conferences because I have not seen any copy of this work.
5. Quirino, *Memoirs*, pp. 49, 50, 53–54.
6. Ibid., pp. 54, 61, 67, 71. See also Salvador P. Lopez, *Elpidio Quirino: The Judgment of History* (President Elpidio Quirino Foundation, 1990), p. 117; *MC*, 18 January 1949.
7. Leon Ma. Guerrero, *Today Began Yesterday* (Manila: National Media Production Center, 1975), p. 26.
8. Melecio Arranz to Leon Ma. Guerrero, 11 March 1949; "Memorandum for the Acting Secretary of the Senate"; "Clearance Letter"; "Leave Computation" and Cesar de Larrazabal to Leon Ma. Guerrero, 21 May 1949 in *LMGFPF*. The list included volume 17 of *Corpus Juris Secondum*, three volumes: 3, 4 and 6 of Macquillan's *Municipal Corporations*, three volumes: 37, 31 and 18 of *American Jurisprudence*, *International Executive Agreements* by McClures, *The Law of Nations — Cases, Documents and Notes* by Briggs, *Decisions of the Court of Industrial Relations* and *United Nations Bulletin*.
9. Quirino, *Memoirs*, pp. 131, 133, 135–38, 153–54, 180.
10. *Green and Gold Law Annual* (Senior Class, Institute of Law, 1948), pp. 21–31, 33–67, 95.
11. Vicente J. Francisco assisted by Leon Ma. Guerrero, *Legal Thesis Writing and Forensic Literature* (Manila: East Publishing, 1950), pp. v–vi.
12. Leon Ma. Guerrero to Salvador P. Lopez, 18 May 1949, Salvador P. Lopez Papers (hereafter cited as *SPLP*), University of the Philippines Main Library.
13. Ibid.
14. *OD 1950*, p. 12; "Certificate of Appointment as of 1 July 1949", "First Endorsement to Budget Commissioner, 9 August 1949", "Oath of Office, 2 August 1949", in *LMGFPF*; Quirino, *Memoirs*, p. 149; Lopez, *Elpidio Quirino*, p. 118.

15. Teehankee, "A Testament …", in *In Memoriam*, p. 9. For the full text of the Supreme Court decision, see *Araneta v. Dinglasan et al.*, G.R. No. L-2044, 26 August 1949.
16. *Government Manual 1950*, p. 136.
17. Leon Ma. Guerrero, *Today Began Yesterday*, p. 25; Quirino, *Memoirs*, pp. 154–56; Carlos Quirino, *Apo Lakay: The Biography of President Elpidio Quirino of the Philippines* (Manila: Total Book World, 1987), pp. 122–23.
18. Leon Ma. Guerrero, "Senator Vicente J. Francisco in 'The Bench and Bar in News'", *The Lawyers Journal* (25 December 1949), p. 668.
19. Carlos Quirino, *Amang: The Life and Times of Eulogio Rodriguez, Sr* (Quezon City: New Day Publishers, 1983), pp. 129–31.
20. Pedro Padilla, *Arsenic & I* (Manila: Self-published, 1962), p. 75.
21. "Certificate of Appointment as of 31 January 1950", "Certificate of Appointment as of 29 April 1950". "Certificate of Appointment as of 1 July 1950", "Certificate of Appointment as of 30 September 1950", "Certificate of Appointment as of 1 November 1950", in *LMGFPF*; Quirino, *Amang*, pp. 131–33; *OD 1950*, p. 11.
22. Alegre and Fernandez, *Writer and his Milieu*, p. 80; Leon Ma. Guerrero, *The Young Rizal: A Translation of Memorias de un Estudiante de Manila by Jose Rizal with Translations of Rizal's Early Poems, Along the Pasig and the Council of the Gods* (Manila: Bardavon Book Co., 1950) copyright page, pp. 10, 11.
23. Ibid., pp. 16, 221–23; Leon Ma. Guerrero to Horacio de la Costa, no date, Horacio de la Costa papers (hereafter cited as *HDCP*).
24. Guerrero, *The Young Rizal*, pp. 8–9.
25. Ibid., pp. 1, 3; *Daily Mirror* (hereafter cited as *DM*), 29 December 1951.

10

The Foreign Policy Critic and Spokesman

Outside his work in the Senate, Guerrero closely monitored world events, a habit which eventualy earned him a reputation as a well-known political analyst who aired his views on current international affairs, particularly the emergence of the Cold War. Since the Philippines was closely allied with the United States, the Cold War demanded special attention from Filipino policymakers and analysts. Before the Malolos Rotary Club in late July 1950, he disclosed how Russia would engage in "little wars" to further its world domination in places like Indochina, Greece and Iraq by using its allies, thus weakening the United States. Russia, he said, was not ready to start a war against the United States but in due time, Russia could challenge the United States with the aid of new weapons of war. In the case of an atomic war, however, the United States, he believed, had the advantage over Russia since the former stockpiled atomic bombs. Guerrero stressed the importance of the United Nations in the maintenance of world peace.[1]

At the Manila Overseas Press Club, he graced the inaugural meeting of the Manila Round Table, a group interested in international and national issues, discussing American policy in the advent of communism in Asia. At the Y's Men's Club, on its special United Nations Week programme, he spoke about a new United Nations that had emerged from the old one established in San Francisco since the outbreak of the Cold War, before flying to Dublin, Ireland to fulfil his function as member and secretary of the Philippine delegation to the International Parliamentary Conference. Special to the *Philippines Herald*, he wrote his sharp impressions of Europe in a series of articles at a time when Europe was slowly taking steps towards a European Community.[2]

The following year, in a regular weekly luncheon meeting of the Manila Rotary at the Manila Hotel, speaking before diplomatic and consular representatives of Southeast Asian countries, he characterized Asian nationalism as anti-Western and anti-capitalist in the wake of India's rejection of the San Francisco peace treaty and Iran's agitation for the nationalization of its oil industry. He made clear why Russian socialism was closer to the hearts of Asian peasants than American capitalism because the American way of life was an impossible, unreachable dream for the Asian peasant who lacked experience and understanding of it. The Philippines, he said, could be "the light of Asia" only when Asian nations could look up to its example of a "self-controlled nationalism", contrasting it to Iran's "uncontrolled nationalism" or to French Indochina's "foreign-controlled nationalism".[3]

His lecture attracted the attention of a student editor of a university magazine and a former president of the Rotary Club of New Haven in Connecticut. The editor asked his permission to reprint his article in its December issue which he acceded to, and in January he received three copies along with a note of appreciation from the president.[4]

In late September 1951, the Harvard Club invited Guerrero to speak on Spain's legacy to the Philippines in which he acknowledged the positive contributions of Spain in its more than three centuries of colonial rule, naming them as the Catholic religion, agriculture and the moral bases of democracy while also pointing out that the present inherited "the great evils of anti-clericalism, servility and a tradition of civic irresponsibility." He likewise asserted that "the Filipino nation itself is the work of Spain" for oppression galvanized the different tribes to rise up against Spain and that a national culture was born distinct from the Iberian character. His talk was timely for President Quirino was scheduled to visit Spain.[5]

He was fast becoming a popular speaker, receiving invitations from different clubs and organizations. He had to reject one invitation coming from the Rotary Club of Cebu because he had a prior commitment.[6]

As the election in November 1951 was fast approaching, the two political parties readied their respective slates. Laurel was drafted for senator in the opposition party. Re-electionist Cuenco ran under the Liberal Party. In one of the rallies sponsored by the National Movement for Free Elections (NAMFREL) in Luneta, Guerrero exhorted students to be intelligent voters. Nine Nacionalista candidates won all the Senate seats, to the chagrin of the majority party.[7]

The victory of the Nacionalista Party was also a victory for Guerrero who had become its foreign policy spokesman and its legal counsel since April. Speaking before the Rotary Club of San Fernando in Pampanga in mid-December, he argued that in a Cold War setting: "One world is better than two worlds, but two worlds are better than none." In the light of American and Russian proposals for disarmament and the recent ceasefire negotiations in Panmunjom, a village in the border of North and South Korea, these in his analysis were bound to be artificial, illusory and ephemeral as long as the two parties would not settle issues between them. "The nations," he discerned, "will not disarm while they have every reason to remain armed ..." but "they need not come to blows if they will come to terms". In late December, he spoke on "Freedom and the World" in a six-day student conference in Baguio City. When the Rotary Club of Cebu reiterated its invitation, he did not hesitate this time to go there and talk on "the constitution or related topics".[8]

GUERRERO VS LOPEZ: FOREIGN POLICY DEBATE BETWEEN RECTO AND ROMULO

At the fifth floor of the Filipinas Building in Escolta, besides attending to legal papers that once needed the help of de la Costa in a case involving the Aglipayan Church, Guerrero also served as Recto's speechwriter or, in the vulgar term, ghost writer. He would write drafts of speeches but Recto would rewrite them to the extent that he could no longer recognize it as his own. The close relationship with his mentor dated back to June 1949 when he described Recto as the "archetype of that present-day Filipino nationalism which is said to scare the striped pants off foreign capital". It was at this time that he "broke politically with Don Elpidio [Quirino]" when he crossed over to the other side, the Nacionalistas. Later, he would be recruited to the faculty when Recto was the dean of the newly established Lyceum School of Law and would be elected secretary of the Philippine Bar Association when Recto was the elected president.[9]

But the most profound phase in their relationship occurred in his work as speechwriter during the foreign policy debate between Recto and Romulo that no doubt shaped his career as a diplomat later on. He recalled in a speech in 1960: "Recto, almost alone, decided to fight in the field of foreign policy, and inevitably nationalism. I had the privilege of being associated with that campaign and I remember that it was opened with a memorable indictment of what he considered the colonial party's foreign policy of mendicancy and subservience to the United States."[10]

He was alluding to Recto's University of the Philippines commencement address entitled "Our Mendicant Foreign Policy" in early April 1951 that provoked a debate between Recto and Romulo. Recto, among other things, mentioned the Korean War where "small nations must still pay the price of quarrels between great powers", in particular, Philippine-American relations. Recto lambasted Philippine foreign policy because it was conducted on the "erroneous assumption of an identity of American and Filipino interests, of the desirability, and even the necessity, of subordinating our interests to those of America". Romulo, then Secretary of Foreign Affairs, in reaction to Recto, delivered his rebuttals before the graduating classes of the University of the East in late April. He defended the administration's foreign policy and categorically denied that such a policy of mendicancy existed. Recto had a chance to answer Romulo at a convocation speech held at Manuel L. Quezon Educational Institution in early May. On that same day, Romulo spoke about the international situation before a joint meeting of the Foreign Affairs Committees of both Houses. Before students and faculty of the FEU, Romulo again asserted on 25 May the positive attributes of Philippine foreign policy. The following day, he spoke again in defence of Quirino's foreign policy at the town plaza of Lucena in Quezon that Recto attacked in an address sponsored by the Iloilo Rotary Club two weeks later. The debate showdown scheduled between the two at Plaza Miranda was a great disappointment to many because Romulo did not honour his promise to be there.[11]

The cancellation of the great debate was not only disappointing to Recto but also to Guerrero who wrote the drafts of these speeches. Guerrero, through the person of Recto, was in fact debating with his friend, S.P. Lopez, who was Romulo's speechwriter. Lopez, still in New York, followed the "great debate" with interest but was relieved to have been told that it was over for "it was really beginning to look like a 'fishwives quarrel' rather unedifying from this distance at least." In this same letter to his boss, Lopez revealed that he was scolded by Romulo and it would be better to quote it to know the feelings in the other camp:

> I have read the text of the Lucena speech, with the pointed notation addressed to me: "This is how a rebuttal should be written." This, following your disappointed remark over the phone that you thought the FEU speech a weak "rehash" which must have been "written by Narsing," comes as a complete surprise to me — a painful one, too, because I had somewhat conceitedly expressed the opinion that it would completely demolish the adversary. Well, I suppose nobody is ever a good judge of his own work, and also, being far removed from the heat and tumult of the battle, we here are inclined to favor a calmer, more detached (more statesmanlike?) approach to the issues involved. This could have been a fault, since we could not wholly enter into the spirit of the fight at such a great remove. But from the beginning, my concept of the "debate" was that you should maintain an attitude of being "above the battle" or even "too proud to

fight." — You could refute the critics by simply referring to the record, letting the facts speak for themselves, instead of a head-on collision with someone who, after all, is a mere private citizen.[12]

Lopez was right to the extent that Recto was "a mere private citizen" but the following year, Recto won his electoral case and got his seat in the Senate. It was in this context that Guerrero, when interviewed in 1981, said bluntly:

> No, I don't think S.P. and I will ever meet in full, head-on collision, except we always met in full head-on collisions as ghost writers. He was the ghost writer for Romulo; I was the ghost writer of Recto. That's when we used to meet, really. All gloves off; we'd claw at each other. Naturally, being shapely behind our masks, what the hell did we care? Oh dear. I used to enjoy that very much, because I knew that he was writing Romulo's speeches, and I was writing Recto's, so that was all right. More than a match for each other.[13]

THE FOREIGN POLICY SPOKESMAN

In the ensuing reorganization in the Senate, the jockeying for positions by the Liberal and Nacionalista parties resulted in the successive elections of three presidents within a four-month period until the end of the session. President Pro-Tempore Paredes took Cuenco's place as acting Senate president. Because of the change in leadership and more so of his desire to engage in private legal practice, Guerrero resigned from his post as legal adviser in December 1951.[14]

When he left the Senate, the Senate leadership underwent a series of deadlocks. Both majority parties were evenly represented with eleven Nacionalista plus one minority party, that of Tañada's Citizens Party whose sympathy went to the Nacionalista, and twelve Liberals. Paredes held the gavel for only forty-two days. With the entry of Claro M. Recto, the complexion of the Senate changed radically. Paredes was forced to resign but wanted Osias to take the position. After hurdling the obstacles, Osias was elected Senate president but he lasted for only about two weeks because the Nacionalistas manoeuvred to elect Eulogio Rodriguez in his place. Guerrero was invited to work again in the Senate starting mid-June 1952 as legal counsel and technical assistant in the office of Senate President Rodriguez until he was caught up again in the vicious cycle of partisan struggles.[15]

Prior to the power struggles, in tandem with Chitang who wrote about foreign diplomats stationed in Manila, Guerrero wrote articles on Philippine diplomatic relations with more than ten countries for *Sunday Times Magazine* starting from August, collecting them under the title *Our Foreign Relations*. He was trying to live up to the promise of being called

Recto's "Undersecretary of Foreign Affairs" as he was once introduced in a Manila Rotary Club's weekly meeting the previous year.[16]

The range of countries he surveyed demonstrated the breadth of his knowledge of Philippine diplomatic map during the Quirino administration. The Vatican, which he noted as one of the "Great Powers" for its millions of adherents in many countries, was for him "a logical and indisputable ally of those governments, like the government of the Republic, which are aligned against communism."[17]

Between the Philippines and Indonesia, he saw it as one of competition not only in the world market for sugar and copra but also in the need for foreign capital. He recommended, apart from the ratified general treaty of friendship, the signing of a non-aggression pact or an agreement coordinating sugar and copra production and prices.[18]

He described the reaching out of Spanish diplomacy as "diplomacy of atonement" for past misdeeds in more than three centuries of colonial rule. Philippine-Spanish relations were mainly cultural, for trade between the two countries was negligible. As for Philippine policy towards Spain, he stated that there was none.[19]

About the emerging Italian penetration of Philippine market in a bid to strengthen Philippine-Italian relations, he recounted the politics behind the sudden cancellation of the Maria Cristina Hydroelectric contract in 1950 awarded to Compagnia Generale Impianti, leading him to conclude that the Philippine market was a closed market except towards the Americans, and thus to argue for alternatives to the U.S. market and capital. He noted that after six years of political independence, the Philippines had yet to sign treaties of commerce with other countries except the United States with the Bell Trade Act.[20]

As for Philippine relations with Thailand, which is a rice-exporting nation, he believed it should focus on eliminating problems affecting the importation of rice, a veiled criticism directed at the Philippine legation in Bangkok.[21]

Regarding Philippine-U.S. relations, Guerrero made a dispassionate appeal for a policy of "readjustments to changed conditions" between two sovereign nations on a more equal footing. In terms of security and trade, the Philippines was always on the losing side as the Philippines "was in no position to bargain". The military alliance stipulated in the military defence pact provided no automatic guarantee of U.S. retaliation in case of invasion. In the field of economic relations, U.S. goods could enter Philippine market duty and quota-free until 1974 but Philippine copra had to pay an increasing duty and subjected to quota limitations from 1954. The Philippine peso was tied to the U.S. dollar. While U.S. citizens and corporations could have the same rights as Filipinos in the Philippines, Filipinos had no equal rights in the United States. In contrast to U.S. policy on Filipino migrants, special immigration quotas were given to Americans in the Philippines. These observations marking his prescience would eventually draw a sympathetic ear among Filipino policymakers.[22]

Australia's snubbing of the Philippines in its non-inclusion to the ANZUS (Australia, New Zealand, United States) conference of a "Pacific Council", a tripartite defence pact, in Hawaii was a "diplomacy of isolation".[23]

Calling it "diplomacy for a transition", the Philippine policy of non-recognition towards the three associated states in Indochina, as he discerned, veered away at least from the U.S. position, which was done "to avoid any criticism of subservience to U.S. policy and betrayal of Asian interests and [the Foreign Office] considers it safer to do nothing as long as it can be helped."[24]

The Dutch Embassy in the Philippines had at one time put pressure on the Philippines not to recognize Indonesia but the Philippines had its way in the end when international law deemed it appropriate. Guerrero's contention however, was that instead of waiting for the right time as the law would dictate, the Philippines could have gained recognition like India had it taken the risk of intervening on behalf of its Indonesian brothers.[25]

The Philippine legation in Argentina earned Guerrero's slight censure when he said that its only justification was the study of Peronism since Philippine-Argentinean commerce was far from substantial if not nil.[26]

He saw the recent establishment of a Belgian mission in the Philippines as a "diplomatic listening-post", which they could afford in order to assess the situation here that might affect their country, aside from taking care of Belgians who were mostly priests and nuns. But he said the proposed setting up of Philippine legations in Cairo and Mexico City would be similar to the posts in Buenos Aires, London, Paris, Rome, and Karachi "where there are no visible Philippine interests to protect, and no discernible Philippine policy to promote".[27]

After touching on the Philippine-Belgian relations, he discussed the development of diplomacy in history and on being a diplomat. The development of diplomacy happened in four stages. In the first stage, the diplomat was a "herald" sent to the enemy camp to push for truce but, in many instances, he was killed before he could deliver his message of peace and so he was given a temporary immunity. In the second stage, as in ancient Greece, an Athenian diplomat was an orator and an advocate sent to plead its city's cause before an enemy's assembly contemplating on declaring war. A diplomat became a negotiator and bargainer in the third stage, busy bribing to foment rebellion, spying, flirting with the Queen, and stealing state papers. In the fourth, the modern diplomat was more of a reporter than a messenger, orator and spy.[28]

What then was a modern diplomat? To Guerrero, the modern diplomat showcased the uncongenial and seemingly degrading qualities inherent in the history of the profession. First, since he submitted protests and admonitions from the home office, he was no other than a messenger. Second, he delivered speeches to promote goodwill and trade and so he acted like a press agent or a public relations officer. Third, diplomacy by conference in the United Nations transformed him into a politician and lobbyist. Fourth, he reported to the home office so he must be a good journalist or newsman. Fifth, he was a "legman" rather than a "commentator" or "analyst". Finally, a diplomat was tasked:

> ...to get the facts, and get them straight. He should be able to discount hypocrisy, self-justification and self-praise, the innuendo of prejudice, the exaggeration of the press agent. He should have an innate curiosity, an habitual skepticism, a fundamental honesty, a sincere liking for people and an ability to mix in any company.[29]

Notes
1. *MT*, 31 July 1950.
2. *MT*, October 1950; 1 November 1950; Leon Ma. Guerrero, "As Others See Us"; "Differing Concepts on PI"; "Pride and Prejudice"; "Is Heaven Enough?"; "Imperialism in Decay"; "Imperialism in Reverse"; "Kingless Kingdom"; "How to be Neutral"; "The Future of Europe", *PH*, November 1950, no exact dates and page numbers (the month is author's extrapolation) in Leon Ma. Guerrero Papers (hereafter cited as *LMGP*), Dasmariñas Village, Makati City.
3. *MT*, 7 and 29 September 1951; *DM*, 6 September 1951.
4. Toribia Maño to Leon Ma. Guerrero, 19 November 1951 and 30 January 1952; Frederick Franz to Leon Ma. Guerrero, 12 January 1952, *LMGP*.
5. *MT*, 29 September 1951.
6. Simoun Almario to Leon Ma. Guerrero, 16 November 1951, Leon Ma. Guerrero to Simoun Almario, no date, *LMGP*; *MC*, 28 November 1951; *MT*, 1 December 1951.
7. Quirino, *Amang*, pp. 134–37, 275 endnote 5; *PH*, 11 November 1951 and *MT*, 11 November 1951.
8. Teehankee, "A Testament...", in *In Memoriam*, p. 9; Andres A. Guanzon to Leon Ma. Guerrero, 4 December 1951, Manuel L. Carreon to Leon Ma. Guerrero, 11 January 1952; Simoun Almario to Leon Ma. Guerrero, 15 January 1952 and Simoun Almario to Leon Ma. Guerrero, 20 January 1952, *LMGP*; *MT*, 19 December 1951; *PH*, 18 December 1951.
9. Leon Ma. Guerrero to Horacio de la Costa, 19 October 1953, *HDCP*; Agoncillo, *The Fateful Years* 1, p. 424 note 103; Leon Ma. Guerrero, "Claro M. Recto: A Study in Filipino Nationalism", *Philippine Trends*, 15 June 1949, p. 38; Quirino, "Introduction" to *The First Filipino*, p. xviii; *TG*, March 1952.

10. Leon Ma. Guerrero, "Recto and Filipino Nationalism", *MT*, 7 October 1960, p. 10A.
11. Emerenciana Y. Arcellana, *The Social and Political Thought of Claro Mayo Recto* (Manila: National Research Council of the Philippines, 1981), pp. 97–156.
12. Salvador P. Lopez to Carlos P. Romulo, 6 June 1951, *SPLP*.
13. Alegre and Fernandez, *Writer and his Milieu*, p. 88. Leoni collected these speeches in *The Great Debate on Philippine Foreign Policy: Carlos P. Romulo versus Claro M. Recto* and his essays in *We Filipinos* both published by the Graphic House. See *Sunday Times Magazine* (hereafter cited as *STM*), 16 December 1951. I have not seen these publications either in libraries or in the possession of the Guerrero family.
14. Leon Ma. Guerrero to Honourable Quintin Paredes, 30 December 1951; Quintin Paredes to Leon Ma. Guerrero, 9 January 1952, *LMGFPF*.
15. "Service Record of Leon Ma. Guerrero", "Certificate of Appointment as of 11 June 1952" in *LMGFPF*; Quirino, *Amang*, pp. 136–39; Remigio Agpalo, "Under the Third Republic", in Petronilo Bn. Daroy, ed. *The Philippine Senate* (Manila: DBE, 1997), pp. 148–51; Jose P. Abletez, *Foundations of Freedom: A History of Philippine Congresses* (Manila: Merriam & Webster, Inc., 1989), pp. 48–60. Much of Agpalo's account, however, is based on Quirino's *Amang* while Abletez's work is poorly documented.
16. *DM*, 6 September 1951.
17. Leon Ma. Guerrero, "The Philippines and the Vatican: The diplomacy", *STM*, 31 August 1952, pp. 4–7.
18. Leon Ma. Guerrero, "The Philippines and Indonesia: Diplomacy for a competitor", *STM*, 14 September 1952, pp. 4–6.
19. Leon Ma. Guerrero, "Diplomacy of atonement", *STM*, 21 September 1952, pp. 4–6.
20. Leon Ma. Guerrero, "The Philippines and Italy: Diplomacy for a closed market", *STM*, 19 October 1952, pp. 4–6.
21. Leon Ma. Guerrero, "The Philippines and Thailand: Wanted — rice diplomacy", *STM*, 12 October 1952, pp. 4–6.
22. Leon Ma. Guerrero, "The Philippines and the United States: Diplomacy of readjustment", *STM*, 25 October 1952, pp. 4–6.
23. Leon Ma. Guerrero, "The Philippines and Australia: Diplomacy of isolation", *STM*, 3 November 1952, pp. 4–6.
24. Leon Ma. Guerrero, "Diplomacy for a transition", *STM*, 14 December 1952, pp. 10–12.
25. Leon Ma. Guerrero, "The Philippines and the Netherlands: Diplomacy and law", *STM*, 7 December 1952, pp. 8–10.
26. Leon Ma. Guerrero, "The Philippines and Argentina: Diplomacy and politics", *STM*, 30 November 1952, pp. 9, 10.
27. Leon Ma. Guerrero, "The Philippines and Belgium: Diplomatic Listening-Post", *STM*, 23 November 1952, pp. 6, 7.
28. Ibid.
29. Ibid.

11

"Asia for the Asians" or How to Leave Arlegui in Six Months

About this time, Guerrero became a regular patron of the Philippine Artists Gallery showcasing Filipino neo-realist painters. The gallery exhibited paintings of his brother Mario who was serving as the president of its board of directors. Mario's wife, Helen Roces, held one of her own exhibitions in November 1952. Guerrero bought art pieces by Arturo R. Luz, Romeo Tabuena and Fernando Zobel. He was also taken in as one of the judges for the second Palanca awards for the short story division in December at the Manila Hotel.[1]

Together with Senator Recto and opposition leaders in February 1953, Guerrero demanded the final judgment from the Supreme Court on the Emergency Powers Act filed back in 1949. The Supreme Court justices declared it void in favour of the petitioners as well as invalidated the Executive Orders allotting about PHP50 million for public works and typhoon relief, which was only intended for election purposes. It was a patent victory for the opposition who was wary again of Quirino's dirty tactics as the incumbent president was trying his last-ditch efforts to win again in the coming elections in November.[2]

In commemoration of his grandfather's birth centenary, Guerrero spoke on behalf of the family before University of Santo Tomas (UST) faculty and students in March. Rather philosophical, he tried to impart the special message he found in his grandfather's life. As botanist, his grandfather looked for the "flower of happiness". As pharmacist, he sought the "recipe for happiness". In both instances, he said, his grandfather succeeded for he believed "he was happy". Did his generation fail to be contented? His own answer was a reflection of his long years in public service when he said: "We belong to a money-minded generation and a generation that is obsessed with politics, not as a means of public service but as an opportunity of personal advancement." In effect, he was assessing his first-hand experiences in the Senate, a six-year witness to Senate intrigues, quarrels and grandstanding.[3]

What then was the solution to this lack of happiness that made the world around pregnant with violence and lawlessness? He told the audience that "The real secret," which might have been his secret until the end of his life,

> the solution that we have lost in our generation, is the sense of proportion, the sense that enables us to see our defects, our proper field of action and of service, and the limits of our capabilities .... We need that sense of proportion to accept the fact that not all of us can have wealth, fame, and power in equal proportions.

In conclusion, he related a story that could have been told to him by his grandfather that in the garden of life, there were four types of flowers: "flowers of pleasure", "flowers of fame and earthly honours", "flowers of worldly power" but the last was "flower of happiness", which in order to seek it, one had to "crossbreed, grafting one on the other, by cleft, splice, saddle and side" the other three flowers. Few men were given this type of flower for God bestowed it only on those worthy of the honour.[4]

From mid to late April, Guerrero was on leave when senators were wrangling over an ill-timed reorganization. By a vote of eleven as opposed to seven, Osias became Senate president with Zulueta as Senate president *pro tempore*. After less than a week, Osias yielded the presidency to Zulueta to fulfil an agreement with Nacionalistas. That would explain the return of Guerrero as legal counsel and technical assistant in the office of Senate President Zulueta. He would stay in that office until the last week of May after Rodriguez was back in the Senate rostrum as the Senate president.[5]

His Senate job over, Guerrero was recruited by Senator Laurel to be a part-time professor of private international law at the Lyceum School of Law in Intramuros. Recto was his dean and Laurel his chairman in the Department of Political Law and International Law. Apart from teaching, he continued to be the legal counsel of the Nacionalista Party. He was involved in June in the filing of a temporary writ of injunction as lead counsel on behalf of Senators Laurel, Rodriguez, Recto and Tañada on the execution of any warrant for their arrest. The new Defence Secretary Oscar Castelo threatened to arrest Recto and Laurel for alleged communist sympathies while the Bureau of Internal Revenue (BIR) demanded Rodriguez, Laurel, and Recto to pay taxes for their supposedly undeclared incomes. Castelo's aggressive attacks against the opposition senators were thwarted as the Supreme Court granted the petition.[6]

Guerrero was still teaching at Lyceum and acting as legal counsel of the opposition when he was pulled into the campaign trail for Ramon F. Magsaysay. A secret agreement was signed in November the previous year that Magsaysay would be the official presidential candidate of the Nacionalista party with Recto, Laurel and Tañada agreeing to withdraw from the race. In fact, Guerrero was sent as emissary as early as August to sound out Magsaysay the offer to join the party. Magsaysay's resignation from the Quirino cabinet in February 1953 was the first step prescribed in the said agreement. The Nacionalista Party convention was held in April in the Manila Hotel at its Fiesta Pavilion. The Ateneo rah-rah boys including Guerrero were very supportive of Magsaysay's candidacy and were responsible for the colourful and fantastic reception of the delegates.[7]

Magsaysay won the nomination against Osias but in the other camp, Quirino got the nomination over Romulo who bolted out of the party to start his own, the Democratic Party. The campaign for Magsaysay kicked off with money coming from the U.S. Central Intelligence Agency (CIA). Guerrero spoke at several campaign rallies convincing the crowd that he saw in Magsaysay that ideas could "be realised with deeds". He also supported Carlos P. Garcia's candidacy describing him as the "fitting running mate" for Magsaysay. Being the Nacionalista counsel and spokesman, he denied the accusation that the party violated the electoral code when it asked for its senatorial candidates to contribute to the campaign funds. He charged the Liberal Party of accepting money from Chinese businessmen for their campaign funds. In mid-October, he was privy to the agreement between the Nacionalista and the Democratic Party senators to not proclaim a presidential candidate who obtained his victory through fraud and terrorism. He intimated to legal circles that the Senate president could assume the presidency should the vice president remain unqualified.[8]

In support of Magsaysay, Guerrero kept on attacking Quirino's foreign policy blunders. In a speech before the Rotary Club of San Pablo City, he criticized the release of more than eighty Japanese convicted of war crimes. While recognizing it as an act of Christian charity, it was, to him, a diplomatic mistake. Looking at it as leverage in the forthcoming negotiations on war reparations with the Japanese, he believed as Recto did, that "the basic motivation of any foreign policy is national interest" because "we are a small weak nation"; "we are living in an ungoverned world where by and large, might makes right" and finally "we shall have to take care of ourselves."[9]

He continued writing on various subjects, probably delivered speeches, and even attended a farewell party where he candidly told the wife of an American forester who was planning to write a book about Filipinos that she would only write about their servants — cook, washerwoman, houseboy and driver, say something about the elite, and very little about the state of affairs in the countryside about the *tao* and the cacique. In an insightful article on "The American Influence", he acknowledged the pervasive influence of America in Philippine life but was quick to say that Filipinos did not owe them Christianity or even democracy. To say that Filipinos were pro-Americans, he said, was begging the question for, in fact, Filipinos were "part-American", "cultural *mestizos*" and "*pensionados*" with scholarships for Americanization. American influence in the Filipino character could be seen in the way they passed onto them the American native temper, tolerance, sense of equality, techniques of good government and the material comforts of civilization. These influences brought what he called the "secularization of our national life" leading to spiritual conflicts. About the Cold War, the cut-throat rivalry between America and Russia brought the precarious balance in the world to uncertainty leaving the United Nations in a state of utter uselessness. This situation prompted him to ask if the United Nations was still necessary. Although cynical about the United Nations, he still kept his hope that it could fulfil its mandate to preserve peace.[10]

Towards the fourth quarter of the year, he was given a regular column in the *Manila Chronicle* in tandem with Chitang's "My Humble Opinion". Calling it "Past and Present", he explained: "History does not repeat itself, and considering the things men do, this is probably a good thing. However, human nature being more or less unchanging, one may learn from the past what to expect from the present or find suggestions for the future in the experiences of the past." Again, he was trying to understand the situation he found himself in the heat and tumult of Philippine politics. To do so, he had to delve into the Philippine past.[11]

On the Chinese immigration racket that scandalized the Quirino administration, he found an interesting Spanish account relating that each Chinese immigrant was required to pay for a licence, a rampant source of corruption in those days. So what is new? He wrote on Filipino historical figures such as Graciano Lopez-Jaena, Gregorio del Pilar and others. On the five Luna brothers, he focused on Juan, the painter and Antonio, the pharmacist turned general. "Why is Juan Luna a national hero?" he asked. The answer he found was "as a Filipino he had been the first painter to prove to Europe what all his countrymen so passionately wanted to establish in every field of endeavour... With his 'Spoliarium,' Juan Luna became an authentic hero of Filipino nationalism; his triumph at the exposition was a feat comparable to a victorious battle." The assassination of General Luna, "plotted or at least permitted" by Aguinaldo, had put the nation in danger because of the "resurgence of that regionalism which had enabled the Western colonizers to rule by playing off one tribe against another". Devoting an article on "the great plebeian" on his birth anniversary, he recognized the paucity of details on Bonifacio's life, asking: "What do we know, for instance, about the private life of Andres Bonifacio?" He tried to discern what the hero might have learned from the books he read. *Les Miserables* "showed him that injustice and tyranny know no boundaries". *The Wandering Jew* "fed his Masonic hatred for the religious orders". On civil and criminal law books, he read it as "a wise precaution". On his reading of international law, he read it "in the faith that his revolution would succeed". On Carlyle's *French Revolution*, he ventured to suppose that Bonifacio might not have read its next to the last chapter on the reign of a dictator for the "Soldier's Sword ... would be raised against him by Emilio Aguinaldo".[12]

His interest in history was heightened by a book project in collaboration with de la Costa, the new dean of Ateneo College of Liberal Arts. Skeezix, whom he addressed as "S." because "somehow I do not feel quite at ease in addressing you as Skeezix", was in Spain doing research on a "source book". For this project, Guerrero was willing to prepare the list for the post-revolutionary period. Expecting from de la Costa some text and documents, he reminded him of the Burgos trial records.[13]

Then the elections came. Magsaysay won, edging out Quirino with over 1.5 million vote difference. Five Nacionalista senators — re-electionist Rodriguez and Cuenco, Emmanuel Pelaez, Edmundo Cea and Alejo Mabanag — were elected along with the coalition party candidates such as Ruperto Kangleon and Lorenzo Tañada. Preparations were made for the inauguration in December. Days prior to President Magsaysay's twenty-five minute inaugural address at the Luneta Grandstand on 30 December, Guerrero, still working at Recto Law Offices, laboured on the president's speech gone over by Emmanuel Pelaez, the elected senator, and others.[14]

Upon the election of Magsaysay, Guerrero was given the choice of two Cabinet portfolios — Undersecretary of Foreign Affairs or Undersecretary of Justice. He chose to be back in Arlegui. Based on the agreement signed in 1952, Magsaysay would choose his Cabinet members with the approval of Nacionalista Party and the Citizens Party, a toned down version of the first draft in which the selection of Cabinet members and key officials would be absolutely in the hands of the Nacionalista Party. Though Recto backed Guerrero's appointment, as Magsaysay confided to Guerrero, it needed a nod from the U.S. Embassy Minister William B. Lacy. Magsaysay's victory in the polls was also a victory for Ateneo. The Ateneo rah-rah boys were very supportive of Magsaysay during the elections. After the elections, it was payback time. Besides Guerrero who got the portfolio of undersecretary of Foreign Affairs, other Ateneans crowded the Cabinet.[15]

UNDERSECRETARY OF FOREIGN AFFAIRS

It was early in January 1954 when Guerrero was appointed and sworn in as Undersecretary of Foreign Affairs by President Magsaysay in Malacañang along with Vice President-elect Carlos P. Garcia, the concurrent Secretary of Foreign Affairs. He had just come from being a member of the board of judges in the Rizal Day Committee English Essay Contest. He succeeded Felino Neri who later became Magsaysay's special adviser in Foreign Affairs. After he was sworn in, he immediately announced that he would file his statement of assets and liabilities within twenty-four hours. His first task was to resolve pending administrative charges against Foreign Service personnel. Trapped in the hurly burly of the office, he missed the trial of a case he was handling. The department had forgotten to send official notification by cable or letters of appointment of the new top officials to the embassies abroad.[16]

Vice President Garcia made the revamp of the Foreign Office a priority at a meeting with Guerrero, Neri, and two other officials. The conference in the Manila Hotel took up the reorganization of the administrative set-up by weeding out undesirable personnel and also the redeployment of career officials. It also corrected administrative imbalances by relocating some of the officers of overstaffed departments to under-manned divisions such as the Division on Passports and Visas. Garcia also favoured the rotation once every three years of career officers as provided by law. The reorganization caused alarm to the department personnel, particularly career officers wary of losing their jobs. Guerrero, who was given full powers to reorganize the Foreign Office by Garcia, was quick to point out that any revamp would be in accordance with present laws. Only political appointees of the past administration would be subjected to the revamp. Career officers were relieved from the announcement that Nacionalista favourites would not replace them. However, a rotation among four counsellors or the reassignment of career officers from abroad to the Home Office was not unlikely.[17]

A few days after his appointment, Guerrero received a letter from S.P. Lopez who was still in New York as a member of the Philippine delegation to the United Nations. Lopez extended his congratulations and support: "It has been a long time since we last discussed how you could be 'mustered' into the foreign service under a hostile regime ... I am happy for you and the Department and the Foreign Service as well ...". He said that Garcia and Guerrero "are in a position to approach administrative and policy problems with fresh insight, and thus tighten up the machinery ... into a well-oiled functioning unit". "I do not envy you," Lopez intimated, "the tough, heart-breaking job that must be done to achieve this. But the opportunity is there, and I am sure also the will and the capacity to make use of it."[18]

Indeed, being undersecretary was no joke, neither was it enviable, for Guerrero in the next three weeks after he assumed his post was busy attending to job requests. As he told Lopez in a late response, he had to work at home to stay away from them. "This was to be expected, of course," he reasoned, "after seven years of famine, but it may have serious consequences for the foreign service." Being undersecretary, he was privy to the secret dealings, new appointments being made, reorganizations being planned. The department, for instance, wanted to amend the Foreign Service Act to accommodate new appointments. "The justification will be," he speculated rightly or wrongly, "that the new administration needs personnel of confidence". There was a plan to separate one administrative unit, again to fulfil campaign promises, into two offices, each to be designated with an ambassador as head. Carlos P. Romulo was offered the post in Washington while the UN position was promised to Felixberto Serrano who would use it as a launching pad to the Senate in 1955. All these he relayed in confidence to Lopez. As for the news about Serrano getting the UN post, he was actually saying that Lopez's job was at stake, up for grabs to the new claimants. That was the reason Lopez wrote to Guerrero in January asking for his "sympathy and support". Lopez was only a step away from becoming the chief of the Philippine delegation to the United Nations but as Guerrero wrote,

> [t]here is going to be a general scramble for missions abroad. And I do think that it will be a shame and a very heavy loss to the foreign service if you do not get what you deserve. Are you interested in the New Delhi post? ... Let me know as soon as possible what you want your friends to do (and you can count me as a sincere one.) I am also especially interested in what Narcising [sic] Reyes wants. Would he consider coming back to the Department? We are badly in need of his services.

Guerrero offered the New Delhi post because Ambassador Narciso Ramos resigned or would resign. Lopez confided to him that once he wanted Djakarta but it was offered to former Senator Fuentebella who wanted the Tokyo post but it was already given to former Undersecretary and Acting Secretary Felino Neri. Narciso "Narcing" Reyes, also a newsman turned diplomat, was working with Lopez in the United Nations.[19]

Under Vice President Garcia, Guerrero took part in the formulation of a new policy in the Foreign Office. Garcia wanted amendments to Republic Act No. 708 or the Foreign Service Act to make the reorganization smooth. Guerrero was partly right in that it was needed to pave the way for new political appointments. To achieve his vision, Garcia contended that men in his confidence should be placed in the department noting that the department was created and at present staffed by Liberals. The emphasis of the new policy was economic rather than political, which had long dominated the policy of the past administration under Quirino and Romulo. The law had several flaws necessitating amendments. In terms of promotion and allowance, it engendered discrimination. Although it provided for an examination as a basis for the appointment of career officers, nobody had passed the examination. It failed to provide for any Foreign Affairs officer specializing on trade. Provision for the rotation of personnel was unsatisfactory while the provision for the removal of officers was ambiguous and knotty. As a result, a bill in Congress was introduced to reorganize the Foreign Service. Once it became law, it would create two levels of Foreign Service officers: highly confidential and technical, which consisted of Foreign Affairs Officers (FAO) Class I-IV, and confidential and highly technical, which referred to staff officers. It also gave full powers to the secretary to revamp the Foreign Office.[20]

Guerrero continued writing his column for the *Manila Chronicle* and in one of his articles he made a distinction between "careerists" and "career men" in the Foreign Service. Lopez mentioned it in his letter saying Mauro Mendez, Narciso Reyes and he "had a good laugh" but he mistakenly attributed to Guerrero a reference to "glorified roving newspapermen diplomats", of whom in fact, Guerrero was also one. The distinction Guerrero made prompted Lopez to comment: "If you don't mind, we prefer to belong to the category of career men, and this despite your naughty allusion to our being press agents of somebody who also happens to be an ex-newspaperman", referring to Romulo. In reply, Guerrero wrote: "I own to making the distinction between 'careerists' and 'career men', but surely you can have no doubts as to the category into which you would fall." In parting, he wondered if Lopez caught the issue he wrote in his column two days before his appointment "about that wretched trip we made on the night of the 1st January 1942 out into the bay on an ammunition barge." "Anyway, the point is that," he added, "we shall always be in the same boat," affirming the friendship borne after that night, which had since then become close and sincere.[21]

One thing he did as undersecretary was to help Jose Garcia Villa. He was willing to give him a job in the Foreign Service after a senator cabled him about Villa's predicament. Having read it in the newspaper, Lopez apprised him about Villa who was "in dire straits" in the United States because he was out of work but had a family to support. It was possible, according to Lopez, that his siblings robbed him of his legitimate share of the family property. Anyway, Lopez assured Guerrero that he could help Villa get a job either in the mission or in the consulate "since he must live and work in New York" but "can't do this too soon". He suggested looking into two vacancies with the aid of the department's staff. In another letter from Lopez, Villa's case was taken up together with Mrs Lydia Arguilla, wife of the late writer Manuel Arguilla and herself a writer. Lopez suggested that the two could be accommodated in the cultural section, subject to the approval of the Home Office. He again urged that the two vacancies he mentioned in his previous letter be given to Villa and Arguilla. "Between the two of them, they could do a lot of good things," he stressed, "for they have excellent connections with writers and artists." Since they were already in New York, Lopez argued, rather than bringing two people from Manila, the Foreign Office could save money this way. By March however, Lopez was still inquiring about these requests, suggesting that although Guerrero was doing something about it, he was busy with official matters in the department.[22]

Besides Villa, Guerrero was also looking into the case of Reyes whom he brought up in his letter to Lopez. Confident in but concerned about Reyes, Lopez wrote at great length to convince Guerrero that Reyes was willing to work with him in the department, but should be given a full position in the top-grade of Class II and should serve first at the mission for one more year before his transfer to the Home Office. Guerrero had discussed this request with Romulo when the latter was still in Manila, but Lopez reiterated his request in March that Reyes be given the "promotion to top grade of FAO, Class II" with the possibility of appointing him as political counsellor in the department. It was not Guerrero's fault that the wheels of the bureaucratic mill turned slowly. Further, Reyes became a victim of a manipulation of the Foreign Service posts. Somebody got his post as second secretary in the mission. After several appeals, Reyes was recalled back to the Home Office and became the president's speechwriter.[23]

Guerrero tried to get the New Delhi post for Lopez. However, Lopez had appealed to Garcia to let him stay on in the New York Mission. "I continue to hope that the President's decision regarding this post will be made with full regard to the requirements of this Mission and the requirements of justice." Lopez was amenable to a post either in Paris or New Delhi provided that these were upgraded to embassies. "It would be less painful to be kicked upstairs than down, you know," he lamented. He would rather stay put in the mission but what could Guerrero do when his superiors were committed to promises made during the elections? As usual, postings in the Foreign Service were subject to political concessions rather than merit. Lopez's case dragged on for two months that it became a subject of conversation among Romulo, Garcia and Guerrero. A "compromise proposal" was suggested in consideration of Lopez's predicament by making him head of the Paris legation. Romulo relayed it to Lopez, who informed Guerrero that he had "no strong feelings" about it but the Foreign Office should take into account that he still had some responsibilities in the New York mission and the expediency of his family especially the schooling of his children whose classes would end in June. He also requested for a home leave after staying for four years in New York, before going to Paris. Guerrero understood the pain that Lopez felt. Lopez was for less than a year the acting Permanent Representative to the United Nations because he could not get Romulo's job and now he was seemingly being banished to Paris. Guerrero became the emotional absorber and confidant for the fears, worries and hurts of his friend. What could a friend do but to listen and do something about it if he could. Aside from this, he looked into Lopez's clothing allowance, a request that had been sent in the first week of January but until March had not been taken care of.[24]

Among other things, Guerrero made sure that Philippine interests in the United Nations as well as in other fields were promoted. For instance, he notified Lopez about the possible re-election of the Philippines to the Executive Board of the United Nations Educational, Scientific and Cultural Organization (UNESCO) to which Lopez dutifully replied. According to Lopez, in his talk with top officials of the UNESCO, election would be based on whether a candidate had previous experience in the United Nations or in UNESCO, and because of the principle of rotation, they might choose a new candidate. Indonesia was given the chance to secure the position which it accepted. Nonetheless, he asked for Guerrero's imprimatur for his name to be included among the list of nominees to replace former Senator

Geronima Pecson. His nomination, however, was to be made only if he was to be posted in Paris where the UNESCO had its headquarters.[25]

As a respite from his official duties, Guerrero attended a number of conferences and meetings of various clubs and organizations. The Philippine Historical Association invited him as guest of honour and speaker for its first regular luncheon meeting in early January at the Philippine Columbian Clubhouse where he was made a member of the association. FEU invited him to be the guest speaker at the Fourth Inter-Institute Oratorical Contest in late January. A day before the "Asia and America" speech, he was a guest speaker at a Community Chest programme. At the Philippine Columbian Association hall, Guerrero pointed out the not-so-apparent dangers of charity at the macroscopic level or at the level of rich nations aiding small, poor countries. A rich nation might succumb to complacency and think of itself as better than other nations while beggar nations would slowly develop an inferiority complex and become dependent on aid making them timid, lazy and docile. As in the case of plain alms-giving, he said, foreign assistance must aim at making aid unnecessary in the long run by training people or nations to become economically independent.[26]

"ASIA FOR THE ASIANS": REORIENTING PHILIPPINE FOREIGN POLICY

Just a month into administrative work, Guerrero was drawn into a controversy. When Romulo in New York was quoted by the press reminding Americans that "leavings of Japanese propaganda were still alive in Asia" in reference to Indian Prime Minister Jawaharlal Nehru's adoption of the "Asia for the Asians" slogan, Guerrero, in good faith, decided to speak on "Asia and America" so that "our neighbors in Asia" would not misunderstand, "the character and temper of the new administration". Before the faculty and students of the Manila Law College on their 55th Anniversary celebration, he declared: "I believe I can say with truth that this administration is not only Nacionalista but *nationalist*. It believes in nationalism, not only for itself but also for others. It believes that *Asia belongs to the Asians for the same reason that the Philippines belongs to the Filipinos* [emphasis added].[27]

His belief regarding nationalism in Philippine foreign policy drew flak from the administration fearing that the United States would be hostile to the policy. But Senator Recto defended the policy and even attacked Romulo in a press statement. Recto's support of Guerrero's stand could be understood in the light that the two during the previous administration were one in condemning its "subservient" foreign policy. Guerrero made a snide remark about it in the same speech when he said: "Let us not turn our backs on Asia. The tragic blunder of the past administration was precisely that, and we do not intend to repeat it." Romulo who replaced President Quirino as Secretary of Foreign Affairs, became their object of attacks that ultimately led to the "Great Debate" in Philippine foreign policy. Now that the Nacionalista Party was at the helm of power, Recto understood that he would be directing Philippine foreign policy based on non-alignment and non-ideological friendship with all nations.[28]

Forced to clarify his position amidst the confusion that arose from his foreign policy declaration — some said that it was not cleared by Magsaysay — Guerrero stressed that it was in consonance with the Asian policy of the president contained in his inaugural speech, which he helped to draft, and also with Garcia's policy statements. He admonished Filipinos to stop having an attitude of "suspicion, a groundless assumption of superior knowledge and virtue, and even apprehension regarding their fellow Asians": "We are going to be in Asia for a long, long time, and the sooner we realize it, the better." In another forum in Manila Overseas Press Club's "Meet the Press" aired over DZRH, he elaborated on the meaning of the new policy. Eliminating the suspicion of Asian countries towards the Philippines needed a change of orientation by fostering close relations through trade and cultural interactions with them. Like a master of his own house, he said the Philippines must determine its own independent policy outside of the United States in accord with the independent aspirations of a united Asia against any form of colonialism. Garcia saw no reason not to support his undersecretary. Senator Francisco Delgado of the Senate Committee on Foreign Relations, Paredes of the Liberal Party and Tañada of the Citizens Party lent credence to the policy reorientation. Senator Laurel supported it to be the cornerstone of Philippine foreign policy. Liberal Party President Eugenio Perez announced his party's opposition to the slogan.[29]

A few days after his speech, Guerrero irritated Congressman Diosdado Macapagal when he punned the lawmaker's name as "Britisher Mac-Pagal" in a radio talk. He even made fun of Congressmen Cornelio Villareal and Ferdinand Marcos' names as Dutch Van Villareal and American Ferdinand Marchusen. Macapagal reproved him in a press statement. Guerrero maintained that there was nothing personal in it. These three congressmen would strongly oppose the slogan. In the lower house, Godofredo P. Ramos, vice chair of the House Committee on Foreign Affairs, asked the permission of the House Speaker to read Guerrero's speech in a privilege address. After being given the go-ahead, Ramos said that the policy did not mean alliance with communist countries but the maintenance of friendly relations with free countries in Asia. Macapagal of the opposition took the issue personally and along with his Liberal Party mates condemned the slogan and denied the insertion of Guerrero's speech in the congressional records. Marcos described it as ridiculous, inconsistent and deceitful for if the Philippines were committed to fight communism, the slogan would ally the regime with communist states in Asia. Villareal interpreted it as saying to the Western powers to pack up and leave Asians on their own. Other congressmen called for Guerrero's resignation in a House resolution.[30]

The controversy over the slogan was brought about by the plausible interpretation that Recto and Guerrero were advocating neutralism, an interpretation Macapagal had discerned in Congress as involving the recognition of Communist China and the re-examination of military and economic relations with the United States. Reportedly the U.S. State Department knew about it but intended to ignore it; however, the U.S. Embassy requested a clarification from President Magsaysay. They were thus alarmed with its implications if indeed it was true that their loyal ally had begun following its own lead in international affairs. Magsaysay, elected with overwhelming support from the Americans especially the Central Intelligence Agency (CIA), could not afford to displease his patron. This would antagonize Recto, the "great dissenter" against Magsaysay's pro-American foreign policy.[31]

Was Guerrero advocating the opening of relations with Communist China? Two years ago, he recognized the necessity of living with China as a Great Power but insisted that recognition could not be given since it had called the Philippine Republic a puppet of the United States. Two years later, in the heat of the controversy, he clarified his position amidst interpretations that he was for the recognition of Mao Zedong's government. He denied such an allegation, and maintained that recognition was given to the Chinese in Taiwan but stated ambiguously that the opportunity has arrived to execute a balanced foreign policy embracing not only America but Asian peoples, whom the Philippines has ignored that it had become isolated.[32]

Consequently, on 22 February, after hosting a luncheon for American officials headed by U.S. Ambassador Raymond E. Spruance in Malacañang, President Magsaysay flew to Clark Air Base to speak at a Washington Day event. He acknowledged the pro-Asian policy of his administration but he did not approve of using any slogan liable to distortion. The reference to distortion was made because of reports that Radio Peiping and other Communist propaganda outlets were utilizing it to broadcast what seemed to be the growing anti-Americanism in the Philippines, which he emphatically denied and said it was a lie. There was no incompatibility, he said, between pursuing close relationship with Asian countries and maintaining warm relationship with the United States. Recto was dissatisfied with Magsaysay's dropping of the slogan. Guerrero shared Recto's dissatisfaction. Both were displeased with the president's giving priority to Philippine-American relations over the extension of Filipino friendships and goodwill to Asian countries. To Recto, the site and the occasion when the pronouncement was made revealed Magsaysay's side on the issue. He believed that the president was speaking on his own rather than for the entire party.[33]

Within the Nacionalista Party, the controversy generated partisan conflict and the Liberal Party took advantage of the situation. At a caucus of coalition senators in anticipation of a meeting with the president on 10 March, Recto was instrumental in making the meaning of the slogan specific and definite. The draft written by Laurel and submitted to Magsaysay at that breakfast meeting clarified that the Philippines stood for self-determination of all countries in Asia; it believed in closer cultural and economic relations with them and in the creation of a regional bloc according to the framework of the UN Charter and that colonialism would never be tolerated in any form in Asia. Magsaysay accepted these propositions but made it clear that the points he made at Clark Air Base were to be incorporated. The same day, he issued a statement embodying Laurel's draft and his main points, which was penned by Guerrero, and shown to Minister Lacy who agreed with it.[34]

Reactions to the statement were varied. In the United Nations headquarters in New York, Romulo cabled Magsaysay congratulating the latter for the "masterly handling" of the whole affair. Recto felt vindicated, for the statement affirmed the policy which Guerrero and himself had advocated but believed that the statement was diluted to placate particular interest groups, obviously referring to the U.S. Embassy. Garcia stood by Guerrero as the Department of Foreign Affairs would still be subscribing to the enunciated policy. When Liberals were claiming that the president was dropping the slogan, Senator Delgado rose to its defence and rebuked them. Guerrero was unaffected by all these noises. "A rose by any other name," was his curt remark with his eyes gleaming with satisfaction.[35]

THE ACTING SECRETARY DISAGREES WITH RECTO

Beginning March, Guerrero witnessed Recto's offensives in Philippine foreign policy with Magsaysay as his unwitting whipping dog, from the question of ownership of U.S. military and naval bases in the Philippines; the Senate's pending ratification of the Japanese peace treaty along with the reparations issue; support of U.S. policy on Indochina; to the forging of military alliance with the United States and other countries through the Pacific Treaty Organization (PATO). It was the beginning of his unleashing of his pent-up resentment that Guerrero was privy to when he was robbed of the presidential nomination by Magsaysay in 1953 notwithstanding his patriotic sensibilities. Things were going smoothly for Magsaysay in the provinces when Recto drummed for war. When U.S. Ambassador Spruance claimed that the United States owned the bases in the country, it provoked an angry retort from Recto who argued to the contrary and concluded that if such was the case, then Philippine sovereignty was incomplete and impaired. He then called for the abrogation of the U.S.-RP military bases agreement. Magsaysay favoured the resumption of negotiations with the Japanese reparations mission necessary for the ratification of the peace treaty with Japan, but Recto upon learning of a rumour that PHP30 million was being used to push for its approval, filed resolutions to upset the move. He assailed Garcia when the latter issued a statement that the Philippines would join the United States in warning against communist aggression in Indochina. When the United States brought up the possibility of forming the PATO with the Philippines, he called for its rejection. He also criticized the Philippine trade relations with the United States as "not really free and reciprocal but unfairly one-sided", which pushed him further to argue later on for the repeal of the Bell Trade Act. Magsaysay could not hold his peace any longer. In a position contrary to Recto's, he said that his administration was ready to go along with the United States in a united front against communism in Southeast Asia. Guerrero got entangled in a quarrel between his two superiors — his mentor versus his president. The break happened when Magsaysay did not invite Recto to a military congressional conference in Baguio. Magsaysay "personally instructed" Guerrero "that the meeting had been postponed indefinitely" when in fact during that conference, Magsaysay made his decision to commit the country in the defence against communism.[36]

Meanwhile, Garcia was meeting with Minister Ohno Katsumi of the Japanese reparations mission and on 15 April, a Garcia-Ohno memorandum was signed between the Philippines and Japan. Garcia wired President Magsaysay who was resting in Castillejos in his home province. He wired back that if the plan was all right with the Nacionalista leaders then he would give his approval. Garcia called a meeting with Senators Laurel, Recto, Delgado and Tañada but only Rodriguez could come, with Ohno present.

Rodriguez was on the whole agreeable to the agreement except for the twenty-year term for payment, which he wanted cut to ten years. Ohno with the consent of his superiors compromised on a ten-year period extensible to another ten years. On the evening of Good Friday, the president was briefed on the details of the agreement at Garcia's residence, with Guerrero in attendance. After satisfying himself on the details of the proposal, Magsaysay gave his consent. On 16 April, the press release of the Garcia-Ohno agreement elicited a strong reaction from Recto in alliance with eleven senators, who felt that the agreement shortchanged the Philippines and called for its rejection. The US$400 million reparations services were deceptively presented to be worth US$1 billion, the amount which Recto and other senators had insisted on. Magsaysay appointed Laurel to head the negotiation panel to settle the final matters on the reparations, which also drew a sharp reaction from Recto who argued that there would be conflict of interests if a member from Congress designated to negotiate the terms should later become one of those to ratify the treaty. Since Garcia flew to Geneva to attend a United Nations conference concerning Korea and Indochina, Guerrero, appointed acting secretary, was left behind to defend the integrity of the agreement that his superior had signed, which he had witnessed. The opportunity came when he was summoned at a Senate caucus on 20 April in what he called his "inescapable duty".[37]

The reparations plan was an agreement between the Philippines and Japan whereby Japan would pay the Philippines at least US$1 billion out of an estimated US$8 billion as war damages. Garcia and his counterpart, Minister Ohno, chief of the Japanese mission in Manila, had straightened out in three months the differences in the said plan, but Guerrero that morning was quick to point out that everything was provisional for the negotiators on both sides would hammer out a final agreement that would be mutually acceptable. In simple terms, he told the senators that Japan agreed to deliver US$1 billion worth of economic reparations but the crux of the problem was: Japan would only pay US$400 million. To disabuse them of the idea that the Japanese wanted to shortchange the government as charged by Recto, he would give an illustration to settle their doubts and reassure the senators that Garcia had done his best to ensure that the plan coincided with the national interests amid some doubts that the plan could hurt the national economy or would resurrect the wartime Greater East Asia Co-Prosperity Sphere. Guerrero pointed out that under the plan, the Japanese were not allowed to own property or other rights and they had to turn over all material investments to the government after ten years. As to the question of who would decide what industries would be put up, he told them that the government should be the one based on what he had witnessed in the negotiations. On the question of control and management of the projects, he pointed out that the Japanese were given the task and were obligated to see that the US$1 billion goal could be attained. He left the senators to decide whether to approve the plan but without failing to suggest that any delay of the reparations since Japan's surrender would be a loss in itself. It was only when Garcia sought to end the stalemate that the plan was put into shape, although it was still subjected to more negotiations and modifications by both parties.[38]

The caucus did not clear the way for understanding. Recto was adamant on his position, thus Guerrero and Recto disagreed. Guerrero felt obliged to consider the issues raised by the senators. Thus, in a note to Ambassador Shozo Murata, the new chief of the Japanese reparations mission, he stated the Philippine position of neither honouring the Garcia-Ohno memorandum nor the Murata draft. Murata in his reply insisted that those memoranda were binding to both the Philippines and Japan. Murata's note prompted Guerrero to mention publicly the vague interpretation of the term "services" in the memorandum that made it somewhat unacceptable. In another note to Murata, he reiterated his position and described the meetings before as merely "exploratory conversations". The agreement, he argued, subject to the ratification of the 1951 San Francisco Peace Treaty, was not binding without the approval of the Senate. The other side stuck to its position. Guerrero announced to the public a new strategy that was not revealed "for strategic reasons" but the following day the next conference with the Japanese mission was cancelled. Alongside these developments were Murata's tactless statements regarding the agreement to the press, possibly out of his disgust with the stalled negotiations. Senators called for Murata's recall. Condemnations from the public and the press were heard and read. The negotiation could have been postponed indefinitely but was saved by Magsaysay's decision to send a fact-finding committee to Japan to determine the latter's capability to pay. Guerrero's hand in the matter was transferred to a group headed by Finance Secretary Jaime Hernandez who flew to Japan and stayed there for thirty-six days.[39]

BANISHED TO LONDON

In early June, it was announced that Guerrero would be made ambassador to the Court of Saint James. The appointment, however, prompted the rumour that he was being "purged" as the reason for his demotion. Denials were issued and pointed to the fact that it was he who asked for the London reassignment. He allegedly sought this arrangement to avoid becoming a "sacrificial goat" in bitter foreign policy differences between President Magsaysay and Recto. His appointment was accompanied by the news that the Philippine legation in London would be raised to embassy status based on the agreement the previous year between the governments of the Philippines and Great Britain. As to who would replace him as undersecretary, he recommended S.P. Lopez to Magsaysay. Felino Neri's name also cropped up as a possible nominee. Guerrero would replace Jose Romero who resigned to become the Philippine Sugar Association's representative in Washington. Although named as ambassador, he would still be acting secretary for another month until the return of Garcia from Geneva. The news of his appointment was greeted with elation by the diplomatic community. The Indonesian charge d'affaires and Mrs Tjokroadisumarto invited him and Annie to a dinner at the Indonesian Embassy. To display his earnestness towards his new assignment, he started acquiring an Oxford accent, probed into English history, imitated the sartorial elegance of Anthony Eden and read Winston Churchill's speeches.[40]

During the last two months that Garcia was absent, Guerrero steered the Foreign Office administratively. Amidst attacks that the revamp was made to accommodate "political protégés", he defended it by saying: "If politics is playing any part in the reorganization, it is to save career men from being thrown out." When ten Foreign Affairs officers were bypassed by the Commission on Appointments, he sought the opinion of the justice secretary to protect these career officers from losing their jobs. When the Retail Trade Nationalization bill restricting retail trade to Filipinos was put up for the president's consideration, he handled protests from various foreign diplomatic establishments in Manila that did not prevent Magsaysay in June from signing the bill into law. He clarified the position of U.S. business interests with respect to Republic Act No. 1180; that based on the Trade Agreement of 1946, the U.S. president, upon claiming that the law was discriminatory, could suspend its effectiveness, making Philippine position "extremely vulnerable".[41]

One issue touching his career as acting secretary was Romulo. Romulo was appointed as "special and personal representative of the President with the rank of Ambassador", a strange title earning Recto's disapproval. Recto opposed the arrangement that Romulo was only accountable to Magsaysay and not to the Department of Foreign Affairs. Guerrero might have felt the same way as Recto. When there was intrigue that Recto was opposed to Romulo's appointment as ambassador to the United States, he denied that such existed, and clarified Recto's stand that an immediate appointment of an ambassador was necessary to correct the abnormal situation. Romulo, however, remained in that odd designation until September 1955.[42]

The following month, Guerrero and his successor were sworn in by President Magsaysay. Raul S. Manglapus would replace him as undersecretary. In other words, Magsaysay rejected Guerrero's recommendation of Lopez. Manglapus had an edge over Lopez because he was the Magsaysay for President Movement (MPM) campaign director, thus making his appointment politically coloured. Guerrero would leave for his new post in London on 24 July.[43]

Embers of Guerrero's "Asia for the Asians" policy continued to burn when in July, Senator Edmundo Cea, chairman of the Committee on Commerce and Industry, favoured limited trade with Communist China on items such as foodstuffs and lumber. Cea's defence of his position was reminiscent of Guerrero's when the former said that the Philippines was inseparably linked with every single Asian country. Although Guerrero maintained that he did not mean recognition of Communist China in clarifying the policy, he was neither against nor for the opening of trade relations. Recto supported Cea but the proposal did not prosper. The proposal came a month before the Laurel mission went to the United States to negotiate the revision of certain iniquitous provisions of the Bell Trade Act. With this as consideration since 1954 was the last year of free trade with the United States under the said act, the implicit relevance of Guerrero's policy speech was the broadening of Philippine foreign and trade relations to soften the impact of economic readjustment between the Philippines and the United States.[44]

A week prior to his departure for London, Guerrero was feted by his former law classmates and professors. The Philippine Law School class of 1939 gave a farewell luncheon in his honour. He was also invited as speaker before the Pasay Lions Club during its Independence Week celebration. In his speech on this occasion, he declared that the Filipino nation was born when Filipinos discovered themselves; and discovering themselves to be one people, they achieved liberty, and emphasized that they were the first Asians to attain nationhood, to rise against Western colonialism and to establish a modern democracy. Though Americans came with "the promise of freedom" and then the Japanese, who left them "robbed and mangled on the wayside", still the Philippine Republic was born. Guerrero issued a challenge — that in renewing allegiance to the Filipino nation, Filipinos should do so in the name and spirit of freedom.[45]

Six years of voluntary banishment from the Senate was not a bad thing. It was there that he developed a distaste for politics where political assassination and black propaganda were common in the scramble for power.

It was also during this period that he developed a close relationship with Recto, born during Ateneo alumni gatherings and gradually flourished during the war when Recto was head of the Ministry of Foreign Affairs. There was no doubt that his nationalism and his ideas in foreign policy bore the imprint of Recto, just as the latter was also influenced by the brilliant young legal adviser's convictions. Recto was also influential in his reappointment to the Foreign Service to be the undersecretary of Foreign Affairs. It was also a piece of writing, his "Asia and America" speech that called for a balanced Philippine foreign policy, that this time caused him to be exiled to Europe.

Notes

1. *7 years of the PAG: A Report Covering Seven Years of Philippine Contemporary Art as Noted through the Philippine Art Gallery* (Manila, 1958), pp. 8, 53, 54, 56, 60-ap 1, ap-6, ap-7, ap-11; *An Anthology of Carlos Palanca Memorial Awards Winners* (Manila, 1976), pp. xiv–xv, 215.
2. Teehankee, "A Testament…", in *In Memoriam*, p. 9; Rodriguez et al. vs. Gella et al., G.R. L.-6266, 2 February 1953. See also Jorge R. Coquia, *The Philippine Presidential Election of 1953* (University Publishing, 1955), pp. 136–42.
3. Leon Ma. Guerrero, "The Flower of Happiness", *Journal of the Philippine Pharmaceutical Association* 40, no. 2: 83–85.
4. Ibid.
5. "Certificate of Appointment as of 30 April 1953", Sofronio Quimson to Leon Ma. Guerrero, 26 May 1953 in *LMGFPF*; Quirino, *Amang*, pp. 139–40.
6. *The Lycaean* (Lyceum of the Philippines, 1954), p. 25; "History of the College of Law", *College of Law Catalogue* (Lyceum of the Philippines, 2006), pp. 5–6; Teehankee, "A Testament …", in *In Memoriam*, p. 9; Lewis E. Gleeck, Jr, *The Third Philippine Republic 1946–1972* (Quezon City: New Day Publishers, 1993), pp. 135–36; Coquia, *The Philippine Presidential Election*, pp. 31, 150–51.
7. Quirino, *Apo Lakay*, p. 175; Quirino, *Amang*, pp. 147–48.
8. Ibid.; Leon Ma. Guerrero, "Ramon Magsaysay: A Memoir", in *Alternatives for Asians: The Philippine Experiment* (London: Philippine Embassy, 1957), p. 26; Leon Ma. Guerrero, "Carlos P. Garcia", *Weekly Women's Magazine* (hereafter cited as *WWM*), 2 October 1953, pp. 4, 39; Coquia, *The Philippine Presidential Election*, pp. 217, 225–26, 245; *PFP*, 11 July 1951, p. 3.
9. Leon Ma. Guerrero, "A Christian Mistake", *WWM*, 14 August 1953, pp. 54–55.
10. Leon Ma. Guerrero, "The American Influence", *SMM*, 8 August 1953, pp. 5–6, 8–9; "Is the UN necessary?", *SMM*, 7 October 1953, pp. 5–6, 8; Agnes N. Keith, *Bare Feet in the Palace* (Little Brown, 1955), pp. 114–17.
11. *MC* beginning 14 September 1953 until 4 January 1954.
12. On the Luna brothers, see the issue on 23 October. Also published in Leon Ma. Guerrero, *We Filipinos* (Manila: Daily Star Publishing, 1984), pp. 125–28. About Bonifacio, see *MC*, 30 November 1953.

13. Leon Ma. Guerrero to Horacio de la Costa, 19 October 1953, *HDCP*; *TG*, 6 July 1953.
14. Quirino, *Amang*, p. 150; Gleeck, *The Third Philippine Republic*, pp. 141–42; Jose V. Abueva, *Ramon Magsaysay: A Political Biography* (Manila: Solidaridad Publishing House, 1971), p. 279; A.V.H. Hartendorp, *History of Industry and Trade of the Philippines* (American Chamber of Commerce of the Philippines, 1958), pp. 12, 15. For the full text of the inaugural address, see J. Eduardo Malaya and Jonathan E. Malaya, ... *So Help Us God: The Presidents of the Philippines and Their Inaugural Addresses* (Manila: Anvil, 2004), pp. 172–76. The speech carried the words: "For this young and vigorous nation of ours, nothing is really impossible! Let us have faith in ourselves, the same faith that fired the heroic generation of revolution. They waged and won their struggle with nothing but bolos in their hands and courage in their hearts. Without political training and experience, they wrote a constitution comparable with the best and established the first republic in Asia. Our own generation was told by doubters and enemies that we would never have independence from the United States. We live today under a free and sovereign Republic. Our faith was fulfilled".
15. Abueva, *Ramon Magsaysay*, pp. 225, 227, 388, 293; John H. Romani, *The Philippine Presidency* (Institute of Public Administration, University of the Philippines, 1956), p. 195; *TG*, 23 January 1954.
16. *MT*, 4 January 1954; *Manila Daily Bulletin* (hereafter cited as *MDB*), 5 January 1954; *MT*, 6 January 1954; Salvador Lopez to Leon Ma. Guerrero, 12 January 1954, *SPLP*; *Palileo v. Cosio*, G.R. No. L-7667, 28 November 1955.
17. *MT*, 6, 8, 9 January 1954.
18. Salvador Lopez to Leon Ma. Guerrero, 12 January 1954, *SPLP*.
19. Leon Ma. Guerrero to Salvador P. Lopez, 22 January 1954, *SPLP*.
20. *MT*, 12 and 23 January; 10 February 1954.
21. Salvador Lopez to Leon Ma. Guerrero, 12 January 1954; Leon Ma. Guerrero to Salvador P. Lopez, 22 January 1954, *SPLP*.
22. Salvador P. Lopez to Leon Ma. Guerrero, no date; Salvador P. Lopez to Leon Ma. Guerrero, 8 February 1954 and 8 March 1954, *SPLP*; Nick Joaquin, *Doveglion and Other Cameos* (National Book Store, 1977), p. 215.
23. Salvador P. Lopez to Leon Ma. Guerrero, no date and 8 March 1954, *SPLP*; Narciso G. Reyes, *Memories of Diplomacy: A Life in the Philippine Foreign Service* (Pasig City: Anvil Publishing, 1995), pp. 21–22.
24. Salvador P. Lopez to Leon Ma. Guerrero, no date and 8 March 1954, *SPLP*.
25. Salvador P. Lopez to Leon Ma. Guerrero, 19 April 1954, *SPLP*.
26. *MT*, 15, 24 January, 4 February 1954; Leon Ma. Guerrero, "Dangers of Charity", *STM*, 14 February 1954, pp. 26–27.
27. *MDB*, 8 February 1954; *MT*, 6 February 1954; Abueva, *Ramon Magsaysay*, p. 393.
28. Renato Constantino, *The Making of a Filipino: A Story of Philippine Colonial Politics* (Self-published, 1969), p. 198; Abaya, The Making of a Subversive, p. 105; Abaya, *The CLU Story*, p. 78.

29. *MT*, 11 February 1954; Abueva, *Ramon Magsaysay*, pp. 388, 393–94.
30. *DM*, 12 February 1954; Meyer, *Diplomatic History of the Philippine Republic*, p. 193; Republic of the Philippines, Congressional Records, House of Representatives, Third Congress, First Regular Session (25 January 1954 to 20 May 1954), First Special Session (19 July 1954 to 3 August 1954), *1954 Index and History of Bills and Resolutions* (Manila: Bureau of Printing, 1965), pp. 141, 201.
31. Ibid.; Abueva, *Ramon Magsaysay*, p. 394; *MT*, 17 February 1954.
32. Leon Ma. Guerrero, "The Philippines and China: The Diplomacy", *STM*, 7 September 1952, pp. 4–6; *MT*, 8 February 1954.
33. Abueva, *Ramon Magsaysay*, pp. 395–96.
34. Ibid., pp. 397–98.
35. Ibid., pp. 398–99.
36. Ibid., pp. 385, 399–403.
37. Ibid., pp. 403–4.
38. Leon Ma. Guerrero, "The Reparations Plan", *MT*, 21 April 1954, p. 3.
39. *MT*, 23, 24, 25 and 26 April 1954; Abueva, *Ramon Magsaysay*, pp. 405–6; Meyer, *Diplomatic History of the Philippine Republic*, pp. 207–12. See also Takushi Ohno, *War Reparations and Peace Settlement: Philippines-Japan Relations 1945–1956* (Solidaridad, 1986).
40. *DM*, 5 June 1954; *MT*, 5 June 1954; *MDB*, 17 June 1954; *Sunday Chronicle* (hereafter cited as *SC*), 13 June 1954.
41. *MC*, 15 June 1954; *MT*, 5 June 1954; Meyer, *Diplomatic History of the Philippine Republic*, p. 197; *MDB*, 17 July 1954; Frank H. Golay, *The Revised United States-Philippine Trade Agreement of 1955* (Southeast Asia Programme, Department of Far Eastern Studies, Cornell University, 1956), p. 31.
42. Meyer, *Diplomatic History of the Philippine Republic*, p. 189; *MT*, 1 June 1954.
43. *DM*, 8 July 1954; Abueva, *Ramon Magsaysay*, p. 241.
44. Meyer, *Diplomatic History of the Philippine Republic*, p. 199.
45. *MT*, 8 and 16 July 1954; Leon Ma. Guerrero, "The Filipino Nation", *MT*, 4 July 1954, p. 4.

IV

London and Madrid:
The Philippines in a Resurgent Asia

West of the chancery, I see the saffron sun
Burning like Gotama bathed in gasoline
(Or perhaps like an effigy of Uncle Sam
Whose flames are fanned by Marxist winds) ...
And then I think of falling dominoes
And Asia's seething politics ...

Federico Licsi Espino Jr., Cogitations of a Diplomat

"Our role is simply to be ourselves, instead of being caricatures of our former rulers, to participate honestly and conscientiously in the building of our people's welfare and happiness and in the greatness of Asia."

Vice President Emmanuel Pelaez,
concurrent Secretary of Foreign Affairs (1961–63)

12

At the Court of Saint James

As scheduled in late July 1954, Guerrero and Annie left the Philippines aboard *S.S. Free State Mariner*, which had a stopover in Hong Kong before embarking on the long voyage to London. His "sainted" mother had an injunction "that under no circumstances must … [he] become an Anglican, which to her mind was somehow connected with having several wives, like Henry VIII." More than Shakespeare and Belloc of his college days, Guerrero had an extensive knowledge of British history. About Philippine-British relations, he knew that the Philippines suspended its North Borneo claim. At Palace Green, they were greeted by a birch tree at the gate of "an old English two-story building with a small front garden" that would be their home.[1]

Here in an exclusive street close to Kensington Gardens, Guerrero had to wait for more than two months to present his credentials to the queen. Although his stint in Tokyo could have helped in his preparations, being ambassador-designate was a different matter. London was home to various embassies from countries all over the world. The process of presenting the credentials of fewer than a hundred chiefs of mission would take months as the Chief of Her Majesty's Protocol would have to schedule them. Thus, on 13 October, the trip aboard the two state carriages to the Buckingham Palace was pleasant as he presented his credentials to Her Majesty Queen Elizabeth II. British Foreign Secretary Anthony Eden met Guerrero and Annie before they separately met the queen who chatted with them. In Whitehall, Eden received and interviewed the new Philippine envoy.[2]

The letter of credence from the president as the "embodiment of the sovereign power of his people" and the acceptance of host country made

Guerrero the personal representative of President Magsaysay to the Court of Saint James. As the ambassador of his people, he had to present the views of his government on matters affecting the national interest or on seemingly uncomplicated subject as the atomic power. Speaking before an international dinner hosted by the Institute of Atomic Information at Claridge's Hotel, Guerrero optimistically remarked on the new hope that the atomic power could raise to alleviate poverty in underdeveloped countries — the key to economic development in countries such as the Philippines. In mid-November, he visited Hunting Aerosurveys and sent a special box of Manila cigars to Sir Winston Churchill.[3]

"WE FILIPINOS ARE ONE ASIAN PEOPLE"

To make a link to the local community, Guerrero, with the help of Annie who was a fabulous hostess, spearheaded dinner parties at the embassy. It was during one of these dinners in February 1955 when his agenda for Philippine-British relations took shape. In the course of the party, at the dinner table, the usual voluble Guerrero talked with the guests. He asked them where they thought the Philippines was, whether it was near Jamaica, Hawaii or Formosa (now Taiwan). To his surprise, nobody, not even by a fluke, offered the correct answer. On every map in Great Britain, the Philippines was nowhere. In fact in the ensuing years, he regularly received letters, cables and official documents with incorrect spellings of the Philippines either spelled with two *l*s or one *p*. Some were even addressed to the American Embassy apparently thinking that the Philippines was still a colony of the United States.[4]

At every opportunity, Guerrero told Londoners about the Philippines. When the British Legion of Hammer Branch invited him to speak at their meeting, he made it a point to air his views about the role of the Philippines in a changing Asia, a theme he had already touched on back home. In Haslemere, Surrey, he demystified European misconceptions about "the so-called inscrutable Oriental mind": Asians would confront the world the way Europeans would; an Asian nationalist would protest against the intrusion of a foreign power on his country's sovereignty in the same degree that a European nationalist would. A new Asia was emerging, he said, being reborn from the ashes of the old; that contrary to the popular view, it was now Europe that had become "ancient". He related the incident at the dinner table. It was a reflection of the Philippines' standing in the Western world he said, but: "I do not take that as a final word, for, in all modesty, we Filipinos sincerely believe that we have made, and can still make, a not entirely worthless contribution to the common task." He made known the greatness of his nation as having launched "the first national democratic revolution in Asia" and that Filipinos did not learn democracy from the West. He asked: "What does this mean for Asia?" "It means we Filipinos are one Asian people" experienced in the ways of democracy, which gave them practical advantages in dealing with elections and in encouraging business enterprises under a regime of law and order. He ended with high hopes that Asia would be in a position to carry out its objectives without reverting back to its image of "shrunken Asia of the despot ages".[5]

To publicize the Philippines, Guerrero organized the Philippine Society of London. Within a month, the society was inaugurated "to spread knowledge and understanding of the Filipino People as Asians". Scheduled on the anniversary of Magellan's landing in the Philippines in 1955, he turned the inaugural address into another venue for explicating what he called "The Philippine Experiment". In the context of the Cold War, he said, non-communist countries in Asia such as the Philippines had a choice resting on their relations with the West but filled with contradictions in matters of sovereignty and security, of economic development and economic independence. The Philippines, a former American colony, surrendered its economic independence for free trade that spelt instant prosperity, and its sovereignty by granting military and naval bases as guarantee of its security, making it "a test case for Asia". If such Philippine choices, which made "the Philippines the most hospitable country in Asia for Western capital and Western policy", turned out to be good choices, then he believed Asians would follow the Philippine experiment.[6]

His efforts to inform Britons about the Philippines paid off. The Royal Geographical Society and the Shell Company sponsored a photographic exhibition about the Philippines. He accepted the invitation to grace its opening on 22 March. At the society's office at Kensington Gore in London, he explained to the audience how well suited Filipino houses and clothing were to the hot climate, and regarding mountain tribes, he warned that "our antagonists", meaning to say, American imperialists, broadcast pictures of these peoples to downplay clamours for independence. He pleaded to look at them in the context of the entire nation, being the first Asian state out of colonialism and the first to proclaim and organize a democratic republic. Turning his thought to the fitting title of the exhibition, "Pearl of the Orient", he compared the pearl — the product produced when a foreign body intrudes into an oyster covering it with glossy secretions — with Western invasion of his country, the Philippines which absorbed Western culture to produce the Pearl of the Orient.[7]

PROMOTING TRADE IN GERMANY AND SCANDINAVIAN COUNTRIES

Eight days later, Guerrero flew to Germany to head the Philippine trade mission in their talks with German counterparts in Bonn. Diplomatic relations between the Philippines and West Germany were restored in July 1954 and a Philippine consulate was opened in Hamburg in November. The Philippine Government was mulling over a commercial treaty that it rejected when Germany proposed it in 1951. A trade protocol was signed on 25 April 1955 that would give way to a general treaty.[8]

In July, Guerrero and Annie celebrated for the first time the day of Philippine independence, which will become a ritual in the years to come. Instead of holding it in the evening, they made the reception at noon with diplomatic representatives from the fifty-eight embassies as well as Lord Reading, the minister of state for foreign affairs, members of the opposition led by Clement R. Atlee and Hugh Gaitskell in attendance. Guerrero and Annie decided to wear the Philippine national dresses of *barong tagalog* and *terno*, marking for the first time they were worn at an official function.[9]

Intrigues in the Foreign Office did not spare Guerrero. Confidential rumours about reassignments swirled in the Foreign Service. It happened when Romulo's appointment as ambassador to the United States was signed by Magsaysay. Felixberto Serrano, the permanent representative to the United Nations, was to be demoted to being the vice chairman of the United Nations delegation and would eventually lose his post to Romulo. As a compromise, Serrano might be transferred to London while Guerrero, in the words of Romulo, "may find himself either in the Vatican or in some unknown place". The plan to transfer Guerrero did not materialize. Ambassadors normally stayed in their post for three years after which the rotation rule was followed. Surely, Garcia did not allow it to happen.[10]

Guerrero was also appointed as minister to Sweden, Denmark, Norway and Finland. In late September, he and Annie flew to the land where Gil Hilario's wife, Miss Universe Armi Kussela came from, presenting his credentials to Finnish President Juho Paasikivi. Pressed by reporters on the couple, his response made headlines in Helsinki: "Armi and Gil have brought Finland and the Philippines so close together that we should now begin trading something else besides romance." The following week, they went to Copenhagen to present his credentials to King Frederick IX. After the brief ceremony at the Royal Palace, they met Queen Ingrid. In mid-November, he presented his papers in Oslo and Stockholm. In Sweden, he presented books on Philippine archaeology to the king who was an amateur archaeologist. The very limited Philippine interests to be promoted in these countries — all constitutional monarchies except Finland — justified his designation as non-resident envoy.[11]

When Lopez was appointed as Philippine representative to go to Liberia for the signing of diplomatic relations between the two countries in December, he informed Guerrero about a personnel arrangement while he was away involving one of Guerrero's staff who was to be detailed in Paris for a brief period, which Guerrero acceded to. Intrigued by Lopez's trip to Monrovia, Guerrero asked: "Was this something that the Liberian Mission to Manila after Bandung Conference wangled out of the Department? I can think of no other justification for the trip and I assume you have no personal interest in it." In fact, the recognition of Liberia was not met with approval by the Foreign Office. It was only when Romulo intervened in Washington that President Magsaysay was persuaded to endorse it. According to Romulo, both the Liberian ambassadors in Washington and Spain had "jointly talked" to him about it. Lopez was not the original choice, as Neri had suggested Guerrero to be sent to Monrovia. Romulo had Lopez appointed from a phone booth in the United Nations.[12]

In early March 1956, Guerrero flew back to Germany to present his credentials to Professor Theodor Heuss, the West German president. He had high hopes, he said, that the recently signed trade protocol would result in closer commercial cooperation and also thanked the German people for having welcomed Rizal during his days in Germany. While there, he and Annie went to Heidelberg and stayed at an inn close to the university so that he could relive Rizal's experience in Germany. Jose D. Ingles replaced him as ambassador in mid-November and two years later, both countries elevated their consulates to embassies.[13]

Not only did Guerrero spearhead the opening of trade relations with Germany in line with Garcia's economic policy, but an opportunity came for him to pursue the negotiation of a trade treaty with Norway. He was in Oslo in late July for the sixth International Bar Association convention that saw him elected as vice president and chairman of the Appeals Committee. Before he flew to Copenhagen, he spoke before the Norwegian diplomatic corps, cabinet ministers, shipowners, businessmen, and the press. At the Oslo Grand Hotel Rococo Room he disclosed that a treaty was under negotiation between the two countries. The treaty was mainly concerned with Norwegian technical assistance to Philippine interests on hydro-electric power, paper and pulp manufacture, and shipping.[14]

MAKING IT TO PARIS

Guerrero had just returned to London from Germany when Lopez invited him to Paris. In fact, Lopez had been invited to London but had to cancel the visit because he had to hurry to Paris. The invitation was inopportune because in April 1956 Guerrero had to attend meetings of that "wretched" International Sugar Council. His hands were tied with his work at the embassy and outside commitments. Expressing his thanks and regrets, he wrote: "I envy you your presidential chores — it must have been very interesting both in Liberia and in the Vatican." Then, he cajoled him: "Now that you have the blessing of His Holiness you can run for the Senate!" "I do hope I shall be able to visit you sometime this summer or autumn; Annie has never been to Paris. Besides, I want to visit Sulka's and take advantage of their export schemes. Also, how is the new Citroen? I am looking for a new small car, something like the Volkswagen." He was planning to learn from French trading approaches possibly as a source of comparison for future trade agreements with Norway or Great Britain. Guerrero was a car aficionado. He was enjoying London very much. He had been seeing Shakespearean plays. On the night of 19 March, he went with Annie to watch *Othello*, a refreshing spectacle from the dramatic reading he performed as Othello way back in May 1953 with Daisy Avellana as Desdemona at FEU. He had already seen *King Lear* and others in the past and "[these] made me feel (retrospectively) like a silly fool", quite a reasonable feeling for someone who was once "King Lear".[15]

Between March and July, Guerrero was committed to a number of speaking engagements and projects in and out of the embassy. Some months before, he received an invitation again from the British Legion, apparently satisfied with his performance in Haslemere, but now upon the request of the Surrey Council. In the second week of April, he was at the legion headquarters at Ripley to speak again on the "new Asia", which had become "a veritable minefield" referring to the wars and insurrections across Asia. But the West should contend with a new Asia, he said, the Asians who do not want to take sides — the Asian neutrals. The West must catch up with Soviet Russia and Communist China, which had come to terms with the new Asia with their offer of "competitive coexistence" vis-à-vis the West, which would offer a higher bid in the "marketplace of neutralism", but it — he was actually hinting at America — might neglect its friends in Asia. He was confident however that it would honour that friendship.[16]

Work at the embassy made it impossible to decide if he and Annie would go to Paris. Among other things, he received a request from the National Waterworks and Sewerage Authority inquiring about the prices of pipes and other items. He notified Lopez about this, asking if his friend received a similar request and attaching his letter to the agency for guidance. Another matter that cropped up was the production of a forty-five-minute television programme about the embassy and the Philippines — billed *Afternoon Out - Tea at the Philippine Embassy* — which Guerrero had to supervise. The first in a series to be inaugurated for Independent Television company, he was able to invite the renowned ballerina Margot Fonteyn and made a show "around her reactions while watching a performance of the *tinikling*".[17]

When the Suez Canal crisis broke out, Guerrero was finally able to visit Paris but only on an overnight stopover before catching a flight to Manila to report on the crisis. Lopez managed to reserve an accommodation at the luxurious Hotel George V. Arriving at almost noon, Guerrero on seeing the extravagant suite exclaimed, "SP, what have you done? This suite must cost at least three times our measly $25 per diem. And what am I supposed to do all alone in this enormous suite?" "Leoni," SP replied, "in Paris as in London loneliness is not a problem." Before going to lunch, the two sat down for half an hour to talk about the crisis in between sips of scotch for Guerrero and dry martini for Lopez.[18]

REPORTING ON THE SUEZ CANAL CRISIS

In mid-September 1956, Guerrero was suddenly summoned home when the Suez Canal crisis escalated. It was his first time to go home after staying more than two years in Europe. Before flying to Manila, he passed through Paris to get a report on the French side of the issue from Lopez who wanted to go home for consultation regarding the crisis and for a visit to his aging mother. The decision to turn down Lopez's request was farsighted considering the criticisms regarding expenses that met Guerrero's return. Upon knowing that he was being summoned, Guerrero gathered and studied pertinent British Government documents. A day or two before he took his flight, he sent a coded cable to Garcia about the implications of the crisis in which he sensed an opportunity for Philippine foreign policy actions to be based on three principles: first, American connection, second, friendship towards other small Asian and African countries and third, adherence to the principles of international law and order. Besides closely monitoring developments on the crisis, Guerrero had some conversations with the British minister of state for Foreign Affairs and other government officials, and colleagues in the diplomatic corps. In a confidential dispatch to Garcia, he placed high hopes on the Egyptian Government under Gamal Abdel Nasser that it could operate the canal efficiently, would not politically discriminate against certain nations, would only collect tolls reasonably and not raise them to finance the Aswan Dam project.[19]

At the local airport on 17 September, Guerrero was met by Press Secretary J.V. Cruz and Undersecretary Raul S. Manglapus. The following day he briefed Garcia and Magsaysay on the crisis. At Camp Murphy, Magsaysay reconvened the joint meeting of the Council of State and the National Security Council, postponed due to the delayed receipt of a report. The briefing was called to ascertain the Philippine position regarding the crisis. Guerrero was in a position to provide an effective report that would guide Philippine policy with the help of reports from his colleagues. He made a thorough discussion on the historical antecedents since 1869 when the canal was opened and the treaties that governed its use, to the events in July leading to its nationalization. The crux of the crisis, as he pointed out to the convened councils, was not ownership of the canal but rather its "control, operation, and maintenance". Although the British and French governments refused to accept the legality of the nationalization decree, the London conferences had accepted it as a fait accompli. Fears on their side stemmed from potential threats that the decree might impose on the passage of ships carrying cargoes of oil and other essential goods. He believed, however, that it was only a question of confidence and trust as he had reported before to the Foreign Office. Was there a danger of war between the two protagonists? In his view, the likelihood of war was nil as "both sides have retreated from their original positions." Yet, the present situation may affect Philippine trade interests with Europe because 17.92 per cent of exports went to Europe while only 9.06 per cent constituted the imports coming from Europe apparently through Suez. Aside from the two powers, the United States and Soviet Union, refraining from initiating a conflict to maintain the "balance of terror", Guerrero suggested the best course was to support whatever action the United Nations may take in maintaining a system of international law and order.[20]

A day after the briefing, he spoke before the Manila Rotary Club at their luncheon meeting at the Manila Hotel about the international situation as regards the Suez Canal crisis. Taking his cue from the report's conclusions he authored, he said that only by maintaining Winston Churchill's "balance of terror" that the Philippines could help preserve world peace, for the United States no longer had a monopoly on nuclear weapons. Maintaining the balance, he said, meant using the bases and the Southeast Asia Treaty Organization (SEATO) "not as means to *fight* the next war but as means to *prevent* it [his own emphasis]". In direct opposition to Recto, although he did not mention Recto's name, Guerrero said that the issue of whether the bases would invite or deter attack was of secondary relevance. On the issue of SEATO, again in reference to Recto, that the Philippines profited nothing from it and that it already had an alliance with the United States, which made it unnecessary, was nonsense, he said. The case of Suez was a threat to that balance and the threat would continue as long as the West failed to understand the nationalism of Asian and African nations. Philippine nationalism was prepared, he believed, on maintaining that balance not only because it would serve its own self-interest but also the common interests of mankind.[21]

He had a Suez Canal crisis hangover a week after he flew to Rome en route to London. At the International Cultural Exchange Programme held at Mahatma Gandhi Hall, Fitzroy Square in London, he realized that while in the plane on his way to London, he believed the concept of a "One World" was feasible, possible and reasonable, but once the plane descended to refuel, the idea of unity was instantly shattered as the "network of nationalities and sovereignties ... divide the world and alienate men from one another." In any case, the proof that unity was still possible, he said, was the gathering. Although differences and divisions existed among men, the point was "to make a beginning" in making friendship and understanding possible.[22]

The aftermath of the Suez consultation did not favour Guerrero's prediction that the danger of an impending war had finally receded. Garcia directed the Philippine Mission in the United Nations to vote for the Canadian resolution calling for an international force to oversee troop movements in West Asia. Garcia initially committed the Philippines to share the burden of costs. Guerrero, Lopez and Serrano were of the same thinking in not taking sides in that conflict. The pressure from the Muslim groups reversed Garcia's posture when President Magsaysay sent fifty volunteers to commit the country militarily.[23]

EAST ASIAN ASSOCIATION

Possibly in connection with Suez, Guerrero visited in November 1956 the Marquess of Reading, the minister of state in the British Foreign Office for a discussion on the international situation. He had a high regard for the marquess for he was accessible to East Asian diplomats like himself in matters affecting their respective countries.[24]

Thus, when the marquess retired as minister of state, the East Asian diplomatic community honoured him at a dinner at Claridge's Hotel in late January 1957. Guerrero paid tribute to the marquess who made sure that

East Asia was as important as Europe to Her Majesty's Government. The gathering of East Asian diplomats in honour of Lord Reading formally gave way to a non-political "East Asian Association". In early February, eleven nations — Burma, Indonesia, Korea, Laos, Thailand, Cambodia, Nepal, Afghanistan, Vietnam, Communist China and Japan — elected Guerrero chairman of this new diplomatic grouping to promote relations between Asian embassies and the British Foreign Office. To stress its non-political objectives, one diplomatic source was quick to point out that as a group they do not see eye-to-eye with China; the object was to facilitate their work in East Asia with consent of all the members.[25]

The election of Guerrero marked the recognition accorded to him as spokesman of Asia. To make known what he termed as "Alternatives for Asians" that would become the title of his book, he decided to compile his speeches — "[t]he lazy way to write a book...". He sought a foreword from his esteemed colleague in the diplomatic corps, Vijaya Lakshmi Pandit, the high commissioner of India in London and president of the Sixth UN General Assembly, who considered Ambassador Guerrero among her personal friends and admired "the catholicity of his mind and the clarity of his convictions". She called him "truly representative of Asian sentiment" on varied issues confronting Asian peoples and the world.[26]

THE COMMON MARKET AND THE US-UK MILITARY BASES AGREEMENT

With the proposed European Common Market being deliberated pending its implementation by ratification of the Rome treaty, the Foreign Office immediately tasked the embassy to make a survey if the "common market" would affect Philippine copra exports to Europe. The proposed common market covered France, West Germany, Italy and Belgium, the Netherlands and Luxembourg (Benelux), and their colonies. Once implemented, the fear was that Philippine copra exports, which yielded favourable trade balances for the country, might be threatened in direct competition with duty-free copra and oil seeds from French West African colonies, Belgian Congo, Dutch New Guinea, and French Oceania and New Caledonia.[27]

In a report submitted to the Foreign Office in June 1957, Guerrero stated that those fears, though reasonable, were unfounded. The common market would not pose any threat to Philippine exports to Scandinavian countries mainly because they were not covered by it. There were reasons for optimism on Philippine copra exports alongside the common market. Common tariff and special trade arrangements for agricultural products would be introduced gradually within a transition period of twelve to fifteen years. Between 1950 and 1956, imports of vegetable and oil seeds rose by 60 per cent with 8 per cent average annual increase. The increase, however, could not be augmented by their colonies because of the high costs of production, so Philippine copra could maintain and even increase its share in the European market. Contrary to the apprehension, the report assured copra farmers and businessmen of their profits.[28]

His report was in full contrast to Lopez who had been "bombarding the Department with 'philippics' on the grave dangers of the Common Market". Based on a study that Guerrero reported to the Foreign Office, Philippine copra had displaced Indonesian copra in the European market. It was brought about by the trade promotions of Philippine embassies in Europe no less to the London embassy. As a consequence, the Philippines had become the main supplier of copra to Sweden.[29]

Calling it the "emergence of Europe", the European Common Market, he believed, was the manifestation of Germans, French, Italians, Dutch, and little by little the British, thinking or imagining beyond their limited nationalities to become Europeans. He identified its four main causes — first, the economic consequences of World War II; second, the fear of communist aggression and subjugation that led to the formation of the North Atlantic Treaty Organization (NATO); third, the resentment to America, which he deemed unfair because American money and nuclear protection enabled Europe to attain their present state but the resentment was the cause of imperial pride; and fourth and last, calling it the "withdrawal of Europe", was the growing antagonism between Europe and their former colonies, now wielding in the United Nations the power that was once only in Europe's possession.[30]

In October, he was instructed by Arlegui to report on the status of US forces in the UK. As usual, he diligently studied the pertinent documents and reported to the Home Office that the US-UK military accord was superior to Philippine-US military bases agreement. He made it a point to confer with British defence minister and other officials.[31]

DEFENDING GARCIA AND PHILIPPINE ELECTIONS

After the tragic death of President Magsaysay in March 1957, Garcia as the vice president assumed the national leadership until the November elections. He won over other four candidates including Recto while his running mate, Jose B. Laurel Jr lost to Diosdado Macapagal. During the heat of electoral counting, the *Manchester Guardian* said that Garcia and his party "are unlikely to be able (or even willing) to remove — the grime from the face of the Philippine body politic".³²

Guerrero was closely watching developments at home when he read the paper's editorial "Magsaysay's Heirs" on its 16 November issue. No doubt, it was a rash verdict forcing him to write a letter saying that Garcia's ability "should be left to the test of time. To question his willingness a priori is not only unfair but unwarranted." In an editorial note at the foot of his letter, the paper said: "We shall be very happy to see President Garcia better expectations."³³

His letter, however, dealt with Philippine elections described by the paper as "a delirious parody" of American elections. Granting that it was true, he wrote,

> it is due to the fact that the adult literate Filipino can vote as freely as any American and more freely than many Eastern and Western Europeans who are herded to the polls in 'orderly' and no doubt 'peaceful' silence to drop a conspicuously marked colored card. The Filipino voter can choose from a variety of candidates. He must be persuaded. He cannot be dragooned.

The slant of the editorial, he concluded, was the logical outcome of reading too much American news magazines. Prior to this, he corrected the eminent British historian, Arnold Toynbee, by pointing out some minor inaccuracies in the latter's article about the Philippines in the *Observer*.³⁴

SPOKESMAN FOR ASIA

In February 1958, the British Broadcasting Company (BBC) slated him for three consecutive weeks on its "Third Programme" talks, a confirmation that indeed he had become the spokesman on Asian affairs correcting misconceptions about Asians.

His first broadcast dealt with wrong assumptions about Asians by the West, which had become too suspicious of the new countries in Asia that would not fit into either the "free world" or the "socialist camp". Those countries, which attended the Bandung Conference in 1955, were "an open field" not only to the West but also the Kremlin. Demystifying the assumptions made by George Kennan in the fifth Reith Lectures, insofar as Afro-Asian nationalism was concerned, it was "not necessarily anti-Western". The degree of hate and distrust towards the West depended on the colonial policies imposed in one country or another. Inevitably, colonialism taught its subjects the principles that would lead them to rebel, to cry for independence. It was not obligatory for the West to feel "cosmic guilt" towards developing countries as Kennan had claimed but, he said, the present plight of these nations was made possible due to the colonial trade set-up. However, one could not make generalizations on the nature of this nationalism. To brand and put them in one category as either pro-Western or pro-communist when these countries received aid from either camp was utterly erroneous. Kennan's accusation that these non-communist countries were using their position to play one against the other was not true. "They ask and accept help wherever they can get it because they must if they are to survive." The real challenge was how Asians could cope with the withdrawal of the West. If India and other countries would fail in their respective experiments in development, communism, he predicted, "would then become a political imperative", both a danger to the area but an incentive for the West to engage.[35]

On his second lecture, Guerrero described the leadership in new Asia as revolving around a cult of personality, which might explain the problems Asia was facing. Many of these leaders led their country in national revolutions against the West. Jawaharlal Nehru of India and Soekarno of Indonesia or Gamal Nasser of Egypt were exemplars of this kind of leadership built around a cult figure. The creation of a cult, he pointed out, was due to the lack of trained bureaucratic personnel and absence of alternative leadership. Such conditions could lead to the situation confronting some countries in Latin America where feudal aristocrats or military dictators grabbed power. Peronism might tempt Asian leaders who must try to resist for all its faults. He doubted the possibility of military interventions in Asia similar to those in Latin America for a number of reasons: the armed forces of these new Asian states had "a tradition of obedience to constituted authority". Nevertheless, he predicted that because of developments in the Middle East and in Indonesia, the armed forces would "become magnet of popular hopes" when "the cult of personality will become the cult of force." After eight months, his prognosis came true; the military took over governments in Iraq, Pakistan, Burma, Thailand and Sudan.[36]

The third and last of his broadcast in mid-February dealt with the so-called "unfinished revolution", of which the subjects of his two previous lectures on economic development and personality cult, were its mere symptoms. It was not a simple question of establishing complete sovereignty by getting rid of foreign bases and a colonial economy but "the beginning of a vast and complicated process ... all this under pressure of the Cold War". The process of becoming modern states at par with the civilized world, he said, was not easy for these Asian countries, which must get rid of feudalism. It was also complicated by religion as in the case of Indonesia or India and Pakistan. Secularizing the state was a means by which India, stratified by castes and religion, wanted to achieve a basis for modern democracy. Experiments in self-government, he argued, were fraught with risks and failures as Asians "must work it out themselves". The West must realize, he argued, that what interested Asians most in their pursuit of economic development were not "political, military, moral or even psychological solutions" but "scientific technique", which communism had tried to offer.[37]

In connection with his second lecture, he wrote a letter to *The Observer* amidst the uncertainty and instability in the recent military takeovers in Iraq, Pakistan, Burma, Thailand, and Sudan. In the whole of Asia, Guerrero observed, in an effort to enlighten the London public, the Philippines and India were by Western criteria the only working democracies. In the case of the Philippines, he saw three possible reasons precluding a similar scenario from happening. First, he said, a martial tradition and a professional military caste were absent or lacking in the Philippines. The Philippine Army, for all intents and purposes, was a "citizen" army. Second, the two-party system for more than half a century of experimentation provided the basis for the peaceful alternation of power, with the losing party "fiscalizing" the administration or offering an alternative leadership. Third and the last, during the Magsaysay administration, military officers were appointed in civil administration or they ran for public office. Thus, they learned how to run a civil bureaucracy in the process, but it also showed to the people that "military men are neither geniuses nor angels in the administration of affairs."[38]

A DIPLOMAT'S SECRET WEAPON

The success of Palace Green as the place for dinner parties, informal talks and meetings was made possible by Guerrero's wife, Annie. Her parties were not the usual staid and stiff formal affairs but rather, quite an innovative departure from those she had to go through with her husband. Her dinner guests would sometimes include a mix of theatre people, Guerrero's intellectual friends, members of parliament and ambassadors. If there was a need to prepare for luncheons, dinners or cocktail parties, she was always ready with the support of the staff and her Portuguese cook. In late February 1958 she prepared a very successful dinner reception in honour of British Foreign Minister Selwyn Lloyd who visited Manila to attend the fourth meeting of SEATO council of ministers.[39]

Annie shared her causes with her husband. She convinced him to draw her two pet Siamese cats named "Ming" and "Fabian" for an art exhibit for the International Save-the-Children Fund due to an invitation, which came to the embassy. As a fund-raising activity, the diplomatic corps in London wanted to display art from under a hundred embassies. A day prior to his second talk over the BBC, Guerrero attended the opening of the art exhibit where his cat drawings were displayed. Besides becoming an instant artist, he was also the subject of a pencil drawing by the Laotian ambassador who was also a prince.[40]

Annie took care that guests at the embassy were looked after, especially relatives like Guerrero's cousin Vic who, while on a world trip as correspondent to a Manila newspaper, visited London. It was during the time when the "common market" was the embassy's paramount concern, and Guerrero had been helping Vic who was reporting on it exclusively to the daily. On an early Sunday morning, Guerrero and Annie went with Vic who brought along his movie camera to film the visit, to attend Mass and Communion at an old Catholic Church near Kensington Park. After the church services, Guerrero "a hot-rod driver" drove them on a tour to the countryside west of London. From Henley by the Thames to Oxford, from Windsor Castle to a side trip to Eton, Guerrero acted as the tourist guide, spicing their travel with titbits of English history, with Annie making sure everything was provided for.[41]

SEATO AND THE SUGAR COUNCIL

At a dinner in January 1959 given by the Thai ambassador for SEATO Secretary-General Pote Sarasin who was in a trip to forge links with the North Atlantic Treaty Organization (NATO) and the Baghdad Pact — the British brainchild for the common defence of Arab states, Guerrero spoke as the senior SEATO diplomatic representative in London. Belying the charge that it was a Western plot to intervene in the affairs of Asian countries, he underscored SEATO's mission in the long term, which was to encourage cooperation among free Asian countries in the spirit of a community, citing President Garcia's vision of economic and cultural collaboration among non-communist countries in Southeast Asia. He clarified that SEATO did not mean to foster economic cooperation but rather as self-defence against aggression; he suggested that SEATO must not lose touch with other like-minded Asian countries.[42]

After meeting Sarasin, Guerrero attended an International Sugar Council meeting that got him elected — the first Asian to be so — in early February, as vice chairman of the council. Serrano, now the Foreign Affairs secretary, cabled his congratulations while Garcia wired him conveying his elation as he saw Guerrero's election as an indication of the Philippines' growing importance in the world sugar market. His election was a compromise of sorts for the elected chair was from the importing countries while he represented the exporting countries.[43]

But his election did not delight Guerrero. To distract himself from it, he pushed for the plan of organizing a series of performances by the Bayanihan dance troupe for the London public. When a "Bayanihan" portfolio arrived in late February, he gave it to a London impresario who was responsible for the successful performances in London of other Asian cultural groups such as the Peking Chinese Opera and the Japanese Kabuki troupe. Guerrero was trying to promote "*tinikling*" to Londoners as a Filipino dance but he knew that it has "cultural limits". To overcome the difficulty, he proposed "that it be performed with Rock-'n'-Roll steps to the appropriate music in order to complete the historical cycle".[44]

His five-year stay in London had its rewards because based on the diplomatic list of precedence, he was eighth and could have become a doyen, if circumstances had allowed. In view of the rotation rule, he had a gentleman's agreement with Lopez that he was open to giving up London for Paris, which did not happen in the long run.[45]

ANOTHER TRANSLATION BUSINESS

As it turned out, Guerrero's idea of translating Rizal's novels got him commissioned by Longmans, a prestigious London publisher, to translate the two novels, perhaps in view of Rizal's birth centenary. He had toyed with the idea three years before because he found the latest translations unreadable and absurd at a time when a bill, later passed into law mandating the teaching of a course on Rizal, was being debated in Congress. It occurred to him several months after he unveiled a historical marker in the house where Rizal lived in Chalcot Crescent and when he was asked by Serrano to write "a patriotic travel guide" to Europe, a brochure billed *Rizal's Europe*. Of course, he was fascinated with Rizal since childhood. Like his early translation of Rizal, he did not render the text literally but rather idiomatically because, to him, "fidelity to language is often infidelity to thought and emotion." He had just read Theodore H. Savory's *The Art of Translation* and found two of his twelve principles in translation agreeable, namely the sixth and the eighth respectively: "A translation should possess the style of the translator" and "A translation should read as a contemporary of the translator." In February 1959 when he was more than halfway through his translation of the *Noli Me Tangere*, he asked his friend de la Costa if he was agreeable to writing the introduction. He would be forced to write the introduction himself.[46]

Putting aside his translation chore, he arranged a trip to Stockholm in mid-March to meet and discuss with a number of Swedish industrialists and businessmen ways to increase trade on both sides. An unwanted consequence of this trip was an inadvertent misunderstanding involving the supposed visit of an important politician to London. As Philippine embassies must always be ready to offer their hospitality, Guerrero was understandably bothered by this and told Lopez about it. Rationalizing why he was unable to entertain the said politician, he said he was trying to project London as a "difficult" city.[47]

As usual, Guerrero had to set aside *Noli* again as he had to attend a commissioner's dinner of the Boy Scouts Association of England on the last week of April. Speaking on behalf of the Philippines, the host for the Tenth World Jamboree, he said that the sending of the 110-man British contingent to the jamboree shall be matched by Filipino hospitality. Although he was glad to announce that 200,000 Filipino boys had taken the oath and that they were always represented at every world gathering, he appealed to the scout commissioners not to forget the peasant boys of underprivileged Asia "to whom scouting must try to give a share in the hopes and pleasures of their age".[48]

Postponing the translation of *Noli*'s last chapters, he wrote to the *London Times* in defence of the country's charter and democratic institutions when it obliquely questioned Filipino democracy by stating that: "When the real test is applied perhaps only Malaya and possibly India and Japan are democratic in Asia." Guerrero was provoked to respond: "I wonder what your correspondent's 'real test' for democracy is." Listing why he believed democracy was working in the Philippines that included freedom of religion and the press, which in his estimation, had "few equals in Asia or, in fact, in Western Europe and America", he snapped, "If this is not democracy, what is?"[49]

Notes

1. *MT*, 26 July 1954; Reyes, *Memories of Diplomacy*, p. 51; Leon Ma. Guerrero, *Alternatives for Asians: The Philippine Experiment* (London: Philippine Embassy, 1957), p. 23; Leon Ma. Guerrero, "The Philippines and Britain: Diplomatic Might-Have-Beens", *STM*, 9 November 1952, pp. 6–7.
2. *DM*, 13 and 14 October 1954; *MT*, 14 October 1954; "Ambassador Guerrero meets the Queen", *PFP*, 30 October 1954, pp. 32, 36.
3. Reyes, *Memories of Diplomacy*, p. 47; *MT*, 23 October 1954; *MC*, 17 November 1954; *SC*, 19 November 1954.

4. Guerrero, *Alternatives for Asians*, p. 11; Leon Ma. Guerrero, "Seven years in London", *MT*, 13 January 1962, p. 12-A.
5. Guerrero, *Alternatives for Asians*, pp. 9–12.
6. Ibid., pp. 12–15; *DM*, 17 March 1955.
7. Guerrero, *Alternatives for Asians*, p. 28.
8. Hermogenes E. Bacareza, *A History of Philippine-German Relations* (QC: self-published, 1980), pp. 140–49.
9. *PH*, 9 July 1955.
10. Narciso G. Reyes to Salvador P. Lopez, 26 September 1955 and Carlos P. Romulo to Salvador P. Lopez, 24 September 1955, *SPLP*.
11. *MC*, 25 September and 18 November 1955; *MT*, 1 and 13 October 1955; Joaquin, "The Guerrero Family's Ambassador", p. 121.
12. Leon Ma. Guerrero to Salvador P. Lopez, 15 December 1955; Carlos P. Romulo to Salvador P. Lopez, 29 December 1955, *SPLP*.
13. Bacareza, *A History of Philippine-German Relations*, p. 157; *MT*, 12 March 1956; Joaquin, "The Guerrero Family's Ambassador", p. 122.
14. *MT*, 1 August 1956.
15. Leon Ma. Guerrero to Salvador P. Lopez, 21 March 1956; Salvador P. Lopez to Leon Ma. Guerrero, 12 January 1955, *SPLP*; Daisy H. Avellana, *The Drama of It: A Life on Film and Theater* (Manila: Anvil, 2009), pp. 50, 66.
16. Guerrero, *Alternatives for Asians*, pp. 15–20.
17. Leon Ma. Guerrero to Salvador P. Lopez, 29 May 1956, *SPLP*; Joaquin, "The Guerrero Family's Ambassador", p. 121; *MT*, 10 June 1956.
18. Lopez, "The Laughter of Leoni", p. 4.
19. Carlos P. Garcia to Salvador P. Lopez, 19 October 1956, *SPLP*; *MT*, 13 and 23 September 1956; Leon Ma. Guerrero, "Extracts from a report on the Suez Canal situation to the Council of State and the National Security Council" (Manila, 1956), pp. 1, 7, 10, 15 in Leon Ma. Guerrero Folder at Lopez Museum and Library (hereafter cited as *LMGF*). These documents were the original "firmans" or charters of concession in 1854 and 1856 granted to the construction company; the 1888 Constantinople Convention on the right of any nation to pass through the canal; the 1936 Anglo-Egyptian Treaty; 1954 Suez Canal Base Agreement; nationalization decree of the Egyptian Government; some documents from the first London Conference on Suez Canal held in August; correspondence between the president of Egypt and the conference committee published at the behest of Her Majesty's Stationery Office; Egyptian proposal for a new conference; and the communiqué issued at the Second London Conference.
20. Guerrero, "Extracts from a report on Suez Canal Situation", pp. 1–14; *MT*, 27 September 1956; *MDB*, 18, 19, 27 September 1956. Among those present in the meeting to listen to Guerrero's briefing were Senate President Eulogio Rodriguez, Garcia, Magsaysay, Former President Sergio Osmeña, Manglapus, Mrs Amparo Villamor, Senator Gil Puyat, Budget Commissioner Dominador Aytona, Commerce Secretary Oscar Ledesma, Representative Numeriano Babao, Defence Secretary Eulogio Balao and Executive Secretary Fortunato de Leon.

21. Leon Ma. Guerrero, "A Personal View of the International Situation" in *LMGF*; Guerrero, *Alternatives for Asians*, pp. 20–22; *MT*, 28 September 1956. The first was the original speech incorporated with extracts from the report while the second was an edited version.
22. *MT*, 1 October 1956; Guerrero, *Alternatives for Asians*, pp. 31–32.
23. Salvador P. Lopez to Carlos P. Romulo, 17 November 1956, *SPLP*; Meyer, *Diplomatic History of the Philippine Republic*, pp. 216–17.
24. *DM*, 29 November 1956; Guerrero, *Alternatives for Asians*, p. 23.
25. *MT*, 6 February 1957.
26. Alegre and Fernandez, *Writer and his Milieu*, p. 86; Guerrero, *Alternatives for Asians*, pp. 5, 7.
27. *MT*, 19 June 1957.
28. Ibid.
29. Salvador P. Lopez to Leon Ma. Guerrero, 1 July 1957, *SPLP*; *MC*, 27 August 1957; *PH*, 27 August 1957.
30. Guerrero, "Seven Years".
31. *MC*, 1 November 1956.
32. *MT*, 22 November 1957.
33. Ibid.
34. Ibid.; *The Observer*, 6 January 1957.
35. Leon Ma. Guerrero, *An Asian on Asia: Three BBC "Third Programme" Talks* (London: Philippine Embassy, 1958), pp. 5–10.
36. Guerrero, *An Asian on Asia*, pp. 10–15, 21.
37. Ibid., pp. 16–20.
38. Ibid., pp. 21–22.
39. Rosalinda I. Orosa, "Her parties make news in London", *Woman and the Home*, 19 June 1958, pp. 8–9; *MT*, 26 February 1958.
40. *DM*, 14 February 1958; *MT*, 14 February 1958.
41. Vicente F. Barranco, "Leon Ma. Guerrero: The Hot Rod Driver as a Tourist Guide par excellence", *Philippine Panorama*, 11 July 1982, pp. 18–20.
42. *MT*, 15 January 1959.
43. *MT*, 4 February 1959; *DM*, 18 March 1959.
44. Leon Ma. Guerrero to Salvador P. Lopez, 5 March 1959, *SPLP*.
45. Ibid.; *MT*, 25 October 1957.
46. Leon Ma. Guerrero to Salvador P. Lopez, 29 May 1956, *SPLP*; Alegre and Fernandez, *Writer and his Milieu*, p. 76; Teodoro M. Locsin, "The church under attack", *Philippines Free Press*, 5 May 1956, pp. 2–3, 34–35; Guerrero, *Alternatives for Asians*, p. 24; Guerrero, *The Young Rizal*, p. 13; Theodore H. Savory, *The Art of Translation* (London: Cape, 1957), pp. 49–50; Leon Ma. Guerrero to Horacio de la Costa, 20 February 1959, *HDCP*.
47. *DM*, 18 March 1959; *MT*, 19 March 1959; Leon Ma. Guerrero to Salvador P. Lopez, 27 April 1959, *SPLP*.
48. *MT*, 4 May 1959; *DM*, May 1959.
49. *MT*, 8 May 1959.

13

A Verbal Tussle in the UN

Romulo's schemes to discredit Guerrero had finally lost their power. Serrano appointed Guerrero member of the UN delegation for the Fourteenth Session of the General Assembly starting on 15 September 1959 headed by former Senator, now Ambassador Francisco Delgado, with Lopez as the vice-chair. He could have gone to the Twelfth Session when his name was removed from the list of members because Romulo insisted to Garcia to revoke the appointment. Prior to his departure, in the wake of the Serrano-Bohlen military bases negotiations, Guerrero urged Serrano via cable to advocate an affirmative SEATO action to the communist problem in Laos to test SEATO's reliability if the need arose in the Philippines.[1]

At the United Nations in New York, Guerrero was having a good time when on the last day of September he got involved in a verbal tiff with Walter Robertson, a member of the American delegation and former Assistant Secretary of State for Far Eastern Affairs. At a U.S.-hosted diplomatic luncheon for the General Assembly's Special Political Committee in one of the U.N. dining rooms where diplomats from Japan, the Netherlands, Canada and several other nations were also seated, he was listening to Robertson on the issue of Tibet scheduled to be tackled in the following week. Then, he joined in saying that some Asian nations were hesitant to have a full-blown debate on Tibet because it would revive Cold War issues into the assembly when the East-West relations were starting to relax. The talk came to the issue of Communist China. Known for his pro-Chinese Nationalist views, Robertson boasted that the United States was the only defence against communist aggression and that he believed that countries had to avail themselves of "free world" security.[2]

It turned to Philippine-American relations dealing with those irritants that continued to vex the bilateral relationship, but Robertson argued that America had taken an altruistic policy towards the Philippines. Guerrero replied that the Philippines offered parity rights in exchange for the war damage payments, where full settlement was still wanting. Robertson remarked that Guerrero's views echoed "the Recto line" to which Guerrero retorted, "I don't care if it is the Recto line. That's my line, too." "You're not used to hearing Filipinos speak to you frankly," he added, "You're used to listening to Romulo. You're used to hearing only what is pleasing to you." He was angered by Robertson's sniping reference to Recto. Then, another member of the U.S. delegation butted in. More irritated than ever, Guerrero said, "Mr Secretary, I'm not going to be forced into an argument with a first or second secretary." Robertson retorted: "You are very rude ... you know, you are the first Filipino who has ever spoken to me like this." Guerrero riposted: "The trouble is that you are not used to Filipinos talking back to Americans."[3]

The aftermath sparked a heated verbal clash. Speaking before the press, Robertson denied the arm-twisting and reference to Recto, and described Guerrero as the rudest young man he had ever met. Guerrero was determined to expose the lies clouding the issue by stating categorically that the delegation was being pressured by Robertson to perform his errands. As to the denial of having mentioned Recto, he said that as a young man he had a good hearing and Robertson would remember that he familiarly referred to Recto as "Don Claro".[4]

News about the incident created a wide following. Back home, Serrano did not issue his comment pending a report from Delgado. A Nacionalista Party spokesman saw the event as in line with Garcia's "Filipino First" policy. Senator Lorenzo Sumulong and Representative Ramon P. Mitra, chairmen of the Senate and House Foreign Relations Committee respectively, said that Guerrero deserved praise from his people if he was quoted right. Meanwhile, Guerrero received cables of congratulations from the Philippines and a telegram from a Cleveland industrialist and financier.[5]

As the issue had become the content of tittle-tattles in UN corridors, Delgado met halfway the U.S. delegation to resolve the impasse by expressing the delegation's regrets over the incident, downplaying it as personal issue between the two and wished to maintain the same cordiality that existed before with the U.S. delegation. Ambassador James J. Wadsworth, the acting head of the U.S. delegation, issued a statement agreeing to the maintenance of cordial relations between the two delegations.[6]

The Guerrero-Robertson affair was far from a closed book. Robertson issued a mild rebuke to the Cleveland industrialist whom he described as very eager to get international publicity. Guerrero got a letter from a baseball fan, one of the "big sheaf of messages" he received from both Filipinos and Americans, all expressing support of his stand. Fresh from Indonesia, Senator Recto sent a cable for his "superb patriotic performance". Soviet Russia even used the incident to lambast the United States on its insistence to include among the general assembly's agenda the Irish-Malayan-sponsored full debate on Tibet. At the home front, Senators Tañada and Recto who provided their respective analysis on the issue, rose to Guerrero's defence. Tañada noted that it was not Guerrero who displayed "rudeness" but Robertson who made offensive remarks about an absent Recto and violating diplomatic protocol by issuing publicly his complaint against Guerrero. It was about time, he said, for Americans to get rid of their patronizing attitude toward Asians and begin treating them as equals. Recto pointed the accusing finger at Robertson as he was inclined to believe Guerrero more than Robertson. Guerrero's charge that Robertson was putting pressure on the Philippine delegation, he said, was beyond doubt true with the ardent nationalism of the Filipino ambassador having defeated the imperialistic behaviour of the former assistant secretary of state.[7]

Back in New York, Guerrero appeared briefly as guest on the Columbia Broadcasting System's programme *The Saturday News*. Before introducing him, the host said that the incident proved that the Philippines was far from being the United States' "most stable" ally in Asia, making it possible for America to withdraw its bases because of policy differences over American military personnel, the unsettled war damage claims and other irritants in Philippine-American relations. Referring to them as having "traded insults", he asked Guerrero the reason behind the Filipino bitterness towards his country. "I myself would not have phrased [it] that way," Guerrero reacted. "The Filipinos," he said, "desire to work out a new relationship with the United States." "They have for a long time under the spell of the old colonial connection" as many Americans, he observed, still thought of the Philippines as its colony, not as an independent country. These Americans, he said, felt that Filipinos must follow their line as there were still Filipinos who were thinking that their country should "go to the United States for a handout when we get in trouble." Americans, he added, must contend now with the "strength and impact of this new nationalism" which was neither anti-American, communist nor neutralist. The present differences, he said, was the consequence of different approaches to the same problem.[8]

The incident did not in any way interfere with his job as member of the Philippine delegation. At the opening of the general assembly's

Special Committee, he spoke in Spanish to second the nomination of an Argentinean delegate to be committee rapporteur. He said that Philippines shared with Argentina the Hispanic legacy and that both countries, having maintained close cultural and political ties, were one in their desire for peace. In support of small free nations, he took the floor in the U.N. Ad Hoc Political Committee, firmly rejecting the Soviet stand that before dealing with the expansion of the UN Security and Economic and Social Councils (SC-ECOSOC), Red China's representation should first be settled. He warned Soviet Russia that its "requisite conditions" were prejudicial to the interests of the world's underdeveloped countries, those of Asia and Africa, which were becoming impatient to gain larger representation in these councils. As a temporary measure to this inequality in the case of ECOSOC, he suggested that these countries be invited by virtue of Article 69 of the UN Charter but on the condition that they could sit on the council without voting privileges.[9]

THE DUEL'S SECOND ROUND

In mid-October 1959 the issue came alive when the debate on Tibet was being tackled by the assembly. Henry Cabot Lodge, the chief of the U.S. delegation, after finishing his speech on Tibet, passed by the Philippine delegation before returning to his seat. Delgado, who was near the aisle, congratulated and shook hands with Lodge. Lopez seated next to Delgado also offered a friendly handshake to Lodge who started chatting with them for a while. Seated next to Lopez, Guerrero who was said to be busy taking notes on the debate neither spoke to Lodge nor extended his hand. The press reported that Lodge ignored Guerrero, insinuating that it has something to do with the incident. Two weeks after, Lopez, the vice-chair of the Philippine delegation, denied that snubbing occurred.[10]

A few days after Lodge was reported to have snubbed Guerrero, Robertson, not contented with the media presentation of his account, wrote to Richmond's *News Leader* giving the lie to Guerrero as having talked back to him as it was he who talked back to Guerrero. The antagonist had suddenly become the protagonist. He said he challenged Guerrero on charges against U.S. policy of imperialism. Guerrero declined to comment. Yet Robertson kept on, sending his letter this time to the *New York Times*. Robertson in his version said to the *Times* that the episode in the dining room was personal and did not in any way affect Philippine-American relations. Guerrero in reply accused Robertson of trying to underrate its repercussions on account of strong Asian and South American reactions against him. The retired State Department employee described Guerrero as being in a provocative mood during the luncheon, which he denied. Policy differences were the root cause of the quarrel for everything was going right until their exchange on U.S.-Philippine and Asian policy. Insisting that he did the right thing, Guerrero said that he had the support of an Asian and an African delegate, victims of Robertson's past browbeating. Robertson's letter, he complained, treated him as his social inferior by refusing to give him the courtesy of being called "Mister". As to the accusations that he leaked the story to the press and that press reports about the incident were misleading, Guerrero challenged Robertson to prove his allegations. In his final retort, he said that Robertson during that infamous luncheon displayed his "appalling ignorance of Philippine-American relations", contrary to his claims of having been personally involved in his past relations with Filipinos on a "whole gamut of Philippine-American problems".[11]

Provoked from his home in Richmond, Robertson issued another statement calling Guerrero the Philippines' "Tokyo Rose". Tokyo Rose, a female broadcaster in the employ of the Japanese, urged the Allied forces over the air to surrender and aired propaganda to weaken their morale. Alluding to his work as Ignacio Javier during the war, Robertson accused Guerrero of conducting a bitter propaganda campaign against the United States. The issue was beside the point. The curious thing was whom did he consult for this dirty trick? Was it the State Department or the Philippine Embassy in Washington? Safely ignoring the first point, Guerrero said that he was never tried for treason either by the Philippine Government or American authorities. The People's Court cleared him of any charges. It was not true that he hated the United States prior to the war for he fought for the United States in the Philippine Army. "Where was Mr Robertson," he asked, "when I was in Bataan and Corregidor and the concentration camp of Capas?" As a final note, he said he was not interested in engaging in a controversy with Robertson; he was only using his right to reply and he would finish whatever Robertson had started.[12]

Serrano, closely watching the match's second round at home, issued for the first time a warning. Guerrero agreed with Serrano to bury the whole incident. It was perhaps over with Robertson but not yet for the U.S. State Department when its spokesman challenged Guerrero's charge that the United States had put a price on Philippine independence. Insofar as Guerrero was concerned, it was at last over.[13]

On his last address at the U.N. Special Committee following the announcement of his return to London to attend Sugar Council meetings, Guerrero expressed his fear that apartheid or racial segregation in South

Africa would be a danger to world peace. The European minority's policy of putting the Bantus in a separate community would certainly cause resentment, he said. Nationalism, he pointed out, must in no way promote racial discrimination; that citizens of one country must be treated equally just like any other without discrimination on the bases of race, sex or religion. The Philippines was among those countries which sponsored a resolution asking for South Africa to abolish apartheid. Later, Guerrero would refuse to attend an invitation to a party to celebrate South Africa's Union day in London and would call for the Philippine government to sever ties with South Africa.[14]

As announced, Guerrero went back to London on 1 November. Attending the International Sugar Council's fourth session in Tangiers, North Africa, he was elected the new chair for the coming year. News of his election was greeted with cables of congratulations from home.[15]

Notes

1. *MT*, 2 and 3 October 1959; Carlos P. Romulo to Carlos P. Garcia, 25 and 27 August 1957, *Carlos P. Romulo Papers*, University of the Philippines Main Library; Carlos P. Romulo to Salvador P. Lopez, 5 September 1957; Salvador P. Lopez to Carlos P. Romulo, 2 March 1957, *SPLP*; Lewis E. Gleeck Jr, *Dissolving the Colonial Bond: American Ambassadors to the Philippines, 1946–1984* (Quezon City: New Day Publishers, 1988), p. 110. In a confidential cable from New York, Romulo sent to Garcia: "Aye object to having Guerrero in delegation PD must have Salvador Lopez PD he is man of my confidence and aye cannot trust Guerrero neither can you …."
2. *MT*, 2 and 3 October 1959; *DM*, 2 October 1959.
3. Ibid.
4. *MT*, 3 October 1959.
5. *MT*, 3 October 1959; *DM*, 3 October 1959.
6. *DM*, 3 October 1959; *MT*, 4 October 1959.
7. *MT*, 6 and 7 October 1959; *DM*, 6 and 10 October 1959.
8. *MT*, 5, 6 October 1959.
9. *MT*, 9 October 1959; *DM*, 8 October 1959; *MT*, 18 October 1959.
10. *DM*, 13 and 23 October 1959.
11. *DM*, 17 October 1959; *MT*, 18 October 1959; *MT*, 19 October 1959. For the complete text of this letter to the *New York Times*, please see *MT*, 21 October 1959.
12. *MT*, 20 October 1959.
13. *MT*, 22 October 1959.
14. *MT*, 1 November 1959; *DM*, 28 April 1960; *MB*, 18 June 1960.
15. *DM*, 28 October and 5 December 1959.

14

The Biographer

Coming back from Africa, Guerrero devoted the rest of December 1959 to translating *Noli Me Tangere* (hereafter *Noli*) he finished on Rizal Day. The following year it was published by Longmans. He agreed to the offer of David Medalla, a rising Filipino artist who had just arrived in London, to draw its cover design. As soon as he was done with *Noli*, he worked on *El Filibusterismo* (hereafter *Fili*). Before Longmans published *Noli*, he sold the rights to the *Manila Times* for publication in instalments. What speeded up his translation was the deadline set by the publisher. "I always like to write against a deadline, because I'm very lazy," he admitted. Thus he did finish translating *Noli* and then *Fili*. The catch to selling his rights to the daily of *Noli* was the exclusion or omission from publication the debate on purgatory between philosopher Tasio and Don Filipo or some parts of chapter fourteen. People noticed it, and many accused him of deliberately suppressing the section. His justification was that it did not help the story. His loyalty to the Church was at stake. It can be said that he was merely protecting himself or trying not to hurt the interest of the Church. His translations met both praise and condemnation. He "desecrated" the language the author used making it unfaithful to the original. But he justified that each generation needed its own translations and that he tried to provide a *Noli* as Rizal had written it for the present generation of Filipinos. Instead of using outdated terms usually accompanied by notes at the bottom or a glossary, he replaced them with contemporary expressions such as the "guardia civil" with "constabulary" or "alcalde mayor" with "governor" so that a new generation of readers could imagine Rizal and his characters in the novels in the context of the turbulent sixties and the coming decades. He had expected the criticism. Romulo, however, wrote to the *New York Times* that Guerrero successfully preserved the original flavour by modernizing outmoded terms.[1]

His translations in time for Rizal's birth centenary got him reacquainted with Rizaliana literature, forcing him to write a biography of Rizal. He wrote an introduction to these translations containing a brief account of Rizal's life. From that "brief account", it became a biographical study of the foremost Filipino. As early as February 1959, he was already intimating to write the biography for he asked from de la Costa his Rizal lectures. He decided to work on it on the last week of January 1960, when he revealed to de la Costa that he was "perhaps rashly contemplating a new biography of Rizal for the centennial contest closing [on] the 30th or the 19th of June this year". He started working on it after the three-week performance of the Bayanihan Philippine Dance Company which he succeeded in inviting members of the British royal family and most of the diplomatic corps to the gala performance. Former National Library Director and Member-Director of the Jose Rizal National Centennial Commission (JRNCC) Luis Montilla, pressed him to enter because the JRNCC has not received any entry for the biography contest.[2]

Even before the actual writing of the biography, Guerrero saw Rizal not as destined hero working single-handedly but reacting to a context of a disunited expatriate community and unclear Spanish policy. He had a theme to start with: "The First Filipino". Regarding Rizal's disputed retraction, he was convinced it was genuine but it did not repudiate Rizal's work, in contrast to Palma's emotional arguments. His perception of Rizal was that prior to his death-cell conversion he was a deist, a romantic rationalist in which scepticism or indifference shaped his tolerance. He was interested in Rizal's religion in the period covering the Ateneo sodality and the Jesuits' confession. He was sure that it was not Masonry for Rizal seemed to consider it unimportant. He had questions however: Did Rizal play safe or was it nostalgia for an innocent past that he retracted?[3]

From late January to 19 June, he wrote based on what had been gathered a decade after he first translated Rizal's childhood memoirs. For a month he followed a writing schedule from 3:00–7:00 a.m. that caused him migraines, finishing the first draft of the last chapter. This five-month period, however, allowed him to read and take notes from the sources, relying a great deal on Rizal, his diary, correspondences and other writings, leading him to consult Teodoro M. Kalaw's edited *Epistolario Rizalino*. Because he eschewed hagiographical biography, he used primary materials on Rizal extensively with the objective of letting Rizal "speak for himself". He submitted his entry under the pseudonym "Aries" within the deadline.[4]

Guerrero read other works to make it appropriate to laymen readers and scholars. He had, of course, read the basic biographies of Rizal by Wenceslao Retana, Rafael Palma, and Carlos Quirino. Quirino, whom he recommended for membership of the Royal Geographic Society of Great Britain, would later write the introduction to his biography of Rizal. He would find Cesar A. Majul's *Critique of Rizal's Concept of a Filipino Nation* as having "broke new and fertile ground" while José Ma. Cavanna's *Rizal and the Philippines of His Days* "gives the Catholic version" of Rizal's life. To understand Rizal in the context of Spanish metropolitan politics and colonial policies, he read Salvador de Madariaga's *The Rise of the Spanish American Empire* and *The Fall of the Spanish American Empire*, Melchor Fernández Almagro's two-volume *Historia Política de la España Contemporánea*, F. Soldevilla's multi-volume *Historia de España*, Antonio Ballesteros' *Sintesis de Historia de España*, and Rafael Altamira's *A History of Spain*. *Enciclopedia Espasa* and *Diccionario de Historia de España* became handy references. To situate Rizal in his relation to his fellow propagandists and his place in Philippine colonial history, he consulted the collected letters of Marcelo H. del Pilar and Mariano Ponce, speeches and articles of Graciano Lopez Jaena, Retana's edited *Archivo del Bibliofilo Filipino*, and Mabini's memoirs on the Philippine revolution, memoirs of José Alejandrino and Maximo Viola, Antonio Luna's *Impresiones*, *La Loba Negra* he attributed to José Burgos, and Pedro A. Paterno's novel *Ninay*. He deemed "indispensable" José Montero y Vidal's three-volume *Historia General de Filipinas*, John Leddy Phelan's *The Hispanization of the Philippines*, Teodoro A. Agoncillo's *The Revolt of the Masses*, John Foreman's *The Philippine Islands*, Kalaw's *Philippine Masonry*, and eleven other works.[5]

Guerrero's Jesuit best friend de la Costa helped him in many ways by sending him a bibliography. When he asked for guidance on sources, de la Costa, although busy with his religious and secular involvements, went out of his way to give him advice. Director Montilla sent the transcript of Rizal's *Datos para mi defensa*. Pedro Ortiz Armengol furnished the academic records of Rizal from the archives of Academia de San Fernando. Since he did not know German, the former Czech ambassador to London, Dr Jiri Hajk, translated materials on Blumentritt, and Maximo Viola and Rizal's visit to Leitmeritz. Chitang sent historical materials from Manila to London. Margaret Burke, his personal assistant and secretary, typed the manuscript.[6]

Besides reading primary and secondary sources on Rizal, Guerrero translated Rizal's essays, letters and other Spanish documents into English.

He also read books on translation. Working on the biography was done alongside his translation of *Fili* "off and on", so that it took him another year to finish the biography and its publication. Annie typed the whole manuscript of *Fili*, pointing out his "lapses into Hispanisms". Biographical writing was a literary genre he was most familiar with, yet, he read John A. Garraty's seminal work *The Nature of Biography*, firming his resolve to depart from the usual hagiographic trend in the Philippines.[7]

His narrative of Rizal's life succeeded in bringing out the hero's humanity. He would recount Rizal's boyhood romances and his early poetic inclinations. He described Rizal's close relationship with Paciano as "more of a second father than an elder brother" or with Ferdinand Blumentritt as "Rizal's dearest confidante and most trusted counsellor", finding in their exchange of letters, "the evolution of a purely intellectual friendship". He would find Rizal in his first voyage outside of the Philippines as "a nostalgic young man, not yet twenty-one, a medical student uncertain of his vocation, almost penniless in a new world". He would aptly call him as "the reluctant revolutionary" for his ambivalence toward independence, divided between reformism and revolution; and weave other fascinating moments of Rizal's life into the biography.[8]

At first, Guerrero seemingly underestimated Rizal's importance in a letter to de la Costa: Bonifacio brought about the revolution; Del Pilar was "surely a more effective polemicist, a shrewder politician, a more savage enemy of the friars". Yet Guerrero was convinced that Rizal "was considered the leader of the Filipinos, or at least of the nationalists. He was not wholly American-made." Rizal was the originary Filipino because

> it was Rizal ... who taught his countrymen that they could be something else, Filipinos who were members of a Filipino Nation. ... the first who sought to "unite the whole archipelago" and envisioned a "compact and homogeneous" society out of the old tribal communities from Batanes to the Sulu Sea ....[9]

Guerrero expected his biography to provoke condemnations both from the Rizalists and the nationalists on account of some assertions in his book. Rizal, to him, retracted, was shot and died a devout Catholic, an image contrary to the beliefs of most Rizalists but accommodating to the interest of the Church. Still, his depiction of the friars would invite indignation from Catholics. But to Guerrero, Rizal was in the end neither an agnostic, a materialist nor an atheist but a Protestant, the first to be so.[10]

THE PRIVATE SECRETARY AS *DULCE EXTRANJERA*

But a woman had helped shape his ideas on the foregoing, particularly on Rizal's retraction.

When Guerrero felt that a hand could assist him finish all the tasks — ambassadorial or otherwise — he decided to hire a private secretary. She was Margaret Burke, an English woman with Irish descent from Blackheath and who studied on scholarship at St. Ursula's Convent School in Greenwich, South East London. She was picked among several candidates fluent in both Spanish and English who responded to an advertisement of a vacancy in the embassy.[11]

Margaret was tasked to type the corrected draft by Guerrero — typed on his favourite and "lucky" Royal typewriter he had since the 1930s — on a standard typewriter. After handing the clean copy, Guerrero would again tinker with it and Margaret would have to retype. She was also sent to the library to research on characters related to the life of Rizal. As an Englishwoman, Margaret explained to Guerrero the nuances of English culture, particularly Rizal's stay with the Becketts. For instance, she explained that Tootie means "little one".[12]

As his sounding board, Guerrero would spend hours conversing with Margaret on controversial aspects in the life of Rizal. Rizal's relationship with Josephine Bracken, his "sweet foreigner", found resonance in Margaret as they both found the relationship "fascinating". Josephine's relationship with the Rizal family particularly with Rizal's sisters when they treated her coldly was a subject of their conversation and Margaret herself would know the feeling years later. And thus the manuscript became a mute witness to a couple in love. Guerrero once asked her whether or not Rizal recanted at the end of his life. Educated as Catholic, Margaret believed that Rizal returned as a loyal son of the Catholic Church. Guerrero, then, made up his mind on the issue that through grace Rizal found the courage to reconcile with the church.[13]

Margaret resigned from her job at the embassy. The following year in 1961 on 5 April, she gave birth to a son, Leon Xavier, later known as David. Guerrero closely followed the delivery of his son who was expected to arrive on 23 April. He sent a colourful baby greetings telegram to Margaret addressed at the maternity ward of St Mary Abbot's Hospital in Kensington, London and even composed a verse: "Most grateful magnificent performance; another Aries after all; all love fond = Father +".[14]

DEFENDING "FILIPINO FIRST"

When Garcia's "Filipino First" was the object of resentment and anxiety among British businessmen, Guerrero defended the policy. Enunciated in August 1958, the policy, which aimed to give preference to Filipinos in Philippine economic development, was met by diplomatic protests from eleven Asian and European countries presumably including Britain by mid-1959. Addressing the Philippine Society of London during its annual ball, he said the policy was a clear indication that Filipinos wanted to be masters in their own home, in their own country.[15]

Still in connection with the "Filipino First" policy, two British leading journals criticized a Philippine legislation limiting the activities of overseas and insurance companies in the Philippines. Again defending the policy, Guerrero wrote to *The Economist* that because Filipinos had long been last that the National Economic Council had enunciated it. It seemed premature, he said, to complain when legislation was still in the hands of Congress. He could not see the logic behind the complaint since the proposal would bring foreign insurance firms into line with local ones. He asked why foreign firms should enjoy greater privileges than local ones in their own country. The Filipinos could not be contented as second best. It would be better, he said, if the British would not allow themselves to be dampened by policies geared towards Filipino self-interest. In a letter to the *London Times*, he observed that while Philippine exports to Britain stayed at the same level between 1954 and 1958, British exports to the Philippines doubled in the same period. Allaying fears of instability on foreign investments, he said that in recent years foreign investments had not been hampered. He further believed that the filipinization of services held by foreigners was in keeping with the national interests. The idea was to prevent foreign traders from pressuring the government, which had been done in the past.[16]

HONOURING A FATHER AND A MENTOR

In September 1960, Guerrero decided to go home. It was a son's filial obligation to his father. When he learned that his father was suffering from a lingering illness, he filed for an indefinite leave of absence. On 21 September aboard the Philippine Air Lines (PAL), he flew home with a brief stopover in Hong Kong.[17]

In that city-state, while waiting for his flight to Manila, he told newsmen that the United Nations should move its headquarters from New York to a city of a neutral Asian country. He cited New Delhi, Rangoon, Colombo or Hong Kong but ruled out Manila because the Philippines was too much committed to America, thus to the West.[18]

From Hong Kong, he arrived at night at the Manila International Airport where he refused press interviews stating that his was an unofficial visit. For this reason, he made a call on Serrano who had been apprised of the situation. He went home to Donada Street in Pasay where he met his mother, Chitang and Mario with their respective families. His visit to his seventy-four-year-old father, a retired professor of medicine at the Manila Central Colleges, which would later become the Manila Central University, would be his last because his father died two years later, before he could go home again.[19]

While he was attending to his sick father, Recto who was on a trip abroad even passed by the London embassy, died in Rome due to a heart attack. Grieving over the sudden death of his friend and mentor, Guerrero in an address before the Manila Rotary Club traced the development of Filipino nationalism in the life of Recto. It was Recto, he believed, who entirely moulded a new phase in Filipino nationalism, starting with his fight in the field of foreign policy. Recto's nationalist ideas were first received as heretical and subversive in the decade between 1949 and 1960, which had now become accepted or taken for granted. He declared that the nationalism of the Garcia administration was the legacy of Claro Recto. Filipinos including himself, he said, were all Recto's heirs and he prayed to God for strength never to disclaim the inheritance with all the burdensome obligations. As a fitting ending to his eulogy, he hoped that Recto's sacrifice would not be rendered meaningless; for enemies of Filipino nationalism were still to be vanquished, but if its cause should go along with his death, then it would deserve to die.[20]

ANOTHER BOOK IN THE MIDDLE OF A REVISION

After more than a month of stay in which he fulfilled some speaking engagements, Guerrero went back to London. Flying to Mexico in November 1960, he presided over the Sugar Council's upcoming elections and lessened his duties by transferring them to his successor. It was summer of 1961 when his nieces, Gemma Cruz and Nina Nakpil, daughter and stepdaughter of Chitang, went to London for a visit. Annie and he, of course, attended to their every need. In April, he was the first Filipino honoured to be the guest speaker on the birth anniversary of Shakespeare in Stratford-on-Avon. In late May he made a short visit to Madrid on the occasion of Rizal Week, where he told a news conference that the United States would recognize Red China but the Philippines would never do so.[21]

Upon his return from Madrid with the celebration of Rizal's birth centenary at the embassy in his mind, that will be attended by people from the diplomatic community, he was greeted by the decision of the panel in the biography contest that his entry won the first prize. Yet a member of the panel, Dr Leoncio Lopez-Rizal, the hero's nephew, protested with a long register of objections. Guerrero was compelled to reply with his clarifications sent to Lopez-Rizal. He asked de la Costa to borrow the complete entry from UP Professor Nicolas Zafra, the head of the revision committee, as he would like his opinion in view of the objections. Lopez-Rizal was anti-retractionist but Guerrero would maintain his retractionist view.[22]

The objections shaped the final narrative of the biography. Lopez-Rizal had to read a copy of the three-part entry in two volumes which he annotated, underlined some questionable passages, encircled some vague words, wrote notes in the margins, and even suggested that some passages be deleted. For instance he enclosed in red ink the word "native" scattered throughout the text which was replaced with "Filipino" by Guerrero. The doctor turned critic also disputed Guerrero's assumption that there was an official changing of the family name to Rizal because family members continued its use; pointed out incorrect dates; false attributions, like a poem allegedly written by Rizal but, to him, was written by his brother Antonio; improper names (Segunda, not Segundina); British spelling (civilisation, honour, etc.); or raised questions on specific passages.[23]

At this time, Guerrero requested de la Costa to send him his book on Rizal's trial published by Ateneo and his history of the Jesuits in the Philippines published by Harvard. This last he warned in jest to his friend: "I cannot wait [for the local edition], and I am afraid that you will have to send me a duly autographed copy post haste! In fact, I'll have your head on a silver platter if I do not get it by the next diplomatic pouch." He attached a list of seven questions, one dealing with the present-day monetary value of the peso, peseta, duro, Mexican dollar and real in Rizal's time and their real value or purchasing power, and another on the meaning of "*Dimas Alang*". Until its publication in 1963, the original manuscript underwent revisions addressing the issues raised by Lopez-Rizal and other matters relevant to the biography, which he might have missed. He had time to read another book on biography, the very recently published *Biography as an Art: Selected Criticism, 1560–1960*, edited by James L. Clifford, treating biography as a literary genre and as an art.[24]

His biography was not yet off the press but Guerrero was already planning another book about the British occupation of the Philippines. Although he had been reading about it for the past six years, he was still weak on the Spanish texts and needed de la Costa's help, asking him urgently for a copy of his Jesuits' history or his Jesuit-Augustinian non-collaboration movement notes, or pointers on relevant files and others in Seville. He had an avid interest in history which he shared with de la Costa. He had just published an article about German attitude and policies right after Dewey's defeat of the Spanish fleet in 1898 when a German naval squadron was stationed in Manila Bay.[25]

A welcome respite from the revision came when a nephew who was taking glass technology at a university in Sheffield visited him and stayed in the chancery for a week. Also in early November, the American Chamber of Commerce in London invited him to talk about the "Filipino First" policy of the Garcia administration. Big foreign business interests opposed it for it allegedly ran counter to the provisions of the Philippine Constitution on parity rights. As in every instance, he defended the Garcia policy of filipinization, arguing that the policy would be good for the Filipinos as well as for American businessmen. The justification by the Philippine Government was the improvement in the living standards of the Filipinos, he said. The goal of nationalization or what he called "Filipinization" was to share with the people the profits that had long been channelled into the bank accounts of foreign traders. In the case of retail trade being nationalized, the Philippine case, he said, was not an exception to the rule in the whole of Asia and there was a growing trend of giving protection and preference to nationals in the export and import trades. Filipinization was also the Philippines' way out of merely supplying raw materials and consuming finished goods.[26]

LONDON OF SEVEN YEARS

After the talk, Guerrero had to attend a cocktail party, events that he sometimes found depressing and funny for the conversational pattern seldom changed. It was his seventh year in London but the Philippines was still not widely known, although there was a marked improvement over the preceding years.

One dinner party, however, shattered this hope. A guest greeted: "How do you like our English weather?" He answered perfunctorily: "I find it delightful, so full of surprises, one might say witty!" "How long have you been here, may I ask?" "Oh, seven years." Then, the same guest asked: "Is the climate in your country like ours? Where do you come from?" "The Philippines," he curtly replied with a sense of frustration. "Oh, I always thought you said Philippines." A desire to please was evident in the guest's eyes but he was not expecting too much. "Oh, I love your country; I have always meant to go there someday. All those lovely girls dancing in their grass skirts on the beach!"[27]

Ignorance about the Philippines was not surprising for even the *London Times* the previous years correctly identified Manila as the site of the SEATO Conference but the Philippines was left out from the names of participating countries, according to him, because of the perception that the country was still a U.S. colony. The publicity on the Philippines was not as bad now as it was before. Nonetheless, stories about the Philippines during the month of October 1961, as he noted, were limited to cholera deaths, the elections and one item about the confiscation of allegedly communist propaganda by the Philippine postmaster-general. It was "embarrassing", for those pamphlets were in fact anti-communist materials designed to warn of parliamentary seizure of power by communist techniques published by London's anti-communist intelligence agencies.[28]

RIZAL DAY SPEAKER: FILIPINOS MUST DESERVE THEIR FREEDOM

Having been declared winner in the Rizal biography contest, Guerrero was invited by the Jose Rizal National Centennial Commission (JRNCC) to be the Rizal Day speaker on 30 December 1961. At the Luneta, he talked on the relevance of Rizal 150 years after his death.[29]

"We have come here in homage to a man whose name is often on our lips but whose life, after a hundred years, is perhaps losing meaning and significance for new generations." Playing the devil's advocate, he asked why single out Rizal when he seemed to be ignorant about communism and irrelevant to the nuclear age. It was about time, he said, to reassess Rizal and ourselves.[30]

Instead of trying to recount his life again, which had become familiar during the centennial, he said, he would appraise Rizal in the context of the times. He said that Rizal believed in man as a rational being free to make his own choices but must be constrained by his free will because of the blind excesses of power. He saw in Rizal's novels one theme — the Actonian dictum that power corrupts; and absolute power corrupts absolutely. That was the nature of power during the bygone colonial years but had it changed when Filipinos took power?[31]

The folly and tragedy of our people, he said, was that upon learning that Capitan Tiago, Doña Victorina, Quiroga, and Don Custodio were still around, we were still waiting for another Rizal. Quoting Father Florentino's famous oration on government as the image of its people, on how to win freedom and the correlation of independence with slavery, he declared in a series of questions that they were still relevant to the times. The significance of Rizal's centenary, he said, was for the Filipinos to determine that they make themselves deserving of their freedom.[32]

He had something to say to the newly elected President Diosdado Macapagal which was that he hoped his presidency could match the qualities and virtues of the people.[33]

Staying until mid-January 1962, Guerrero attended a welcome dinner in Ermita with his relatives. At a local bookstore, he autographed copies of his English translation of *Noli Me Tangere*. Under the auspices of the UP Student Union, he spoke before the University Student Convocation.[34]

THE DIPLOMAT AS NATIONALIST AND PUBLICIST

The speech at the UP was instructive of his years in London, but most importantly it was his sober realization of the character and role of a diplomat. An ambassador, thus an expatriate, had difficulty integrating into the national community because firstly, his mind was for too long preoccupied with the outside world called foreign affairs, and secondly, he had lost touch with what was happening at home. What was the role and nature of a diplomat?

> ...it has been his mission to present the best side of his country and people. There is no nationalist more fervent than the expatriate, who sees his nation with all the enchantment lent by distance and absence; and there is no expatriate more nationalist than an ambassador of whom it might be said that he is almost a nationalist by occupation, a professional nationalist, whose mission is constantly to promote the national interest among competing national interests, and to project the most flattering image of his country...[35]

The next line: "...project it, one might add in the case of the Philippines, against a black screen", was charged with frustrations. In the first years of his stay, it was as if the Philippines was obliterated from the face of the earth. Through various means of publicity, he was happy to note that it had changed for the better.[36]

Though the Philippines lacked publicity, he noted that the Foreign Service had chiefs of mission who were formerly newsmen. The present organization from top — meaning the Foreign Affairs Secretary — to ambassadors to various countries such as Lopez to France, who was now appointed undersecretary, were formerly press people like himself. The tasks of an ambassador, as he heard some of his colleagues in London complain, were not extraordinary — cipher clerks, drafters of correspondence, diplomatic couriers or travel agents at unholy hours to meet a VIP at the airport. Being a newsman had its own advantages for the embassy of a small country, which he referred to as a "listening post", for he was a professional gatherer of facts, a sifter of rumours, an accurate and unbiased reporter and lucid and forceful articulator of the views of his government and people.[37]

PREPARING FOR MADRID

His flight back to London was to finish commitments and also to prepare for the next assignment, which needed some arrangements for the important packages to be brought to Madrid. The last of his speaking engagements as the dean of the Asian diplomatic corps was before the Military Commentator's Circle of London. In his talk, he doubted Peking's ability to create an Asian communist empire. The bases of his conclusion were the limited achievements in securing their frontiers in North Vietnam and North Korea. Although they might succeed with Laos, in other countries in Southeast Asia, they made little progress. Their failure to intervene in Taiwan was an indication, he said, that they were afraid to take the risk of nuclear attack by the United States. Asian problems, he declared, neither needed American nor communist solution but must be solved "in their own terms".[38]

At the end of his career in London but the onset of another in Madrid, Guerrero said in a press interview that there were three main problems in Philippine-British relations: Britain's attitude towards SEATO; Britain's application to the European Common Market and finally, the North Borneo sovereignty issue. In the case of SEATO, he said dissatisfaction was high because Asian countries felt that Britain and France were not as cooperative as expected. Nonetheless, he said, "I have given our viewpoint to the British Government" receiving "very sincere assurances that the United Kingdom would fulfil all its commitments". As for the North Borneo claim, started two years ago, he received instructions that it was a private claim. There were private negotiations done since 1960 but the Foreign Office did not instruct him to officially intercede.[39]

Being a full-fledged ambassador with a facility in the Castilian language gave him more weight than anyone else considered for Madrid. Looking back at his post, he had publicized the Philippines; organized the Philippine Society of London; promoted trade with countries under his jurisdiction; defended Philippine sugar interests; and stood up to defy American intrusion in Philippine matters in the United Nations. It was in London where he produced his translations of *Noli* and *Fili* and his prize-winning biography of Rizal whose revision he would carry to Madrid. By having himself appointed in London, and now Madrid, he was, in effect, saying to Philippine foreign policymakers that there was a world outside America where Philippine interests would benefit, economically and culturally — in Europe.

Notes

1. Jose Rizal, *Noli Me Tangere* (Translated by Leon Ma. Guerrero) (Guerrero Publishing, 2004), pp. ii, xiii, xv; Jose Rizal, *El Filibusterismo* (Translated by Leon Ma. Guerrero) (Guerrero Publishing, 2004), pp. xii–xiii; Alegre and Fernandez, *The Writer and his Milieu*, pp. 78–80, 85; quoted in Qurino, Introduction to *The First Filipino*, p. xiv; Guerrero, *The First Filipino*, p. xii; "Guerrero's Translation of the 'Noli'", *PFP*, 29 July 1961, p. 17. For a recent criticism of Guerrero's translations, see Anderson, "Hard to Imagine", pp. 81–118, cited previously in the prologue. Also republished under the same title in Benedict Anderson, *The Spectre of Comparisons: Nationalism, Southeast Asia and the World* (Quezon City: Ateneo de Manila University Press, 2004). It was first published first in two parts, "Rereading Rizal: The translator as propagandist", *MC*, 26 September–2 October 1992: p. 1; "'Noli' Bowdlerized", *MC*, 3–9 October 1992, p. 10.
2. Guerrero, *The First Filipino*, p. xii; Leon Ma. Guerrero to Horacio de la Costa, 20 February 1959 and 26 January 1960, HDCP; "Bayanihan in London", *STM*, 17 April 1960; "Memorandum", 3 January 1958; "Minutes of the Meeting of the Executive Board Held at the Headquarters of the JRNCC on Canonigo-Isaac Peral Sts. on 16 June 1958, 3:10 p.m."; "Memorandum for the Commission, 9 February 1961", in Jose Rizal National Centennial Commission Papers (hereafter cited as JRNCCP), National Historical Institute, Manila; Alegre and Fernandez, *Writer and his Milieu*, p. 78.
3. Leon Ma. Guerrero to Horacio de la Costa, 26 January 1960, HDCP.
4. Alegre and Fernandez, *Writer and his Milieu*, p. 79; Guerrero, *The First Filipino*, pp. xiii, 509–12.
5. Guerrero, *The First Filipino*, pp. 509–11; *PH*, 27 June 1958.
6. Guerrero, *The First Filipino*, pp. 12, 49, 78, 87, 120–21, 160, 168, 194, 436, 475; Aries, "Introduction", *The First Filipino: A New Biography of Rizal*, Part One, copy

submitted to the Jose Rizal Biography Contest, Jose Rizal National Centennial Commission in *Lopez-Bantug Collection*, Dela Salle University Library; Margaret Burke Guerrero, interview by the author, Dasmariñas Village, Makati City, 29 April 2006.
7. Rizal, *El Filibusterismo*, pp. vi, xii; Guerrero, *The First Filipino*, p. 512.
8. Guerrero, *The First Filipino*, p. 31 and passim.
9. Leon Ma. Guerrero to Horacio de la Costa, 26 January 1960, *HDCP*; Guerrero, *The First Filipino*, p. 501.
10. Guerrero, *The First Filipino*, pp. xiii; 437, 471.
11. Carmen Guerrero-Nakpil, telephone conversation with the author, 19 April 2006; Gemma Cruz-Araneta, interview by the author, Makati City, 16 August 2006; Margaret Burke Guerrero, interview by the author, Dasmariñas Village, Makati City, 5 May 2006; Jane Bordas, "Diplomats' Wives also sweat it out", *DFA Review* 1, no. 4 (1974): 8.
12. Margaret B. Guerrero, "The writing of *The First Filipino*: A memoir of Leon Ma. Guerrero, Rizal Biographer, Translator, Author and Statesman", *Flip* 2, no. 2 (March 2003): 29–31, 92.
13. Ibid.
14. "Baby greetings telegram from Leon Ma. Guerrero to Margaret Burke", no date, *LMGP*.
15. Agoncillo and Guerrero, *History of the Filipino People*, p. 600; Meyer, *Diplomatic History of the Philippine Republic*, p. 251; *MT*, 24 April 1960; Leon Ma. Guerrero, *Prisoners of History* (New Delhi: Embassy of the Philippines, 1972), pp. 267–70.
16. *MT*, 28 April 1960.
17. *MT*, 20 and 22 September 1960.
18. Ibid.
19. Ibid.; "Dr. Alfredo Leon Guerrero", *Science for Schools* 6, no. 11 (November 1962): 8.
20. Leon Ma. Guerrero, "Recto and Filipino nationalism", *MT*, 7 October 1960, p. 10A; *Diplomatic Bulletin* (hereafter cited as *DB*), 1 October 1960.
21. *MT*, 31 October 1960; *MC*, 23 November 1960; *PH*, 1 December 1960; *MT*, 16 April 1961; *The Evening News and Star*, 6 May 1961; *DM*, 24 May 1961; Gemma Cruz, "People I have known — II 'Uncle Leoni was fun'", *MC*, 24 September 1964, pp. 1, 5. See also Leon Ma. Guerrero, "Visit to Shakespeare's hometown", *Kislap Graphic*, 2 October 1957, pp. 12, 13, 23.
22. "Memorandum for the Jose Rizal National Centennial Commission, 9 February 1961", in *JRNCCP*; *DB*, 1 July 1961; Leon Ma. Guerrero to Horacio de la Costa, 8 August 1961, *HDCP*; Luis M. Montilla to Justice Alex Reyes, no date, *Lopez-Bantug Collection*, Dela Salle University Manila; Aries [Leon Ma. Guerrero], *The First Filipino: A New Biography of Rizal*, Part Three, copy submitted to the Jose Rizal Biography Contest, Jose Rizal National Centennial Commission, 1960, pp. 185, 211 in *Lopez-Bantug Collection*, Dela Salle University Library.
23. Aries, *The First Filipino*, pp. 14, 33, 39, 58, 75, 86, 224.

24. Leon Ma. Guerrero to Horacio de la Costa, 8 August 1961, *HDCP*; Guerrero, *The First Filipino*, p. 512.
25. Leon Ma. Guerrero to Horacio de la Costa, 3 February 1956 and 8 August 1961; Mr and Mrs Leon Ma. Guerrero to Horacio de la Costa, no date [1954 or 1955], *HDCP*; Leon Ma. Guerrero, "The Kaiser and the Philippines", *MC*, 24–28 August 1960. The article was submitted to the *Republic Cultural Heritage Committee*, a copy of which was deposited in Filipiniana Vertical Files, University of the Philippines Main Library.
26. Roberto Ma. Guerrero, "David Guerrero: Preserving a father's legacy", *MT*, 29 June 1995, p. B18; *DM*, 9 November 1961; *MT*, 10 November 1961.
27. Guerrero, "Seven years".
28. Ibid.
29. *MT*, 25 December 1961; Leon Ma. Guerrero, "Rizal: after 100 years", *MT*, 31 December 1961, p. 15A.
30. Ibid.
31. Ibid.
32. Ibid.
33. Ibid
34. *MDB*, 3 January 1962; *DM*, 12 January 1962; Guerrero, "Seven years", p. 12A.
35. Ibid.
36. Ibid.
37. Ibid. Compare this to his previous characterization of a Filipino diplomat as tackled in the previous chapter about his article "The Philippines and Belgium: Diplomatic Listening-Post", *STM*, 23 November 1952, pp. 6–7.
38. *MT*, 11 March 1962; *DM*, 10 March 1962.
39. *DM*, 29 March 1962; *MT*, 30 March 1962.

15

At Franco Country

As early as January 1962, the Foreign Office had notified Madrid of Guerrero's assignment to Spain, which was accepted late that month. He was in Madrid in May the previous year when he delivered a lecture on the occasion of Rizal's birth centenary. Delivered in the midst of writing Rizal's biography, his lecture dealt with Rizal's Hispanism as reflected in his novels. Those novels, he said, were a dialogue between two ambivalent Rizals. Rizal had a love-hate relationship with Spain, but this ambivalence gave birth to his love for his beloved nation; he created a nation because the Spanish nation repudiated him.[1]

A week or two before his departure from London, Guerrero and Annie packed clothes, books and research materials to be brought to Madrid. Annie donated five parcels to the Save the Children Fund. Then, she fell ill, exhausted from all the packing, and was brought to the Priory Clinic. Hearing about Annie's illness and their departure, their close friends and acquaintances wished her a speedy recovery and thanked Guerrero for the outstanding services he rendered to the Philippines and Britain. After Annie's recovery, the couple attended an official farewell lunch given by the Marquess of Landsdowne, the foreign undersecretary of state, and his wife. Instead of a formal lunch, usually given for arriving and departing ambassadors, the marquess agreed to make it informal among close associates of the couple.[2]

While preparing for the next post, Guerrero thought it was opportune to be awarded the Knight Grand Cross of Rizal before the presentation of his credentials but in an unprecedented way. He had the Grand Cross of the Lion and Grand Cross, Order of Dannebrog from the Finnish and Danish governments respectively for meritorious services as ambassador to these countries. He was a Knight of Rizal. Now that he had his prize-winning biography and translations of Rizal's novels to his credit, he thought he was qualified for the award. Upon learning later that the unorthodox way of bestowing it would create a controversy with the oldest members, he gave it up as mere *"vanitas vanitatum"*. But it was not a lost cause for in another assembly of the Order in the same year, his nomination was approved, with the awarding ceremonies to be made in February the following year.³

On 4 April, the couple boarded the plane for Spain. It was night when the plane landed at the airport. Philippine Embassy officials and officials from the Spanish Foreign Ministry were there to welcome them. Immediately after staying in a hotel, they went looking for a house. Having found one at Velazquez, they went to the office of the embassy at Plaza de Alonso Martínez and met the staff — one of them he brought along from London — for the new ambassador's requisite orientation. The following week, he was interviewed by the Spanish press, including television and radio reporters. His message to the Generalissimo was aired over a hundred radio stations.⁴

While trying to acquaint himself with his work, Guerrero came across two cases in the embassy files. An Augustinian friar did a 4,200-page *"catálogo razonado"* of all documents relating to the Philippines in his Order's archives, and gave the original copy to the then ambassador, Pedro Sabido, for publication in the Philippines and a copy to Dr Domingo Abella. Guerrero inquired about this case in a letter to Dr Montilla. The other case was the historical materials presumably given at the behest of the Spanish Government to Dr Jose P. Bantug but their whereabouts were unknown.⁵

In early May, the long wait for the presentation of credentials was over. Guerrero and Annie went to the Palacio de Oriente at Calle Bailen. Generalissimo Francisco Franco received Guerrero's credentials in the presence of Foreign Minister Fernando María Castiella and other members of the Spanish Foreign Ministry. Upon his presentation of his credentials, Guerrero delivered in Spanish an address saying he desired "to know and understand the Spain of today and enable Spaniards to know and comprehend the present Philippines" because Philippine-Spanish relations lived too much in the past, in history, or in his own words, *"vivimos demasiado en la historia"*.⁶

PREPARING FOR "THE GREAT PAMPANGO'S" VISIT

His presentation was recorded in photos, which Guerrero decided to send some for publication hoping that "it might be timed for the eve of the Great

Pampango's visit to Spain (if and when)." Franco sent a letter of invitation to President Diosdado Macapagal on 20 May through the Philippine Embassy in Madrid. It was not yet known when Macapagal would go to Spain on a state visit.[7]

After the "spectacular" meeting with Franco, Guerrero was back on his desk reading the situation in Madrid. Spain in the post-civil war after more than two decades of harsh authoritarian rule was different from the Spain he knew in the 1930s. Franco mellowed in an effort to improve the Spanish economy, emphasizing on tourism but remaining the head of a national-syndicalist state with one official party, the Falange Español Tradicionalista. Fascinated with the regime, Guerrero sent dispatches to the Home Office noting in the London papers but not the Madrid dailies, that Franco faced the most serious threat against him on labour and industrial fronts since 1939.[8]

One of the first visiting Filipino dignitaries whom he attended to was Romulo, now president of UP, who was to deliver a lecture at the Instituto de Cultura Hispánica at the Universidad Central de Madrid during its Filipino Week. That afternoon, he introduced Romulo flatteringly but made it a point to describe him as the "favourite son of the Americans", a man who personified a generation in the Philippines made in the United States. The Filipinos, he said, lived in three worlds, the American, Spanish and Asiatic worlds and it was Romulo who had linked these three. Romulo, after relating his life, about his generation formed and moulded differently from Recto, Quezon and Osmeña, pointed out in his lecture that the Philippines was situated between three worlds and that relations between Spain and the Philippines must be strengthened.[9]

Guerrero was closely following events at home through Manila newspapers sent through the diplomatic pouch when the United States House of Representatives on 9 May did not approve the war damage payment bill, resulting in popular indignation. Macapagal cancelled his trip to the United States and moved to change the date of Philippine independence from 4 July to 12 June, the day Gen Emilio Aguinaldo proclaimed Philippine independence. Americans as well as Filipinos saw it "as an act of resentment" but Macapagal retrospectively justified that the timing for the action had arrived for a decision made. Thus, Macapagal presided over the celebration of independence at the Luneta on 12 June with a joyful Aguinaldo as the guest of honour.[10]

Guerrero justified the action of the Philippine Government without a second thought. In an article submitted to *Arriba*, a Madrid newspaper, he believed that the presidential decree changing the date of Philippine independence vindicated Spain. It was on 12 June that the Philippines discovered itself as a nation:

> The Filipinos, born of Spain, declared themselves independent and emancipated themselves when they believed they had reached maturity, but having succeeded in leaving the family home, they found themselves converted into an apprentice and pupil in the house of another. Thus, today the Philippines ought to love the United States as one loves a good teacher and patron, but it simply ought to love Spain simply as mother.[11]

The change of date presaged the development of closer relations with Spain in light of President Macapapal's planned state visit to Spain. Guerrero conferred the Philippine Legion of Honour on an education minister during the awarding ceremony in the embassy on 19 June, in recognition of his exemplary services not only in promoting scholarships and other facilities to Filipino students in Madrid but also the restoration and gift to the Filipinos of Juan Luna's prize-winning painting *Spoliarium*.[12]

Having been informed by the Foreign Office of the state visit on 30 June, Guerrero prepared for it, his first since former President Magsaysay and Garcia did not visit Her Majesty the Queen while Guerrero was in London. He coordinated with the Spanish Foreign Ministry through Foreign Minister Castiella. Lasting for seven days, the visit consisted of state dinner at the Generalissimo's palace, a formal dinner under the auspices of Foreign Minister Castiella, a dinner given by the Mayor of Madrid, a *corrida de toro* with the Chief of State and First Lady in attendance, a speech at the Instituto de Cultura Hispánica, visits to the Valle de los Caidos, a memorial to the dead of the civil war, and to a labour university, a trip to Barcelona, a press conference in Spanish and a state dinner again with the *El Caudillo* and his wife.[13]

At the airport, Guerrero met Macapagal and his entourage, which included the First Lady and the children, Secretary of Commerce and Industry Rufino Hechanova, Foreign Affairs Undersecretary S.P. Lopez and Colonel Victor Dizon. Spanish Ambassador to Manila Jaime Alba Delibes and his wife went with them for the trip. Generalissimo Franco and his wife Doña Carmen met them at the airport. Franco gave Macapagal "*un abrazo*". As they rode to the Palacio de Moncloa where they would stay, enthusiastic crowds greeted them along the highway. The week-long visit did not hit snag. On the last day of the visit, Macapagal and Franco issued a joint communiqué strengthening the ties between the two countries.[14]

The communiqué listed down the areas where the Philippines and Spain could cooperate. It noted the respect and affection of each sovereign towards each other; their desire to reaffirm the existing ties of both their countries; their determination to share with each other not only knowledge and experience in economic and cultural aspects but also views affecting their interests, which included UN questions; and their resolve to fight international communism seen as threat to security and people's freedom. It also recorded the exchange of diplomatic notes between the two countries made during the visit, the first dealing with the assurance on the right of permanent residence of both its citizens in the other country on a reciprocal basis and the second dealing with the abolition of consular fees for tourists and business visas of both visiting citizens of the two countries. It also mentioned the discussions made on the need to complete two pending negotiations on questions of nationality reconciling the provisions of the Spanish civil code and the Philippine Republic Act No. 2639 of 1960, and a commercial agreement giving administrative and tariff concessions on both countries to certain products for greater trade. Other matters that were subject of the communiqué were the Spanish offer to collaborate with Macapagal's Socio-Economic Programme, scholarships for Spanish teachers in the Philippines and also a limited number of scholarships in the Diplomatic School of Madrid, and a project involving the UNESCO and other Hispanic countries establishing a centre in Manila for the propagation of Hispanic culture.[15]

The success of the state visit encouraged Guerrero to confer decorations on Spanish officials. He suggested a new rank, that of Datu, in the Order of Sikatuna befitting officials of cabinet rank. On the initiative of the embassy, the first to be awarded for the "cordial welcome and successful state visit" was Foreign Minister Castiella.[16]

RUNNING THE EMBASSY

The rest of the year preoccupied Guerrero with personal and administrative concerns. When floods wrecked havoc in Barcelona in September 1962, he sent dispatches to suggest strongly that the Home Office should make a cash donation for the relief of the victims, which the government did. But in early October, he learned of his father's death after more than two years of lingering illness. Since he could not go home this time, he called his mother by telephone to lessen the grief of a widow. Though mournful, he delivered a short memorable address in a gathering of Madrid's diplomatic community on 12 October, *el día de la Hispanidad*. By mid-October after an exchange of notes was made in Manila, he accompanied Central Bank Governor Andres V. Castillo to the Ministry of Commerce in Madrid to sign a credit agreement. When the government denied visas to the Yugoslav basketball team which led to the cancellation of the world championships in Manila on 1–15 December, upon instructions from the Foreign Office, he invited and secured the participation of the Spanish national team in the special games in Manila. His *Fili* translation was released by a U.S. university press in November and by the year end, he was awarded the Rizal Presidential Award, an award he failed to get in the previous nomination. Since he could not attend the ceremony, he sent his brother Mario.[17]

One of Guerrero's concerns was the welfare of Filipino students in Madrid. Speaking before the Asociación de Universitarios Filipinos on the inauguration of its new officers in December, he pointed out to them, after relating Rizal's student life in Madrid, that in contrast to other Filipinos, their mission was to save Spanish culture in the Philippines as well as restore a sound balance in national development. On New Year's Day 1963, he presided over a small gathering of Filipino students in the embassy where he encouraged them to study the Spanish language, "the voice of our history". On this same day, he delivered a message to Filipino students on "Bonifacio and the Filipino Youth" commemorating the hero's birth centenary. Although Bonifacio did not know the privileges enjoyed by them, he said, he was relevant to the present age because Filipino students could follow in their own limited ways the patriotic work he started.[18]

Ever accommodating to students and academic community, he was invited to speak on "The Filipino University Student" in early March and on the similarities and differences between the Philippines and Latin America, and the legacies of Latin America to the Philippines in early April during the Filipino Week. Delivered at the university dormitory of San Fernando in the city, his talk highlighted the passion for education in Philippine society producing a mentality of "excessive individualism and materialism" in the Filipino student, but wished the birth of a social conscience among Filipino university students in the service of the Filipino people. The ties that bound the Philippines and Latin America, he said, were not only through Spain but also through Mexico. Though the Philippines belonged to Asia, there was something, however, that separated it from the rest of Asia; this it shared with Latin America, he said.[19]

Another of Guerrerro's concerns was the Sabah claim. Since he was detailed to advise the Philippine delegation, he flew to London in late January 1963 to join Vice President and concurrent Foreign Affairs Secretary Emmanuel Pelaez, Undersecretary Lopez and a host of others in their talks with British representatives. In fact, after receiving a directive from the Foreign Office the previous year, he ordered embassy personnel and commissioned researchers to search the archives of the Spanish Foreign Ministry and other archives in Spain to bolster the Philippine claim. For five days from 28 January, the Philippine delegation defended the validity of the Philippine claim that rested on the lease, not cession, of Sabah. The British North Borneo Company administered Sabah from 1878 to 1946 upon the consent of the Sulu sultan, which in the Confirmatory Deed of 1903, recognized the sultan as the sovereign of Sabah. Pelaez declared that the North Borneo Cession Order of 1946 was illegal and consequently, Great Britain has no right to turn over Sabah to Malaysia.[20]

On 12 June, Philippine Independence Day, Guerrero put forward the idea in the *ABC*, the largest and most influential daily in Spain, of a tripartite international commission consisting of the Philippines, Spain and Mexico to commemorate the fourth centenary of Philippine-Spanish relations since the arrival of Legazpi in 1565. As part of its mandate, the commission would take charge of the reconstruction of Fort Santiago, the conversion of Legazpi's manor house into a museum, the publication of a commemorative book of essays, and a compilation of historical documents about this event found in Spanish archives. The sovereignty of Spain over the Philippines commenced with a blood compact between Katunaw — not Sikatuna or Cicatuna — and Legazpi, and ended in another blood compact among the brotherhood of Andres Bonifacio's Katipunan. An invigorated brotherhood between Filipinos and Spaniards, he said, could be done through this commemoration. "These shall be 'covenants' in word, paper and stone but no less valuable and lasting than those covenants that 'bled' Legazpi and Katunaw."[21]

The embassy under Guerrero extended protection to Filipinos in matters dealing with inheritance, repatriation, burial, pardon or detention. The embassy interceded officially in the initial investigation of a case, later withdrawn, involving the Compañia General de Tabacos de Filipinas, the principal offended party, in Barcelona where a case of falsification of Philippine internal revenue (cigarette strip) stamps was discovered. Guerrero took up the suggestion of Carlos Quirino, now the director of public libraries, on the exchange of publications between the Philippines and Spain by exploring its possibility. The embassy began compiling a list of publications that might interest Spanish agencies concerned. When the Spanish Foreign Ministry issued a circular penalizing diplomatic agents for traffic violations, Guerrero protested to authorities that such action contravened international practices and convinced the Foreign Office to do the same for Spanish diplomatic agents in Manila. Upon the request of the Juan Luna Centennial Commission, he commissioned a painter to reproduce Luna's *La Batalla de Lepanto* which hung in the former Spanish Senate's session hall, and shipped it to Manila. He entertained Vice President Pelaez who, after a SEATO Ministers Conference and the Conference of Philippine Ambassadors in Paris, made a private visit to the embassy. He was to meet Pelaez in Paris but due to illness he was unable to attend.[22]

Guerrero closed down the Philippines' honorary consulate in Alicante but opened another in Seville; recommended that trade promotion attachés fluent in Spanish be sent to the embassy since only two Foreign Affairs officers and himself shared the burden of the task and directed his staff to study and submit reports on important developments in Spain which might have significance back home. Two of these concerned the Spanish social security system, "one of the oldest (since 1908) and most comprehensive in the world", and the 1967 Spanish Economic Development Plan.[23]

Notes

1. *MC*, 28 January 1962; Leon Ma. Guerrero, *El Sí y El No (Estudios Historico- Sociales)* (Madrid, 1963), pp. 20–32.
2. *The Evening News and the Star*, 27 March 1962; Harold Davies to Leon Ma. Guerrero, 27 March 1962; Countess Jellicoe to Anita Corominas, 13 April 1962, *LMGP*.
3. Leon Ma. Guerrero to Horacio de la Costa, 31 March and 13 April 1962, *HDCP*; Department of Foreign Affairs, *Biographic Register* (Manila: Bureau of Printing, 1970), pp. 37–38; *Supreme Commander's Annual Report and Yearbook 1962* (Manila, 1962), pp. 4, 5, 19.
4. *MT*, 5 and 15 April 1962; Leon Ma. Guerrero to Horacio de la Costa, 13 April 1962 and Leon Ma.Guerrero to Horacio de la Costa, 30 November 1963, *HDCP*; *OD 1963*, p. 62; *Annual Report of the Embassy Spain for the Fiscal Year 1962–1963* (hereafter cited as *Annual Report 1962–1963*) (Madrid: Philippine Embassy, 1963), inside back cover. The embassy personnel were Jose S. Estrada, Counsellor; Rodolfo Severino, Consul General; Juan Atienza, Vice Consul; Vicente Guzman Rivas, Third Secretary; Julius G. Maloles, Attaché; Maria Virginia Boncan, Assistant Attaché (Finance Officer); Enrique V. Togle, Assistant Attaché; Arturo Soler, Private Secretary; Pedro de Guzman, Property Officer; and Araceli Larrarte. The alien personnel were Maria Josefina Caminero de Rodriguez, Josefina Serantes, J. Bautista Rosado, J. Antonio Rasilla and Felix Sanz.
5. Leon Ma. Guerrero to Horacio de la Costa, 13 April 1962, *HDCP*.
6. *MDB*, 23 May 1962; Guerrero, *El Sí y El No*, p. 8.
7. Leon Ma. Guerrero to Abe [Emilio Aguilar Cruz], no date, *LMGF*; Diosdado Macapagal, *A Stone for the Edifice: Memoirs of a President* (Quezon City: Mac Publishing House, 1968), p. 341.
8. Leon Ma. Guerrero to Abe [Emilio Aguilar Cruz], no date, *LMGF*; Leon Ma.

Guerrero, "Midnight in Spain", *PFP*, 17 July 1937, p. 8; "RP shows renewed enthusiasm for Spain", *Examiner*, 19 August 1963, p. 15.
9. "Palabras del Excmo. Sr. D. Leon Maria Guerrero, Embajador de Filipinas en España, presentando al Excmo. Sr. Dr. D. Carlos Romulo Peña, Conferenciante durante la semana Filipina de la Universidad de Madrid en el Instituto de Cultura Hispanica, 11 de Mayo de 1962"; "Conferencia pronunciada por el General D. Carlos P. Romulo, presidente de la Academia Filipina de Ciencias y Humanidades, en el Instituto de la Cultura Hispanica el dia 11 de Mayo de 1962 con motivo de la celebracion de la Semana Filipina" in *LMGF*.
10. Macapagal, *A Stone for the Edifice*, pp. 248–50.
11. *MT*, 14 June 1962; Guerrero, *El Sí y El No*, pp. 9–13.
12. Guerrero, *El Sí y El No*, pp. 45–46.
13. Macapagal, *A Stone for the Edifice*, pp. 341–42.
14. Ibid.
15. Ibid., pp. 344–45, 529.
16. *Annual Report 1962-1963*, p. 5.
17. Ibid., pp. 2, 5–6; *MC*, 8 October 1962; *MT*, 8 and 9 October 1962; *MC*, 10 September 1962; Jose Rizal, *The Subversive (El Filibusterismo): A Sequel to The Lost Eden* (Bloomington: Indiana University Press, 1962); *Supreme Commander's Annual Report*, pp. 5, 8; *MC*, 29 December 1962; *EN*, 29 December 1962; "Committee on Rizal Awards created on 15 March 1961" in *JRNCCP*.
18. Guerrero, *El Sí y El No*, pp. 68–72.
19. Ibid., pp. 57–68; 73–78.
20. *Annual Report 1962-1963*, p. 3. For a broad discussion on the validity of the Philippine claim, see the *Philippine Claim to North Borneo Volume I* (Manila, 1964). Anchoring on the law on prescription, Great Britain and Malaysia rejected the Philippine claim since the Sultanate of Sulu, according to them, did not exercise effective sovereignty over North Borneo. See Mohammed bin Dato Othman Ariff, *The Philippine Claim to Sabah: Its Historical, Legal and Political Implications* (Kuala Lumpur: Oxford University Press, 1970).
21. *Annual Report 1962-1963*, pp. 13–19; *MT*, 19 June 1963.
22. *Annual Report 1962-1963*, pp. 2–6, 26.
23. Ibid., pp. 6–8, 10–18.

16

In Search of the Burgos Trial Records

During his visit to the Philippines in December 1962, Guerrero discussed with de la Costa a project on nineteenth century Philippines and along with it was the objective of recovering the Burgos trial records. In London before he left for Madrid, he saw the Spanish ambassador, the Marquess de Santa Cruz, who suggested to him to get in touch with key Spanish officials. In the first quarter of 1963, he inquired about the Burgos trial records and communicated to the Army Ministry but they were evasive.[1]

Once the records were available to the public, the rewriting of Philippine history, at least from 1872 onwards, would be logical. The trial of Burgos was still shrouded in mystery for almost a century because no Filipino or even Spanish historians had accessed the trial records. Gaining access to these *procesos* would be boon to their project. Towards this end, he reread Montero y Vidal's *Historia General de Filipinas*, which took him to the movement of Apolinario de la Cruz and recognized its Katipunan resemblance, particularly its restriction to Tagalogs, making him conclude that Filipino nationalism was based on racial resentments. Rereading the same, he realized almost on the eve of the Philippine Revolution, that the Spanish conquest never succeeded in the mountainous north and in the southern islands. On Montero y Vidal's account, he said it "reads just as badly as Zaide et al. sometimes; all those decrees — but his footnotes are often amusing and some of his accounts of historical events most readable." After Montero y Vidal, he wanted to read Sinibaldo de Mas' *Informe sobre el estado de las Islas Filipinas en 1842*, a copy of which he was looking for, but he had instead Martinez de Zuñiga's *Estadismo de las Filipinas*. For the Spanish background of nineteenth century Philippines, he enjoyed

La Política y Los Políticos en el Reinado de Carlos III, leading him to two other books.²

In all these readings, he began to question the beginning of the nineteenth century in the Philippines:

> The roots of the modern era would seem to go as far back as the Ilustracion under Carlos III and the Sociedades de Amigos del Pais. Or one might, like Rizal, start later with the definite triumph of Liberalism (Maria Cristina, Isabel II, Espartero and all that) leading to the Republic, Carlos Ma. de la Torre in Manila and the consequences in Cavite! Until de la Torre I have not come across any instance of a change of regime in the Philippines — the usual time-lag, I suppose. This would go along with the traditional theory on what Zaide et al. would call the birth of Filipino nationalism.

Based on his acquaintance with a number of sources the nineteenth century was "overcrowded" so that he suggested to de la Costa to split the nineteenth century into two.³

Besides this research project, he accepted the writing of another biography, that of Jose Abad Santos, so that he could have some writing done during the summer. He had gone through the 700-page Hayashi-Kawaguchi trial of Abad Santos, that, to him, was "fascinating stuff" but it provoked questions such as: "Was Abad Santos shot because he was confused with his brother Pedro the Communist? Who really issued the order of execution (plainly illegal because there was no court-martial)? Why was Roxas saved and not Abad Santos?" Reading the trial made him conclude that a possible article could be made out of it for *Philippine Studies*. Yet, with regard to Abad Santos' earlier life, he was at a loss. To remedy this, he decided to try to contact his former boss George Vargas, Quintin Paredes, Jose Yulo and other "survivors", also Pepito and Ossie Abad Santos and one of the latter's living brothers.⁴

TROUBLING TEETH AND FOOT

Events at home were relayed to Guerrero fast. After holding a grand reception for the Philippine Independence Day at Hotel Ritz in Madrid in which he wore an *americana cerrada* that raised hackles at home, he was shocked to learn how President Macapagal subjected Pelaez to harassment and defamation through Justice Secretary Salvador L. Mariño. In fact, Macapagal thought of recalling Guerrero for Home Office job but was dissuaded when he was convinced by Palace advisers that Guerrero might resign and return as an oppositionist broadcast commentator. The investigation of Harry Stonehill over alleged pay-offs of high-ranking officials of the government made the headlines. In a series of radio-television broadcast, Mariño in his "It appears" speech singled out Pelaez as one of those listed in the voluminous Stonehill files. Later on, Pelaez was said to have had a legitimate transaction. Pelaez resigned as Foreign Affairs Secretary on 21 July 1963 accusing Mariño and Macapagal of having "borrowed his honour". He also left the Liberal Party and joined the opposition. For political, or rather electoral purposes, on the eve of the senatorial elections, Macapagal partly succeeded in weeding out possible contenders for the next presidential elections. Pelaez, a party mate, was perceived to be seeking the Nacionalista nomination. Upon Pelaez's resignation, Macapagal appointed Lopez as Foreign Affairs Secretary.[5]

In the middle of this abrupt change, Guerrero's dental problem had gone from bad to worse. His teeth in his upper jaw were extracted and for this reason, he had to wear a denture. On the strong recommendation of his dentist, he needed to purchase a powder to keep it in place. Since the doctor's powder had to come from the United States, even via diplomatic channels it would take much time. This was an emergency as the doctor told him, but he was constrained to tell his "deep dark secret" for he did not dare ask the embassy staff to do it for him. He had no other choice but to contact his friend who was in London on a research fellowship at the School of Oriental and African Studies (SOAS). "Don't think I have made you a purchasing agent in London ..." he wrote to de la Costa explaining the details and imploring: "... I beg you to run, not walk, to the nearest apothecary's to get them for me for this senile classmate of yours if only as an experiment."[6]

Having received them, he was relieved to do his work. When the Spanish press carried news about the Malaya-Indonesia confrontation regarding the creation of a Federation of Malaysia, and the Manila Summit taking place from 31 July to 5 August, he clarified the issues in the Spanish press about President Macapagal's idea of a Malayan confederation consisting of the Philippines, Malaya, Borneo territories and Indonesia. On the morning of 6 August, he received a Jesuit Fulbright scholar doing his doctoral research on the Propaganda Movement with whom he enjoyed talking with, giving him leads on available materials in Spain, one of which was a catalogue in the Augustinian Colegio de Filipinos in Valladolid. He continued working on the project now codenamed "the Grand Design", discarding the idea that the nineteenth century should be split into two.[7]

After the dental problem, in late August he felt pain on his left foot that impaired his walking. His Spanish doctor who revealed himself to be an author of a book, told him that he was suffering from gout. Derailed for a while from continuing his research on the Abad Santos project for health reasons and also because he was still waiting for the development of his request to de la Costa on the project, he went to Valladolid to do research in the Augustinian archives. As for the Burgos trial records, the army archives in Madrid seemed to be unmanned while the archives in Segovia, the *Archivo General Militar* was closed until September. He was hoping that the Foreign Office would keep him in Madrid long enough to recover the Burgos trial records.[8]

NEW HEAD IN PADRE FAURA

The resignation of Pelaez cleared the way for Lopez to become the top official now in Padre Faura after the transfer from Arlegui, news that got a *Free Press* cover story. Sent a copy of the issue and after reading it, Guerrero was moved to write Lopez: "Odd that Nick Joaquin should pair us off briefly on Corregidor and nowhere else: what happened to 'the only two intellectuals in the Foreign Service'? I would have been rather pleased if he had mentioned the fact that I strongly recommended you as my successor when I left the Department in 1954. You would have been Undersecretary and perhaps Secretary nine years earlier!" He continued:

> Anyway, congratulations again both on the occasion of the Free Press cover story ... and on the Manila Conference itself.... As one of the original "Asians" I was, of course, delighted by the move to "restore Asia to the Asians."[9]

The Manila Conference, or the Manila Summit, was the meeting of three heads of states from Malaya, the Philippines and Indonesia on Macapagal's proposal to create a regional grouping of Malayan peoples. Upon the resignation of Pelaez, Lopez took on the task of negotiating with his counterparts such as Indonesian Foreign Affairs Secretary Subandrio and Deputy Minister Tun Abdul Razak, which led to the signing of the Manila Accord and the establishment of Maphilindo. Guerrero would later learn that Britain and Malaya went ahead with their plan of establishing the Federation of Malaysia on 31 August, prejudicing the Philippine claim to Sabah and without waiting for the result of the plebiscite marked with irregularity.[10]

Reporting to the new head in the Foreign Office, Guerrero updated Lopez on the condition of the embassy in Madrid. He had already sent a confidential dispatch on the reorganization of the staff as well as a telegram on the impending personnel shortage. He had no objection to a leaner workforce in adherence to the post's importance. He knew the rationale behind keeping the vacancies in the embassy, which was to let the next successor have the option to appoint his own people. Elections were due in the coming November for senatorial offices. That being the case, he entreated Lopez, without forgetting his mission regarding the Burgos trial records to "... give me a fair warning and let me finish the search for the Burgos trial record. Otherwise history (or at least historians) may never forgive you!"[11]

When S.P. Lopez was formally appointed as secretary of Foreign Affairs in December, Guerrero sent two telegrams congratulating him on what he termed as "*vindicalon* [sic] [vindication] of intellectualism in service of country's paramount interests" followed by the enigmatic phrase "Now we are three." Surely, they were the two of the three but who was the third — the late Claro Recto?[12]

BONIFACIO AND RIZAL, THEN AGUINALDO

Knowing the significance of the 1960s in Philippine history starting with the Rizal centenary, Guerrero in August 1963 considered publishing a monograph or pamphlet on the Bonifacio centenary. He had three options: first, he could translate into Spanish important documents in Agoncillo's collection of Bonifacio's writings; second, he could publish the material relating to Bonifacio in Valladolid; and third, he could make use of the materials in the military archives in Madrid. He was also thinking of newspaper or friar accounts in Valladolid or elsewhere. Documents on the Philippine Revolution found in the Spanish archives were awaiting publication, but because of the lack of funds, Guerrero did not push for a pamphlet or a monograph. Instead of doing away with the usual parties, a diplomatic reception was held at his residence on 30 November, the only Philippine diplomatic post that did so.[13]

Although Guerrero could not come to the Annual Rizal Lecture in December hosted by the Philippine Centre of International P.E.N., an organization of Filipino writers, they insisted on him giving a lecture even though he could not deliver it personally. In choosing the comparative lecture on Rizal and Bonifacio, he explained that it was to commemorate Bonifacio's centenary (perhaps to "atone" for that aborted pamphlet) and to pay homage to Recto — "that parfait knight of Filipino nationalism" — the first to deliver the lectures. A time would come, he said, when a lecture may be conceived on the parallel lives of Rizal and Recto.[14]

The following year when Emilio Aguinaldo died in early February, the Philippine Government in honour of the president of the First Philippine Republic declared a fifteen-day national mourning. Guerrero organized a memorial service in the Instituto de Cultura Hispánica auditorium at the Avenida de los Reyes Católicos in Madrid. He invited three distinguished Spaniards: Manuel Ballesteros, professor of History at the Universidad Central de Madrid; Blas Piñar, former director of the Institute; and Lieutenant General Mariano Alonso who personally handed to Aguinaldo the Spanish Army's Sword of Honour prior to his death. Guerrero delivered his tribute centring on his thesis that Aguinaldo died twice, hence his title in Spanish "Las Dos Muertes del General Aguinaldo". The first, "a political death", occurred when Aguinaldo was captured in Palanan on 23 March 1901. Honour was returned to Aguinaldo, he said, when the date of independence was reverted to 12 June and with his death, his second, he gained the acceptance of the people as a national hero. Texts of the speeches were published in a small pamphlet, something that was not accomplished during the Bonifacio centenary.[15]

IRONY OF THE ZOBEL PRIZE

In September 1963, Guerrero decided to publish another collection of his speeches and lectures; some were translations of his lectures delivered first in English. Manuel Fraga Iribarne, the Spanish Minister of Information and Tourism, whom he asked to write a short foreword for the book, wrote that its publication "without doubt, would help in the strengthening of the ties that bind Spain to the noble Filipino nation …". Familiar with the annual Zobel literary contest, Guerrero submitted his book, which was favourably received and reviewed by the Spanish press and distributed to Spanish cultural institutions. The board of judges decided to award him the Zobel literary prize. He was quite elated that he won, sending Mario to represent him in the awarding ceremonies at the Spanish Embassy in Manila in late February 1964. After being awarded the prize, Filipino students in Madrid paid homage to him at the embassy.[16]

It was April when the repeal or amendment of the Spanish Law, known also as the Cuenco Law, made headway in the Philippine Congress. Yet, as early as March 1962, Filipino college students were advocating the law's repeal. Among the reasons were its impracticality to engineering and science students, and the compulsory twenty-four units in Spanish for all college students as intended by the amendment was not only unreasonable but also a waste of time to those who could not even see its application to their career. News about it was watched with interest in Spain. The embassy in Madrid received and noted official and unofficial protests from unexpected quarters. Spanish-American countries also sent their protests over the said controversy.[17]

It was rather ironic that after getting the highest literary prize in Spanish, Guerrero had to face the rising clamour against Spanish by Filipinos. One of the things he did was put the issue in its proper context, both historical and educational. He did this in a speech to the Ateneo Barcelonés in mid-April, which he described as "risky and quite imprudent for a diplomat" to tackle "the problem of Spanish language in the Philippines". He synthesized his ideas in two concepts: misgivings and yearning. Spanish friars had misgivings about teaching Spanish to the natives despite their yearning to learn the language. As a result, when the Americans arrived, only a few knew Spanish, and English became the language of convenience in business and government, making Spanish impractical to the new generation.[18]

Why did Guerrero choose to speak in Barcelona? "I have dared to say these things in Barcelona that frankly I would have not been allowed to say in Madrid." Indeed, Catalans had their own language and their sympathies might side with the Filipinos. In an apt conclusion, he said: "Perhaps, the Filipino of our days no longer speaks the Spanish language but he still thinks and feels in Spanish. You, Catalans, would understand that it is possible to love Spain in Catalan — and in Tagalog — the same way as it is possible to hear mass without knowing Latin." A day after his lecture, the Spanish Syndicate of University Students presented him a Silver Swan, one of its highest decorations for his "ardent defence" of the Spanish language in the Philippines.[19]

His speech could have enlightened a part of the Spanish public but the controversy continued to affect the causes of the embassy. The placing of commemorative markers where Rizal had stayed in Madrid and Barcelona like what he did in London was put on hold. Since these markers were not installed on Rizal's birth centenary under the auspices of the Centennial Commission, the embassy had to oversee its completion. The recovery of the Gomburza and Rizal trial records encountered resistance from authorities in Madrid and Seville. Guerrero in his confidential negotiations with them could not secure the originals or even photostatic copies of the trial records.[20]

Mulling over the consequences that the controversy had created, Guerrero suggested the establishment of a Philippine Institute of Spanish Culture. While he favoured the move to repeal the Cuenco Law, it was unwise to let this motivate the "unnecessary weakening" of sympathies from Spain and Latin American countries. Spanish culture could be disseminated through other venues through this institute in time for the fourth centenary of the evangelization of the Philippines the following year. The objectives of the institute were threefold: the publication of works in Spanish as part of Philippine national literature and history, the creation of prizes and grants to nurture the growth of this great literature, and the encouragement of research on historical documents about "unwritten" Philippine history through funding.[21]

But the controversy did not affect the esteem Guerrero held among his colleagues. He was honoured by Latin Americans on board the replica of Columbus' ship, *Santa Maria* in Puerta de la Paz in Barcelona. He donated a bronze bust of Rizal to the Sociedad Cervantina in Madrid in commemoration of the 368th death anniversary of Miguel de Cervantes.[22]

RESHUFFLE IN THE HOME OFFICE

The latest reshuffle in Padre Faura in May 1964 saw the appointment of Ambassador to Japan Mauro Mendez as Foreign Affairs Secretary, replacing Lopez who will take the place of UN Ambassador Jacinto Borja. The reshuffle prompted Guerrero to write to Mendez: "You have inherited a rather difficult situation ... I am relieved that so far, you have not yet become a political target, something to be expected on the eve of a presidential election ...". Lopez was sent to the United Nations to follow up the Philippine claim to Sabah. The reason for the Cabinet change was that Lopez was accommodating to Communist USSR and China while Mendez was a resolute anti-communist who did not see any profit in the Soviet Union-China rift. Actually, Lopez wanted to establish ties with the USSR. It was like a repeat of what happened to Guerrero ten years ago. Now Lopez was being banished not to London but to New York. Guerrero might have sensed the parallelism and his sympathies went with Lopez. Both were serving an administration whose foreign policy was inflexibly anti-communist.[23]

The embassy remained unaffected by the change. The limited jurisdiction of the Madrid embassy impelled Guerrero to suggest to the Foreign Office to accredit him as concurrent ambassador to Morocco, Algeria, Tunisia and Libya. His justifications were first, it would expand the embassy's limited field of activities; second, the accreditation would not entail additional appropriation; third, the London embassy, where he was previously assigned to, was accredited to several countries and applying this to Madrid would be a boon to the country's limited resources; and fourth, accreditation to these countries was based on the historical connection since North African Moors ruled Spain for centuries. He also suggested the possible accreditation of the Madrid embassy to Portugal and the Republic of Ireland. He knew for a fact that Ireland disallowed the accreditation of a London envoy to Dublin. Portugal's Lisbon was of course nearer to Madrid than Dublin or Rabat, aside from the fact that Spanish-Portuguese relations were close in view of the Iberian Pact, and Portugal was also the only country that Franco had visited. A year later, only Algeria and Morocco were accredited to the embassy. Guerrero sent dispatches, telegrams and other official communications to the Home Office reporting on Spain on "balance of payments, industrialization, foreign investments, inflationary trends, food shortages, labour unrest, military cooperation with or dependence on the U.S.A. etc." He directed the minister-counsellor to make a summary of the Spanish Socio-Economic Development Plan for a four-year period, promulgated in December. The embassy suffered two losses when two of its members died.[24]

Aside from dealing with administrative matters, Guerrero had to deal with other personal concerns and undertakings. He acceded to the request of de la Costa to reprint passages from his two essays in a book of readings tentatively entitled, *A Philippine Reader*, renamed *Readings in Philippine History*. When he heard the news about his niece Gemma Teresa Guerrero Cruz, daughter of Chitang, winning the Miss International crown, he was rather surprised, in contrast to Annie who was all along confident that Gemma would win. He even wired Chitang when he heard Gemma was joining the contest: "*¡Basta ya de barbaridades!*" because beauty contests in Spain were considered "rather vulgar".[25]

Notes
1. Leon Ma. Guerrero to Horacio de la Costa, 13 April 1962; 27 July 1963, *HDCP*.
2. Leon Ma. Guerrero, "Memorandum on the 19th Century Project" enclosed in ibid.
3. Ibid.
4. Leon Ma. Guerrero, "Memorandum on Abad Santos Project" enclosed in ibid.
5. *EN*, 25 January 1963; Lina O. Sevilla, "Guerrero in 'cerrada' at Madrid reception", *MT*, 28 June 1963, p. 12A; Leon Ma. Guerrero to Horacio de la Costa, 27 July 1963, *HDCP*; Macapagal, *A Stone for the Edifice*, p. 16; Gleeck, *The Third Philippine Republic*, p. 299.
6. Leon Ma. Guerrero to Horacio de la Costa, 29 July 1963; 6 August 1963, *HDCP*.
7. *Annual Report 1962–1963*, p. 3; Leon Ma. Guerrero to Horacio de la Costa,

6 August 1963, *HDCP*; Father John N. Schumacher, interview by the author, Ateneo de Manila University, 12 May 2006.
8. Leon Ma. Guerrero to Horacio de la Costa, 24 August 1963, *HDCP*.
9. Leon Ma. Guerrero to Salvador P. Lopez, 23 August 1963, *SPLP*.
10. Gleeck, *The Third Philippine Republic*, pp. 294–98. See also Gerald Sussman, "The Sabah Claim and Maphilindo: A Case Study of Philippine Foreign Policy Decision-making" (MA thesis, Philippine Center for Advanced Studies, University of the Philippines, 1975) and Michael Leifer, *The Philippine Claim to Sabah* (Zug: Inter Documentation, 1968).
11. Leon Ma. Guerrero to Salvador P. Lopez, 23 August 1963, *SPLP*.
12. Leon Ma. Guerrero to Salvador P. Lopez, [telegrams] 21 and 22 December 1963, *SPLP*.
13. Leon Ma. Guerrero to Horacio de la Costa, no date, *HDCP*; *Annual Report of the Embassy Spain for the Fiscal Year 1963-1964* (hereafter cited as *Annual Report 1963-1964*) (Madrid: Philippine Embassy, 1964), p. 6.
14. Leon Ma. Guerrero, "Rizal and Bonifacio", *Philippine International Law Journal* 2, no. 4 (October–December 1963): 534–44.
15. *Homenaje a Emilio Aguinaldo* (Madrid: Embajada de Filipinas, 1964), pp. 3, 12–15, 19, 22, 33–40, 45–58; *Annual Report 1963-1964*, pp. 6–7, Annex II.
16. Guerrero, *El Si y El No*, pp. 4–5; *MT*, 26 February and 16 April 1964; *DM*, 15 April 1964; *Annual Report 1963-1964*, p. 7.
17. Ibid., pp. 3–4. On the controversy on the Spanish law, see R.V. Mapile, "The Spanish Law Controversy", *Weekly Graphic*, 15 April 1964, p. 12 and Augusto Gatmaytan, "The case against Spanish", *PFP*, 31 March 1962, pp. 18, 20, 22, 24, 69, 71.
18. *Annual Report 1963-1964*, p. 4. See Annex III of this report for the speech entitled "Recelo y Anhelo del Castellano en Filipinas".
19. *Annual Report 1963-1964*, p. 4; *MT*, 18 April 1964.
20. *Annual Report 1963-1964*, pp. 4–5.
21. Ibid., pp. 10–11.
22. D. Guerrero, *LMG*, pp. 348–49.
23. Ventura, *Mauro Mendez*, p. 132; Gleeck, *The Third Philippine Republic*, p. 310; Felipe Landa Jocano, *Philippines-USSR Relations: A Study in Foreign Policy Development* (NDCP Foundation, 1988), p. 47.
24. *Annual Report 1963-1964*, pp. 3, 11–12, Annex I, Inside Back Cover; *Annual Report of the Embassy Spain for the Fiscal Year 1965-1966* (hereafter cited as *Annual Report 1965-1966*) (Madrid: Philippine Embassy, 1966), p. 8.
25. Horacio de la Costa to Leon Ma. Guerrero, 25 September 1964, *HDCP*. See also Horacio de la Costa, *Readings in Philippine History: Selected Historical Texts Presented with a Commentary* (Makati: Bookmark, 1992), pp. x, 242, 262–63, 267; *MT*, 17 August 1964; Nick Joaquin, "1974 and all that", *PFP*, 20 March 1965, p. 81.

17

Home Leave in Preparation for a State Visit

From Madrid with a brief stopover in Bangkok, Guerrero arrived with Annie in Manila on 20 February 1965, to participate in welcoming the Marques and Marquesa de Villaverde, the son-in-law and only daughter of Generalissimo and Mrs Franco, and Spanish Foreign Minister Castiella. The visit was to return the generosity accorded to President Macapagal when he visited Spain three years ago. Originally scheduled in April in time for ceremonies celebrating the Christianization of the Philippines in Cebu, the state visitors arrived on 24 February.[1]

In an interview about the American debacle in Vietnam the following day, Guerrero said that if the United States were to leave Vietnam, the Philippines could assume an important and strategic role in the American defence map and if that happened, the Philippines would be in a much greater bargaining position to gain more concessions from the United States. At that time, the Americans were negotiating with the Philippine Government for the revision of the 1947 Military Bases Agreement. He likened the situation of the Philippines to that of Spain. The United States negotiated with Spain for another ten-year extension of the bases agreement for which it obtained massive assistance as it bargained for more concessions.[2]

The week-long state visit was both a success and a failure. Guerrero was supposed to arrive with the state visitors but he deliberately came two days earlier to arrange for them to meet Filipinos, not Spaniards. He had told them: "You are going 10,000 miles to the Philippines and I do not want to spend your visit there with other Spaniards. I want you to know and meet the Filipino people." They did not, for they spent their time with other Spaniards. He also wanted them to go to Pansol or to Pagsanjan to meet the real Filipinos who revolted against Spain. He would have wanted them to walk on Azcárraga. "How can you find Filipinos in Forbes Park, for goodness sake! It's really stupid. What idea will they have of Filipinos if they mix only with the Zobels and the Elizaldes and so forth?" He succeeded in one thing, that of taking them to the Senate for them "to see Philippine democracy in action". They were calling on Senate President Ferdinand E. Marcos but as they entered the Senate Hall, Senator Arturo M. Tolentino was on the rostrum assailing not only the president but also Marcos. Guerrero was, nonetheless, contented with the state visit for the visitors were impressed with Filipino hospitality; he himself was charmed.[3]

The visit was doubly significant. Annie has not gone home for eleven years. Both of them were impressed with the development that was happening in Manila. Guerrero was "astounded". He felt he would not mind living in Manila again. Annie, for instance, could not find her way around. When she was accompanied by Chitang to a hairdresser, she asked where they were when they were at Mabini Street in Ermita where she used to live. The experience taught her that it was not good to stay away for too long. Guerrero also missed Filipino food such as *toyo* and *patis*, *daing* and *tuyo* for there was no Filipino food in Madrid, making him lose his appetite and his weight. He realized that "patriotism is in the stomach, nationalism is in the stomach."[4]

LESSONS IN FRANCO DIPLOMACY: FILIPINOS MUST SPEAK FOR THEMSELVES

To fulfil a string of speaking engagements, Guerrero stayed for two more weeks. On 5 March, at the Arts and Sciences Theater of the UP, UP President Romulo introduced him before he spoke in a lecture on Philippine-American relations subtitled, "There ain't no Santa Claus". However, he did not talk about Philippine-American relationship but instead discussed about Spanish diplomacy, what and how the Philippines could learn from it in dealing with the United States, particularly as the military agreement was up for revision. He began by relating his admiration of Spanish diplomacy on its handling of Gibraltar, then Franco's diplomatic foresight during the war and, finally, the negotiation on the U.S. military bases in Spain.[5]

The Spanish Government in spite of being diplomatically isolated and economically and militarily disadvantaged in Western Europe, got its wishes of a Spanish-American command over the military bases under Spanish sovereignty with a right to determine the utility and purpose of these bases, and received aid that jump-started the Spanish economy towards development and industrialization. He observed that no single Spaniard had been shot at the American base in Spain, unlike the Philippine situation when in November and December 1964, two Filipinos were shot at Subic. Restricted to last for only ten years, the agreement, which could have been automatically extended for another ten years, was subjected to another round of negotiations. Again, the Spanish Government bargained for and succeeded in getting U.S. assistance for the modernization of its armed forces.[6]

What was Guerrero's conclusion to all of these examples of Spanish diplomacy at its best? Was Spanish diplomacy in any way accused of ingratitude? Filipinos tended to see states as individuals; it should not be the case. He pointed out that a state having no feelings had to only serve its interests. Thinking of their interests, Europe, he said, established the European Common Market as a protection against American competition; France, followed by Spain, was moving away from the dollar-pound-sterling system to return to an international gold standard; France, following Great Britain, recognized Peking; again France, the United Kingdom and the Federal Republic of Germany were seeking political and commercial relations with the Communist states of Eastern Europe. He emphasized that Filipinos must learn like the Europeans that there was no permanent ally, no special relations that can be placed above the national interest.[7]

To underscore his point, he gave an anecdote about British Prime Minister Neville Chamberlain. As Chamberlain was defending his disastrous policies during the war, a member of his majority party from the bench shouted: "Speak for England!" On that issue alone, Chamberlain fell from power, replaced by Winston Churchill. "Why speak for our enemies," Guerrero ardently asked, "or even our friends, or even our allies? They can speak for themselves. Rather, let us now speak for the Philippines, speak for the Filipinos, speak for ourselves."[8]

BUNDY AND PARITY

Three days after the speech at UP, a statement by an American foreign assistant secretary for Far Eastern Affairs caught Guerrero's attention. William P. Bundy, who came to preside over an Asian conference of American envoys in Baguio City, issued a statement about Philippine-American ties dealing with the parity rights. The parity would expire in

1974. Bundy said that their side would not be seeking an extension but assumed that the pre-1974 rights would be protected. Guerrero read it in the press but was not deceived. He seized the opportunity to expose the veiled ambiguities of the American assistant secretary.[9]

Before the Manila Lions, impatient Guerrero first stated that he was speaking as a private citizen, not as an ambassador, on the "curious" statement made by Bundy. He claimed that the statement could not be binding as both governments could, if they want to, extend parity. He discerned that such a statement, which he described as Bundy's "sweet lullaby", was issued to mollify Philippine nationalism by taking out one of the serious and sensitive irritants in Philippine-American relations. The parity amendment was made to spur Philippine economic development but it did not achieve its purpose because it wanted to protect American vested interests in the country. Guerrero discerned the meaning of "rights" in Bundy's statement, either American properties were to be protected from confiscation under the "due process" clause of the Constitution, or that parity rights would remain permanent even after its expiration.[10]

If he was correct, he likened it to U.S. Attorney General Herbert Brownell Jr.'s assumption that Americans had sovereignty and property rights over the American bases. Brownell claimed in 1956 that the United States had sovereignty over the U.S. bases in the Philippines. Recto furiously denied that such was the case by extracting from the then Vice President Richard Nixon on a visit to the Philippines a statement that supported Recto's position. A clarification was needed, Guerrero appealed, and Bundy should volunteer to explain his side to avoid misunderstandings in Philippine-American relations. Did they assume, he asked, that even after 1974, Americans would be exempted from any form of discrimination as between Filipinos and aliens? He ended it wittily: "Surely 28 years of parity are long enough! Shall we have parity forever?"[11]

The impact of his speech could not be ascertained but that Friday when he was beginning to pack for Madrid, Filipino protesters went to the U.S. Embassy to demonstrate against the bases and the parity rights with one placard bearing: "Asia for the Asians!" On the turn of events, he was surprised for he never thought this would happen, something impossible ten years ago. The agreement on the military bases was the first agreement that the Philippines and the United States had entered into. As he himself had witnessed, neither party should be blamed for it as neither had a clear idea of what should go into it, he said. He believed that the change of attitude was a demonstration of Filipinos becoming more nationalistic. Still, Filipinos would accord success to those who became a president or senator, but not to a poet or scientist. It was a repeat of his inaugural lecture at UP following his induction as a member of the Philippine Academy of Sciences and Humanities.[12]

BACK TO WORK

On 13 March 1965, Guerrero and Annie flew to Madrid. Two days later, he celebrated his fiftieth birthday. He resumed his usual activities meeting his colleagues in the diplomatic community, entertaining them once in a while at his residence and chatting with them about the latest news and gossips in Madrid. It was only about a month later that he appeared in a nationwide televised news conference — the first foreign ambassador to do so. He reported on the arrangements being made for the Spanish airline, Iberia, in cooperation with Philippine Airlines towards the establishment of regular scheduled flights between Madrid and Manila. Asked by a member of the panel on its "Meet the Press" programme about communism in the Philippines, he singled out Catholicism as one of the best defences of the Philippines against communism. He said that the Philippines was an ally of the United States and a member of the Afro-Asian community. Regarding Spain, he said that the former motherland had a special place in the heart of every Filipino, a feeling that could not be compared with other Hispanic nations. When he was interviewed for the *Mundo Hispánico* on its *coloquios semi-diplomaticos*, he stated that "the Philippines should be interpreted as coming from a resurgent Asia."[13]

From April until October, he attended to a number of gatherings and other ambassadorial concerns. In the absence of an international conference as suggested by Guerrero to mark the fourth centenary of Philippine-Spanish relations, the embassy in cooperation with Spanish officials and agencies commemorated it with gatherings in Barcelona and Valladolid, where he was the closing speaker and guest speaker respectively. The embassy in cooperation with the Instituto de Cultura Hispánica, also held the Semana Filipina with array of activities. Towards the middle of the year, he arranged for the visit of his niece Gemma, who went there to promote Philippine tourism and to get married to Oxonian Antonio "Tonypet" Araneta in the City of Ávila where the Aranetas traced their roots. As expected, her visit created tremendous publicity for the Philippines. A Franco general who was a blood relation — in fact a grand-uncle of the Guerreros — attended the wedding, making it a family reunion of some sort. It would not take long before Guerrero was to act as pall-bearer at the general's funeral. Guerrero then left for Geneva as head of the Philippine delegation to the United Nations Sugar Conference, staying there until the third week of October. Before flying to the sugar conference, he said to the Spanish publication, *3e*, that since the privileged position held by the United States in the Philippines would expire in 1974, Spanish exporters should increase trade with the Philippines by testing the Philippine market with their products.[14]

A week after his return from Geneva, he followed the newspapers for the November elections. *Ya*, one of Spain's largest newspapers, speculated that a return of the Nacionalistas would mean a turn towards neutralist policy in Philippine foreign policy. Immediately taking up his pen, Guerrero wrote to deny that possibility. Although acknowledging the Nacionalista party's tendency to extricate the country from American involvement in Asian conflicts, he said that newly elected President Ferdinand E. Marcos was reported in his first press conference, that he supported U.S. President Lyndon Johnson's policies in Vietnam, taking into account other possible political solutions. He denied that the reason Marcos left the Liberal Party was due to Macapagal's "excessive pro-Americanism". He said that foreign policy was never an issue in the electoral campaign, which gave emphasis to economic issues. He also clarified the assumption made that the return of the Nacionalista would mean an "autonomous" Philippine foreign policy, which would not be "in Washington's tow". Independent or dependent, Philippine foreign policy, Guerrero said, would require a reassessment of Philippine national interests in light of the danger of communist expansion in Asia, the balance of power in the Cold War and other considerations. The claim for an "independent" foreign policy, he said, was made in relation to the pending bilateral negotiations between the Philippines and the United States.[15]

DEBATING WITH AN AMERICAN PATRIOT

It was about the same Philippine-American relations that he debated with Frederic Marquardt, his former associate editor at the *Free Press*. Now an editor of the largest newspaper in Arizona, Fritz — as Guerrero would call Marquardt by nickname — visited Madrid in 1965. Guerrero saw to it that Fritz would enjoy his visit to the embassy but they mostly argued about American foreign policy. The same debate continued when Fritz sent him a clipping about Philippine-American relations, which induced Guerrero to send a copy to the then U.S. Ambassador to Spain.[16]

But the American patriot did not want to yield, writing to Guerrero after the visit that a strong anti-communist policy rather than a neutralist or pro-communist policy would serve better Philippine nationalism. Fritz also believed that it would be beneficial if American and Philippine nationalism would go down the same road. Guerrero, who had neutralist sympathies, replied that he was "inclined to agree" about communism, yet stated that "In the historical context of Philippine-American relations, I also think that a certain 'aggressiveness' is inevitable in asserting that nationalism is psychological 'compensation' for what might be called the 'double allegiance' of most Filipinos."[17]

Nevertheless, the debate continued in another time and place and mutual respect remained between the two nationalists.

NEW PRESIDENT, NEW POST

After the elections, the newly elected Philippine president prepared for his inauguration. In early December 1965, Guerrero wrote the memorandum of an ambassador-designate who was instructed to open a diplomatic mission in Brasilia. On 27 December, Annie and he gave a Christmas party for 1,000 schoolchildren attending the elementary school Grupo Escolar Islas Filipinas. On 30 December, the day of the inauguration, he decided to write to President Ferdinand E. Marcos what could have been the "shortest wire" and "a little of Kennedy" as one columnist said: "Dear Mr. President: Heartfelt congratulations. What can I do for my country? — Very truly yours, Leon Ma. Guerrero." He also wrote to Vice President-elect Fernando Lopez in which he said in part: "You are a perfect gentleman. That is why you are Vice President a second time. What greater proof of your abnegation and that you can be trusted?" Lopez was President Quirino's Vice President. Guerrero was compelled to write to the president due to the political intrigues in his department that often abound after elections. Since he was not a "political" diplomat as one columnist had said, he was safe but sometimes "career diplomats got sacrificed because of cliques in the Foreign Service."[18]

His fate was not yet decided when he learned of the death of Foreign Affairs Secretary Mauro Mendez in January 1966. He wrote immediately a letter consoling Pacita, the bereaved widow. He said that the *disgustos* in the Foreign Office raised difficulties for Mendez but in the end managed to carry on all along. Pacita did not forget to thank Guerrero. "Yours," she honestly told him, "is one of those I appreciate the most, especially because you wrote it only minutes after you received the sad news." She added: "Mauro was [an] admirer of your excellent writing style. Also I can tell you now that he rose to your defense on more than one occasion…."[19]

Waiting anxiously for his new appointment, Guerrero attended the twenty-first session of the International Sugar Council in London in late January and instructed the embassy staff to extend all possible assistance to the Philippine delegation to the First Hispano-Luso-American-Philippine Assembly on Tourism held in Madrid. Then, on the fourth week of April, President Marcos approved his assignment to New Delhi. That same day, Guerrero and Annie entertained Dame Margot Fonteyn, the famous ballerina-wife of Roberto Arias, former ambassador of Panama to London and a close friend, at a special party held at the chancery. The following month, the Government of India accepted his appointment as ambassador-designate to replace Ambassador Mauro Calingo. Guerrero even loaned some books from his library in late May for the Spanish Annual Book Fair where one booth was allocated to the Philippines.[20]

Before he left for New Delhi in mid-June after the Independence Day celebration, he paid his farewell calls on Generalissimo Franco in the El Pardo Palace, on the Vice President, Captain-General Agustin Muñoz Grandes, Foreign Minister Castiella, the Papal Nuncio, the Mayor of Madrid, the Indian Ambassador, and Director Marañon. Generalissimo Franco by a decree signed on 21 May in his capacity as the Grand Master of the Order of Isabela La Católica and countersigned by Foreign Minister Castiella as Chancellor of the Order awarded Guerrero the Grand Cross of the Order. He attended a number of farewell parties and dinners given by his colleagues in the diplomatic corps. He was honoured by his Latin-American colleagues when they organized a dinner for him and Annie at Restaurante Commodore. The dinner was a clear indication of the esteem that Guerrero and the Philippines had among the Latin American countries.[21]

As an ambassadorial post, Madrid's success outweighed its failure. Guerrero strengthened Philippine-Spanish relations by supporting and organizing conferences and gatherings, promoting trade, and ensuring that the reciprocal visits of Philippine and Spanish dignitaries in Spain and the Philippines were successful. It was still as productive as London for he was contributing articles and letters to Spanish dailies, and conducting research for two books. But it could be called a failure in a limited sense because he did not attain his objective of securing the Rizal and Gomburza trial records. It proved to be his greatest disappointment in Madrid hoping that after a century since the execution of Burgos and the trial of Rizal, Spain would let Filipinos know what really happened. Nonetheless, Spain must have signified to him the return of a "son" to a "mother" who gave birth to the Filipino nation — an enduring belief he held since his Ateneo days, and that alone was more than a rewarding experience.[22]

Notes

1. Feliciano Macaraeg, "Envoy Discusses Plans: To solidify Philippine-Spanish ties", *Mirror*, 30 May 1964, p. 30; *DM*, 19 February 1965; *MT*, 20 February 1965.
2. *DM*, 19 and 25 February 1965.
3. Joaquin, "1974 and all that", p. 79.
4. Ibid., pp. 79, 81.
5. *MC*, 4 March 1965; Leon Ma. Guerrero, "There is no Santa Claus", in *We Filipinos*, pp. 188–94.
6. Guerrero, "There is no Santa Claus", pp. 191–92.
7. Ibid., pp. 192–93.
8. Ibid., pp. 193–94.
9. Joaquin, "1974 and all that", p. 80.
10. Ibid.; Leon Ma. Guerrero, "Parity Forever?" *MT*, 16 and 18 March 1965, no page indicated in *LMGF*.
11. Ibid.
12. Joaquin, "1974 and all that", pp. 2, 81; Carlos P. Romulo, "Diplomacy and Arts and Letters" typescript in *LMGP*; Leon Ma. Guerrero, "Standards of Success", in *We Filipinos*, pp. 36–39.
13. *PH*, 4 March 1965; *DM*, 14 April 1965; *MT*, 15 April 1965; *Mundo Hispánico*, April 1965.
14. *MC*, 26 April 1965; *PH*, 27 April 1965; *MDB*, 15 December 1966; *Annual Report 1965–1966*, pp. 2–5, 7–8, 11; Nakpil, *Legends & Adventures*, pp. 87–88.
15. *MT*, 18 November 1965.
16. Frederic S. Marquardt, "Remembering Leoni Guerrero", *Bulletin of American Historical Collection* 11, no. 2 (April–June 1983): 38.
17. Ibid.
18. *Annual Report 1965–1966*, pp. 5, 12–13; *PH*, 12 January 1966; *MC*, 11 January 1966.
19. Paz P. Mendez to Leon Ma. Guerrero, 14 February 1966, *LMGP*.
20. *Annual Report 1965–1966*, pp. 4, 7, 14; *Daily Express* (London), 26 April 1966; *PH*, 28 April 1966; *MB*, 26 April 1966.
21. *MT*, 10 May, 20 and 21 June 1966; *DM*, 9 May and 2 June 1966; *Annual Report 1965–1966*, p. 9; Iberian-American Diplomatic Corps to Leon Ma. and Anita C. Guerrero, *LMGP*.
22. Joaquin, "1974 and all that", p. 79.

V

New Delhi to Belgrade: The Philippines towards Non-Alignment

"In international affairs, we shall be guided by the national interests ... Today, as never before, we need a new orientation toward Asians; we must intensify the cultural identity with our ancient kin ... For this we shall require the understanding of ourselves and of Asia that exceeds acquaintance ..."

President-elect Ferdinand E. Marcos,
First Inaugural Address, 1965

"We have fought in wars that are not of our own making. We shall do so no longer. We shall cease to be mere pawns in conflicts involving the Great Powers. We shall refuse to be drawn into the quarrels of the great. We shall cut our own path, independent of ideological encumbrances."

President Ferdinand E. Marcos,
Speech before the UNCTAD IV, Manila, 1976

18

Homecoming to Asia at Nehruvian India

From the Iberian Peninsula, Guerrero crossed to India, a homecoming to Asia after more than ten years of exile in the heartland of Europe. Great Britain and Spain combined, almost a quarter of India's total land area, was no match to a subcontinent. India was the cradle of human civilization older and more ancient than the West. He had been to London, the metropolis that during the heydays of empire ruled colonial India until its independence in 1947. Writing about Philippine-India relations in 1952, Guerrero noted how the two countries diverged, never to converge, in their way of looking at world affairs. India maintained diplomatic relations with the United States and the USSR, choosing not to side with either camp; it recognized Communist China instead of Taiwan and backed its entry to the UN — the exact opposite of Philippine policy — but with an anti-communist posture on the domestic front, the only similarity between Indian and Philippine foreign policies. In 1966 the template in those relations changed from an attitude of suspicion during the height of the Cold War to a meeting of minds with the upgrading of legations to embassies, increase in technical cooperation, intensified cultural and student exchanges, and state visits — the favourable situation Guerrero would find himself in June.[1]

Guerrero and Annie stayed at the embassy residence located in Friends Colony (West) with the chancery situated at B66, Greater Kailash I. Unlike the London and Madrid embassies, the New Delhi embassy moved from one place to another. Under Ambassador Narciso Ramos, now the Foreign Affairs Secretary, it had offices at Suites 32-37 Indra Palace Building, Central

Ring, Connaught Place. Then, during the terms of Ambassadors Manuel A. Alzate and Mauro Calingo, it moved to the third floor of the Thapar, Thipar or Thaper (different spellings in the directories) Building, 124 Jan Path. The mission had jurisdiction on a non-residential basis over the Kingdom of Nepal and oversaw honorary consulates in Calcutta, Bombay and Madras, the only three in the whole of India. The importance of the mission, as noted by Guerrero himself, was that it was:

> ... one of the world's most important listening posts, New Delhi being not only the capital of the world's largest democracy but also a strategic point of contact of the two "ideological worlds" and the so-called "third world", which are represented in New Delhi by 76 diplomatic missions, not including the U.N.O. and its specialized agencies for Asia.

Guerrero held office at the ground floor of the chancery which had an adjoining room for his secretarial staff, a reception room, a room for consular interviews and store rooms. It had separate rooms with air-conditioning and private bathrooms for the personnel.[2]

ACQUAINTING WITH INDIA UNDER INDIRA

His presentation set on 1 August, Guerrero absorbed himself in reading books on Indian history and culture. At home now with English as in the London days, though in Madrid he had almost forgotten it, he read Percival Spear's *A History of India* and Madeleine Biardeaus' *India*. Fascinated with Indian pre-independence political and revolutionary leaders because of their seeming familiarity with the personalities of Philippine political history, he found Rizal in Ram Mohan Roy (1772–1833), a writer and linguist who led the fight for his countrymen's political and civil rights. In the persons of Gopal Krishna Gokhale and Bal Gangadhar Tilak, leaders of rival "moderates" and "extremists" in the Indian National Congress, he found their political persuasions and strategies similar to the opposing personalities of Rizal and Bonifacio, and Quezon and Osmeña. Since India was predominantly Hindu, he read up on Hinduism and tried to understand Islam and Sikhism.[3]

The realities of India's domestic and international policies, which had dramatically changed since China's attack and the death of Nehru, did not escape him. India under Prime Minister Indira Gandhi, daughter of the late first Indian Prime Minister Jawaharlal Nehru, overhauled Indian foreign policy of non-alignment opening military and economic negotiations with the United States and USSR for the sake of economic development and security. Indira Gandhi, as he read from the newspapers, was accused of totally going against her father's policies by approving the participation of foreign capital in the fertilizers industry; devaluing the rupee allegedly because of American pressure; and supporting allegedly agricultural development in the coming four-year development plan in exchange of U.S. shipments of grains. Gandhi's visit to Moscow in July 1966 did not escape criticism from right-wing opponents for she had supposedly offended Washington and West Germany by supporting the joint communiqué which contained references to "imperialist aggression" in Vietnam and to the existence of "two Germanys". It was a delicate balancing act for Gandhi to stand by her policy. In the case of Vietnam, the Indian consul-general in Saigon was recalled when he justified the American bombing in North Vietnam to the Hong Kong press. While calling for an end to hostilities in Vietnam, her Foreign Office was assigning a consul-general to Hanoi. Even though India maintained relations with the two Vietnams, it called for the reactivation of the International Control Commission under its chairmanship and the Geneva Conference to initiate a new peace settlement in Vietnam. Despite the initiative for peace in Vietnam, Peking still denounced her as a tool of American "imperialism".[4]

AT RASHTRAPATI BHAVAN

On Monday morning, Guerrero, Annie and the embassy staff drove to the official residence of the president of India, the Rashtrapati Bhavan with its magnificently laid out Mughal gardens and an imposing aura of the building's architecture of 340 rooms and 37 fountains. Dressed in white suit and black pants, and wearing his black-rimmed spectacles, Guerrero presented his credentials to President Dr Sarvapalli Radhakrishnan in the presence of the Ministry of External Affairs officials led by Shri T. N. Kaul. At the Ashoka Hall, upon the presentation of his credentials, he delivered a brief speech, manifestly the upshot of a month of reading and acquainting with his new post.[5]

Referring to the past Philippine-India relations as suffering from suspicion and fear using an Indian metaphor for seclusion, *purdah*, he underscored their commonality in culture, the problems on economic development and social justice they were confronting and the parallelism in the evolution of their nationalism with the difference that India was an ancient civilization and the Philippines a young nation but "the first Asian people to defeat a Western colonial power and to proclaim the first Asian democratic republic". Though both countries, with their own *dharmas*, had pursued different policies, he hoped that the Philippines and India would share lessons and experiences; offer sympathy and assistance to each other, "in a comradeship ... with no room for condescension or disdain, recrimination or suspicion, self-righteousness or a pathetic self-satisfaction that would avert its eyes from mud of [their] common humanity".[6]

A week after the interview by the *Times of India* in which his "disarming habit of greeting foreign friends in their native 'lingo'" he said earned him the honorary citizenship of Zummarraga in Spain, Annie and he went to Rashtrapati Bhavan to attend the afternoon ceremonies of 15 August independence celebrations, a ritual they would keep in the following years. Guerrero would meet his colleagues in the diplomatic corps, developing close relations with Asian and Latin American envoys like the Mexican ambassador to India, the poet Octavio Paz who was years ahead of him in India and, for a time, became the dean of the corps. Guerrero would come to know Paz more than it met the eye. For him, Paz was "a rather queer character" involved in a widely known scandal and subject of gossips in the diplomatic community, when he fell in love with the wife of a French cultural attaché, whom Guerrero had met and described as "quite attractive". Eventually both left their spouses and married each other. But as a consequence, Guerrero observed, the wife of the French ambassador could never receive the wife of the Mexican ambassador.[7]

BUILDING THE CHANCERY

One of the first things Guerrero did as chief of mission was to check if the staff was adequate for the mission's needs. Out of the total personnel, the alien staff consisted of a translator-interpreter, a stenographer-typist, two typists, three messenger-clerks, one driver, one gardener, and one watchman. Their tasks were tight for a post like New Delhi, so he recommended for the assignment to the mission of a records clerk and a confidential stenographer-typist. Since he was chief of mission, Class I, and considering the importance of the post, he recommended to the Home Office the upgrading of the embassy to Class I. He also sent a dispatch to the Home Office suggesting that Afghanistan, which was accredited to the ambassador to Pakistan, be accredited to his post because Afghanistan and Pakistan had a dispute on Pushtunistan, putting the ambassador assigned to both countries in a difficult position.[8]

He spearheaded the transformation of the New Delhi mission from its nomadic existence to having a building of its own. It was 1955 when the embassy, still a legation then, acquired a lot in the diplomatic enclave in New Delhi, but it was only during his term that the building of a permanent structure to house the chancery and the ambassador's residence was pursued. In consultation with the Home Office, he went to Manila to get funds and plans for the embassy edifice on the last Sunday of August 1966. Meanwhile, Annie flew to London to meet old friends, staying there until the end of September.[9]

Reporting to Padre Faura regarding the funds for the embassy compound, he also followed up on his request for the accreditation of Afghanistan to his post, which had been approved a few days ago. However, he later learned that an acting chief of the Division of Ceremonials, whom he would meet, was allegedly opposing his credentials. At a party that night, an inebriated Guerrero who became noisier in his banter with the protocol ladies until a protocol officer accosted him to go home, saw the young officer and said: "Be sure to be in your office tomorrow morning." In the office, Guerrero asked about the accreditation, listening to the officer about bureaucratic procedures to be followed. Losing his patience, he threatened: "You are forcing me to denounce your ignorance to the media. Do you want Senator Manglapus to raise a fuss in the Senate?" Undaunted, the acting chief said that he refused to do anything illegal. Stunned that a junior talked back to him, he settled for a compromise. As far as the case was concerned, Guerrero's action had a streak of arrogance of a superior over a low-ranking officer. Impatient over bureaucratic procedures, he thought that those did not matter. In the end, he had his way when Padre Faura recommended his accreditation to the president. The Royal Kingdom of Afghanistan approved his nomination a year after. Yet he would never forget the incident with an assertive subordinate.[10]

TOYING WITH NON-ALIGNMENT: FILIPINO SOLUTION TO FILIPINO PROBLEM

Whenever he went home since his days in London and Madrid, Guerrero would speak on international affairs to comment obliquely on Philippine foreign policy. Thus, before the Junior Chamber of Commerce (Jaycees) luncheon meeting in Manila, he spoke on the international situation in Asia in the context of what he called "the view from New Delhi" to provoke Filipino policymakers about the possibility of non-alignment.[11]

The struggle for Asia, he said, was easily dubbed as the struggle between India and China; whether Asia turned to communism or not depended on which socio-economic system — either the Indian or the Chinese — would be more effective in solving the manifold problems of its people. It was not "aggressive expansionism" that motivated the Chinese to invade India in 1962 but the frustration and disruption of India's economic development plan. The Chinese succeeded because the Indians were compelled to redirect their resources for economic projects to defence and security. There was no need for open warfare just to impose communism because the masses would clamour for it and even die for it if, in the case of India, the leadership failed to uplift them from poverty, he said, concluding that the "security gap" in Asia was no more than an "economic gap". This realization was not hidden from Washington or to the other rich countries in the generous economic assistance they showered on underdeveloped countries.[12]

"The view from New Delhi cannot be the same as that from Manila" Guerrero told the audience, for while the Philippines was in total alignment with Washington, Indian policy was, as one commentator had coined, "bi-alignment" — no longer non-aligned because it openly asked for economic and military aid from Washington and Moscow. Yet, he said, it was still non-alignment for India maintained its independence. He noted that the implementation of this policy was not easy, recounting how Prime Minister Gandhi faced criticisms of her new policy. The difficulties, however, were compensated by its achievements. India had the advantages of both worlds: Russian and American jets, tanks and ships, making India never dependent on any sole power for its security. On the other hand, the British, Germans and Russians were helping India build its steel mills and industrial complexes. Americans, Japanese and other member countries of the Aid India Club were giving generous financial aid.[13]

On the possibility that India would fall into the hands of Chinese Communists if the economic problems of its teeming millions were not solved, he quoted Jawaharlal Nehru, saying that communism did not strike a chord in the national feeling. With this backdrop and on the issue of Vietnam, he said Filipinos thought rigidly in terms of a bipolar world, either black or white with no in-between. Implicitly disagreeing with President Marcos' speech in the U.S. Congress committing the Philippines to the war, Guerrero subscribed to the view expressed by UN Secretary General U Thant that the Vietnamese problem was not ideological but one of national identity and survival. The view from New Delhi was also this;

that the solution to any Indian problem was neither an American nor a Russian solution but an Indian solution.[14]

EXPLORING INDIA

Before he flew back to India, Guerrero was interviewed about latest developments in Philippine diplomacy on television. Back in New Delhi, he met Indian Foreign Secretary T.N. Kaul to assure New Delhi about the upcoming Manila conference on Vietnam. President Marcos after his state visit to Washington where he pledged his support for U.S. President Lyndon Johnson's policy on Vietnam, prepared for the five-day conference to be held on 23–27 October 1966. Guerrero explained that the seven-nation summit — which included the United States as the chair, the Philippines, South Vietnam, Thailand, South Korea, New Zealand and Australia — was Asian in character and was gathered to think about plans for South Vietnam's economic and social development. It also aimed, he said, to discuss ways on how to strengthen the representative government in that country.[15]

New Delhi was a historic city that fascinated Guerrero. Situated on the Jamuna River, India's modern capital had a twin, the Old Delhi, both comprising the 573 square mile (1,484 sq km) Union Territory of Delhi. Eighteen years before the British decided to transfer the capital from Calcutta to this city in 1931, New Delhi was conceived as an expression of imperial grandeur with its tree-lined streets, parks, fountains and magnificent buildings. Old Delhi retained its ancient flavour with its narrow streets, crumbling walls and gates but still teeming with commercial life as an Indo-Islamic city. As modernity was creeping into the city of fewer than three million people with the building of residential and industrial enclaves, New Delhi was losing its character as a garden city.[16]

In any case, New Delhi continued to charm Guerrero and Annie. A number of historical places dotted its landscapes: Rashtrapati Bhavan, Chandni Chowk, a busy thoroughfare where great and exciting festival processions passed through this main road; Red Fort, a magnificent royal palace complex; Jama Masjid, the biggest mosque in the whole of India; Ashoka's Pillar, a tall column containing Ashoka's edicts; Qutb Minar, a tower where New Delhi could be viewed from the top; Humayun's tomb, a royal family's mausoleum; Parliament House, the building home to the Lok Sabha and the Rajya Sabha; and the Secretariat, a building complex of the Indian Government.[17]

A BRIDGE CALLED UN

Definitely, India was not New Delhi. Guerrero was to discover this in Varanasi, southeast of New Delhi, when the Lions Club invited him there by the end of October 1966 to speak on the twenty-first anniversary of the United Nations, his first speaking engagement as Philippine ambassador outside the capital. In his address at the Clarks Hotel, though admitting he had little to say about the United Nations that has not been uttered before, he tried to unravel the ills afflicting the organization. He saw the United Nation's impotence in the ongoing Vietnam crisis and also in the Suez Canal crisis. He realized that international relations were no longer relations between nation-states, the theory that founded the United Nations; rather, they had become ideological and party conflicts and relations, citing the rift between the USSR and the People's Republic of China. This kind of conflict, he felt, was not foreseen by the UN founders who were thinking of preventing clashes among different competing national interests.[18]

But the United Nations might justify its existence by becoming the bridge to reconcile the division between rich and poor countries through the United Nations Conference on Trade and Development (UNCTAD), first held in Geneva, then now in New Delhi. Having read some Indian legends of the city weeks before he arrived, Guerrero expressed his hope that "these two worlds may someday merge like your rivers Varana and the Asi, which sprang where the Goddess Durga cast away her warlike sword." He likened the gathering of 121 nations in the United Nations to the yearly pilgrimage made to the Ganges River, with India leading the nations "to the temples of justice and peace".[19]

BANQUETS AND STATE DINNERS

If Guerrero was not looking after administrative concerns, he and Annie would be attending banquets. One was given by the president of the Czechoslovak Socialist Republic in November 1966 held at Ashoka Hotel. When not at a banquet, he would be reading newspapers monitoring events at home. In mid-December, he caught an article mentioning his name. A senator exposed to the public an irregular transfer of land to a private corporation. It was a case he looked into back in Spain which he learned with regret had come to nought, as the private company came into possession of the 16,800 hectares of government property. Now, the good senator was lambasting the agency concerned for ineptitude. It was December and Christmas was fast approaching. Guerrero and Annie sent a number of personalized cards to the Home Office. Two of these cards were sent to the Protocol Office. As a matter of respect for a principled argument, he sent a card to the junior officer who stood up to him.[20]

The Guerreros attended state dinners in the "Malacañang of New Delhi" as Guerrero called the Rashtrapati Bhavan. He was dismayed that Indians never served hard drinks but only fruit juices but not Annie who was a non-alcoholic drinker. One evening while at a dinner, Guerrero and his colleagues were getting bored. Next to him was the French ambassador who told him, "All this juice … I'm getting dizzy." Beside him was Octavio Paz's French wife who said: "I'm very bored, and you know what I'm doing?" He said: "No, what are you doing?" The Ugandan ambassador who used to be a football player was in front of her. She replied: "I'm imagining what he looks like — naked!" Of course, diplomats like ordinary people talked about the most mundane to the most complex of things — the affairs of nations.[21]

Notes

1. Leon Ma. Guerrero, "The Philippines and India: Diplomacy for Peace", *STM*, 16 November 1952, pp. 6–7; Ajit Singh Rye, "A Survey of Philippine-India Relations in the Post-Independence Period", *Asian Studies* 6, no. 3 (December 1968): 271–85.
2. *OD 1955*, p. 35; *OD 1959*, p. 50; *OD 1963*, p. 61; *OD 1965*, p. 60; *OD 1966*, p. 86; *OD 1968*, p. 124; *Post Report 1967* (New Delhi: Embassy of the Philippines, 1967), pp. 1, 4.
3. Joaquin, "1974 and all that", p. 2; Leon Ma. Guerrero, "Votive Lights on a Dark River", *Prisoners of History*, pp. 25, 27–28; *Times of India*, 7 August 1966.
4. Guerrero, "The View from New Delhi", in *We Filipinos*, pp. 50–51.
5. "Presentation of Letter of Credence, 1 August 1966", in *LMGP*; *Times of India*, 2 August 1966; *MC*, 3 August 1966.
6. *Philippine Embassy in India Annual Report for the Fiscal Year 1966–1967* (hereafter cited as *Annual Report 1966–1967*) (New Delhi: Embassy of the Philippines, 1967), Annex a, pp. 1–4.
7. *Times of India*, 7 August 1966; "Invitation to India's Independence Day Celebration", in *LMGP*; Alegre and Fernandez, *Writer and his Milieu*, pp. 77–78.
8. *Post Report 1967*, pp. 1–3; Ambassador Juan A. Ona to DFA Tattlers, email, 20 January 1998; *Annual Report 1966–1967*, p. 8.
9. *MC*, 30 August 1966; *MT*, 1 September 1966; *The Diplomatist*, October 1966.
10. Ambassador Juan A. Ona to DFA Tattlers, email, 20 January 1998; *MT*, 8 November 1967; *DM*, 8 November 1967.
11. *MDB*, 23 September 1966; L.M. Guerrero, "The View from New Delhi", in *Prisoners of History*, pp. 47–56.
12. Ibid., pp. 47–49.

13. Ibid., pp. 49–52.
14. Ibid., pp. 52–56.
15. *MT*, 3 October 1966; *The Hindustan Times*, 20 October 1966.
16. *Post Report 1967*, pp. 8–10.
17. Ibid., pp. 11–14.
18. *Annual Report 1966–1967*, Annex b, pp. 1–8.
19. Ibid., Annex b, pp. 8–11.
20. "Various invitations to Leon Ma. Guerrero", in *LMGP*; *MDB*, 15 December 1966; Ambassador Juan A. Ona to DFA Tattlers, email, 20 January 1998.
21. Alegre and Fernandez, *Writer and his Milieu*, pp. 77–78.

19

"Diplomacy of Development" and Other Speeches

Philippine foreign policy was the subject of Guerrero's lecture delivered before the Indian Foreign Service Probationers in early January 1967, at the Indian School of International Studies at Sapru House in New Delhi. At the outset, he observed that although the Philippines and India had rather similar problems and aims, and both had shared the benefits of democratic processes, they had enunciated different foreign policies. Regarding the foreign policies of developing countries such as the Philippines and India, he noted that each country has to solve a diplomatic problem according to their unique circumstances. He coined here the term "diplomacy of development" that Philippine foreign policymakers would later adopt.[1]

Sources of Philippine foreign policy, he said, were uniquely different from the foreign policies of its Asian allies and neighbours. Neither inflexible nor unchanging, Philippine foreign policy was being re-examined, alluding to the latest pronouncements of President Marcos. It was a policy that was mostly concerned with Philippine relations with the United States, which he discussed by tackling the historical underpinnings of Philippine-American relations in a nutshell. The Philippines' anti-communist stance was the result of policies taken such as having American air and naval bases in the Philippines as well as the threat of communist rebellion. He did not believe that it was possible for the Philippines to have chosen a different path by severing ties with the United States and to start anew after the war since, unlike the Germans and the Japanese, the Filipinos still left in the farm without technical skills, were unable to industrialize.[2]

He discussed Philippine-American economic relations, particularly on the free trade, expiring in 1974. In an echo of his speech to the Manila Lions Club two years ago, Guerrero said that there was growing realization in the Philippines about the relevance of the parity rights, which aimed to help the Philippines build its shattered economy but never generated substantial American investments. Moreover, Filipinos realized that American assistance was never proportionate to Filipino loyalty and American aid was niggardly and less to the Philippines than to other countries. This kind of economic nationalism found its expression in the "Filipino First" policy. Guerrero said that it was incorrect to say that Philippine foreign policy was "veering away" from America. In fact, the Philippine Civic Action Group (PHILCAG), was sent to Vietnam "in an American war" out of "an historic necessity" as he put it, for the Philippines was desperate for foreign assistance. To sum it up, he said that while foreign policy should protect the national interest, there was a price to be paid for foreign aid when economic need outweighed the need for political independence, especially for Filipinos who were "prisoners of [their] history."[3]

SPEECHES, MORE SPEECHES

At Ashoka Hotel, Guerrero and Annie attended the banquet in late January 1967 given by the king and queen of Afghanistan to whom he would present his credentials in November. They entertained Narcing Reyes, the Philippine ambassador to Indonesia when he visited them at the embassy, introducing him to their friends in the diplomatic community and with Annie preparing delicious Filipino food for lunch. What Guerrero had missed in Madrid he found in abundance in New Delhi. In mid-March, he and Annie were invited for lunch by the governor of Maharashtra and Shrimati P.V. Cherian at Raj Bhavan in Bombay, the capital of a constituent province southwest of New Delhi.[4]

On the same day, he was invited to give a talk at the dinner-meeting of the Bombay Rotary Club at the Taj Mahal Hotel. Since he knew that after-dinner speeches would make people sleepy, fittingly, he chose to share the story of "The Conference that Fell Asleep" culled from the book of essays by an English writer, J.B. Priestley. As the story went, a summit conference was attended by leaders of the great powers to decide the fate of the world. Suddenly, one by one fell asleep for no apparent reason. Speeches were not heard as the world went on its normal business.[5]

Taking issue with Priestley's simplistic caricature of a peaceful world of sleeping leaders, Guerrero pointed out that in reality, human ambition would rush in to take their places. But far from being sources of conflicts themselves, leaders of the modern world contributed to the promotion of understanding in the world. Priestley's point was when follies among world leaders were put to sleep we can achieve a better world. To Guerrero, what stood in the way of greater world understanding was the predatory character of big and rich countries towards small and newly independent countries, alluding to the U.S. intervention in Vietnam and the cut-throat competition between the United States and USSR in the Cold War.[6]

As distinguished from the other two, he saw a means towards greater world understanding in the case of churches, away from their violent past, when they gathered and met together to reconcile in an ecumenical movement in religion. Still, international understanding was difficult to achieve even though the premier of USSR had met the Pope the previous year and the queen in Buckingham. He mentioned the U.S. involvement in the Vietnam War and the Chinese menace. But quoting Nehru's speech inscribed on two granite slabs at Buddha Jayanti Park in New Delhi, he said that cooperation in a conflict-ridden world was possible.[7]

In another gathering four days after the speech to the Bombay Rotary Club, Guerrero and Annie were the guests of honour at an international luncheon-meeting of the International Club of India at Hotel Ambassador, where members of the diplomatic corps and Indian businessmen were present. The president of the club, a former railway minister, welcomed and introduced him. In line with reducing dependence on the United States, Guerrero said, Indian businessmen had opportunities to export goods to the Philippines. The Philippines and India shared common problems and he promised that he would bring the two countries closer in trade and cultural cooperation.[8]

Indians were not the only ones receptive to his speeches. They were also read by his colleagues in the Foreign Service, in the Home Office. His sensational cables, with one read by amused Secretary Ramos and colleagues, were said to be "fantastic, terrific". Reyes, who recently visited him after reading his "brilliant and perceptive speech" in Bombay and "subtly needling report on 'The Diplomacy of Food'", wrote to him that he ought to be "in the center of national affairs". Chuckling while reading it, he remembered he was once in the "center of national affairs" but was sent to London, in exile, because of his too nationalist stance in Philippine foreign policy. Did he ever entertain the thought of going back, not to Arlegui but this time to Padre Faura? He was told by a special assistant to the secretary that he was being considered by many for the top post after Ramos. Guerrero really disliked politics but in May, he met his esteemed friend back in London, Vijaya Lakshmi Pandit who was now a politician, a member of the Lok Sabha and was to be conferred a Doctor of Laws degree by the UP.[9]

A VISIT TO TAJ MAHAL

India was so big that Guerrero could not let it go unexplored. One night, Annie and he drove to Agra to visit its most famous landmark — the Taj Mahal. Southeast of the capital, Agra was the capital city of the district of the same name. As they arrived at the site of the monumental tomb built by Shah Jahan for his wife Mumtaz Mahal, they were disappointed to find so many tourists and other people around. Leaving anxiously their shoes in the care of a child, they went inside the Taj with other chattering tourists, a guide with his flashlight used for looking at obscure inscriptions on the walls, and a tomb attendant who asked for a rupee for a religious incantation.[10]

They came back in the morning and felt it was better to go there by daylight. As they approached the Taj along one of the pools, they noticed a commotion in one of the side gardens. A group had gathered around something.

> We joined the group and, peering over heads and shoulders, saw a man lying on the swept path. Presently an old woman came running across the lawn, weeping and screaming, a ladle in her hand — for she had obviously been interrupted in the middle of some domestic task — and threw herself on her knees beside the body.

They learned that the dead man, a retired government clerk, regularly took a walk in the gardens of the Taj after breakfast and that he had suffered a heart attack. The woman was his wife, now a widow. "I was surprised," said Guerrero, "to find this incident incongruous; I felt it almost indecorous; for the curious thing about the Taj is that it does not have the atmosphere of death...." They continued touring the Taj with its domes and minarets and the garden beside the river. It was a visit worth remembering for the romantic couple.[11]

The visit to the Taj became a subject of Guerrero's conversation one evening with the Syrian Ambassador, Omar Abou-Riche, one of his few close acquaintances in India. A renowned Arabic poet whose verses were copied and reproduced all over the Middle East, he was three-time ambassador to India. He was not the only poet in the diplomatic corps, where intellectual and literary brilliance were common and ordinary as to give one "a formidable inferiority complex" as Guerrero once admitted. Abou-Riche told Guerrero that he really loved India. They were talking about the visit, particularly the surreal scene of a woman grieving over her husband, when Abou-Riche told him about his latest play on the Taj. It was a remarkable play; the Indian Government commissioned special paintings as illustrations of the published edition. The playwright-ambassador told him that the play was part historical and part fiction, starting with Shah Jahan grieving over his dead wife, promising to build her a tomb for her to be remembered. The fiction involved the construction of the Taj, which lasted for eighteen years, so that the emperor forgot what it had been intended for — a tomb for the empress. After the construction of the Taj, the emperor was again planning to build another on the opposite bank of the river. Thus, the secret of the Taj was that it was also a testimony to Shah Jahan's megalomania. Aurangzeb, his son, would rebel against him, imprisoning him in a prison-tower.[12]

THE IGNORANCE OF MR CHAUDHURI

In August 1967, Guerrero greeted with elation the Philippine participation in the founding of the Association of Southeast Asian Nations (ASEAN) in Bangkok, in line with the Philippine president's policy of orienting the country towards Asia. However, in New Delhi, as in London, Filipinos were unknown Asians and more often than not misrepresented in the press. It happened that while he was reading a daily at his desk in mid-October, he caught an article with slighting reference to the Philippines written by an Indian author whose books he had read all but one. Nirad C. Chaudhuri in "The Hindi-English Conflict" said that it was inappropriate to compare the continued use of English in India to the Philippines or the new African states, which had no original civilization of their own and if there were, it was derived from English, since giving up English would mean returning to headhunting or the kraal. In a letter addressed to the editor of the *Times of India*, Guerrero slammed Chaudhuri's ignorance about the Philippines. He said Chaudhuri needlessly insulted the Filipinos, whom he could not dismiss for they had the second-highest literacy rate after Japan. If the Indians were to renounce English, would they, he asked, go back to widow-burning? Despite his wide reading, he added, Chaudhuri could not even get to know the neighbouring islands.[13]

In refuting Chaudhuri, Guerrero made four main points. First, he said, the Philippine civilization was not derived from the English language. When English arrived with the American forces in 1898, Filipinos had established the first Asian nationalist revolution and the first Asian democratic republic. While he conceded that Spanish was the language of that republic, the language of mass propaganda was Tagalog. The nation formed was built from its Malay foundations under the influence of Spanish liberalism. Second, if anything could be said about Philippine civilization, it was derived from Spain and Spanish but on which it did not depend. Third, Filipinos had a high degree of culture centuries before the coming of the Spaniards as manifested in the many languages preserved and spoken in the country with their own rich literatures. Fourth, the use of language — in the case of the Philippines, English, Spanish or Tagalog — for practical reasons was considered to be the means, not the foundation, of Philippine national culture. The continued use of English as a medium of instruction, he said, was a pragmatic answer to the scant resources that the government had, for priority was given to economic and social development. At the end of his letter, he asked for an apology from Chaudhuri for his "uncharacteristic display of the snobbery of ignorance" to all "unknown Filipinos" including himself.[14]

PHILIPPINE AND INDIAN DEMOCRACIES COMPARED

Whether an apology was issued or not, Guerrero delivered a talk on democracy in Asia in the light of Philippine experience to the Indian Council of World Affairs in Udaipur, a city of Southern Rajasthan in mid-November 1967 re-echoed before the North Ahmedabad Junior Chamber in Gujarat. It happened after his presentation of credentials to King Mahendra of Nepal in Kathmandu in late October in which he underscored the commonalities between the Philippines and Nepal in terms of "national objectives of peace, the safeguarding of our frontiers, the diversification of our trade and social and economic development of our people". Although calling attention to different types of governments in Asia, he disabused his audience into thinking that a constitutional representative form of government was the only way for Asia. Western experiences could not be the sole criterion for Asians who had different traditions and institutions, culture and history that each might evolve a form of government or democracy relevant to its experiences.[15]

Comparing Philippine democracy with India, Guerrero described Philippine political culture with unerring analysis relevant even to the present. Philippine political parties, he said, were not political parties in the conventional sense of having specific political programmes or principles as contending parties could form temporary alliances for electoral purposes. In

India after independence, parties were splintered into the left and the right and other political persuasions. The majority party in the Philippines was split into two not due to ideological but personally motivated reasons: the struggle between two politicians led to the founding of the Liberal Party. An ideological party might have been in the offing, he said, but became a victim of state-sponsored harassment. No true political parties had arisen because the people did not feel any need or did not understand it. Individuals could not think of the collective interest or beyond their personal interest because of personal, parochial and patriarchal politics. Issues in Philippine elections, as in the first, were personal, not principles or platforms. Political opportunism was rampant, for switching parties when a party was about to lose power was not condemned.[16]

Unlike in India where political power rested on the prime minister elected in a parliament, in the Philippines — a unitary state with a presidential form of government — all authority and power flowed from the president, unlike in India where a chief minister of state could exercise executive powers. The Philippine president, the great dispenser of patronage, must be attended to by interested parties and in turn, he must keep their loyalty. A presidential candidate running for election with his presidential programme as his vision for the nation, must not antagonize other sectors for he must embrace a coalition of interests. Guerrero saw in this system both advantages and disadvantages. It had kept the country united but spawned demagogues and charlatans. In an effort to satisfy the interests of all and careful not to antagonize anyone, the government was likely to produce a slapdash programme. Corruption was endemic; favours were more important than political principles. Violence was resorted to because one's economic well-being depended on the political victory of one's patron.[17]

Democracy in Asia differed, Guerrero said, because every democracy was a reflection of its people's desires. When all forms of government failed, when ideology failed, it was a good thing in democracy that people still retained their right to change their leaders. According to an Indian tale set in the ruins of Chittor, a certain Queen Padmini lived in a palace by the lake. Her beauty captivated an emperor who begged to have a glimpse of her in a tower but falling in love, he stormed the palace but the queen threw herself into the flames of the burning castle rather than be with him. Guerrero equated democracy with the queen by the lake: "It seems to me that we in Asia have also fallen in love with the beauties of democracy, as we have glimpsed them in the mirror of the Western world. But we must know of democracy more than a brief and a distant image..."[18]

Notes

1. *Annual Report 1966-1967*, Annex c, p. 1.
2. Ibid., Annex c, pp. 1-6.
3. Ibid., Annex c, pp. 6-11. See also Guerrero, "Prisoners of History", in *Prisoners of History*, pp. 13-23.
4. "Various invitations to Leon Ma. Guerrero"; Narciso Reyes to Leon Ma. Guerrero, 4 April 1967, in *LMGP*.
5. *Free Press Journal (Bombay)*, 15 March 1967; *Annual Report 1966-1967*, Annex d, p. 1.
6. Ibid., Annex d, pp. 2-8.
7. Ibid., Annex d, pp. 8-11.
8. *The Sunday Standard (Bombay)*, 19 March 1967.
9. Narciso Reyes to Leon Ma. Guerrero, 4 April 1967 and Mariano C. Ruiz to Leon Ma. Guerrero, 20 June 1967, *LMGP*; Lourdes Rye, "Philippines-India Bilateral Relations (1950-1980)" (MA thesis, University of the Philippines, 1990), Appendix C2.
10. L.M. Guerrero, "The Secret of Taj Mahal", in *Prisoners of History*, pp. 57-58.
11. Ibid., pp. 58-59.
12. Ibid., pp. 59-61. See also Guerrero, "The Secret of Taj Mahal", *STM*, 6 August 1967, pp. 6, 7.
13. *MDB*, 17 October 1967; Leon Ma. Guerrero, "Letter to the *Times of India*" typescript in *LMGF*.
14. Ibid.
15. *The Rising Nepal*, 23 October 1967; *Gujarat Herald*, 18 November 1967; Guerrero, "Democracy in Asia: Our Lady of the Lake" in *Prisoners of History*, pp. 29-31.
16. Ibid., pp. 34-38.
17. Ibid., pp. 39-43.
18. Ibid., pp. 43-46.

20

The Foreign Policy Rescuer and Again, Critic

As in London and Madrid, in between his work as ambassador, Guerrero was able to finish the research on Philippine church history he started while he was still in Madrid, where he had sought the help of Spanish priests. De la Costa, who was now the Provincial Superior of the Philippine Province of the Society of Jesus, invited him to write the article to be included in a compilation of discursive essays — a belated contribution to the fourth centenary of Christianity in the Philippines. It dealt with the contrasting religious lives of two Spanish priests after the outbreak of the revolution.[1]

At about this time, Guerrero contemplated editing and publishing a monthly for the first time, aimed for distribution in India and other diplomatic posts. After a talk with his colleagues, his poet-friend Abou-Riche suggested the title *Philippine Approaches* subtitled *A Monthly Review of Writing in the Philippines (Fiction Essays, Poetry, Politics, History, Economics)*. It was to make its debut in January 1968. Due to limited funds, the magazine was published bi-monthly. Perhaps it was the first of its kind in the entire Philippine diplomatic establishment that it received a special citation from the Manila Rotary Club during its Second Annual Journalism Awards, citing its role in promoting the works of Filipino writers and artists to people in foreign lands.[2]

ASIAN BLOC, UNCTAD AND ISO

In January 1968, Guerrero received a letter from Lopez, now the permanent representative to the United Nations in New York and concurrent ambassador to the United States, who asked him to seek Indian support for his candidature for chairmanship of the First Committee in the United Nations. Guerrero went to the Indian official at the Indian Foreign Ministry with an *aide memoire* explaining the position of the Philippines on the case. Reacting rather guardedly, the Indian official thought that a decision on the matter could not be reached too early though he understood the necessity of announcing the candidature as early as possible. He was not confident that Lopez would get elected on the basis of the Asian group alone. Having no official instructions from Manila, Guerrero left telling the official to keep in touch with him. He relayed all these to Lopez, including the matter about the head of the UN desk at the Indian Foreign Ministry who approached the head of the Philippine Mission to the UN in Switzerland to support his re-election to the Advisory Committee on Budgetary Questions. The dilemma was that Lopez's deputy chief of mission in the United Nations was also running for the same position. Guerrero's advice to Lopez was: "You should be the best judge whether your candidature will be served by Mr. Jimenez's withdrawal in favour of Mr. Singh or by maintaining the Philippine candidature at least for the time being."[3]

Aside from Lopez's candidacy, which entailed the support of India to strengthen Philippine relations with the Asian bloc in the United Nations, the other matter which Guerrero attended to was UNCTAD. Reporting on his attendance to the session, he believed that "the progress of UNCTAD II does not give much rise to optimism." The Philippines co-chaired with India UNCTAD II held in New Delhi from February to March. During a plenary session in a successful attempt to protest the apartheid policy in South Africa, Guerrero took the chair before the South African delegate could speak and addressed the remaining delegates who did not join the mass walkout that his country also shared the feelings against apartheid. During the conference, Guerrero succeeded in signing a trade agreement with India leading to the arrival of a twenty-five-man delegation from the Philippines to explore industrial joint ventures with the Indians. As he explained to Lopez: "We are in a peculiar position since the general system of [trade] preferences is bound to complicate our negotiations with the USA for a trade agreement replacing the Laurel-Langley Agreement." UNCTAD II adopted a resolution recognizing the "unanimous agreement in favour of the early establishment of a mutually acceptable system of generalized non-reciprocal and non-discriminatory preferences which would be beneficial to the developing countries." Guerrero was right because under the resolution, the United States could not be granted trade preferences on a reciprocal basis the way Philippine-U.S. trade relationship was conducted under the present agreement.[4]

Towards the middle of the year, the Home Office instructed Guerrero to go to Geneva to attend the International Sugar Conference. His attendance to that conference was auspicious for it finally arrived at the 1968 International Sugar Agreement establishing the International Sugar Organization (ISO). For this reason, he urged for its ratification by the Philippine Government as it would benefit the country by the increase of Philippine sugar in the world market and the increase of the Philippine export entitlement to 60,000 tonnes annually. Later, upon the instructions of the Home Office, he went to London to attend the inauguration of the new International Sugar Council. Reports and other communications about the conference and the meeting were as usual sent to Padre Faura.[5]

SABAH: TO BANGKOK IN A RESCUE MISSION

In March 1968 the Jabidah Massacre, in which agents supposedly trained to infiltrate Sabah for the Oplan *Merdeka* were killed, was leaked to the media. The controversy had put Philippine-Malaysia relations in another shaky state of affairs following the severance of their ties in 1963, re-established in 1967. While Malaysia called for an international inquiry and expressed concern to the United Nations, Secretary Ramos expressed the Philippine intention of going back to the negotiating table. Back in Manila, Lopez departed from his boss, calling on Malaysia to submit the dispute to the World Court and arguing that as long as it was unresolved, the issue would upset Philippine-Malaysia relations. Malaysia agreed to have conversation with the Philippine delegation in Bangkok, ostensibly to settle the dispute in June.[6]

In New Delhi, Guerrero watched the developments in Bangkok. The Philippine delegation was instructed to discuss modes of settling the dispute but must press for the settlement of the claim in the World Court. On the other hand, the Malaysian delegation was seeking clarification of the claim. The two delegations met in Bangkok but distrust and suspicion clouded the atmosphere during the negotiation. As the talks progressed, little was achieved. Both refused to yield on procedural matters. The Filipinos suspected foul play when the telegraph and telephone communications with Manila in the Philippine Embassy in Bangkok broke down. The Philippine delegation suggested that the proceedings be tape recorded, which the Malaysian panel objected to but both agreed that the proceedings be transcribed, with the transcription submitted to both governments only.[7]

Stalemate happened when both parties, lacking in agreement, were too careful not to insinuate something with what they had said. The Philippine delegation suffered from the sudden departure of one of its members leaving for Manila because of the death of his brother. Then another became sick because of stomach problem. As the proceedings came to substantive matters, the Philippine delegation insisted that all questions be written and submitted in advance. A recess was declared. Members of the Philippine delegation flew home for documents. By the last day of June, both sides were becoming hopeless until a breakthrough occurred when the Malaysian delegation agreed that after the clarification, they would discuss how to settle the claim regardless of their respective assessment of each other's position. On 8 July, President Marcos summoned and informed the Malaysian ambassador that the talks be recessed without a definite date of resumption. The Malaysian responded two days later that the claim had been suspended long enough and they would like to state their position, but were prepared to resume at a later date. Marcos said the Philippines would like to state its position too and preferred a post-election meeting be arranged after November 1969.[8]

Meanwhile, Guerrero received instructions "belatedly" from the Foreign Office to go to Bangkok to beef up the panel. Before he flew to Bangkok, he studied the pertinent documents for a statement on the Philippine position on the claim. When the editorial of the *Times of India* rebuked the Philippines for pursuing the claim, Guerrero took his pen to write a rejoinder debunking the allegations and pointing out the solid documentary evidences on the Philippine claim. The Philippine delegation was boosted by the arrival of Florentino Feliciano, an international law expert, carrying with him conciliatory message from the president. Guerrero and Press Secretary José Aspiras who was sent to improve the image of Filipino delegation, arrived. As soon as he arrived on 9 July, Guerrero issued a belligerent statement calling the Malaysians "the forced heirs and puppets of British imperialists and neocolonialists".[9]

Two days later, at a press conference luncheon, Guerrero further articulated his views on the legality and validity of the Philippine claim as against Malaysia's accusations and allegations. That he had studied the documents pertinent to the claim was very evident in his exposition. The contract signed between the Sulu Sultanate and the two adventurers was a lease and nothing more. The British North Borneo Company assumed no sovereign powers for it remained with the sultan. Under the agreements with the United States, the sultan did not lose his sovereignty on his territories including Sabah. Upon the withdrawal of the American Government in 1946, Sulu's sovereignty over Sabah by implication was transferred to the new Philippine republic. The British annexation and the transfer of Sabah to the Federation of Malaysia was illegal, quoting in his opening Francis

Burton Harrison, former governor general, who denounced the British unilateral act as "an act of political aggression" against the Philippines. Narrating how the Philippine Government reacted to the annexation up to the creation of Malaysia, he insisted on submitting the claim to the World Court.[10]

The Malaysians found an excuse to break off the talks two days after the Permanent Secretary for Foreign Affairs Tan Sri Ghazali Bin Shafie, head of the Malaysian delegation, made a statement. Ghazali condemned the Philippine delegation for what his delegation saw as a reversal of an earlier commitment to engage in another round of clarification, which the Filipinos had thought was over. Raising questions he thought were insufficiently answered by the Philippine panel, like when and how had the sultan exercise sovereignty over the area and when and how had the Philippine Government acquire sovereignty over Sabah, Ghazali maintained that the claim was baseless and unrealistic and he rejected it, adding that the Malaysian Government was willing to cooperate with the Philippines on economic and security terms but the pursuit of the claim would destroy this cooperation.[11]

The following day, the Philippine delegation through Guerrero and Feliciano replied in the presence of the Malaysian delegation. Guerrero retorted that from the very beginning he discerned the Malaysians were not serious and sincere. Pointing to the statement made, he said the whole clarification was pointless for in fact, the Malaysians already had answers to their questions. Since they had a "predetermined conclusion" that the claim had no legal basis, he said, how long the clarification would take did not matter. He revealed that the Philippine panel was ready to issue a preliminary reply, but the Malaysian delegation misled the press that they were going to discuss the modes of settlement so that they would print the story, which the press did and thus deceived the Philippine delegation. Since they had observed Malaysian "precedents of unscrupulousness" that anything they said was the opposite of what they were planning to do, he said they were not surprised by the turn of events.[12]

The Philippine delegation was bound to reject the unwarranted rejection Guerrero said. He stated that the aim of the Bangkok talks was to implement the provisions of the joint communiqué issued by the heads of both governments, which were to clarify the Philippine claim and discuss the means of settling it. He questioned the authority of the Malaysian representative in rejecting the claim, calling Ghazali's attention to the five agreements which both governments were bound to consider, enumerating them one by one. Finally, he informed Ghazali that his action provoked wide condemnation in the Philippines, with Congress calling for diplomatic rupture with Malaysia and thus imperiling the stability of ASEAN, suggesting to Ghazali to rethink his stance.[13]

The Malaysian delegation did not reconsider. After Feliciano had point by point demolished their legal objections to the Philippine claim, the Malaysians asked the Philippine delegation if there were "other matters of mutual concern" or anything else to add, which Filipinos had not since the aim of the conference was really to find means of settling the claim, they left the room. As Guerrero put it, "the Bangkok talks came to a close."[14]

The aftermath of the failed Bangkok talks was immediate and expected. At the Council of State meeting in Malacañang, Marcos convened top officials of the government including Guerrero to discuss the next move. On 20 July, the Foreign Office sent a note to the Malaysian ambassador listing the "solemn agreements" and stated that the Malaysian delegation did not have the competence to do what it did in Bangkok. It also said that the Philippines was "deeply aggrieved" by the Malaysian rejection to have another round of negotiations. It also announced the withdrawal of the Philippine ambassador and its staff from its embassy in Kuala Lumpur. By September, Guerrero was back in India but still waiting for further developments on the matter. Marcos later signed the so-called Annexation Law delineating the baselines of Philippine territorial sea around Sabah as part of its dominion and sovereignty. The Malaysians abrogated the Anti-Smuggling Pact with the Philippines and recalled its ambassador from Manila.[15]

RIZAL FOR THE FAUSTIAN GENERATION

After the Bangkok talks, Guerrero went back to managing the affairs in the embassy. It was his third trip when he accepted the invitation to talk on Rizal Day for its Second Annual Rizal Lecture in December 1968. Under the auspices of the National Historical Commission whose head now was no other than his sister Chitang, he would deliver one of the three lectures held at the Raja Sulayman Theater at the Rizal Shrine. Foreign Affairs Secretary-designate Carlos P. Romulo who replaced Ramos was the guest of honour at the commission's programme.

Guerrero's lecture began with a draft of a three-act play in which he made Rizal alive running for the presidency but hastened to add in his speech that he was not referring to any particular election year, an obvious reference to the coming elections the following year. In the second act, Rizal ran for the presidency facing all sorts of black propaganda — his age, his citizenship, payment of taxes, immoral relations with Josephine — resulting in a poor showing in the elections, the last among the seven presidential candidates. Guerrero was suggesting that Rizal could not bear the electoral vagaries. But Rizal was still relevant to the times although he might not have prescriptions for the pressing national issues.[16]

Guerrero's main point was Rizal's political philosophy, which he found in Rizal's *Fili* when the dying Simuon asked Padre Florentino what was to be done. "Endure and work" was the reply. Here, he found Rizal's political message, his philosophy of *pagtitiis*. He wondered if this message was acceptable to the present generation whom he called "Faustian", meaning materialistic and less spiritual. The generation which suffered the Japanese Occupation was a case of Rizal's concept of *pagtitiis*. But Rizal and the present generation of hippies had something in common — escapism. He found Rizal very Faustian in his sense of ambivalence as manifested in his life. Rizal was Faustian, too, because he defied conformity, questioned existing beliefs and dogmas, and rejected his own counsel of resignation. For the present Faustian generation, Guerrero commended Rizal. A member of the audience, however, noticed that the Bangkok Talks celebrity "kept mumbling, and lowering his voice to the point of unintelligibility at climactic points."[17]

ADVOCATING RELATIONS WITH SOCIALIST COUNTRIES: FILIPINOS MUST TAKE CARE OF THEMSELVES

A few days later in January 1969, rumoured to be the Philippine's next ambassador to the United Nations and no longer afraid to speak his mind on foreign policy, Guerrero spoke before the Manila Overseas Press Club on the opening of Philippine relations to socialist countries. He was reluctant and uneasy at first, knowing that the subject would invite all kinds of prejudice.[18]

In any case, he knew the exciting phase that Philippine diplomacy was undergoing under President Marcos. Marcos believed that the Philippines must coexist with Communist China, and he lifted the travel ban to communist countries. A congressional mission travelled to the USSR and, in the Enverga Report, recommended the opening of trade relations with socialist countries. In October 1968, Marcos approved a Philippine Chamber of Commerce mission to Moscow to find direct trade links with the USSR. In November, Marcos had intimated to the press that he was considering the opening of relations with Communist China. Opposition from rabid anti-communist sectors was heard against this new foreign policy orientation.[19]

Romulo, recently named the new head of Padre Faura, spoke of a new foreign policy that would be "courageous", "friendly" and "free" but Guerrero, intrigued about the word "free", told of a story of an American marine from Vietnam who found a not exactly free but reasonable Filipina in Angeles; that allusion meant that Philippine foreign policy was no longer willing to give away assets but it was prepared to be reasonable. He could not understand the fear and apprehension of some when they heard that the Philippine Government would follow an independent foreign policy. The Philippines, he said, had always had an independent foreign policy of its own, although it sometimes did not have much of a choice, citing that in 1946 the Philippines could have declined to sign the bases and other military agreements or could have refused to amend the Constitution to give way to the parity rights, but it was not ready to face the challenge of independence. An independent foreign policy was not really independent since it must deal with an interdependent world. Simply, an independent foreign policy as enunciated by the president through his secretary of Foreign Affairs meant the pursuit of national interests. Quoting Romulo that the Philippines should seek to avoid over-dependence on any country in any way, and that Philippine foreign policy would only promote Filipino interests, Guerrero added that the latter was a slogan that Filipinos must nevertheless always be reminded of.[20]

After clarifying the word "socialist" as countries controlled by communist countries, Guerrero said that the Philippines had relations with almost all of them because almost all were members of the United Nations where Filipino delegates were dealing with their communist representatives. He went on to appreciate Romulo's repeal of the regulation forbidding Filipinos from making any contact with communist diplomats as "a timely acceptance of realities", referring to Foreign Service Circular (FSC) 977 repealed by FSC 1-69 or the "Relations of Philippine Diplomatic Officers with their Counterparts". Relations with these countries then would be bilateral in terms of trade and the exchange of diplomatic representations "though not necessarily".[21]

Regarding China, he disagreed with Romulo that opening relations with them depended on that country's attitude. In a sense, he was saying that much of it depended on Filipinos, too. In the case of China with its current state of embassies being sacked and diplomats being beaten, he doubted if Peking would agree to opening relations with the Philippines and for the time being, it needed to be postponed. President Marcos was amenable to opening relations with the socialist countries of Eastern Europe, leaving the USSR for further study. Quoting Romulo once again, who said that once legal obstacles were removed by the Senate, the question was one of implementation but nobody would know how as this could be learned only from experience. He saw the answer in the approval of coconut oil as a trial export to Bulgaria. For many years, there were repeated calls to diversify Philippine markets to improve the Philippines' bargaining position. By opening relations with socialist countries, he said the Philippines would achieve this, open up new markets, and reduce "over-dependence" on one or two countries. Yet it would not be easy, as he related his experiences in international sugar conferences dealing with them, for countries such as the USSR and Cuba, were tough bargainers.[22]

He found it amusing that certain Filipinos in their timidity still saw in every Communist trader or some other a threat to Philippine democratic institutions. He might have remembered that when he was in Spain, President Macapagal did not allow the Russian and Yugoslavian basketball teams to enter the Philippines. It would be in the Philippines' national interest to sell abaca and cordage and to obtain loans from these socialist countries, but Guerrero was quick to say that Filipinos would not know until they had tried. He cited countries that maintained trade agreements with Socialist countries in a number of ways not limited to government-to-government agreements. Spain, he said, did it "through a special banking arrangement", India "through special rupee accounts" and it also traded with Yugoslavia and United Arab Republic.[23]

How to bargain towards our advantage depended on Filipinos. If it was in the national interest to open relations and exchange missions, for example, with Yugoslavia, he asked amid the communist paranoia whether or not Filipinos were ignorant, faithless in their own institutions, their intelligence agents clumsy to allow a Communist embassy to endanger the government. Thailand and Malaysia, he said, maintained relations with the USSR. In India, he observed that aid and trade with the Soviet Union had increased a hundred-fold, but he believed that the Communist Party which was splintered into three groups, was incapable of seizing power. Afghanistan and Nepal, which he noticed was more vulnerable and had more explosive problems than the Philippines, could nevertheless afford to maintain relations with socialist countries. Why could the Philippines not? To this, he was sure of the reason. It was because the Filipinos lacked the nerve to believe that they could take care of themselves, a lack of self-confidence that made them believe they could not survive on their own.[24]

Notes

1. Leon Ma. Guerrero, "Spanish friars in exodus", *PFP*, 9 December 1967, pp. 54, 56, 58, 60, 137–41. Also published as "Nozaleda and Pons: Two Spanish Friars in Exodus", *Studies in Philippine Church History*, edited by Gerald H. Anderson (Ithaca and London: Cornell University Press, 1969), pp. 172–202.
2. *Philippine Approaches: A Monthly Review of Writing in the Philippines* 1, no. 1 (January 1968): 1; 2, no. 1–2 (January–February 1969): 1, 7.
3. Leon Ma. Guerrero to Salvador P. Lopez, 22 February 1968, *SPLP*.
4. Ibid.; *Annual Report 1966–1967*, p. 8; Rye, "Philippine-India Bilateral Relations", Appendix B1; Abdulqawi Yusuf, *Legal Aspects of Trade Preferences for Developing States: A Study in the Influence of Development Needs on the Evolution of International Law* (Brill, 1982), p. 81; *The Hindustan Times*, 23 February 1968. UNCTAD II complicated the negotiations because the United States was unwilling to give up its preferential trade and investment status in the Philippines. The negotiations for a new treaty extended to more than a decade when agreement was reached in September 1979. See Ingles, *Philippine Foreign Policy*, pp. 51–54.
5. *Annual Report 1966–1967*, p. 8; *Sunday Times*, 19 January 1969.
6. Lela Garner Noble, *Philippine Policy Toward Sabah: A Claim to Independence* (Tucson, Arizona: published for the Association for Asian Studies by the University of Arizona Press, 1977), pp. 165–69; Benigno Aquino Jr, "Jabidah! Special Forces of Evil?", in *A Garrison State in the Make and other Speeches* (Benigno S. Aquino Jr Foundation, 1985), pp. 43–60.
7. Noble, *Philippine Policy Toward Sabah*, pp. 169, 171.
8. Ibid., pp. 171–72.
9. *Annual Report 1966–1967*, p. 8; as quoted in Noble, *Philippine Policy Toward Sabah*, p. 172; *MC*, 8 and 9 July 1968. After the Jabidah exposé, Malaysians called on their allies, New Zealand and Australia, to send their warships near Philippine-Malaysia borders. The British were supportive of the Malaysians, the beneficiaries of their project unlike the Americans who stood neutral over the case, drawing bitter Filipino resentment. See Gleeck, *Third Philippine Republic*, p. 353.
10. L.M. Guerrero, "The Right to Sabah: The Philippine Case", in *Prisoners of History*, pp. 111–25. See also *MT*, 18 and 19 July 1968 for the text of the speech.
11. Noble, *Philippine Policy Toward Sabah*, pp. 173–74.
12. L.M. Guerrero, "The Right to Sabah: Reply to Malaysia", in *Prisoners of History*, pp. 127–30.
13. Ibid., pp. 130–33.
14. Ibid., p. 133; Noble, *Philippine Policy Toward Sabah*, p. 174. See also *MT*, 24 July 1968 for text of the speech.
15. Noble, *Philippine Policy Toward Sabah*, pp. 175, 181, 191–92.
16. *DM*, 28 December 1968; L.M. Guerrero, "Rizal for President", in *Prisoners of History*, pp. 159–68.
17. Ibid., pp. 170–76; Jose Lacaba, "Discovering Rizal", *PFP*, 11 January 1969, p. 67. See also L.M. Guerrero, "Rizal and the Faustian generation", *MT*, 1 January 1969, p. 12A and 2 January 1969, no page indicated in *LMGF*.

18. *MT*, 8 January 1969; *MC*, 8 January 1969; L.M. Guerrero, "A Crisis of Confidence" typescript, *LMGF*.
19. Kessler, "Development Diplomacy", pp. 34–35, 229, 232, 234–35, 252.
20. L.M. Guerrero, "A Crisis of Confidence", pp. 1–3.
21. Ibid., pp. 3–4.
22. Ibid., pp. 4–5.
23. Ibid., p. 6.
24. Ibid.; See also L.M. Guerrero, "A Crisis of Confidence", in *Prisoners of History*, pp. 177–87.

21

The Diplomat as Efficient Intellectual-Bureaucrat

Three months later in April 1969, Guerrero hit the news. A daily reported that "Guerrero would scrap annual report". The news was based on the release of his "anti-report" by his sympathetic colleagues in the Foreign Affairs Department, which was actually written in September the previous year. Instead of submitting the usual annual report which he dutifully made his staff do in Madrid, this time in India, he was fed up with it. For his first three years in India, he submitted not an annual report but an "anti-report" because "it is a report against traditional reports ... a report designed to end this type of reports", contrary to the law requiring each embassy and consulate to annually submit 300 copies for the various offices of the government with twenty earmarked for the office of the president. How could he scrap the annual report when he was not authorized to do so? But he did — in New Delhi and perhaps even to his subsequent posts. It was a waste of money and effort costing the government which had seventy-six diplomatic missions. No one read or would read it except the employee assigned to the task or a newspaper reporter or columnist, he argued.[1]

He did not object to the other reports required of each post such as the Post Report, monthly financial reports and quarterly inspection reports. He found it amusing that annual reports recorded the calls the chief of mission did on his colleagues and the trifling details of the visits made by various VIPs. Other contents of the report such as summaries of consular services rendered, financial statements, number of diplomatic notes, telegrams, letters and other communications sent and received, which he described as "the nadir of bureaucratic small-mindedness" as well as requests and recommendations could be taken into account in other reports sent to the Home Office.[2]

Asked in a news conference about it, Romulo said unsmilingly: "Who says nobody reads the annual reports? I do!" Romulo in the following weeks sent Guerrero to London as the Philippine representative to the International Sugar Council's Special Hardship Relief Committee. Based on Article 44 of the council's constitution, the committee granted special concessions to the Philippines and Indonesia. All of the forty signatory countries were subjected to quota limitations but developing countries could have 60,000 tonnes each year with prior approval.[3]

TRANSLATING MABINI

From London, Guerrero returned to translating Apolinario Mabini's less than seventy-page *La Revolución Filipina* commissioned by the National Historical Commission, and finished it a week after May Day "under great pressure of time and official business, and may have suffered in consequence". Similar to his earlier translations, he translated whenever possible Spanish idioms to their closest English counterparts rather than translating them literally, using the Spanish text of Mabini's work published by the Bureau of Printing and edited by Teodoro M. Kalaw. He did not tamper much with the work as other translators were wont to do for he had "kept Mabini's paragraphing and emphasis". He also inserted in italics the variants noted by Kalaw in the several copies made by Mabini of his own work included in the 1931 edition. Kalaw noted that Mabini had translated his work into English. Curious about it, Guerrero tried to locate it but failed. In between his translation, Guerrero read Mabini's Guam memoirs and regretted that a brief biography could not accompany his translation. What he did was to include in his translator's note the notes made by Mabini himself in his memoirs.[4]

His translation of Mabini's work displayed his fascination with the "thin gray paralyzed philosopher", the phrase which he had used to describe Mabini in a pre-war article. In that article, he could not hide his admiration for Mabini's statesmanship. He had already made a reference to Mabini's *La Revolución Filipina* when he alluded to it as "a philosophical history of the Revolution revealing principles that might have guided him [Mabini] in office." His interest in Mabini was no coincidence, for the house where he lived as a young boy in pre-war Ermita was located at Mabini Street. Now translating Mabini's work, he maintained his deep affection for the "paralytic premier" who "lived for his country" when he wrote:

> Righteous, perceptive and farsighted beyond the measure of his contemporaries and successors, the very embodiment of the intellectual in a revolution, he was not intransigent as he was thought to be ... Among the Filipinos, he was one of the few who knew what it was all about.[5]

THE NEW CHANCERY

It was at the new chancery in the diplomatic enclave at Nyuya Marg, Ckarak Yapuki, the chancery that Guerrero was proud of, that in due time would be "the most beautiful not only in New Delhi but in the Philippines", where he would entertain his colleagues and friends. By August 1968 the embassy edifice was nearing its completion so that the following year they could move to the new embassy compound. The excitement over its completion induced Guerrero to order his finance and property officer to burn all furniture, equipment, files, books and records before moving to the newly-built chancery so that "everything must be new!" Was it either a form of superstition or extravagance or both? On both sides of the imposing granite stairs he ordered his gardener to plant cypress trees.[6]

Inaugurated in September 1969, a reception was held there in honour of Romulo who headed the Gandhi Centennial Committee created by President Marcos. Prime Minister Gandhi even broke protocol to attend the gathering. Romulo's visit resulted in the signing of a cultural agreement between the Philippines and India providing for the exchange of books, periodicals, and films; exchange of professionals, scholars and other artists; and the creation of a cultural association and scholarship grants. The agreement was preceded by a technical cooperation on the peaceful use of atomic energy signed in Manila in March.[7]

At the new chancery Annie hosted parties until she became ill. In late November Guerrero brought her home for medical tests and treatment because of a recurring influenza that turned out to be terminal cancer. The unexpected visit raised speculations in Padre Faura that he would be appointed either secretary or undersecretary of Foreign Affairs in line with the president's nationalistic foreign policy. When asked regarding these speculations, he said that he wanted to be left alone in his New Delhi post. In addition, Romulo was the newly appointed secretary early that year.[8]

SYMINGTON REPORT: RE-EXAMINING
PHILIPPINE-U.S. SECURITY RELATIONSHIP

Guerrero stayed for less than a month attending to Annie until after the elections that wasted the Philippine Treasury with Marcos winning his bid for re-election. The complexion of Philippine-U.S. security relations changed radically when U.S. President Richard Nixon announced the reduction of U.S. military presence in Asia, leading Marcos to withdraw the PHILCAG from Vietnam in November 1969. In light of this development, Guerrero spoke in late December on "The Symington Report". Named after Senator Stuart Symington who chaired the Senate Subcommittee on United States Security Arrangement and Commitments Abroad, Symington conducted hearings on the conduct of the war in Vietnam, particularly the role of Asian countries, with the Philippines the first to be examined. The four-day hearing beginning on the last day of September was held behind closed doors as senior U.S. military officers and diplomats revealed widespread corruption, crime and smuggling in the Philippines impugning the Marcos administration. Later the transcript consisting of 1,146 pages was published and released after the elections but sanitized without any references to how Marcos ruled the country and some confidential military matters. This was the report that Guerrero had taken hold of and subjected to his analysis in relation to Philippine foreign policy.[9]

The crux of the speech focused on the credibility of the United States of America in insuring protection for the Philippines. Based on the text of the transcript pertinent to Philippine-U.S. security particularly the testimonies of American civilian and military officers detailed in the Philippines, Guerrero came up with a critical appraisal of the American guarantee. Based on the selected transcript of the first part, the Americans, he said, viewed the threat of Communist China to the Philippines to be minor, but if the Chinese were to develop nuclear missiles, then that would become "quite considerable". He said that the U.S. Armed Forces in the Philippines could not defend Manila from nuclear attack; that if the bases in the Philippines were attacked, the United States would be automatically involved; that the Russian threat was considered to be "relatively theoretical and impractical". He asked: "Even then, would the U.S. be automatically involved?"[10]

In the second part of the selected transcript, he found the answer to be No. Based on the Mutual Defence Treaty with the Philippines, the

Americans were not committed to the automatic defence or retaliation in the event that the Philippines was attacked. The various executive agreements, all promising that any attack "would be instantly repelled" were not binding. Any attack not involving the U.S. Armed Forces would not be "instantly repelled". As he pointed out, the danger of repeating what happened in Bataan in what he called the "Pensacola Syndrome" when weary Filipinos waited for the heavy cruiser Pensacola to bring relief but which never got past Australia, was lurking in the present security arrangement of the Philippines with the United States. The situation demanded an alternative to this insecurity; Guerrero found it in "self-reliant independent neutrality".[11]

The speech was a timely reminder to re-elected President Marcos. The following year Marcos created a Philippine technical panel to study the "unequal provisions" in the military bases agreement with the United States.[12]

REFLECTIONS ON FILIPINO NATIONALISM

That December 1969 Guerrero wrote on "The Strange Ratooning of Filipino Nationalism" gracing the first issue of *The Philippines Quarterly*. Three years before the centenary of the martyrdom of the three Filipino priests — Mariano Gomez, Jose Burgos and Jacinto Zamora, known as Gomburza, who were implicated in the failed Cavite Mutiny of 1872 — he traced the beginnings of Filipino nationalism in the secularization of parishes ending in the garrotte. Filipino nationalism attained an anti-clerical tinge when "native-born reformers" saw the Spanish clergy as vanguards of obscurantism and enemies of political reforms, making them attack the Church. "Anti-clericalism and then nationalism became necessary for reforms, and eventually separatism and independence for democracy." Filipino nationalism during the revolution was "essentially evangelical and xenophobic" until Mabini, Felipe Calderon, Antonio Luna provided it with political philosophy, a modern Constitution, and discipline. This nationalism, he said, became effective only when its purely intellectual and idealistic character ceased.[13]

In a way, Guerrero was reflecting on the evolution of his nationalism from a pro-American generation until caught by the strange ratooning — from the word "ratoon", or shoot sprouting from the main stem of a plant — of Philippine nationalism led by Recto. He was puzzled by the anxiety of some Americans on the growing anti-Americanism, for pro-Americanism for half a century predominated the landscape after the forgotten sanguinary Philippine-American War. Filipino nationalism was brainwashed away through "schools and textbooks, courts and gallows, jobs, profits and perhaps above all, politics." The American regime saw the resurgence of nationalism in the parliamentary struggle for independence. Contrary to American propagandists, the clamour for independence was not the handiwork of demagoguery but a reflection of the desires of the common people. What Guerrero saw in the 1920s and 1930s was that the old nationalism "had been buried long and deep under the accumulating vested interests in a preferential market", kept alive only by Quezon, Osmeña and Roxas but, speaking for himself and his generation:

> ... the new generations, the young Filipinos brainwashed in the public schools and, as well, in the American-dominated sectarian schools, had neither understanding nor memory of the cropped old hardy perennial which was dying with its old men. The truth is that the young Filipinos of the 30s and the 40s were all pro-Americans, automatically and unthinkingly so, they were not aware of any alternative, and they would starve and kill and die for America in the Japanese War, the only Asians to fight as a people for the white man. Thus was the point reached, aided by Japanese brutality, when pro-Americanism among the Filipinos became identified, against all probability, with nationalism, or perhaps more accurately with patriotism. To be anti-American was to be pro-Japanese, to be pro-Filipino was to be anti-American.[14]

The lowest point in Philippine nationalism was during the Japanese Occupation and the liberation when it spawned using what I.P. Soliongco called "the guerilla mentality" and "the collaborator syndrome". The latter, he said, was "the manifestation of a guilt complex" while the former was of "a double allegiance". It was an era that willingly gave Americans whatever they wanted. After three years, meaning 1949, the "strange ratooning" took place when Filipinos began to discern the realities of Philippine independence as something "conditional". But this nationalism, Guerrero said, reflected in the polls of 1958 when Recto only got 9 per cent of the popular vote, "can become possible only if and when it is accepted by Bonifacio's and Aguinaldo's people from the theoreticians". He discerned an interesting parallelism between the 1870s and the 1970s as "Burgos's frustrated coadjutors are now the clever young vice presidents who will never make chairman of the board in Philippine subsidiaries of U.S. corporations; Rizal's reformers are now exercised by parity rights, quotas, unequal treaties and the control of the economy...." Still, the question remained as to the "true springs of modern Filipino nationalism", and echoing Lenin, he asked about the "whom" but more importantly the "who" only after Filipinos had looked more closely at themselves.[15]

GOOD NEWS AND BAD NEWS BEFORE ANOTHER UN

The usual routine activities confronted Guerrero when he returned to the embassy but now more burdensome and lonesome without Annie whom he left in Manila. Having read that "self-reliance is no longer an option; it is our fate" from the inaugural address of President Marcos, he was delighted; he felt that this would translate to a reorientation of Philippine foreign policy. In the first quarter of 1970, the issue on the military bases came up and a wave of student radicalism hit Manila. It was not clear however, if these showed that "a new nationalism was changing the Philippines."[16]

But the good news in Philippine foreign policy was followed by a bad news in the family forcing Guerrero to rush back home in early June to attend a funeral Mass at the Ermita Church. His mother, in her early eighties, died from a series of heart attacks despite Mario's attempts to revive her. Doña Filomena, a loyal wife and a devoted mother, who in her old age became a loyal fan of Ho Chi Minh mainly through the influence of television and newspapers, was first and foremost an admirer of Rizal and Mabini, with her son Leoni continuing her fascination with these two great Filipino heroes. The homecoming was fortuitous for he was able to reunite with Fr. Horacio de la Costa at the Nakpil residence after many years of lost contact. Naturally, they took advantage of the situation talking and conversing a lot to the chagrin of their host.[17]

After his mother's funeral, Guerrero fulfilled a speaking engagement on 26 June. Speaking before the Indian Federation of UN Associations in New Delhi on the topic "The UN and Southeast Asia in the Past 25 Years", he distinguished three United Nations — "the original peace-enforcing UN", the "resolution-passing UN" and the "third UN". It was in the last that Southeast Asia would benefit from the specialized agencies for the promotion of social progress or what he called the "people's UN". He called the UNCTAD, UNICEF, and all those affiliated agencies to the United Nations "an alphabet of hope" for their role in alleviating the suffering of the poor and in implementing projects beneficial to developing countries. For if the first and second UN failed to stop wars, it was the third UN, he said, that "has at least planted the seeds of international cooperation between the rich nations and the poor".[18]

In another UN celebration, the Haryana UN Association at Hissar University invited Guerrero to their Silver Jubilee programme in late October. Hissar was a town in Haryana state, northwest of New Delhi. Getting tired of the subject, he asked what could possibly be said on the United Nations that had not been said yet. Demystifying the idea that the United Nations was a form of world government, he declared that, in truth, the United Nations was a world government under five dominant powers. If they had acted in concert, they could impose their will on any country and even do what the present United Nations had failed to do like abolishing the apartheid in South Africa. He asked if that would be better than the present one. Relating first Aesop's fable of the frogs who preferred to have a stork as king rather than a log but regretted it later, he said: "Better indeed a log of a United Nations than the imperial storks of the superpowers." To stress his point, he told of John Wyndham's story of a dying Amanda who was expecting to go to heaven but was startled to learn from a ghost that heavens were made for men while women were destined to hell. "So also we might say," he said, "that the various concepts of the United Nations organisation as a world government are heavens made by the maxi-powers for the maxi-powers, and they would be hell for the midi-powers, the mini-powers and the un-powers. Let us then be content with what we have got." The United Nations with all its imperfections had made the world better.[19]

IN A LEGAL COMMITTEE AND PANEL OF SCHOLARS

To represent the country in the Asian-African Legal Consultative Committee in late January 1971, Guerrero was sent to Colombo. Clearly a departure from the tired and boring speeches on the United Nations, he was there before legal experts like him to expound on the archipelago concept of the Law of the Sea as it affected the Philippines. He explained that the Philippine position was "that archipelagoes like the Philippines constitute a necessary exception to any general law of the sea" and "that the territorial waters of the Philippines fall into the category of 'historic waters', which constitute another recognized exception to any general law of the sea", a claim that would protect the territorial integrity and security of the Philippines and the livelihood of its people.[20]

When the 1958 Conference on the Law of the Sea discussed the area of the territorial sea of archipelagoes, the convention deemed it an exception the way the territorial seas of separate islands were measured. What Guerrero meant by "historic waters" was the definition set in the Treaty of Paris specifying the latitude and longitude of the Philippine territory that comprised also its territorial sea, and cited various laws thereafter that recognized the provision of the said treaty including Republic Act No. 5466 amending Republic Act No. 3046, which redefined the Philippine baselines to include the territorial seas around Sabah. The Philippine panel obtained support and appreciation for the archipelago concept from several delegations with one opposition coming from Japan.[21]

After coming from Colombo, Guerrero received a request from the Lopez Foundation to be a member of a panel of Filipino scholars headed by Professor Renato Constantino, that would examine original documents from the Philippine Insurgent Records (PIR) compiled by John R.M. Taylor of the U.S. Army. He agreed and the same year the foundation released in several volumes *The Philippine Insurrection against the United States*. Perusing these documents was once in a while set aside to sign this paper or that or to reply in protest of a provision of a circular like the one issued by the Indian authorities that allowed bodily search for passengers including diplomats to avoid a repeat of the Kashmiri-perpetrated hijacking and burning of an Indian plane. Guerrero found the Indian search of passengers in violation of a provision on diplomatic immunity set in the Geneva Convention. Citing the said provision that guaranteed immunity from searches and investigations for diplomats, he protested this in a letter to the Indian Foreign Ministry. Thus, in another trip home in early May 1971, Guerrero might have been spared from the procedure.[22]

EXECUTIVE-LEGISLATIVE ROLE IN PHILIPPINE FOREIGN POLICY

When the Lyceum of the Philippines wrote to Guerrero that they would honour him with a Doctor of Humanities degree with the accompanying obligation of being the commencement exercises speaker, he was glad to accept the invitation for the school in Intramuros that took him as one of its faculty during those fateful years in the Senate. During the months of March and April, he thought of putting in perspective the executive-legislative role in the crafting of Philippine foreign policy. It was his way of commemorating the silver anniversary of the Philippine Foreign Service that year and of understanding more the role of Congress, which had taken an active role in the opening of trade relations with Socialist countries.[23]

On 15 May, dressed in ceremonial toga after the conferment ceremony in which his sister Chitang put the academic hood because Annie was sick, Guerrero spoke before the Lyceum's graduating class. That Saturday night was drizzling and even if that was the case, the graduating class in the open quadrangle remained seated until Guerrero finished his speech. Many believed that foreign policy was the result of executive-legislative department interactions, with Padre Faura, the street where the office of the Department of Foreign Affairs was once located, receiving instructions from Malacañang. This was not true, as Congress or its individual members at Padre Burgos, the street where Philippine Congress once held office, performed a crucial role in the crafting of foreign policy. The "symbiotic relationship" between "Padre Faura" and "Padre Burgos" was evident as he looked into the history of Philippine diplomacy. Starting with the post-war agreements with the United States and following the renegotiations, the legislature was cooperative with the executive. In major treaties and negotiations, he observed that legislators were heads of the delegations rather than ambassadors.[24]

In any case, it would be wrong, Guerrero said, to conclude that "Padre Burgos" was cowed into submission or compliance, citing cases to prove his point. For example, an act of Congress, Republic Act No. 4109, was the stumbling block to the opening of trade relations with socialist states though he believed it was "erroneously" used as an excuse. More important than the collective action of the legislature however, were individual senators or congressmen whom he described as "lonely men [who] stood forth like the prophets and judges of old to open the eyes of rulers and people, to stigmatize subservience, mock at mendicancy, cry anathema on the abdication of our sovereign rights", alluding to Claro Recto. In his view, Congress might participate in the making of Philippine foreign policy "more in terms of consent than of advice" but, as he saw it, international affairs such as the implementation of UNCTAD II on "a general system of non-reciprocal non-discriminatory preferences for selected exports of the developing countries" and the Nixon Doctrine, "leaving Asia to the Asians" in line with U.S. policy of withdrawing from Vietnam, would require its active role in policymaking.[25]

Notes

1. *MT*, 21 April 1969; *Annual Report 1966-1967*, pp. 3-8.
2. Ibid.
3. *MT*, 21 April 1969; *MC*, 5 May 1969.
4. Apolinario Mabini, *The Philippine Revolution* (Translated by Leon Ma. Guerrero) (Manila: National Historical Commission, 1969), pp. v-vi.
5. Ibid.; Leon Ma. Guerrero, "Apolinario Mabini", in *We Filipinos*, pp. 129-35.
6. Alegre and Fernandez, *Writer and his Milieu*, p. 77; Ambassador Juan A. Ona to

DFA Tattlers, 20 January 1998; Jose A. Zaide, *Bababa, ba? Anecdotes of a Foreign Service Officer* (Mandaluyong City: Academic Publishing Corporation, DFA Foreign Service Institute and the Ateneo Alumni Class '60/'64, 2004), p. 118.
7. Rye, "Philippine-India Bilateral Relations", pp. 126, 134–35, Appendix A.
8. *MT*, 29 November 1969; Nakpil, *Legends & Adventures*, p. 183.
9. *MT*, 21 December 1969; Raymond Bonner, *Waltzing with a Dictator: The Marcoses and the Making of American Policy* (Timesbooks, 1987), pp. 73–76.
10. L.M. Guerrero, "The Pensacola Syndrome", in *Prisoners of History*, pp. 209–17.
11. Ibid., pp. 217–28.
12. Ingles, *Philippine Foreign Policy*, p. 25.
13. L.M. Guerrero, "The Strange Ratooning of Filipino Nationalism", in *Prisoners of History*, pp. 149–52.
14. Ibid., pp. 153–56.
15. Ibid., pp. 156–58.
16. J. Eduardo Malaya and Jonathan E. Malaya, *So Help Us God: The Presidents of the Philippines and Their Inaugural Addresses* (Manila: Anvil, 2004), p. 228; Gleeck, *Third Philippine Republic*, pp. 364–65.
17. Carmen Guerrero Nakpil, telephone conversation with the author, 15 March 2007; Nakpil, *Legends & Adventures*, p. 186; Nakpil, *Myself*, p. 19; *MC*, 20 July 1970.
18. L.M. Guerrero, "Alphabet of Hope", in *Prisoners of History*, pp. 87–94.
19. L.M. Guerrero, "The U.N.: King Log", in ibid., pp. 65–73.
20. L.M. Guerrero, "The Archipelago Concept: Our 7,000 Shores", in ibid., pp. 135–45.
21. Ram P. Anand, *Legal Regime of the Sea-bed and the Developing Countries* (Thomson Press (India) Limited, 1975), pp. 151–55.
22. John R.M. Taylor, *The Philippine Insurrection against the United States: A Compilation of Documents with Notes and Introduction* (Pasig: Lopez Foundation, 1971), II: iii; *MT*, 20 March 1971.
23. L.M. Guerrero, "Padre Burgos and Padre Faura", in *Prisoners of History*, pp. 229–39.
24. Ibid., pp. 233–36; *MDB*, 17 May 1971.
25. Guerrero, "Padre Burgos and Padre Faura", pp. 236–39.

22

Endorsing Non-alignment amid Personal Crisis

Two weeks later in June 1971, Guerrero hurried home to attend to his ailing wife, leaving instructions to the embassy personnel. Asked about his opinion on the opening of relations with Soviet Russia which was being opposed by some members of the Foreign Policy Council members, namely Senate President Gil Puyat, Speaker Cornelio Villareal, former Foreign Affairs Secretary Serrano and former President Garcia, he said: "Let's be candid about it. The Russians want to establish diplomatic ties with us, so we set up pre-conditions and get the best deal from such relations." The Philippines, he said, belonged to a group of countries still adamant about opening relations with Russia, such as South Korea, South Vietnam and Nationalist China.[1]

Again, before the same group of newsmen, when asked on the Constitutional Convention which would open the following day, he suggested the scrapping of the boundary provision or the first article in the 1935 Constitution, not only because the Philippines was the only country with definite territorial boundary, but the provision also worked against the Philippine claim on Sabah. Regarding the Tolentino Law, which delineated Philippine territorial waters around Sabah, he asked, "How can a law modify a constitution?" According to Guerrero, it would be better to rescind this law and adopt the archipelago theory he recently expounded early this year in Colombo, which would extend territorial waters from twelve to 200 miles (19.31 to 321.88 kilometres) from the outermost island. His suggestion to excise from the first article on the national territory the enumeration of colonial treaties was heeded by the committee responsible for that provision two years later.[2]

While in the Philippines, he delivered a lecture before the first ASEAN seminar on "The Role of Mass Media in the Development of Southeast Asia". His lecture had no connection with the theme, but it revealed a turning point in the development of his foreign policy thinking. It was in this lecture that he seemed to declare that the economic losses incurred as a result of the military bases' presence far outweighed the economic benefits that these were supposed to bring, citing prostitution, rampant smuggling, and black-marketeering. His lecture was concerned with which foreign policy — alignment or non-alignment — would help in the development of ASEAN or more specifically, towards the region's industrialization programmes.[3]

In his words, "what is or should be the diplomacy in aid of industrial development?" He found that it was not one of alignment or reliance with Western countries. Quoting an Indian economist, he said it was because Western developed countries were reluctant to be aligned to protect their own interests. In the case of non-alignment, he advocated that this course was profitable and advantageous. The USSR and other countries of Eastern Europe were very open to accepting imports of traditional products such as copra, oil and non-traditional consumer goods in exchange for machines, tools and plants for light industries because they had concentrated heavily on industries. Guerrero's support for non-alignment for ASEAN was shaped by his observations of Indian foreign policy. As he revealed to the audience, he was amazed how India exported millions of shoes to the USSR made of hides from sacred cows.[4]

OF POLITICS AND ANNIE

Guerrero abhorred politics. A few days after he arrived, some of his friends nominated him for the Liberal Party senatorial line-up. He immediately wrote a letter to Liberal Party President Gerardo Roxas requesting him to withdraw his name from the list for "I was never meant to be a party politician and had long ago chosen to serve the Republic 'in another part of the forest.'" On why he was nominated, he wrote: "It is not unreasonable to discern a definite purpose in the Liberal Party convention's pattern of nominations. It was to project a new image, glamorous and at the same time radical and populist." Guerrero's refusal of the senatorial candidacy was a fateful decision that saved him from the Plaza Miranda bombing in August 1971, when senatorial candidates such as Sergio Osmeña Jr., Jovito Salonga and Gerardo Roxas suffered from deadly injuries. But he could have also won as all except two were elected in the November elections.[5]

Guerrero's decision was partly shaped by a dying Annie. When he brought her home, Annie met his late mother's doctor at ABM Sison in Pasig. After being diagnosed with cancer, she underwent courses of radiation. Then, she was confined in the hospital. He poured his attention on Annie, "decorating her hospital room with rugs, paintings, carved screens and tapestries, plying her with books, music cassettes, flowers". It was his way of compensating for whatever he had done to Annie in a marriage "full of storms and vicissitudes" but where love conquered all. To hide his sorrow, and tears, he wore dark shades. When she died on 4 July, he had to be admitted to another hospital due to dehydration.[6]

"An incurable romantic", he made a memorial card announcing Annie's death with a quote from Elizabeth Barrett Browning: "'Guess now who holds thee?' | Death, I said, but there | The silver answer rang, | 'Not death, but Love.'" On the day of her interment, he organized "the most moving and theatrical funeral" where all relatives and friends including himself walked in a procession holding torches from Loyola Memorial Chapel in Marikina to her tomb. He was equally morbid for in the tomb inscription his name was already there beside Annie's name minus the day of his death. He took off his wedding ring as a parting gift to Annie. Letters and cards were received from well-meaning friends abroad and in the Philippines. In reply to one of them, he revealed that he "shall really miss her very much".[7]

"TWO CHINAS" POLICY

For the seventh time, Guerrero flew home in early October 1971 on the instructions of Padre Faura, to be part of First Lady Imelda Marcos' entourage on her two-day official visit to India. The First Lady was scheduled to meet Prime Minister Indira Gandhi to discuss "broad outlines of economic cooperation".[8]

While home, the Kiwanis Club of Quezon City invited Guerrero to be the guest speaker at its induction of officers and directors. On 2 October, at Hotel Enrico, he spoke on the government's new China policy or the so-called "Two Chinas" policy. Upon the enunciation of the Guam Doctrine or the Nixon Doctrine, the Philippine Government decided to support the admission of the People's Republic of China (PRC) as the legitimate representative of the Chinese people in the United Nations. "I do not hesitate to say that this was the correct thing to do; and I believed it and said so during the many years when it was not official policy." In the ensuing years, the Philippine Government would exert efforts to open ties with the PRC. While it supported the PRC's admission to the

United Nations, it opposed the expulsion of Taiwan, an ally in the fight against communism.⁹

Thus the new policy was called "Two Chinas" which in his opinion was incorrect. Rather, Philippine policy should appropriately be called "One and One-Tenth Chinas" in allusion to geographic and demographic size or "One China, One Taiwan". He saw nothing peculiar in it, comparing it to the USSR having three votes because of the separate votes given to Byelorussia and Ukraine. Why not accord Taiwan a separate identity and an individual vote? He believed as others did that an accommodation between Peking and Taipei was imminent. Up to the present, however, PRC has a long way to go to keep Taiwan under its suzerainty but Philippine policy remained — an exchange of missions between Manila and Peking was started three years later while cultural offices were established in Manila and in Taipei.¹⁰

MUSLIMS AS FILIPINOS

In the early part of 1972 Guerrero received an invitation from the Mindanao State University in Marawi City to deliver the commencement address in the graduation exercises. Putting aside his usual chores, he absorbed himself in reading books to understand the Muslim insurgency in Mindanao. He would find the friction between Filipinos Muslims and Filipino Christians as "an encounter between two communities with different traditions and rival economic interests, and suffering from different historical hangovers". He would learn that if the Spaniards had been late by fifty years, the Filipinos might have been Muslims; that Filipino Muslims resisted Spain and remained unconquered; that they attained a high culture, "an indigenous culture not derived from Spain or America"; that during the Philippine Revolution and the First Republic, they were not represented; that upon the coming of the Americans, impositions such as the creation of a Moro Province further alienated them from Christian Filipinos; that alienation grew to its worse when Muslims, culturally and economically backward, were unable to cope with the times and, thus, could take the blame for their own plight.¹¹

Under the policy of the regime in Manila, Christian Filipinos, suffering from lack of land and tenancy problems, were encouraged to migrate to Mindanao until eventually the Filipino Muslims were marginalized in their own provinces. However, Guerrero was wrong in assuming that Mindanao was "the traditional Muslim homeland" because it was also home to the Lumads or indigenous tribes, which were neither Christians nor Muslims except those who had converted to either religion. Nevertheless, the encounter came to the point when a religious war was beginning to take shape in the attacks between rival Christian and Muslim outlaw bands. It also brought about the establishment of a "Mindanao Independence Movement". Guerrero believed that integration was the easy answer to the friction, citing the various laws enacted to redress the marginal situation of the Filipino Muslims such as the role of the Commission on National Integration. The failure of the commission's mandate, he found, could not be attributed only to the government for lack of funds but also to the Filipino Muslims' lack of cooperation. The government must allot the needed funds for them to participate in national affairs, and Muslim countries could consider grants in aid to the commission matched by funds from the government. Since one of the main problem was land, he thought that the commission could begin tackling it first by taking a cadastral survey, cooperating with the agency concerned with land reform, and coordinating with the Mindanao Development Authority in the promotion of industrialization projects.[12]

All these were pointed out in his address in late April 1972, which was a splendid dissertation on the subject, a reflection of how he grasped Philippine history deeper than most of the Filipino historians. At the outset, he denied the impression that the government was guilty of committing genocide towards Muslims in reference to the propaganda being peddled to the Arab world by the Muslim insurgents. There was no religious war in the Philippines "or at least, and hopefully, not yet". It would take time and millions of money, he said, for integration to succeed so that Filipino Muslims and Christians might come to terms that they belonged to one single nation.[13]

ANOTHER COLLECTION OF SPEECHES AND A NEW ASSIGNMENT

Upon arrival in New Delhi in May 1972, Guerrero embarked on a project — a compilation again of his speeches, lectures and addresses into a book because "a book is always better than a cocktail party". He intended its publication to promote "mutual understanding between the Philippines and India". He dedicated the book entitled *Prisoners of History* after his lecture at the Indian School of International Studies, to Anita "who was by far the better Ambassador". In the foreword written on Philippine Independence Day, he revealed the special significance of India to his diplomatic career:

> I shall never forget my assignment in India for a very personal reason. But in any case I would have remembered it because of the contrast between what I expected to find and what I actually found. I arrived just after

Tashkent and the devaluation of rupee; I shall be leaving soon after Simla and the triumphant accession to unchallengeable power of Indira Gandhi on the rejuvenation of the historical Congress Party, by all standards a most memorable and decisive period in the history of India. It was an unexpected privilege to serve my country in those years that proved so fateful, and I am grateful to those who made it possible.[14]

Before leaving for Mexico on the other side of the world, he would still represent the country as head of the Philippine delegation to the Twenty-second Consultative Meeting of the Colombo Plan in New Delhi from 30 October to 10 November. He also directed the release late in the year of a National Media Production Center booklet on the Philippines with nineteenth-century Spanish lithographs.[15]

Guerrero asked for the New Delhi posting because of the profound changes about to take place in the Foreign Service by the new administration hinted at in President Marcos' inaugural address in 1965. Asia had become the central thrust in Philippine foreign policy. What had been regarded as blasphemy more than a decade ago was being made the cornerstone of policy. India proved to be exciting and stimulating. Sent to various international gatherings including the Bangkok Talks dealing with the Sabah claim, Guerrero fought steadfastly for Philippine honour and interest. Before clubs and organizations, he spoke on Philippine foreign policy and it was during one of these speaking engagements that he endorsed non-alignment as the basis of Philippine foreign policy in keeping with the country's economic programme of industrialization. He promoted Philippine trade with the Indians without forsaking his love for writing, for aside from the usual dispatches and speeches, he managed to translate Mabini's brilliant treatise on the Philippine Revolution and wrote about the exodus of two Spanish priests during the Philippine revolution. But a part of him died in New Delhi.

Notes
1. *MB*, 1 June 1971.
2. *MC*, 1 June 1971; Emmanuel T. Santos, *The Constitution of the Philippines: Notes and Comments* (Manila: Self-published, 2001), p. 55.
3. L.M. Guerrero, "Alignment and Non-Alignment: Alternatives for Development", in *Prisoners of History*, pp. 189–94.
4. Ibid., pp. 194–200. See also *MC*, 27 June 1971 and *MT*, 27 June 1971.
5. L.M. Guerrero, "Ambassadors and Politics", *PH*, 27 June 1971, p. 5; Gleeck, *Dissolving the Colonial Bond*, pp. 255–57.
6. Gemma Cruz-Araneta, interview by the author, DZRJ 810 AM Studio, 16 August

2006; Letters of Condolence to Leon Ma. Guerrero, *LMGP*; Nakpil, *Legends & Adventures*, pp. 183–84. Anita died either from cancer of the stomach or intestine, Carmen Guerrero Nakpil, telephone conversation with the author, 15 March 2007.
7. Nakpil, *Legends & Adventures*, pp. 183–84; Marquardt, "Remembering Leoni", pp. 36–37; *MC*, 10 August 1971.
8. *MT*, 1 and 9 October 1971.
9. L.M. Guerrero, "Chinese Arithmetic", in *Prisoners of History*, p. 95.
10. Ibid., pp. 96–98. See also *MT*, 4 October 1971.
11. L.M. Guerrero, "The Muslims in the Philippines: Encounter of Cultures", in *Prisoners of History*, pp. 241–52.
12. Ibid., pp. 251–64.
13. Ibid., pp. 241–42, 263–64.
14. L.M. Guerrero, *Prisoners of History*, pp. 5, 9–10.
15. *MT*, 19 September 1972; *The Philippines* (New Delhi: Embassy of the Philippines, 1972), pp. 1–28.

23

Flirting with Dictators

Besides having visited Mexico to attend a Latin American conference the year Philippine-Mexican Friendship Year was proclaimed in which he visited Guadalajara and Navidad where he unveiled a monument to Legazpi and Urdaneta, while posted in Madrid, Guerrero understood the historical antecedents of Philippine-Mexican relations. In 1963, speaking in Madrid, he discussed with extraordinary erudition the close relations, deep connections and the surface differences between the Philippines and Latin America, or to use his term, Iberian America. More than the differences, superficial at best, were those lessons learned from Latin American experiences. Pointing out the Malolos Constitution as having derived its inspiration from the constitutions of Costa Rica, Mexico, Brazil, Nicaragua and Guatemala whose common roots were found in the French Constitution, Guerrero disclosed that the 1935 Philippine Constitution contained safeguards and guarantees owing to the political history of Latin America. Among those were the provisions banning the re-election of a president to prevent the perpetuation of one-man rule, and the care of the national defence placed under a civilian secretary to forestall military takeovers.[1]

But, again greater than these lessons, Guerrero uncovered "the depth of Philippine-Iberian American kinship" in political concepts, that distinguished the Philippines, although Asian in biology and destiny, from the rest of Asian countries but inevitably linked it with Latin America. The Philippines and Latin America shared problems common in underdeveloped countries almost possessing a commonality found in Hispanic culture, in

> an individualistic culture that is at the same time catholic, that is to say, universal; a culture that protects personal conscience, the freedom

of individual to be lost, and at the same time submits it to a universal system of beliefs, to dogmas and doctrines outside of which there is no possible salvation ...

producing a political and social human prototype in the manner of a Don Quixote and Don Juan. This political culture manifested once when Filipinos under Quezon, Osmeña and Roxas thought that political independence was able to "fix everything, when in truth it was going to reveal and to put everything out of order" because economic independence was left out of the equation.[2]

Whether Guerrero asked for his appointment to Mexico or whether it was at Romulo's discretion, the decision to send him as the next envoy was apt. After a four-year stay in the early to mid-1960s in Spain, the motherland of Hispanic nations including his own, he was rightfully sent to Mexico to savour Hispanic culture in a former crown colony. Guerrero stayed in the mission, which was upgraded to an embassy in 1961, at a time when Mexico was being made the "base" for the expansion of Philippine diplomatic map in Latin America, as part of its focus on building up relations with the Third World. Guerrero's assignment to Mexico was also significant because it coincided with the beginning of what President Marcos called "New Directions in Philippine Foreign Policy": the Philippines would open ties with any country regardless of ideology — the very incarnation of a policy of non-alignment that Guerrero was preaching. It did not matter then, that three years earlier, the press had speculated that Guerrero would become either the next Philippine ambassador to the United Nations since his friend, Salvador "S.P." Lopez, had been appointed president of UP, or the next chief at Padre Faura to replace Romulo. Again in early January 1971, he was reported to become the first envoy to Moscow following the negotiations between the Philippines and the USSR by way of India, which he spearheaded by contacting his Russian counterpart, since mid-October 1970.[3]

SECOND MARRIAGE WITH PERMISSION

Before he arrived in Mexico, widowed Guerrero married Margaret Burke, his former private secretary who was ten years younger than him, on 30 November 1972 at St James's Roman Catholic Church, Spanish Place, Marylebone in London. It was witnessed by select Filipinos including people from the London embassy. To proceed with his marriage to an alien, he had to ask permission from the Foreign Office.[4]

Guerrero maintained communications with her during and after his stint in London. When he was posted in Madrid, Margaret decided to move to

Spain, with their son David. David as a toddler even appeared as an extra in the film *55 Days at Peking* — when the producers were looking for a baby with Asian features — that starred Charlton Heston, Ava Gardner and David Niven and shot at a studio in Las Rozas de Madrid in 1963. Staying for five years, they went back to London when Guerrero was assigned to New Delhi. Although Margaret was financially independent with her successful secretarial firm, he, nonetheless, sent allowances from time to time to Margaret and David. He sent telegrams and letters inquiring about them, telling Margaret about his activities and sharing his thoughts on whatever fancied him. One letter he wrote as a father to David — who was attending Bishop Challoner School in Bromley, Kent after his studies at St. Edward's School at Marylebone — expressed his joy on his son's first communion, related his first communion when he was six years old, advised his son to be better than him in playing football and hoped that "the next time I am in London we must have a conversation". From Delhi he would arrange for the delivery to David a scooter as gift on his seventh birthday. David, at the time of marriage, was attending a boarding school in Devon, England. To make his son legitimate in the eyes of the law, Guerrero had all the necessary legal niceties done before leaving for Mexico with his second wife.[5]

Since Margaret was new to the duties of an ambassador's wife, she tried to learn some diplomatic protocol. Guerrero oriented her to the duties and obligations of a hostess to parties, dinner luncheons and gatherings in the embassy. Her two-year stay in Madrid, part of her training as translator, at least facilitated her access to her husband's peers and their wives. In less than a year as hostess, she learned the protocol on seating arrangements, that the dean in the diplomatic corps should receive preference. Their stay in Mexico was a period of breaking the ice for them to know each other more. As it turned out, they were a study in contrast. She was an active person, young in her early thirties. She was used to walking. On the other hand, Guerrero was physically lazy. He did not like to exercise. He hated walking. Regarding this awkward situation, she said: "It's quite an amiable arrangement, really, since we both approve of each other enough to laugh about what I call his arrant laziness and what he calls my horrendous nervous energy."[6]

A MISSION OVER TEN CITIES

The mission had offices at Sierra Torrecillas, Lomas de Chapultepec in Mexico City exercising jurisdiction over honorary consulates in Guadalajara and Acapulco. When Guerrero and Margaret arrived in Mexico, they confronted a nation gripped in insurgency and terrorism. Presenting his credentials in mid-January 1973 at the Palacio Nacional located at the city's main square, Plaza de la Constitución, to President Luis Echeverría, Guerrero argued for the renewal of the historic and cultural ties between the Philippines and Mexico and stated that his special mission was to transmit to this government "the historic and contemporary experiences of Mexico that will serve as a guide or model, for the reforms that the President is instituting in the Philippines". The presentation was made after a series of bank robberies followed by political kidnappings of a university rector and the director of the country's airport. A U.S. consul-general in Guadalajara, a British honorary consul, a wealthy Guadalajara businessman and a daughter of a Belgian ambassador were also kidnapped.[7]

Accredited as a non-resident ambassador to Colombia, Ecuador, Venezuela, Honduras, Nicaragua, El Salvador, Guatemala, and Costa Rica, Guerrero and Margaret would visit his jurisdiction scattered in nine cities when necessary. Adolfo Molina Orantes, the mission's honorary consul in Guatemala City, made sure they were looked after on their visit there; they went to Guatemala Antigua, the former capital that was ruined by an earthquake, and toured the ancient Mayan ruins of Tikal in the middle of the jungle. Orantes became a close friend and even personally gave David a book about the Mayans. The change of government in Guatemala did not prevent Orantes from extending his friendship to them after his appointment as Foreign Affairs Minister. Guerrero and Margaret reciprocated Orantes' hospitality when he visited Manila. By the end of his stint, Guerrero was awarded the Grand Cross of the Order of Quetzal, the highest Guatemalan honour.[8]

The unstable conditions in Central America obligated Guerrero to send many dispatches to the Home Office. In El Salvador, the Philippine honorary consul in San Salvador was assassinated on the steps of the university where he was teaching. Both he and Margaret had the opportunity to see the jungles, volcanoes, pre-Colombian ruins and lakes of Central America but they "were distressed by the injustices which abound".[9]

READING LATIN AMERICA

In August 1973, Guerrero was busy studying the international treaties that might interest Philippine authorities. One of these was his study on the Treaty of Tlatelolco or the Treaty for the Prohibition of Nuclear Weapons in Latin America. According to him, the treaty "may well serve as a model and a precedent for the proclamation of a 'nuke'-free zone in our own region to complement and reenforce the long mooted ASEAN zone of peace and neutrality". The Philippines was signatory to the declaration that ASEAN be recognized as a Zone of Peace, Freedom and Neutrality (ZOPFAN) in November 1971. Although there were eighteen states party to the Tlatelolco treaty including the nuclear powers with the exception of the USSR, Guerrero recognized its inherent limitations for it "do[es] not have the means to compel the two superpowers [namely the United States and the USSR] to respect its prohibitions or indeed even to detect any violations". This provision might also apply to a similar treaty being contemplated for ASEAN in the future.[10]

In his private study, Guerrero began to acquaint himself with Latin American literature. He read Colombia-born Gabriel Garcia Marquez, the Peruvian Mario Vargas Llosa, the Mexican Carlos Fuentes, the Cuban Alejo Carpentier and the Argentinian Jorge Luis Borges. About these authors, he believed: "You can't stop with Gabriel Garcia Marquez; there are so many wonderful authors, you know. Really you can't imagine! You must read them in the original, of course, or it wouldn't make any sense. You have Mario Vargas Llosa…. And of course Borges; Borges can drive you mad…." Among these writers those who really inspired him were Gabriel Garcia Marquez, Carlos Fuentes, and Alejo Carpentier.[11]

Reading literature brought back his interest in history, particularly Philippine-Mexican relations. Back in 1964 he became involved in preliminary research and studies on the Manila galleons — ships that brought the Philippines closer culturally and politically to Latin America — and the return voyage, the *el tornaviaje*, which Andres de Urdaneta had discovered facilitating trade contacts between Asia and Latin America since it became the traditional route these ships had taken from Manila to Acapulco or vice versa. When the city of Manila was contemplating on writing a new history of Manila he was immediately taken in as member of the research committee.[12]

More essential than these activities to his work were his sharp observations regarding countries in which he was accredited to. He took note of Echeverría instituting left-wing policies that restricted foreign investments and alleviated poverty, and his efforts to identify Mexico with the Third World, even denouncing the United States for its dominance in the hemisphere. The election of Colonel Carlos Arana Osorio, military commander of the anti-guerrilla campaign, Guerrero observed, did not end the right-wing terrorism in Guatemala but, with government connivance, terrorism escalated, culminating in the killing of the entire Guatemalan Communist Party leadership in 1973. Guerrero reported on Colonel Arturo Armando Molina's successful infrastructure programme following the coffee bonanza in the midst of a harsh crackdown against leftist dissidents and the opposition, which was set off by the military occupation in July 1972 of the University of El Salvador for being a hotbed of Marxist indoctrination. He found Honduras again in the hands of Air Force General Oswaldo López Arellano who staged a coup in December 1972 (after having an elected presidency in 1965 to 1971) posturing a nationalist and developmentalist policy.

Guerrero arrived in Managua still reeling from the devastating earthquake a day before Christmas 1972 and under a political transition that would give way again in 1974 to the administration of Anastasio Somoza Debayle who ruled Nicaragua from 1967 to 1972. He learned of the severe drought affecting Costa Rica and the increasing unpopularity on the eve of a presidential election of President José Figueres Ferrer who led the 1948 revolution and became president for three non-consecutive terms. In Caracas, he became acquainted with the policies of President Rafael Caldera reorienting Venezuela to its neighbours leading to the Andean Pact, the regional trade bloc comprising Bolivia, Colombia, Chile, Ecuador and Peru. Ruled by a conservative regime, Colombia at that time when Guerrero arrived in Mexico was also on the eve of a presidential election with contenders who were all the children of former presidents. He gave an account of Ecuador under military rule since 1972 under the leadership of General Guillermo Rodríguez Lara who steered the country's petroleum boom.[13]

DEFENDING MARTIAL LAW

In September 1973 Guerrero flew to the United States with Margaret to attend the autumn sessions of the UN General Assembly in New York as a member of the Philippine delegation, meeting Romulo, the chair of the delegation, Narcing Reyes who was now the Philippine permanent representative to the United Nations, and a coterie of Filipino ambassadors, consuls, and foreign affairs officers. At this time, he and Margaret became close to Beth Day, Romulo's American girlfriend. The four of them would always go out together for dinner or to watch theatre. One day, he commissioned the renowned painter, Federico Aguilar Alcuaz, to separately paint portraits of the three of them — him, Margaret and David. He left New York in October for Paraguay as the president's special representative to the taking of oath of office of General of the Army Alfredo Stroessner on his fifth five-year term as president since 1954, when he led a coup d'etat against Dr Federico Chavez.[14]

Back in New York, Guerrero was apprised of a *New York Times* article written by former Senator Raul Manglapus, now the founder of Movement for Free Philippines in the United States, criticizing the martial law regime in the Philippines. The article coincided with the first anniversary of martial law's proclamation. Romulo instructed Guerrero to write a reply, which he did after delivering a lecture on politics and the military in Southeast Asia at the behest of the Washington Institute of Foreign Affairs in Washington DC. His response to the article was published only after Romulo had convinced the daily's managing editor to do so. "Should the proclamation of martial law in the Philippines prick the American conscience?" Guerrero prefaced his article. "Perhaps," he wrote, "but not for the reasons advanced recently in these columns", referring to the article by Manglapus.[15]

Guerrero seemed to justify martial law by saying that the first Philippine Republic had a revolutionary government ruled by a military dictator before the Americans intervened and imposed an "American form of democracy on an Asian people in a completely different economic and social situation". This, he said, could prick the American conscience since "it led to the political crisis from which … the proclamation of martial law was the only way out." Starting with the post-war politics, he described the alternation of power between two parties as "25 years of Watergate", referring to the scandals that were then plaguing the White House that compared well to the "interminable stream of corruption" that flowed since 1946 — from the U.S. army surplus properties scandal to the Stonehill scandal. "American conscience had not been pricked by the feudal system of land tenure" as after independence, a peasant revolt erupted. With land reform hampered, student riots escalated and poverty worsened. Hope remained in the reform of the political system, even when with a new Constitution it turned out to be a farce with its members as corrupt as the old politicians. A national disillusionment would explain why Filipinos accepted the proclamation of martial law and that:

> No American conscience need be pricked if the Filipinos now agree to seek and find way out of the crisis in which they, like so many other peoples in Asia and the world, are caught. To seek American intervention or even a benevolent neutrality in favor of a coup de force by the armed forces of the Philippines, is, I suggest, the surest way to another Vietnam.[16]

In effect, Guerrero was saying to the Americans to leave the Filipinos to make their own destiny and that any American intervention was an invitation to disaster similar to what the United States was doing in Vietnam. Romulo's decision to have Guerrero write a response in the defence of the martial law regime was unmistakably directed against Manglapus, Guerrero's childhood friend whose pro-Americanism was beyond doubt.[17]

FLYING IN AND OUT OF MEXICO

Insurgency and terrorism in Mexico continued in the early months of the following year when the president's father-in-law, the former governor of Jalisco was kidnapped, producing an atmosphere of fear in the capital. Guerrero and Margaret did not stay at the embassy residence because more often than not, they were abroad.[18]

They flew to Quito, Caracas, San Jose and Guatemala City in March and April 1974 for Guerrero to present his credentials in which he met Ecuadorian President Rodríguez, Venezuelan President Caldera, Costa Rican President Figueres and Guatemalan President General Arana Osorio. Just as he did in Paraguay, Venezuela and Brazil months before, Guerrero, accompanied by his wife and the honorary consul, attended the presidential inauguration in April in San Jose of Costa Rican President Daniel Oduber Quirós of the Partido de la Liberación Nacional, the administration's party. Towards the middle of the year in late May, Guerrero flew to Colombia to present his credentials before President Misael Pastrana Borrero at the presidential palace in Bogotá. He was back in June to host the Freedom Day celebration at the embassy where he entertained U.S. Ambassador John Joseph Jova and Ambassador Hortencio J. Brillantes, who was in Mexico for the UNCTAD working group session.[19]

Again in September, he flew to New York to attend the UN session. It was during the inauguration of the Philippine Center on Fifth Avenue when he suffered public ridicule for his support of martial law. While waiting on the sidewalk to enter the building with Chitang whom Mrs Marcos took along on a UN speaking engagement, he saw on the other side of the street an anti-Marcos group of protesting Filipinos and on a truck holding a mike was Manglapus. Manglapus yelled to them, "What are those two libertarians (naming them) doing there?" Ridiculed in public, Guerrero chuckled, asking Chitang to "Go and talk some sense into Raulito [Manglapus]." Chitang, however, merely smiled and waved to him. The point was, there was no need to publicly deride them as Guerrero was just doing his job serving the Republic the best he could whether Marcos was the president or not.[20]

From New York Guerrero went back to Mexico in late November to oversee the signing of an agreement on technical cooperation in commerce and trade between the Philippines and Mexico. It was the first step in promoting Philippine trade with Mexico, in conjunction with President Marcos' Letter of Instruction No. 217 in early October 1974 directing all government personnel abroad to take an active role in the promotion of Philippine exports. The directive also tasked the Department of Foreign

Affairs to take into account, in the criteria for promotion and assessment of performance of all personnel including chiefs of mission, the amount of trade they can generate for Philippine products. Under the slogan "development diplomacy", a spin-off of what he called "diplomacy of development", Philippine foreign policy "is heavily oriented towards economic ends such as maximizing trade through negotiations, aid through cooperation, and investments through incentives."[21]

The agreement initiated the strengthening of Philippine-Mexican relations that was preceded by the visit to Manila in July of celebrated Mexican painter Rufino Tamayo, Mrs Marcos' guest of honour during the inauguration of the Folk Arts Theater. Making the necessary arrangements for the trip, Guerrero renewed his friendship with Tamayo when the latter was awarded the French Legion of Merit.[22]

By this time, although always out of Mexico, Guerrero was nonetheless informed of the politics within his territory. In Guatemala, following the fraudulent election in 1974, a general, Eugenio Kjell Laugerud Garcia, replaced Colonel Osorio and began a congressional alliance with the moderate Partido Revolucionario. In Honduras, President López Arellano whom Guerrero met in March 1975 for his credentials, was removed in a military coup after becoming implicated in a bribery scandal involving the United Fruit Company, with Colonel Arturo Melgar Castro taking over. The Somoza dynasty in Nicaragua faced growing discontent and opposition that would coalesce in the Sandinista movement. President Carlos Andrés Pérez was elected in Venezuela and began a firmly nationalist and progressive stance. After presenting his credentials in Colombia before President Pastrana Borrero, Guerrero would meet another president, the newly elected Alfonso López Michelsen.[23]

The following year in June 1975, Guerrero held a cocktail party in celebration of Philippine Independence Day but this time with a little difference. The opening of Philippine diplomatic relations with the PRC formally signed by President Marcos in a state visit to Peking only a week earlier freed him from the restriction to invite the Chinese envoy to Mexico, Ambassador Yao Kuang, to the gathering. Days after the gathering, he flew to El Salvador to present his credentials to Colonel Arturo Armando Molina in San Salvador where he greeted schoolchildren after the presentation. In November 1975, he went to Managua and presented his credentials to General Somoza.[24]

Preparation for a string of visits by the First Lady not only to Mexico but to adjacent Latin American countries was added to Guerrero's usual duties. In support of President Echeverría who sponsored the International

Women's Year Conference in Mexico City, Imelda Marcos went in June to address the conference and also meet Echeverría. Guerrero was asked to prepare her speech, which he also did when she made an official visit in July to Premier Fidel Castro for a discussion on re-establishing bilateral relations with Cuba, and also when she made a visit to Caracas in August.[25]

Though Guerrero wanted to promote Philippine-Mexican relations, there was a time when he risked it for the national interest. Mexico had expressed its intention to bid for the venue of an international tourism conference and asked for the Philippines' support. The Philippines, however, decided to bid for it as well, so Guerrero thought that it was only logical for him to withdraw his support for the Mexican bid. He did so and earned himself cool treatment from the Mexican Government.[26]

Notes
1. Homer M. Hill, "Philippine-Mexican relations, 1960–1970" (MA thesis, Philippine Center for Advanced Studies, University of the Philippines, 1975), pp. 73–74, 145; Howard F. Cline, *Latin American history: Essays on Its Study and Teaching, 1898–1965* (Austin: Published for the Conference on Latin American History by the University of Texas Press, 1967), 2: 186; Guerrero, *El Sí y El No*, pp. 57–60.
2. Ibid., pp. 60–68.
3. "CPR Speaks", *The DFA Review* (hereafter cited as *DFAR*) 2, no. 10 (1975): 6; Jose D. Ingles, *Philippine Foreign Policy*, pp. 1–3; *MC*, 8 and 24 January 1969; *MT*, 29 November 1969; *MC*, 7 January 1971; *DM*, 28 January 1971; "The unseen Indian hand in Manila's Moscow diplomacy", *India eNews*, 21 August 2006.
4. Ambassador Juan A. Ona to DFA Tattlers, email, 20 January 1998; Margaret Burke Guerrero, interview by the author, Dasmariñas Village, Makati City, 3 and 5 May 2006; Marquardt, "Remembering Leoni Guerrero", p. 39.
5. David Guerrero, interview by the author, Dasmariñas Village, Makati City, 4 December 2016; Margaret Guerrero to Leon Ma. Guerrero; Leon Ma. Guerrero to Margaret Guerrero, and Leon Ma. Guerrero to David Guerrero, various letters and telegrams, *LMGP*; Gemma Cruz-Araneta, interview by the author, DZRJ 810 AM Studio, 16 August 2006.
6. Jane Bordas, "Diplomats' Wives' also 'sweat it out'", *DFAR* 1, no. 4 (1974): 8.
7. Michael C. Meyer and William L. Sherman, *The Course of Mexican History* (New York: Oxford University Press, 1987), pp. 672–73; *The Ambassador* 4, no. 2 (1973): 37–38; *DFAR* 1, no. 7 (1974): 7; Republic of the Philippines, *Philippine Diplomacy: Chronology and Documents 1972–1981* (Manila: Foreign Service Institute, 1981), p. 58; *Información Nacional*, 20 January 1973; *El Sol*, 20 January 1973.
8. Margaret Burke Guerrero, interview by the author, Dasmariñas Village, Makati City, 29 April 2006; Margaret Burke Guerrero, interview by Alexander Umali, Bel-air, 14 January 2002 (courtesy of David Guerrero).
9. Ibid.

10. Leon Ma. Guerrero, "A Model for ASEAN?", *The Ambassador* (August 1973), pp. 19–24.
11. Alegre and Fernandez, *Writer and His Milieu*, pp. 76, 82, 83.
12. Margaret Burke Guerrero, interview by the author, Dasmariñas Village, Makati City, 29 April 2006; "History of Manila", in *LMGP*.
13. Martin C. Kneedler, *An Introduction to Latin American Politics: The Structure of Conflict* (New Jersey: Prentice Hall, Inc., 1983), pp. 20, 26, 36–37, 45–46, 50, 55–56, 91, 97, 106. About the presidency of Colonel Arturo Armando Molina in El Salvador, see "La herencia de las manitas", *El diario de hoy*, 12 November 2006.
14. *DFAR* 1, no. 1 (1973): 2; *DFAR* 1, no. 2 (1973): 8; *DFAR* 1, no. 9 (1974): 6; *DFAR* 2, no. 10 (1975): 1; Margaret Burke Guerrero, interview by Alexander Umali, Dasmariñas Village, 21 January 2002 (courtesy of David Guerrero).
15. Alegre and Fernandez, *Writer and His Milieu*, pp. 86–87; *New York Times*, 24 November 1973; Leon Ma. Guerrero, "Politics and the Military in Southeast Asia", Lecture delivered at the auspices of Washington Institute of Foreign Affairs, Washington DC, 21 November 1973, *LMGP*.
16. Ibid.; See also Leon Ma. Guerrero, "Pricking the American Conscience", *DFAR* 1, no. 2 (1973): 3.
17. About Manglapus, see Bonner, *Waltzing with a Dictator*, pp. 143–44.
18. Meyer and Sherman, *The Course of Mexican History*, pp. 672–73.
19. *DFAR* 1, no. 6 (1974): 5; *DFAR* 1, no. 8 (1974): 4; *Philippine Diplomacy*, p. 279.
20. Nakpil, *Legends & Adventures*, p. 205.
21. Benjamin Domingo, *Philippine Treaties Index 1946–1982* (Manila: Foreign Service Institute, 1983), p. 66; Ingles, *Philippine Foreign Policy*, pp. 238–39; Manuel Collantes, "Diplomacy for Development", Speech delivered at the discussion series on national development, AIM, Makati, 26 September 1973, *From Mabini to Collantes: The Filipino Diplomat* (Manila: Foreign Service Institute, 1984), pp. 11–12.
22. *DFAR* 2, no. 2–3 (1975): 6.
23. Kneedler, *An Introduction to Latin American Politics*, pp. 37, 46, 50, 94–95, 101.
24. "PROC envoys make their first appearance at Freedom Day rites abroad", *DFAR* 2, no. 7 (1975): 1; *DFAR* 2, no. 6 (1975): 4.
25. *Philippine Diplomacy*, pp. 167, 311.
26. Margaret Burke Guerrero to the author, email, 1 August 2006.

24

Martial Law Propagandist

Though on a tight schedule, Guerrero decided to develop into a booklet his thesis on the raison d'être of martial law he put forward in his *New York Times* article. Romulo launched *Today Began Yesterday* in Manila in early September 1975 and was issued as a newspaper serial in late September in time for the anniversary of the proclamation of martial law. Retitled later as *Why Martial Law?*, Guerrero justified the imposition of martial law in the Philippines, which he hoped would bring about reforms, using Philippine history as a backdrop beginning with the Philippine Revolution against Spain until 1972 in the context of Muslim secessionism and the CPP-NPA-orchestrated communist revolution. "One must seek in Philippine history," he noted, "the nature of these reforms, political as well as social, and the way to bring them about best suited to the traditions and character of the Filipinos." His thesis was that martial law, with its vision of a "New Society", was a long overdue recognition of Rizal's call for "social regeneration" and Mabini's exhortation on "internal revolution", which led Quezon to promote "partyless democracy" in a society Senator Juan Sumulong called "farcical representative government" reigned by "feared and detested oligarchy".[1]

What should the "New Society" accomplish? As if to remind President Marcos, he stated it would:

> would face the task of redressing grievances that had been mocked in the past, and fulfilling desires and aspirations that remained frustrated; of redeeming the peasants from age-old bondage, and giving them the lands that the Revolution had promised; of 'democratizing wealth' and enlisting it to provide tolerable lives for the common people; of assuring equal progress for all in a just society without sacrificing the workers

to the technocratic goals of full and rapid development at any cost; of reconciling the basic human rights and freedoms with the requirements of national discipline and security; of devising a form of representative democracy that would enable the ordinary Filipino, in his village, farm or humble tenement, to make his voice truly heard, and his will effectively participate in the great decisions of his government.[2]

On the reason why he wrote the essay, Guerrero said empathically in 1981:

> What most people don't understand is what I think is the primary duty of anyone in the government service. I am an ambassador, see. If you don't agree with the policy of the government, the only honest thing to do is to resign, to quit. If you stay in the government, so to speak, as the British say, get the king's shilling, make your living out of the government, you had better do what the government wants you to do, otherwise you should get out.

It sounded like a defensive self-justification of his action but he saw in President Marcos the qualities he saw in President Quezon.[3]

Being a bureaucrat, he saw martial law as a "historical necessity" as President Marcos phrased it at that juncture in Philippine history. There were no better alternative to save the Republic than martial law against threats of Moro secessionism and communist revolution. The environment, too, could have shaped his decision. Guerrero was serving a president who was in fact a military dictator and he himself was flirting with dictators — presidents who were strongmen, heirs to the *caudillismo*, the blessing and the curse of Latin America. He had seen them in leaders like Franco and they would not to be the last. In addition, Guerrero was not the only Filipino intellectual who supported and justified martial law because other Filipino intellectuals lent their names to its cause.[4]

His stand in support of martial law was also taken by his sister Chitang and his brother Mario. Both occupied posts in the Marcos bureaucracy with Chitang heading first the National Historical Commission in the late 1960s, then the Technological Management Resource Center as Director-General from 1976 until 1985, while Mario worked as cardiologist at the Philippine Heart Center for Asia. Guerrero's friend Salvador Lopez, took a different and opposite course, and as president of the UP, led the faculty and students into street activism. The Jesuits, one of whom was Father Lorenzo Ma. Guerrero, his cousin-friend from college, were critical of the martial law regime. Guerrero's good friend Father Horacio de la Costa who had just come back from Rome as one of the Jesuit Order's general consultor, issued along with others a statement condemning martial law in October 1975. Thus, there must be truth that martial law divided the Guerrero clan as Wilfrido Ma. Guerrero said: "The February 1986 Revolution also divided the Ermita Guerreros. And all because of the tragic conjugal dictatorship."[5]

In direct contrast to his support for martial law, Guerrero wrote a play, *Tatang*, about a rebel leading his men in resisting the government. Divided into twenty-one acts excluding the ending, it was his first work written in Tagalog, conspicuous in its tortured sentence construction (Guerrero seemed to be translating from English to Tagalog) most probably written back in New Delhi after the declaration of martial law. Using his popular pseudonym, "Totoy", he submitted it as an entry to a contest. In the play, a former guerilla during the war was frustrated with the politics and killed a politician. Tatang — the name of the protagonist — and his men headed to the mountains and planned to buy a large cache of arms for their struggle. In the end, in the middle of a skirmish against bandits, Tatang was injured. As he was dying, he reminded his activist son to fight against excesses of power that could be checked only by the sweat and blood of poor people rising in arms. Was Guerrero commenting on the abuse of power that martial law would instigate?[6]

Then in one of his conversations with Margaret, he expressed his dismay over the New Society. He did not believe it was genuine. When he saw in a magazine that Imelda Marcos was listed as one of the ten richest people in the world, he was outraged.[7]

GEMMA IN MEXICO

But the Guerrero family's support for martial law had had unintended consequences. Antonio "Tonypet" Araneta, husband of Gemma, was arrested by the military after months of hiding but released upon the intercession of Chitang. Tonypet felt that it would be safer for Gemma and their children to go abroad. Thus, Gemma with her two children arrived in Mexico one night in October 1975. Guerrero sent two embassy officials to meet them at the Benito Juarez International Airport. Welcoming his niece and the two children, Fatimah and Leon, his namesake, at Torrecillas Street, he told her that they could occupy the second-floor suite beside his private study room "overlooking a small side garden with a gorgeous flame tree decked out in all its autumn splendor".[8]

The arrival of Gemma and her children was a welcome respite from the daily tasks in the office. In his free moments, he would talk to Gemma not in Spanish but in Tagalog, spending hours gossiping about the family. He would invite her to diplomatic receptions given by the diplomatic corps, and to concerts at the Teatro de Bellas Artes. On weekends, he took her to lunch to places like Oaxtepec, Cuernavaca or Desierto de Leones. When the embassy limousine was not in use, he would let her tour the city for a visit to museums and galleries with the embassy chauffeur. In due time, Gemma would find their own house because her children "needed more space and fresh air". She would work as an English teacher for three years. They would stay long after Guerrero had left Mexico.[9]

APPOINTED TO HAVANA

The official visit to Cuba in July 1975 by the First Lady yielded another jurisdiction to the mission when in September Guerrero was notified by the Cuban Embassy in Mexico that the Cuban Government had approved his appointment to Havana — a historic restoration of the ties discontinued in 1961, when anti-communism was the hallmark of Philippine foreign policy, after the Cuban charge d'affaires in Manila was linked to subversive activities. Again, Guerrero and Margaret flew to New York to be present at the UN session that was attended by Imelda Marcos who spoke on a world code of ethics before the General Assembly.[10]

Finally, in March 1976, Guerrero presented his credentials in Havana to Oswaldo Dorticós, Cuban minister of foreign relations. Fidel Castro had just consolidated his power in the First Party Congress in December 1975 and the Cuban people had ratified a socialist Constitution in February. In Havana, though per diems were allocated, the Guerreros ran short of money. When handed the bill, of almost US$1,000, Guerrero was shocked to learn that they did not have enough to pay. He told them suavely that that was all the money they had scrapping all the Mexican pesos they had, which settled the fuss. While in Cuba for almost four days, he did not personally meet Fidel Castro who was in Africa, which he regretted because he admired the Cuban revolutionary. Margaret, however, had the opportunity to see Castro who called her "la filipina rubia" in a special event among ambassadresses prior to the presentation.[11]

Nonetheless, he visited museums and met leading Cuban poets and one editor Nicolas Guillén induced him to publish a collection of Filipino writings in Spanish. Alongside this plan was the publication of a magazine in Spanish to be named *El Galeón de Manila* in honour of the annual ship that plied the seas from Manila to Acapulco. Guillén was editor of a famous Cuban magazine which had tremendous influence in

Latin America. To realize the plan, Guerrero wrote to people in Manila to send him all the winners of the Zobel Prize and all the poems of the foremost Filipino poets such as Manuel Bernabe, Jesus Balmori and Cecilio Apostol. When he was done checking all these writings, he was of the opinion that there was "nothing, nothing that would not merit the instant contempt of modern Cuban, Mexican, Spanish, Latin-American audiences". He showed them to Guillén who agreed. Thus, the plan was aborted and so was the magazine.[12]

TOWARDS THE NEXT POST

Catering to the needs of the small Filipino community in Mexico, Guerrero and Margaret accepted the invitation to a luncheon hosted by Romeo and Nina Tabuena at their residence in San Miguel Allende. Guerrero owned a number of Tabuena's earlier paintings. As a patron and connoisseur of art, he cultivated relations with Filipino painters and artists. The latter included Filipino conductor, Redentor Romero, who was invited by the Mexico State Symphony to inaugurate the new season. Guerrero gave a farewell reception in honour of Romero. Another painter he patronized was Vicente Manansala; he bought a number of Manasala's paintings. The embassy served as the site of the small gathering in June 1976 when a small get-together was held in honour of the Filipino community. Guerrero conferred the Golden Heart Award on a well-known Mexican cardiologist. Then, in November, he arranged for Romulo's official visit.[13]

Guerrero's years in Mexico were marked by illness and visits to his doctors. He contracted emphysema for he was a heavy smoker, a condition aggravated by the environment — Mexico City had a high air pollution density. In one of his visits to his doctor, he was told to give up smoking but he shrugged it off.[14]

His stay in Mexico nurtured his bond with Margaret and his son. Margaret said of Guerrero: "He was fascinating in conversation. I was never bored with him. We had plenty to talk about. He had enormous laughter roaring like a lion. He was an avid reader." To his son, he was not an indulgent father. Nonetheless, he tried to maintain a link with David by sending postcards because it was only during the holidays that they had opportunities to meet and talk.[15]

After Romulo's visit, Guerrero learned of his assignment to Belgrade as the first resident ambassador. It was in recognition of his pioneering advocacy of non-alignment. The Guerreros flew to Belgrade in late November and stayed during the sickly years of Marshal Joseph Broz

Tito, the recognized leader of the non-aligned nations, and the Socialist Federal Republic of Yugoslavia since 1953. They left Mexico under a threat of economic dislocation as rumours were rife that the Mexican peso was about to be devalued. President Echeverría left the government suffering from a huge balance of payments deficit and a devalued peso to be passed on to the incoming administration of President Jose López Portillo.[16]

As a post, Mexico did not meet the expectations of a higher trade volume and balance in favour of the Philippines. Although Guerrero received in June a Foreign Service circular reiterating to all chiefs of mission their role in promoting Philippine trade, it was too late; more so, the lack of budgetary allocation militated against the effective implementation of the policy. Trade with Central American countries posted a balance in favour of the Philippines except in 1975. However, overall, Philippine trade with Latin America during Guerrero's time posted a negative balance of trade, reaching its peak when the Philippines successfully negotiated for oil with Mexico in 1980. Although the Philippines suffered from the oil crisis in 1973–74 and could have taken advantage of its relations with Mexico, it was only in 1975 when Mexico's oil output surpassed domestic consumption that the next administration used its petroleum assets in 1976 as guarantee for international loans and for export.[17]

Guerrero's appointment to Mexico was timely and appropriate when Philippine foreign policy had recognized and adopted his foreign policy advocacies. He expanded the Philippines' diplomatic map to a dozen countries in Latin America, defended martial law in an environment where *caudillos* were the norm rather than the exception, and tried to maintain his historical and literary inclinations.

Notes

1. "CPR to launch Guerrero book", *DFAR* 2, no. 8 (1975): 1, 8; *Daily Express*, 21–29 September 1975; Guerrero, *Today Began Yesterday*, p. 2.
2. Ibid., pp. 54–55.
3. Alegre and Fernandez, *Writer and his Milieu*, p. 87.
4. Ibid., p. 86. On Latin American politics, see Simon Collier et al., eds. *The Cambridge Encyclopedia of Latin America and the Caribbean* (New York: Cambridge University, 1992), pp. 324–34. One was Onofre D. Corpuz, once Education Minister and UP President.
5. Nakpil, *Legends & Adventures*, pp. 203–206; Sison and Chua, *Armando Malay*, p. 168; Mark R. Thompson, *The Anti-Marcos Struggle: Personalistic Rule and Democratic Transition in the Philippines* (Quezon City: New Day Publishers), p. 73; W.M. Guerrero, *Guerreros of Ermita*, pp. 7, 80.
6. Leon Ma. Guerrero, *Tatang* (In original typescript, University of the Philippines Main Library, 1972), no page number.

7. Margaret Burke Guerrero, interview by Alexander Umali, Bel-air, 14 January 2002 (courtesy of David Guerrero).
8. Nakpil, *Legends & Adventures*, pp. 153–54; Gemma Guerrero Cruz, "A reluctant exile", *STM*, 20 August 1989, pp. 4–8.
9. Ibid.
10. "Guerrero to Cuba", *DFAR* 2, no. 9 (1975): 1; "FL proposes world code of ethics at UN", *DFAR* 2, no. 10 (1975): 1.
11. *Philippine Diplomacy*, p. 58; Kneedler, *An Introduction to Latin American Politics*, p. 82; Margaret Burke Guerrero, interview by the author, Dasmariñas Village, Makati City, 29 April 2006; Leon Ma. Guerrero to Carmen Guerrero Nakpil, 30 March 1976 in D. Guerrero, *LMG*, p. 420.
12. Alegre and Fernandez, *Writer and his Milieu*, p. 83.
13. *DFAR* 3, no. 7 (1976): 5; *Philippine Diplomacy*, p. 167; *Community News*, 11 February 1976; *The News*, 25 February 1976.
14. Margaret Burke Guerrero to the author, email, 1 August 2006.
15. Margaret Burke Guerrero, interview by the author, Dasmariñas Village, Makati City, 29 April 2006.
16. Meyer and Sherman, *The Course of Mexican History*, pp. 675–76. For a discussion on Tito's Yugoslavia, see Fred Singleton, *A Short History of the Yugoslav Peoples* (New York: Cambridge University Press, 1985).
17. Kessler, "Development Diplomacy", pp. 218–19; Ingles, *Philippine Foreign Policy*, p. 150.

25

At Tito's Pre-Balkanized Yugoslavia

It took five years for the Philippines to finally establish a permanent mission in Belgrade since 1972 when an exchange of letters was made between the two governments. The Yugoslav Government in 1973 accredited their Tokyo ambassador as non-resident envoy to the Philippines. After two years, they decided to send a resident ambassador to Manila. From 1972 until Guerrero's arrival in Belgrade in November 1976, there were several diplomatic engagements between the Philippines and Yugoslavia such as the signing of an agreement on waiver of non-immigrant visa requirements in Manila; Romulo's visit to Belgrade; visits to Manila of a member of the Federal Executive Council; a minister of economy and head of the Yugoslav delegation to the Third Ministerial Meeting of the Group of 77, a federal secretary for Finance and the governor of the National Bank of Yugoslavia.[1]

The Yugoslav Government leased a terrace-type building to house the Philippine Embassy and the ambassador's residence. Guerrero was accepted as Philippine ambassador by the Yugoslav government in early January 1977. A few days after, four Yugoslav football specialists arrived in Manila to provide training to more than fifty coaches under the FIFA Coca Cola World Football development programme. From reading English newspapers that had to come all the way from Paris, he learned that Yugoslavia was reeling from an economic crisis. By the end of 1976, the World Bank had loaned more than US$1 billion to Yugoslavia followed by another US$1 billion in two loans in February 1977. In the middle of this uncertainty, he had to come home in March to attend the funeral of de la Costa who died from liver cancer.[2]

FULFILLING A REQUEST

Guerrero attended the funeral in Novaliches to pay his last respects to his best friend. After the funeral, he went to Chitang's house in San Juan. Chitang could not forget that afternoon: "His face had darkened several hues and his eyebrows were knit over downcast eyes. Gone was the sunny smile. His shoulders drooped and he seemed to be dragging his feet to the couch in my living room. We sat together wordlessly for a long time, sunk in sorrow, digesting the fact that, both he and I, had lost someone who was, for us, the best creature to have walked this earth." He went home to fulfil the last of de la Costa's request — to deliver the commencement address before the graduating class of the Ateneo, which was also the centenary of Rizal's graduation.[3]

Still smarting from the loss, tipsy Guerrero talked about his favourite topic, relevant to the occasion, which was about the young Rizal whom he described as "the boy who was nothing", listened to by 400 graduating students. "I address you," he said in tribute to de la Costa, "in the honoured place of one who was my classmate for many years in this school, my boon companion in all manner of scholarly gallivanting, my philosopher and the friend of my youth and over many long separations — Horacio de la Costa." He continued:

> I am told that in his last illness he asked the reverend authorities of this university that I should speak in his stead at these exercises and neither they nor I do less than accept the commission. Yet am I conscious now of the heavy burden, for only his erudition, felicity of perception, and elegance of language would have matched this evening's theme, and I can only attempt in these brief reflexions to venture to convey what he might have thought and said....[4]

The point of his speech was that Rizal was singularly honoured because he was the national hero who came from Ateneo; that when he graduated from Ateneo, he was "a boy who was nothing … But if he was still nothing, he had the capacity to become everything"; that among the twelve graduates, nine *sobresaliente* like Rizal, only Rizal found his greater place in the nation's history because he lived in a time of change and made "the choice for change". He left the graduates with the question if their batch would be commemorated in a similar rite 100 years later, a question he said only they would know the answer to.[5]

FAILING HEALTH, RISING DEBT, PROMOTING EXPORTS

Guerrero flew to Belgrade facing a country in a crisis. In June 1977, another loan of less than US$1 billion dollars was granted for a nationwide agricultural programme. It was the failure of the Five Year Plan caused by factors outside the government's control but also by the complacency of the Yugoslavs, particularly Tito's economic managers who failed to curb the import of consumer goods. Guerrero has just presented his credentials on 14 June to Yugoslav Vice President Steven Dorojski calling for closer relations between the Philippines and Yugoslavia. In any case, he made possible the signing of a cultural agreement in Manila between the Philippines and Yugoslavia in September. It provided for the exchange of books and periodicals, non-commercial films, arts and other cultural forms; exchange of professors, scholars and artists; grants of scholarships to students of both countries; and exchange in the area of sports and physical education.[6]

Once the Yugoslav Foreign Ministry invited Guerrero to an annual party for ambassadors that involved hunting. Upon receiving the invitation, he immediately remembered that the previous year the Austrian envoy has accidentally killed the French ambassador. Knowing how dangerous the sport was, he went to the hunt but did not use a shotgun and instead stayed in the hunting lodge. Tito, a hunting aficionado, once killed a grizzly bear, which upon seeing it, Guerrero was said to have been horrified.[7]

Busy with his usual chores, Guerrero's health got worse. His emphysema troubled him. He had poor appetite because he craved for Filipino food. A Filipina who was stranded in Belgrade and sought help from the embassy provided the opportunity for him to taste Filipino dishes. This lady while en route to Rome via train had her things stolen. The embassy prepared the papers for her departure. While under the embassy's custody, she was able to cook *pancit* and other Filipino dishes. Guerrero, however, ate a little. Having stayed in Belgrade, he was fond of a popular Yugoslav dish — beans stewed in paprika sauce.[8]

Although he was becoming languid because of failing health, Guerrero was never remiss in his duties as ambassador. He managed to host gatherings with the help of Margaret and the embassy staff. For instance, on the celebration of independence in 1978, most of the diplomatic corps members were invited to the Panorama Hall in Hotel Jugoslavija. The overall assessment on the reception was "one of the best, if not the best ever held in Belgrade". He was sent as the Philippine representative to the Non-Aligned Foreign Ministers Conference in Belgrade in July, enabling him to witness the intense lobbying done to prevent Cuba from hosting the next summit; the debates on the meaning of the movement itself and President Marshal Tito himself lambasting "new forms of colonial presence" and "domination" among their bloc, an allusion to the Soviet and Cuban incursion in Africa. His enunciation of non-alignment was realized in August 1975 in Lima, Peru when the Philippines, as guest at the Foreign Ministers Conference, applied for observer status in the movement.[9]

The last two years of his term saw the visits of important Yugoslav officials that strengthened Philippine-Yugoslav relations. One of these was the visit of Federal Executive Council Vice President Branislav Ikonic and Assistant Federal Secretary for Foreign Affairs Kazmir Vidas, delegates to the UNCTAD V in mid-1979. The most important, however, was the state visit of Vice-President Fadilj Hodza made in the same year from 28 June to 2 July, which led to the signing of a joint statement with President Marcos. Vice-President Hodza pledged support for the Philippine application as observer in the Non-Aligned Movement Summit Meeting in Havana in September. Guerrero sent dispatches to the Home Office about the economic instability of Yugoslavia because by the last quarter of 1979 the total indebtedness of Yugoslavia rose to between US$11 billion and US$13 billion.[10]

Along the lines of export promotion following the Foreign Service circular of 6 October 1978 and amplified by another Foreign Service circular in January 1979, Guerrero directed his staff towards this end. During this period (1977–80), the Philippines posted a favourable balance of trade with Yugoslavia while a trade agreement was underway.[11]

Memories of his stint in Mexico came rushing back when he and Margaret learned of the cruel death of a Guatemalan diplomat friend in late January 1980. Adolfo Molina Orantes was applying for visa in the Spanish Embassy to enable him to attend a legal conference in Madrid. The Spanish Embassy, however, was taken over by insurgents and a shoot-out took place between them and the Guatemalan military, which led to the embassy being set on fire where Orantes was burned to death along with others.[12]

LEAST ENJOYED BUT MEMORABLE

Yugoslavia was the post Guerrero least enjoyed among the countries where he had been assigned because, as he confessed, "I was weak in the language. I don't enjoy being in a country where I can't read the newspapers; I can't even listen to the radio; I don't know anything; I'm lost completely." Even newspapers like *The International Herald Tribune* had to come from Paris for him to know the news. Margaret, on the other hand, tried to learn Serbo-Croat. During his stay in Belgrade as in Mexico, he did not publish collections of his speeches. One reason was he did not deliver many speeches. The other reason was his failing health prevented him from doing so.[13]

There was one incident that made Belgrade memorable to him as a father. David, his teenage son, was punched in the mouth by a son of an ambassador, at a party. At first, Margaret and David did not know what to do. Eventually, David appealed to his father to write a letter addressed to the ambassador. Guerrero wrote it, demanding an apology that never came. Nevertheless, it made him closer to David who was attending Dartington, a co-ed school where they did not wear uniforms and where they called each other by their given names. In this school, David was in contact with "kids from the liberal media establishment and free thinkers". Even though separated from each other for many years, the genes could not conceal the likeness of father and son. David, years later, would acknowledge the influence of his parents on him, especially his father: "From my father, I got my perfectionist streak and quest for excellence, and from my mom, my sense of fairness and egalitarianism." Guerrero was very proud of his only son who knew how to play the piano. Although they seldom saw each other except during holidays, Guerrero did not forget to send postcards to David, a habit he started in India and Mexico. When he turned sixty-four, eighteen-year-old David affectionately sang him the Beatles song "When I'm Sixty-Four", making him doubly happy.[14]

AT TITO'S FUNERAL BEFORE RETIREMENT

As proof of President Marcos' confidence in him, Guerrero was appointed special envoy to the funeral service of President Marshal Tito in May 1980 — the culmination of his advocacy for non-alignment. In fact, First Lady Imelda Marcos wanted to attend the ceremony. Sick with a heavy cough and a broken hip, he was concerned about this dilemma so he called his translator and asked her if the Yugoslav Government could accommodate the First Lady and her famously large entourage in a villa. She answered rather correctly that it was better to consult the Foreign Ministry. Immediately, Guerrero explained his position via telex to the Home Office.[15]

That same day, Manila replied that the president was appointing him representative. Attended by heads of states such as USSR President Leonid Brezhnev, People's Republic of China Chairman Hua Guofeng and others, he went to the ceremony, which needed some effort from him because he had to walk for the procession even though he was weak and sick. He deemed that being present was worth the sacrifice for a man of Tito's stature and integrity. He admired Marshal Tito's statesmanship because Tito managed to maintain his country's independence amidst the temptation of being drawn into either side of the Cold War, becoming the leader of the non-aligned countries who was able to withstand pressures from both camps. By being appointed in Belgrade, Guerrero's advocacy for non-alignment was rewarded and again expanded the Philippine diplomatic map to the neglected Eastern Europe.[16]

After celebrating his sixty-fifth birthday in March, also his twenty-sixth year in the Foreign Service since his appointment in 1954, Guerrero realized that he had to retire as all government workers had to. He confided to Margaret that he did not want to for where would he get his income. Unlike other diplomats, he never profited from his postings abroad. Chitang once wondered and asked how he was able to survive from the low salary he was receiving from the government. Laughing at the remark, he told her: "All it takes to succeed in government service is complete honesty, and yes, some patriotism and a little intelligence." Five months after Tito's funeral and capping it with a Grand Cross of the Order of the Yugoslav Flag, he retired from the service, packed their belongings in Belgrade and went home with Margaret to the Philippines in Donada Street in Pasay, the old home built by his father.[17]

Notes

1. *Philippine Diplomacy*, pp. 287–88.
2. *Bulletin Today*, 8 and 11 January 1977; Margaret Burke Guerrero, interview by the author, Dasmariñas Village, Makati City, 9 May 2006; Singleton, *A Short History of the Yugoslav Peoples*, pp. 267–68; Sicam, "A Man for all Seasons", p. 15.
3. Nakpil, *Legends & Adventures*, p. 134.
4. *TG*, 7 July 1977; 29 March 1978; John N. Schumacher, interview by the author, Ateneo de Manila University, 12 May 2006; L.M. Guerrero, "The boy who was nothing", in *We Filipinos*, pp. 100–103.
5. Ibid. See also *Bulletin of American Historical Collection* 6 (January–March 1978): 7–10. After his commencement speech at Ateneo, Guerrero delivered an address on the 35th Bataan Day before Filipino, American and Japanese World War II veterans at the Dambana ng Kagitingan, Mt Samat in Bataan on 9 April 1977. See *Evening Express*, 11 April 1977.
6. Singleton, *A Short History of the Yugoslav Peoples*, pp. 267–68; *Philippine Diplomacy*, pp. 287–88; "Cultural Agreement between the Government of the Republic of the Philippines and the Government of the Socialist Federal Republic of Yugoslavia", *Philippine Yearbook in International Law* 6 (1977): 206–9.
7. D. Guerrero, *LMG*, p. 435.

8. Margaret Burke Guerrero to the author, email, 1 August 2006.
9. *DFAR* 5, no. 6 (1978): 8; Thomas Scott, *The Diplomacy of Liberation: The Foreign Relations of the African National Congress Since 1960* (I.B. Tauris, 1996), p. 99; Ingles, *Philippine Foreign Policy*, pp. 15, 75–76.
10. *Philippine Diplomacy*, pp. 287–88; Singleton, *A Short History of the Yugoslav Peoples*, pp. 267–68.
11. Ingles, *Philippine Foreign Policy*, pp. 76, 239.
12. Margaret Burke Guerrero to the author, email, 1 August 2006.
13. Alegre and Fernandez, *Writer and his Milieu*, p. 90; Margaret Burke Guerrero, interview by the author, Dasmariñas Village, Makati City, 9 May 2006.
14. Margaret Burke Guerrero to the author, email, 28 October 2006; Margaret Burke Guerrero, interview by the author, Dasmariñas Village, Makati City, 29 April 2006; Pennie Azarcon-dela Cruz, "David's Goliath", *Sunday Inquirer Magazine*, 6 January 2002, pp. 3–4.
15. *Philippine Diplomacy*, pp. 287–88; Margaret Burke Guerrero to the author, email, 1 August 2006; Ljiljana Plavsic to the author, email, 7 January 2007.
16. Ljiljana Plavsic to the author, email, 7 January 2007; Singleton, *A Short History of the Yugoslav Peoples*, p. 271; Margaret Burke Guerrero to the author, email, 1 August 2006.
17. *DFAR* 7, no. 10 (1980): 5; Margaret Burke Guerrero, interview by the author, Dasmariñas Village, Makati City, 5 May 2006; *Malaya*, 22 September 2004.

Epilogue

Leon Ma. Guerrero "was one of the best writers in English the country has ever produced".

> F. Theo Rogers, Guerrero's superior in the *Philippines Free Press*

"A distinguished Filipino diplomat, the most eminent and the best equipped in our Foreign Service."

> Claro M. Recto, *Speech before the Chamber of Commerce of the Philippines*, 1956

"Ambassador Leon Ma. Guerrero has distinguished himself in the profession of letters… To Philippine letters he has brought a profound sense of history… His nationalism is the more profound because he has not repudiated the past but rather learned from it."

> Carlos P. Romulo, *Address before the Philippine Academy of Sciences and Humanities*, 1965

Upon his retirement, Leon Ma. Guerrero was the most senior career ambassador in the Philippine Foreign Service. Although he did not want to retire, heavy smoking and hard drinking had taken a toll on his health. His emphysema worsened. Yet, his interest in international affairs did not diminish. Seated or in bed while smoking, he would read Philippine newspapers and *Time* magazine bought to him by his houseboy whom he had difficulty conversing with in Tagalog. He could not walk because of a broken hip so that he had to use a wheelchair.[1]

During the last two years of his life, he suffered from bouts of depression leading him to alcoholism. He would drink tea during breakfast but would skip his meal to drink brandy in the morning. Difficult to feed, he would only eat *sotanghon* with soup, a diet that made him bony and lean. Once, Chitang brought him food for he was said to be pining for Ermita food.

"I brought him," she reminisced, "dishes from a caterer, French galantine, puffy *ukoy* made from rice flour that Mamá used to cook for him, *empanaditas* wrapped in *mille feuilles*, *pasta de mil hojas*, but he would throw them at the wall, fretfully complaining that they were not at all what he remembered." "I lost my patience one day," she continued, "and replied sharply (only to regret it as soon as I'd said it) that *he* was not at all what I remembered either [her emphasis]."[2]

He was becoming a recluse, a hermit in the traditional Ermita sense as Chitang put it. He would entertain once in a while Claudio "Ding" Teehankee, then Supreme Court Associate Justice; his brother, Mario, who occupied the first floor of the apartment in the same compound where they both lived; and Chitang. He agreed to write a preface to a collection of essays by Beth Day Romulo, the American second wife of the general, still playful as to reveal that the marriage caused apprehension in some quarters because of the ongoing negotiations between the Philippines and the United States on the bases and a new trade treaty. One day he allowed an interview by Doreen Fernandez and Edilberto Alegre in the presence of his wife Margaret. He did not allow them to take his pictures because he said he was too thin. He was still the Rizalist who would inquire on the latest studies on Rizal.[3]

He was fascinated with advertisements, how pithy words could draw emotions and motivations from people. He would no longer know that David — who was taking up International Relations at the University of Sussex — would take his fascination even further by becoming a successful adman. He encouraged David to write by telling him to send his pieces to and get published in *Mabuhay* magazine.[4]

In October 1981, he was closely following the Cancún Summit in Mexico where twenty-two countries and their representatives were gathered to thresh out ways to improve the conditions of the Third World as they proposed a "New International Economic Order". Revealing his cynicism about it in an article he wrote for a journal in December, Guerrero called the summit "a masterpiece of diplomatese" because it did not accomplish anything, blaming it on the unwillingness of the developed countries particularly Ronald Reagan's United States, which firmly supported free market policies in direct contrast to Third World aspirations.[5]

In the following months, he was indisposed to eating food. Sometimes, he would skip meals for three consecutive days with brandy as his sustenance. He would stop receiving visitors; he had become a complete recluse. By January 1982, Guerrero stopped smoking but his smoking and drinking had a deleterious effect so that by April until June, he was bedridden. He was able to entertain Lopez who, having heard that he was not well, went to visit him. He greeted his friend as in the good old days, edged with a trademark laughter "full-throated, uninhibited and wholly without malice". But the wasted warrior was at death's doorstep.[6]

In name and deed, Guerrero was the fearless but reckless warrior in diplomacy and letters. The collegiate editor who would clash with UP writers was the same diplomat talking back to a pompous fellow in the United Nations. Or the revisionist historical writer debunking the myths surrounding the Filipino campaign in Bataan was the same undersecretary of Foreign Affairs enunciating the "Asia for the Asians" policy. During these instances, Guerrero was bold and pioneering, qualities that are common in a writer, yet rare in a diplomat who, more often than not, had to toe the line or else face unwanted repercussion. "...[W]riters," he feels, "are often unaware of the consequences of what they write. What they feel as a private vision, a personal revelation, an intimate emotion, often becomes transformed, to their surprise and sometimes to their dismay and doom, into a public truth." But, in later years, he had tempered his pen with prudence and wit of a diplomat.[7]

Writing about the effect of geography on man, he believed that a milieu "does not determine everything a man is". "Because all men have free wills," he further asserted that the environment "does not predestine a human being but does test the strength of his will". In Ermita, the boy who could eulogize coloured people foreshadowed what was to come. Also, the youngster who reaped the most presents out of the Christmas visits showed promise at the negotiating table. Or, the teenager who could stand up against anybody to defend things Filipino foreshadowed the feisty fellow at a diplomatic luncheon in New York.[8]

This element of free will was not always present when Guerrero was growing up in Ermita. Born in a U.S. colony, he was educated under American Jesuits who taught him patriotism in colonial terms — loyalty to the United States is allegiance to the Philippines — and he idolized Hollywood stars. In short, he was a perfect specimen for an Americanized generation. Yet he was not. Knowing Spanish, he understood its legacies, which were the only links to the dying remnants of the Glorious Revolution of 1896, a historical moment alive in the memories of his grandfathers, uncles and aunts, and even his own parents. In that seed of Hispanic heritage grew the Filipino in Guerrero who in his life was searching for what it meant to be Filipino in a generation that was "almost hysterically pro-American" to him.[9]

This became the subject of his conversations with foreign friends, asking them their impressions of the Filipino. Revealing them in his classic essay "What are Filipinos like?" he cited the frequent complaint against Filipinos — their lack of self-reliance and their imitativeness. He would find the reasons for them in colonialism. Filipinos, however, retained their "good humor and the vitality to demand the only possible solution" to their troubles. To him, the Philippines seemed to inspire other nations to save the Filipinos, given the more than three centuries of colonialism, but he optimistically believed that Filipinos have learned that in the end they must save themselves.[10]

Guerrero saved himself in the throes of war by being pragmatic in his approach to his nationalism, enabling him to break free from the pitfalls of double allegiance — loyalty to America was professing allegiance to the Philippines. His association with Claro Recto, his mentor, further deepened and ripened his nationalism in the newly-born republic.

It was only Guerrero who was able to bridge the chasm separating the old generation of 1896 from the new generation accustomed to English and cut off from the mainsprings of Filipino nationalism. As a writer, he was conscious of this heritage enabling him to connect with the past, to link with the old generation and make communion with dead heroes.

In his search for the Filipino, he had to look for him in the lives of Filipino heroes. He would find in Jose Rizal the originary Filipino. He was obsessed with Rizal. Reading the hero's novels during his childhood goaded him to translate first Rizal's juvenile memoirs and novels, then to write Rizal's biography. *The First Filipino* is Guerrero's intellectual contribution — a political manifesto — calling for the integration of all the ethnicities in the building of a cohesive Filipino nation.[11]

That London was an influential milieu in this work was evident in that his spellings were British. Controversial in his treatment of Rizal's retraction, *The First Filipino* was able to engage a number of Rizalist scholars and historians. The least hagiographic and the best of all the biographies written on the national hero, it will continue to engage Filipino and foreign scholars interested in Rizal. Veering away from the hagiographical trend in the writing of Rizal's life by Filipinos, Guerrero established the canon in Philippine biographical writing, underscoring it with craft and style rather than mere enumeration of facts.[12]

With this significant contribution to Philippine literature, why is his place in Philippine literary history ignored and forgotten at present? He rose to prominence as a writer during the 1930s, the so-called "period of growth" or the "period of emergence" in Philippine literature in English.

Unlike previous collections in which one of his essays like the often-anthologized "What are Filipinos Like?" would be included, contemporary anthologies of Philippine literature do not include a sample of his works, no doubt reflecting the tastes of the anthologists finding him outdated. One casually mentioned him as an essayist without a representative essay of his, and he was not listed as a short-story writer. Another noted him only as a translator. As early as 1937, however, he was ranked among the leading short-story writers.[13]

Why is he not known today as a short-story writer? Popular during his *Free Press* days, Guerrero would receive fan mail. Jose Garcia Villa, the self-appointed critic, would issue his final word putting a short-story writer either in good or in bad repute in his "Annual Roll Honour" and "Criminal Record". Guerrero's reputation as a short-story writer suffered as almost every year one or two of his short stories would be listed in the "Criminal Record". Villa conditioned his contemporaries and the next generation of literary critics on what to consider as a "good" short story and who to consider as a "good" writer by getting rid of supposedly "bad" writers. Yet, Guerrero was not after literary eminence when he wrote what he called "Gothic stories". In any case, his "Still Small Voice" was listed in Villa's 1940 "Roll of Honour" for the short stories but Villa's literary canon had stayed on since then, marginalizing other fiction writers and the genres they represented.[14]

One of the genres that was overlooked was detective fiction. With short stories revolving around the exploits of Attorney Toni Tan and two novelettes, *The Case of the Seven Suspects* and *His Dishonor, the Mayor*, to his credit, Guerrero could lay claim to being one of the pioneers in, if not the father of, Philippine detective fiction in English deserving more than a passing notice in the history of Philippine literature in English.[15]

Guerrero's *Twilight in Tokyo* and *Passion and Death of the USAFFE* were eyewitness narratives indispensable in every account of the war. His *Twilight in Tokyo* was both autobiographical and eyewitness story on the fall of President Laurel's Cabinet in Japan until their return to the Philippines. His revisionist *Passion and Death of the USAFFE* was his first serious attempt in historical writing, asserting that Bataan was a Filipino fight and perhaps initiating the idea that Philippine history should be viewed through the eyes of the Filipino.[16]

But the early Guerrero was a humorist both in prose and in poetry — satirizing college life and later national events in "The Times in Rhymes" to great effect, using his pseudonym "Totoy". Deserving of a deeper study, these works are Guerrero's contribution to humorous writing in Philippine literature.[17]

In the field of Philippine diplomacy, Guerrero's place is certain. A prophet literally banished from his own country, Guerrero was either far-sighted — or his superiors behind the times — in advocating a reorientation in Philippine foreign policy towards Asia. Philippine foreign policy since President Roxas was totally aligned with the United States militarily (upon the signing of the Mutual Defence Treaty) and economically (upon the ratification of the parity amendment to the Constitution allowing U.S. citizens equal rights as Filipinos to exploit Philippine natural resources). Guerrero, however, benefited from and even participated in the stirrings for a change in Philippine foreign policy primarily spearheaded by Senator Recto.

In a series of foreign policy critiques from 1949 to 1951, Recto lambasted President Quirino's pro-U.S. foreign policy and urged a refocus of Philippine foreign policy to Asia, leading to the "great debate" in Philippine foreign policy with Foreign Secretary Romulo. As Recto's speechwriter during this debate, Guerrero propounded his ideas, subjected to refinement in articulation by his boss and mentor so that one could say they influenced each other on their respective convictions regarding Philippine foreign policy. But the origins of their Asia-oriented policy could be traced back to during the war at the height of the Japanese-foisted Greater East Asia Co-Prosperity Sphere propaganda when Recto was Guerrero's superior in the wartime Ministry of Foreign Affairs. Prior to his appointment as second secretary, Guerrero as Ignacio Javier had already intimated over the radio that Filipinos should take advantage of the opportunity that the war would present. To him, this meant breaking away from U.S. economic bondage imposed on the Philippines by exploring trading ties with Japan and other East Asian countries. The intellectual camaraderie between Guerrero and Recto, which started during the Ateneo alumni meetings as friendship, bloomed during Guerrero's work as associate attorney in the latter's law offices, as Senate legal and legislative adviser and Nacionalista foreign policy spokesman critical of President Quirino's foreign policy.[18]

Guerrero's policy declaration in redirecting Philippine foreign policy to Asia and re-examining Philippine-American relations had a bearing in the shape and contour of Philippine foreign policy in the next twenty years of his diplomatic career. The policy's significance and acceptance was already conditioned by the nationalist ferment that started at least five years ago through Recto's nationalist speeches. The difference between Recto's and his speeches was that Guerrero spoke in his official capacity (or so he thought, but was disabused shortly) seeking to infuse nationalism in official policy while Recto delivered his as opposition senator. Although Philippine foreign policy was, and still is, largely determined by the president aided by his secretary of Foreign Affairs, a man like Guerrero, a no ordinary career service officer, once an undersecretary of Foreign Affairs and acting secretary, and foreign policy expert, exerted pressures upon the make-up of Philippine foreign policy as presidents were forced to reckon, although belatedly, with his iconoclastic policy recommendations. However, his role in the evolution of Philippine foreign policy was part of a larger movement in Philippine society reacting to the vestiges of Western, especially U.S. colonialism. Those who first opposed Guerrero and his policy declaration, namely former Congressmen Macapagal and Marcos, would be the ones who would carry it out in their respective foreign policy reforms as presidents.[19]

As former UP President Salvador P. Lopez had observed in a lecture on Philippine foreign policy, "the new orientation of Philippine foreign policy toward Asia could no longer be held in check." President Magsaysay directed the establishment of the Institute of Asian Studies in the College of Liberal Arts at UP, later renamed the Asian Center during the late 1960s, to provide "common ground in which to bring together scholars and students in Asia ... for joint endeavors ... to preserve and advance their common cultural heritage". Magsaysay took notice of the importance of regional affairs through the SEATO although only upon the prodding of the United States keen to use it as a security organization against communism. Romulo was sent to the Bandung Conference in 1955 with Asian countries getting apprehensive of Philippine motives. The Philippines lost the opportunity to remove the suspicion among Afro-Asian countries in Bandung and to assume the leadership or share it with Indonesia.[20]

Re-examining Philippine-American relations and Philippine policy towards Asia was timely for, in 1954, negotiations on some of the provisions of the Bell Trade Act, soon to be called the Laurel-Langley Agreement, were underway. The negotiation extended the free trade for another twenty years. Two years later, sectors of Philippine society especially congressmen in an "outburst of nationalism" now insisted on the overall re-examination of Philippine-American relations, precipitated by the failure to solve problems arising from the U.S. military bases. That same year, negotiations on the bases were held amidst the clamour for the inclusion of all issues confronting Philippine-American ties. Lasting for nearly four months, the Bendetsen-Pelaez Base Negotiations failed to accomplish anything and, thus, this particular irritant to Philippine-American relations had to be dealt with among other things by subsequent administrations in an attempt to reassess Philippine-American relations.[21]

There were efforts to acquaint the Philippines with Asia before 1954 by participating in international conferences — the 1949 New Delhi Conference, the 1950 Baguio Conference, and the conferences of the Economic Commission for Asia and the Far East (ECAFE). President Quirino signed treaties of friendship with Pakistan and Indonesia in 1951 and with India in 1952. These developments happened after Recto's verbal assaults on Quirino's Asian policy. The problem remained and it was best summarized by Foreign Secretary Serrano in 1959 when he frankly said:

> There is no consolation in being free when people around us think we are not. In such a degrading environment, we cannot pursue our national destiny with honor and dignity. It is in the light of this new outlook that we have set in motion the forces that will enable us to rediscover the roots of our national soul and revive the mainsprings of Asian identity.[22]

President Garcia actively participated in regional affairs through the short-lived Association of Southeast Asia (ASA), his brainchild resulting from Malayan Prime Minister Tunku Abdul Rahman's visit to Manila in 1958. In 1959 Garcia visited Vietnam and signed a treaty of friendship with that country followed by a cultural agreement with Indonesia. Under the policy of "respectable independence", Garcia continued the re-examination of Philippine-American relations regarding the military bases. And it was during this policy that occasioned a "revolt" in Philippine foreign policy and the implementation of the "Filipino First" policy in Philippine diplomacy. Since 1946 it was a commonly accepted practice in Philippine diplomacy that whatever the U.S. position in international questions, the Philippines should vote as one with the Americans. Because of this, Philippine prestige and honour suffered. One instance of this happened in the UN General Assembly when a resolution on the partition of Palestine was being deliberated. The Philippines initially was against it because it would alienate Filipino Muslims but when the American panel applied tactics of intimidation to the Philippine panel, the vote went to the side of Israel favouring partition. In 1959 Robertson tried to dictate to the Philippine panel the position to be taken on the Tibet question in the United Nations. Malaysia and Ireland, acting supposedly at the behest of the United States, sponsored a full debate on Tibet on China's alleged human rights suppression. Discerning this pressure on the Filipino delegation, Guerrero protested and decried the undue influence, a classic "twisting of arm" by the U.S. delegation on the Philippine delegation in the so-called Guerrero-Robertson duel.[23]

Soon after he came to power, President Macapagal continued the re-examination of Philippine-American relations since Magsaysay, initiating major foreign policy reforms. When the U.S. Congress did not pass the Philippine War Damage Bill, Macapagal cancelled his trip to the United States in 1962 and changed the date of Philippine independence from 4 July to 12 June, the date of Philippine independence from Spain. In another assertion of independence, Macapagal in September 1963 put an end to the agreement stipulated in the Treaty of General Relations, specifically Article III in which the United States can represent the Philippines in countries where there is no Philippine representation. The long overdue negotiations over the U.S. military bases bore fruit when in August 1965 an agreement was signed, giving exclusive jurisdiction to the Philippines over all cases inside the bases.[24]

Vice President and concurrent Foreign Affairs Secretary Pelaez articulated Macapagal's foreign policy towards Asia when he said in a speech before the Manila Rotary, reminiscent of Guerrero's "Asia for the Asians" speech:

> We are a people basically Malay in origin, tradition and culture.... *Our role is not to advance the cause of Western democracy in Asia*, not to be an outpost of anybody or anything in Asia, not least of all to be a leader in Asia. Our role is simply to be ourselves, *instead of being caricatures of our former rulers*, to participate honestly and conscientiously in the building of our people's welfare and happiness and in the greatness of Asia [emphasis added].

Thus, President Macapagal directed major foreign policy initiatives such as the establishment of Greater Malayan Confederation and Maphilindo. These facilitated greater interaction with Asian neighbours, but in fact both were aimed at forestalling the establishment of Malaysia because of the Philippine claim to Sabah. In the end, the plans were only good on paper because the Philippines and Indonesia had to contend with the birth of the Federation of Malaysia. Beyond Asia, Macapagal opened diplomatic ties with African nations; strengthened ties with European countries and actively participated in the United Nations.[25]

Under the five preceding administrations, anti-communism was the hallmark of Philippine foreign policy. However, during the first term of President Marcos, there were attempts to relax the ban on travelling to communist countries. In 1969 Marcos considered opening diplomatic relations with communist and socialist countries, an option that Guerrero had in mind more than a decade ago. The shift in U.S. policy away from

Asia in 1969, known as the Nixon Doctrine, and U.S. President Nixon's visit to Communist China in 1972 paved the way for the establishment of trade and diplomatic relations to communist and socialist countries including China. The Philippine diplomatic map was expanded as trade relations with other countries were looked upon as a source of possible revenues and trade exploration under the rubric of so-called development diplomacy. It was Guerrero who first coined "diplomacy of development" in a lecture on Philippine foreign policy before Indian Foreign Service probationers in 1967 that was given a new twist in 1973 as "development for diplomacy" or "development diplomacy". Alongside this policy was the continued re-examination of Philippine-American relations on matters dealing with security and trade. The opening of diplomatic and trade relations with other countries was also seen as a possible solution to the loss of share in the U.S. market owing to the Laurel-Langley Agreement's expiration in 1974. Within Southeast Asia, Marcos energetically engaged with Asian neighbours resulting in the creation of ASEAN in 1967, soured only by the Jabidah massacre. Romulo, Marcos' foreign minister, lukewarm to the idea of "Asia for the Asians" policy at first, gradually witnessed its incorporation in Philippine foreign policy saying: "As the Philippines has veered away from its ties with the West, it has become more Asian-oriented, and is now more acceptable to its Asian neighbors." That would partly explain the holding of the Fourth Afro-Asian Writers Symposium in Manila in early 1975 because the Philippines was increasingly identified with the Third World, and thanks to Chitang Nakpil who was able to bring it to Manila from Kazakhstan.[26]

During the second half of Guerrero's career coinciding with President Marcos' tenure until 1980, it saw the evolution of Philippine foreign policy as it gradually looked towards Asia and made profound changes. His last three posts were remarkable for they coincided with the foreign policy reforms initiated by Marcos. From 1966 until 1972, he was posted to India and given additional assignments as non-resident envoy to Nepal and Afghanistan, an indication of how Asia had finally occupied a central place in Philippine foreign relations. His next assignment was Mexico and ten other Latin American countries including Cuba from 1972 until 1977, another indication of how Philippine foreign policy had adapted to Philippine economic needs. On his last post, he was assigned to a communist country, Marshal Tito's Yugoslavia, which was a testament to his far-reaching contribution to Philippine foreign policy. Able to assume the vacant position left by Recto as foreign policy critic and analyst, though very careful to add that he was speaking not as an ambassador but as a mere private citizen, Guerrero's foreign policy analyses on the opening of relations with socialist countries, on the lessons to be learned from Spanish experiences on military bases and on non-alignment as a development alternative were, no doubt, read and heeded by the president as well as by other foreign policymakers. In Belgrade, he represented the Philippines in the Non-Aligned Foreign Ministers Conference. It was not only an indication of the trust placed in him by Marcos but also a sign that the Philippines was taking the path towards non-alignment in foreign affairs. But it would take more than a decade, in 1992, a year after the dismantling of the U.S. military bases, before the Philippines was finally accepted as an official member of the Non-Aligned Movement. Guerrero was made and matured as a diplomat during the height of the Cold War. That would explain the preoccupation in his speeches about the resurgence of Asia, the role of the United Nations, its futility and its hopes, and the need to re-examine Philippine foreign policy in the context of international developments. In assessing Guerrero's role in the evolution of Philippine foreign policy, various factors interplayed producing the present template of Philippine diplomacy. Presidents became sympathetic to his cause, perhaps without even realizing it; they were forced to do so because of domestic and international pressures.

No less than President Marcos acknowledged Guerrero's contribution when he awarded to a frail-looking man on his deathbed the *Gawad Mabini*, the highest award in the Foreign Service in the suite specially opened for him by First Lady Imelda Marcos at the Philippine Lung Center. Marcos offered a pension or a book grant but Guerrero only wanted the Mabini medal. It was Rizal's 121st birthday, a very special occasion for Rizal's biographer. In a brief response to President Marcos in the presence of the First Lady, Prime Minister Cesar E.A. Virata, Romulo, Margaret, only son David, Chitang and Mario, Guerrero was still the warrior who could brandish his aged but sharp sword. "I am accepting the award," he declared with effort, "in the name of all career ambassadors of the Foreign Service of the Philippines, past, present and to come. We have been neglected, forgotten and persecuted by the *mean megalomania of our superiors*, but we shall always remember that only you remembered us these many years, and we shall not — I for one shall not — forget [emphasis added]." It was enigmatic because for whom did those words apply? Five days later, he died peacefully. It was as if he had waited for it — the recognition that he deserved. Guerrero still had projects unfinished. He was contemplating on writing a history of the Philippines. He had begun writing his memoirs but started from the wrong end, the beginning. One of his projects, a collection of his essays and speeches, was accomplished by his only son a few years later.[27]

A funeral service was held at the Ateneo College Chapel in Loyola Heights, Quezon City. A few of his colleagues were there to render their tributes because many of his friends abroad were unable to come. Prime Minister Virata, Presidential Spokesman Cristobal, former Secretary Ramos, Minister of State for Foreign Affairs Pelaez, Associate Justice Teehankee and finally Romulo delivered their respective eulogies to Guerrero. David in response gratefully acknowledged the warm tributes to his father.[28]

All were unanimous that Guerrero lived up to his nationalism. He was truly a loyal heir of Recto as Recto was Rizal's.

It is instructive that months before Guerrero succumbed to lung cancer, Lopez wrote a critique of *Today Began Yesterday* when it was re-issued as *Why Martial Law? A Historical Approach*. Lopez found the pamphlet as "more like retrospective justification of the regime. The time may be a little late for that." Accepting the rationale for martial law as one of historical necessity, he conversely asked: "how has the regime measured up to the goals that were set for it?" He did not agree with Guerrero that the difference between American and Filipino reactions to martial law "has a historical or psychological basis" because what happened in 1972 was "a bloodless coup d'etat". Lastly he called Guerrero's assumption that obedience to authority a racial trait "rubbish" because "that would be saying that the Filipino is a born slave, and in so doing, provide a perpetual license for dictators present and to come." The following week after the publication of his critical commentary, Lopez met Chitang who had a message from Guerrero to him and the message was: "I agree." As simple and as mysterious as that but it shed a clue to his disillusionment with Marcos and the martial law regime.[29]

As a writer, Guerrero — versatile yet quite adept in handling different genres, be it verse, short story, radio play, essay or novel — looked at writing as a means to an end in propagandistic terms. Looking at the range of his writings, Guerrero from his college days to being a diplomat showed the evolution of a propagandist. Honing his skills at Ateneo's college paper, he as the editor-in-chief made it the mouthpiece of the school's policies. As member of Chesterton Evidence Guild after graduation, he supported through his radio plays the Jesuit preference for a corporative state and Jesuit ideas on social justice. As a journalist writing for the *Philippines Free Press*, he espoused pro-Filipino though not necessarily anti-American convictions. After the war, he wrote *Twilight in Tokyo* in defence of embattled ex-President Laurel in the wake of his collaboration trial. During the height of martial law, he wrote *Today Began Yesterday* justifying Proclamation No. 1081 as a "historical necessity".

Guerrero in his writings believed in the power of the written and spoken word to bring about change in Filipinos' consciousness of themselves. In *The Passion and Death of the USAFFE*, which reflected a radical break in his thinking towards Americans and their policies following his experience during the war, he went against the belief that Bataan was an American fight; instead he believed it was a fight for and by Filipinos. In *The First Filipino*, his prize-winning biography of Rizal, he reminded "other" Filipinos, heirs to the originary Filipino, of the still continuing and unfinished project of nationhood. His "Asia and America" speech, better known as "Asia for the Asians" speech, called for the reclaiming of Filipinos of their Asian identity so that his posting in New Delhi was a confirmation of that claim. His translations of Rizal's early memoirs and novels, affirmed further by his postings in Spain, and later in Latin America, reminded Filipinos of their Hispanic heritage, and that weaning away from excessive pro-Americanism would mean strengthening ties with these countries. His speech on non-alignment as development alternative affirmed his belief in the aptitude of Filipinos to be self-reliant.

Finally, Guerrero knew the capacity of his writings for subversion. His English translations of Rizal's novels, particularly his method of placing the novel in the context of his times might have invited insurgent readings during the 1970s and 1980s contrary to what has been asserted in a faulty study of Guerrero's translation. His rebellious play, *Tatang*, would seem awkward if placed beside his support for martial law. It could mean, however, that as a government employee he was outwardly loyal but subversive at heart. It also meant that as a writer he could assume two contradictory positions: one that showed his dissident side while the other reflected his stand for the status quo. Thus, he could never be branded as totally pro-martial law, as he hinted to Lopez.

As a diplomat, Guerrero displayed uncommon and common qualities in his approach to international and domestic questions involving his country.

First, he was well informed regarding issues affecting the Philippines and the country where he was assigned to. In London as in Madrid, New Delhi, Mexico or Belgrade, he represented and promoted Philippine interests as they ought to be. He was the only Filipino diplomat among his contemporaries who made a thorough study of Philippine diplomatic relations with at least ten different nations. To wean Philippine foreign policy away from obsessive pro-Americanism, he favoured strong Philippine relations with Afro-Asia, Europe and Latin America.

Second, he had the faculty to speak his mind. Unlike diplomats who were content to parrot what their superiors would say, Guerrero could articulate to the public his position regarding controversial issues such as non-alignment, parity, and U.S. military bases. Although he would say that he was speaking in his private capacity as a citizen of the country, he was still a diplomat. Foreign affairs secretaries and presidents had no choice but to listen and heed his counsel.

Third, he bordered on being impudent, undiplomatic, and tactless on several occasions. Such impudence was necessary in a diplomat who wanted to assert his country's independence as in the case of his verbal duel with former U.S. Assistant Secretary of State Walter Robertson. A certain tactlessness was also imperative in a diplomat who wanted to defend and save Philippine honour as demonstrated during the Bangkok Talks on Sabah.

There was a quality of impulsiveness in Guerrero that was both a boon and a bane to him in his career. It led him to verbal and physical entanglements in his writing and in diplomacy. However, it served him to become assertive in his rights as an individual and as a Filipino.

Historian, translator and biographer, Guerrero managed to put on these hats while working as an envoy in foreign capitals. A loyal and brilliant state servant, he was a rare breed of an ambassador who combined his passion for literary and oral eloquence and his interest in history — a diplomat-scholar.

It is most telling that once when he was entering a building where all were required to deposit their guns at the security desk, Guerrero left his pen, which he believed was his only "weapon".[30]

Thus, here ends my story of Leon Ma. Guerrero, the diplomat-scholar.

Notes

1. Nakpil, *Myself*, p. 53; Nakpil, *Legends & Adventures*, p. 188; Abelardo Caro, interview by the author, Dasmariñas Village, Makati City, 29 April 2006.
2. Abelardo Caro, interview by the author, Dasmariñas Village, Makati City, 29 April 2006; Nakpil, *Myself*, p. 53.
3. Nakpil, *Myself*, p. 53; Leon Ma. Guerrero, "Filipinization of a Hoosier Lady", in *Perspective of a Diplomat's Wife* by Beth Day Romulo (Manila: Foreign Service Institute, 1981), p. iv; Alegre and Fernandez, *Writer and His Milieu*, p. 70; Abelardo Caro, interview by the author, Dasmariñas Village, Makati City, 29 April 2006.

4. David Guerrero, interview by the author, Dasmariñas Village, Makati City, 4 December 2016.
5. Leon Ma. Guerrero, "Conversations of [sic] Cancun Summit on Wealth and Poverty of Nations 1981", in *We Filipinos*, pp. 200–5.
6. Abelardo Caro, interview by the author, Dasmariñas Village, Makati City, 29 April 2006; Lopez, "The Laughter of Leoni", p. 4.
7. Guerrero, *The First Filipino*, p. 103.
8. Leon Ma. Guerrero, "Man and his environment", *SMM*, 27 February 1954, pp. 5, 6, 22.
9. Leon Ma. Guerrero, "Recto and Filipino nationalism", *MT*, 7 October 1960, p. 10A; Guerrero, "Prisoners of History", in *Prisoners of History*, pp. 13–23.
10. Leon Ma. Guerrero, "What are Filipinos like?", in *We Filipinos*, pp. 13–18.
11. Erwin S. Fernandez, "The originary Filipino: Rizal and the making of Leon Ma. Guerrero as biographer", *Philippine Studies* 57, no. 4 (2009): 461–504.
12. Erwin S. Fernandez, "Rereading *The First Filipino*: Interrogating León Ma. Guerrero's Rizal", *Danyag: Journal of Humanities and Social Sciences* 14, no. 1 (2009): 51–60.
13. Victoria Abelardo, "A Survey of Philippine Literature in English", *Philippine Prose and Poetry* IV (Bureau of Printing, 1951), p. 13; Joseph Galdon, *Essays on the Philippine Novel in English* (Quezon City: Ateneo de Manila University Press, 1979), p. 7; Leon Ma. Guerrero, "What are Filipinos Like?", in *Essays : English, American, and Filipino* by Arturo G. Roseburg (Barvadon Book, 1950), pp. 226–31; in *Philippine Contemporary Literature* by Asuncion Maramba (Bookmark, 1962*a*, 1982*b*), pp. 245–52*a*, 251–58*b*, in *Katha: Philippine Writing in English I* (Philippine Writers Association, 1955), pp. 195–204 and in *Looking at Ourselves: A Study of Our Peculiar Social Traits as a People* by Delfin F. Batacan (Philaw Pub., 1956), pp. 248–55; Bienvenido L. Lumbera and Cynthia N. Lumbera, *Philippine Literature: A History and Anthology* (Manila: Anvil, 2005); Asuncion D. Maramba, *Early Philippine Literature: From Ancient Times to 1940* (Manila: Anvil, 2006), pp. 321–22; Bienvenido L. Lumbera and Cynthia N. Lumbera, *Philippine Literature: A History and Anthology* (Manila: National Book Store, 1982), pp. 81, 88; Teofilo T. Del Castillo, *A Brief History of Philippine Literature* (Progressive Schoolbooks, 1937), p. 349. To keep alive his father's literary legacy, David Guerrero began to reprint and republish *Noli Me Tagere*, *El Filibusterismo* and *The First Filipino* after getting the rights to his father's books.
14. See Virginia Moreno, "A Critical Study of the Short Story in English Written by Filipinos from 1910 to 1941 with an Anthology of Representative Stories" (MA thesis, University of the Philippines, 1952); Elmer A. Ordoñez, "The Filipino Short Story in English: From the Commonwealth through the War Years to the Postwar Decade, 1935–1955" (MA thesis, University of the Philippines, 1956); Isagani R. Cruz, ed., *The Best Philippine Short Stories of the Twentieth Century* (Manila: Tahanan Books, 2000). Cruz relied on Leopoldo Y. Yabes' three-volume *Philippine Short Stories*. Yabes was influenced by Villa's Annual Honor Roll. Guerrero's "Hello,

Misinformation? A Short Story" was listed in 1933 "Criminal Record" as well as his "All Questions Answered" and "Anything Can Happen on Xmas" in 1934 and his "Power of Suggestion" in 1935. But his "Enemy of Caesar" got two asterisks, lacking only one for it to be included in the honour roll. His "Gift-Horses" was listed in 1936 but his "Escape" got two asterisks. In 1938, his "Man Who Knew Too Much" and "Three Wives" published in the *Promenade* were fair enough for Villa. See Chua, *The Critical Villa*, pp. 122, 164, 166,175, 177, 218.

15. See Leopoldo Y. Yabes, *Philippine Literature in English: 1898–1957* (University of the Philippines, 1958), p. 351; Leopoldo Yabes, "The Filipino Novel in English", *Herald Mid-week Magazine*, September 1941 in Deanna O. Recto, "A Critical Survey of Literary Criticism in English in the Philippines" (MA thesis, University of the Philippines, 1969), pp. 671–88; Majid, *The Filipino Novel in English*, pp. 40–41; Leopoldo Y. Yabes, "The Filipino Essay in English: A Critical Study with an Anthology of Representative Essays (1912–41) (MA thesis, UP, 1949), pp. 60, 77.

16. Alejandro Lichauco, *The Lichauco Paper: Imperialism in the Philippines* (Monthly Review Press, 1973), p. 70.

17. Gemino Abad cites "Halo-Halo" by Mapagbiro, pseudonym of Tom Inglis Moore, Australian professor of English in UP, published in the *Philippine Magazine* in 1930 as the first verse-column followed by Guerrero, not 1938 as Abad had written but 1934. See Gemino H. Abad and Edna Zapanta-Manlapaz, eds. *Man of Earth: An Anthology of Filipino Poetry and Verse in English from 1905 to the mid-50s* (Quezon City: Ateneo de Manila University Press, 1989), p. 13.

18. Renato Constantino, *The Making of a Filipino: A Story of Philippine Colonial Politics* (Quezon City: Malaya Books, 1969), pp. 128–29, 138, 139, 153.

19. Romani, *The Philippine Presidency*, pp. 149–73. Please see Erwin S. Fernandez, "Decolonizing the Filipino: Cultural-Intellectual Revolution in Contemporary Philippines", *Proceedings of the Asia Youth Culture Camp 2: "Doing Cultural Spaces in Asia" 26–29 October 2006*, edited by Kim Shin Dong et al. (Gwangju, Korea: Asia's Future Initiative, 2006), pp. 313–26.

20. Salvador P. Lopez, "New Directions in Philippine Foreign Policy", lecture given under the auspices of the Department of Political Science, at the Faculty Center, University of the Philippines, 10 June 1975, p. 11; Carolyn I. Sobritchea, "Reflections on the Development of Philippine Studies in the Philippines: The U.P. Asian Center Experience", *Asian Studies* 38, no. 1 (2002): 100.

21. Leon Ma. Guerrero, "The Philippines and the United States: Diplomacy of Readjustment", *STM*, 25 October 1952, pp. 4–6; Meyer, *A Diplomatic History of the Philippine Republic*, p. 175. For an overview of the negotiations, please see Gleeck Jr. *The Third Philippine Republic*, pp. 184–89.

22. *DFAR*, October 1959, p. 52; Agoncillo and Guerrero, *The History of the Filipino People*, pp. 631, 640.

23. Agoncillo and Guerrero, *The History of the Filipino People*, p. 625. For a personal account about it, see Ofreneo, *Renato Constantino*, pp. 90–108. See also Gleeck,

The Third Philippine Republic, pp. 76–77. On Garcia's foreign policy, see Severo C. Madrona, "Respectable Independence: The Foreign Policy of Carlos P. Garcia, 1957–1961" (MA thesis, College of Social Sciences and Philosophy, University of the Philippines Diliman, 2003).

24. The Philippines and the United States soon after the independence ceremonies signed a treaty of General relations that would, in effect, partly define the conduct of Philippine diplomacy and Philippine-American relations. Article III of the treaty, which stated that "pending the final establishment of the requisite Philippine Foreign Service establishments abroad" "... the United States of America will endeavor ... to represent through its Foreign Service the interests of the Republic of the Philippines in countries where there is no Philippine representation". "Excerpts from the Treaty of General Relations between the Republic of the Philippines and the United States of America, 4 July 1946".

25. Emmanuel Pelaez, "Philippines' Role in Asia", *Philippine International Law Journal* 2, no. 3 (1963): 364–65; Josue S. Dizon, "The Foreign Policy of the Philippines with special emphasis on the Macapagal Administration, 1961–1965" (PhD dissertation, American University, 1969), p. 237.

26. Kessler, "Development Diplomacy", passim; Collantes, "Diplomacy for Development", pp. 11–12; Romulo and Romulo, *The Philippine Presidents*, p. 153; Nakpil, *Legends & Adventures*, pp. 161–63. Although Kessler traced the term to Eugene R. Black, president of the World Bank (1949–62), Guerrero could have coined it independent of Black. On the Nixon Doctrine, please see Gabriel Kolko, *Confronting the Third World: United States Foreign Policy 1945–1980* (Quezon City: Karrel, 1988), p. 208.

27. *In Memoriam*, p. iii; Nakpil, *Legends & Adventures*, p. 187; Alegre and Fernandez, *Writer and His Milieu*, p. 88; Margaret Burke Guerrero, interview by the author, Dasmariñas Village, Makati City, 5 May 2006; Guerrero, *We Filipinos*, p. 10.

28. *In Memoriam*, pp. 1–14.

29. Salvador P. Lopez, "Authority and Liberty", *Mr. & Ms.*, 18 August 1981, pp. 6–7; Salvador P. Lopez, "Capsule Story of a Life", *Mr. & Ms.*, 1 September 1981, pp. 6–7.

30. Margaret Burke Guerrero, interview by the author, Dasmariñas Village, Makati City, 29 April 2006. She said that this anecdote came from Beth Day Romulo.

Glossary

Legend

Bu – Burmese   My – Malay
Ce – Cebuano   PhE – Philippine English
Fr – French   Sn – Sanskrit
Jp – Japanese Sp – Spanish
Lat – Latin   Tg – Tagalog
Mr – Maranao

aguinaldo	Christmas presents (Sp)
aide memoire	a memorandum or a note outlining items to be considered in a proposed agreement (Fr)
americana cerrada	a Philippine male dress with a close-necked coat plus a tie (Sp)
anito	idol (Tg)
aparador	cabinet (Sp)
arrabal	village (Sp)
Asociación de Universitarios Filipinos	Filipino University Students Association (Sp)
avenida	avenue (Sp)
ayuntamiento	city hall (Sp)
bahay kubo	nipa hut (Tg)
barong	a Philippine male upper garment costume known as *barong tagalog* characterized by transparent material made of piña threads (Tg)
Basta ya de barbaridades	Enough already of barbarities (Sp)
bibingka	native rice cake (Tg)
Bota Flores	an offering of flowers to the Ermita patroness, Virgen de Guía (Sp)
cacique	native or local elite (Sp)
calle	street (Sp)

carajo	a cuss word, which means "fuck", "shit", "damn it" etc. (Sp)
catálogo razonado	annotated catalogue (Sp)
caudillismo	a system of government in Latin America headed by a *caudillo*, usually a term to denote a strongman or a dictator; it later evolved to mean any unstable or weak government led by a personalistic leader, usually a military; it also means pejoratively as governments ruled by dictators as what happened in contemporary Latin America (Sp)
chaquetilla	small or short jacket (Sp)
colegialas	college girls (Sp)
coloquios semi-diplomáticos	semi-diplomatic conversations (or talks, dialogues) (Sp)
corrida de toro	bullfight (Sp)
daing	dried fish (Tg)
datu	chieftain (Tg)
despedida	farewell party (Sp)
dharma	in Hinduism it means fulfilment of one's duty according to law or custom; in Buddhism it is the law and order in the universe; in Sikhism, it is the path leading to righteousness (Sn)
día de la Hispanidad	"day of the Hispanic World", same as *día de la raza* (Sp)
día de la raza	"day of the race"; refers to the celebration of Hispanic heritage in Latin America held every 12 October annually (Sp)
dinuguan	viand cooked from pig's innards and blood (Tg)
disgustos	troubles, annoyances (Sp)
Dolor de mis dolores	Sorrow of my sorrows (Sp)
Don, Doña	honorific titles for upper class gentlemen or ladies used during the Spanish colonial period in the Philippines (Sp)
El Caudillo	literally, "the chief", referring to Francisco Franco as the paramount leader of the Spanish state (Sp)
empanaditas	turnovers (Sp)
Esclavos de María	Literally, "slaves of Maria", an annual Dominican pilgrimage (Sp)

GLOSSARY 315

fiscalize	a term in Philippine politics, which means to check, examine and scrutinize, particularly policies and programmes of the administration, usually performed by the opposition (PhE)
Gawad Mabini	Mabini Award, the highest decoration in Philippine foreign service, named after Apolinario Mabini, the first Filipino secretary of foreign affairs (Tg)
generalissimo	the supreme commander of the armed forces (Sp)
kris	a dagger with a wavy blade (My)
la filipina rubia	the blonde Filipina (Sp)
lavandera	washerwoman (Sp)
lechon	roasted pig (Sp)
Lok Sabha	House of the People, the lower house of India's bicameral parliament (Sn)
Lolo, Lola	a corruption of the Spanish abuelo and abuela, which means grandfather, grandmother respectively (Tg)
longyi	traditional Burmese clothing resembling the sarong (Bu)
malong	tube skirt usually woven and worn in southern Philippines (Mr)
Mang	term of respect for gentleman similar to mister in English or monsieur in French (Tg)
medianoche	the evening before Christmas (Sp)
merdeka	independence (My)
merienda	snacks (Sp)
mestizo	a racial type in Philippine society, which is the result of marriage between two different races (Sp)
mille feuilles	vanilla slice, custard slice, also known as Napoleon; a French pastry (Fr)
mision civilisatrice	civilizing mission (Fr)
okasan	mother, mum, mummy (Jp)
pagtitiis	passive resignation (Tg)
pancit	Philippine noodle dish (Tg)
panciteria	a market stall selling *pancit* and other street food (Sp)
pasta de mil hojas	Spanish equivalent of *mille feuilles* (Sp)
patis	fish sauce (Tg)
pensionados	student and professionals sent abroad to study

	supported by the Philippine government; in short, scholarship grantees (Sp)
procesos	trial records (Sp)
puñeta	a cuss word for "damn it" (Sp)
purdah	religious and social custom of female seclusion among Hindus of India (Sn)
puyo-puyo	common law husband and wife arrangement or cohabitation between partners without the blessing of the Church or sanction of the state (Ce)
Rajya Sabha	Council of States, the upper house of the same Indian parliament (Sn)
Sajonista	saxonist, pro-American (Sp)
sala	living room (Sp)
sala de armas	armoury (Sp)
salón de actos	assembly hall, events room or auditorium (Sp)
Santo Niño	venerated image of Jesus Christ as a child (Sp)
semana filipina	Filipino week (Sp)
semana santa	holy week (Sp)
sobresaliente	outstanding or excellent scholastic standing (Sp)
sotanghon	cellophane or vermicelli noodles (Tg)
summa cum laude	"with the highest honours", the highest scholastic standing accorded to a graduating university student (Lat)
tao	common people (Tg)
terno	Philippine female garment whose striking feature is the butterfly sleeves (Sp)
tertulias	afternoon meetings (Sp)
tinikling	Philippine national dance involving two sticks of bamboo, which the two dancers had to cross during their dance performance (Tg)
tio	uncle (Sp)
tornaviaje	the return route that Fr. Andres de Urdaneta had discovered from Manila to Acapulco (Sp)
toyo	soy sauce (Tg)
tuyo	dried fish (Tg)
ukoy	shrimp fritters (Tg)
un abrazo	a hug or embrace (Sp)
Valientes Filipinos!	Brave Filipinos! (Sp)
Vanitas vanitatum	Vanity of vanities (Lat)
Virgen de Guía	Virgin of Guidance (Sp)

List of Abbreviations

AAA	Ateneo Alumni Association
AM	Ateneo Monthly
ANZUS	Australia, New Zealand, United States
ASA	Association of Southeast Asia
ASEAN	Association of Southeast Asian Nations
BIR	Bureau of Internal Revenue
CEG	College Editors Guild
CIA	Central Intelligence Agency
CLU	Civil Liberties Union
DB	Diplomatic Bulletin
DFA	Department of Foreign Affairs
DFAR	Department of Foreign Affairs Review
DM	Daily Mirror
ECAFE	Economic Commission for Asia and the Pacific
EN	Evening News
FAO	Foreign Affairs Officer
FEU	Far Eastern University
Gomburza	Gomez, Burgos, Zamora
HDCP	Horacio Dela Costa Papers
ISO	International Sugar Organization
JRNCCP	Jose Rizal National Centennial Commission Papers
KALIBAPI	Kapisanan sa Paglilingkod sa Bagong Pilipinas
KAPINI	Kapisanan ng mga Pilipino sa Nippon
KBS	Knight of the Blessed Sacrament
LMGF	Leon Ma. Guerrero Folder
LMGFPF	Leon Ma. Guerrero File, Personnel Files
LMGP	Leon Ma. Guerrero Papers
LMGPCP	Leon Ma. Guerrero People's Court Papers
LMGPDP	Leon Ma. Guerrero Personnel Data Papers
LSH	League of Sacred Heart
Maphilindo	Malaya, Philippines and Indonesia
MB	Manila Bulletin
MC	Manila Chronicle
MDB	Manila Daily Bulletin
MFA	Ministry of Foreign Affairs

MIS	Military Intelligence Service
MPM	Magsaysay for President Movement
MT	Manila Times
NAMFREL	National Movement for Free Elections
NATO	North Atlantic Treaty Organization
NCAA	National Collegiate Athletic Association
PATO	Pacific Treaty Organization
PFP	Philippines Free Press
PH	Philippines Herald
PHILCAG	Philippine Civic Action Group
PLN	Philippine Liberty News
PRC	People's Republic of China
SC	Sunday Chronicle
SC-ECOSOC	Security and Economic and Social Councils
SEATO	South East Asia Treaty Organization
SMM	Saturday Mirror Magazine
SPLP	Salvador P. Lopez Papers
STM	Sunday Times Magazine
SYIM	See You in Manila
TG	The Guidon
TJ	Times Journal
UN	United Nations
UNCTAD	United Nations Conference on Trade and Development
UNESCO	United Nations Educational Scientific and Cultural Organization
UP	University of the Philippines
US	United States
USAFFE	United States Army Forces in Far East
USFIP	United States Forces in the Philippines
USSR	Union of Soviet Socialist Republics
UST	University of Santo Tomas
WWM	Weekly Women's Magazine
ZOPFAN	Zone of Peace, Freedom and Neutrality

Bibliography

Abad, Gemino H. and Edna Zapanta-Manlapaz, eds. *Man of Earth: An Anthology of Filipino Poetry and Verse in English from 1905 to the mid-50s*. Quezon City: Ateneo de Manila University Press, 1989.
Abaya, Hernando J. *The Making of a Subversive — A Memoir*. Quezon City: New Publishers, 1984.
———. *The CLU Story: 50 Years of Struggle for Civil Liberties*. Quezon City: New Day, 1987.
Abelarde, Pedro E. *American Tariff Policy towards the Philippines, 1898–1946*. New York: King's Crown Press, 1947.
Abelardo, Victoria. "A Survey of Philippine Literature in English". In *Philippine Prose and Poetry* IV. Bureau of Printing, 1951.
Abletez, Jose P. *Foundations of Freedom: A History of Philippine Congresses*. Manila: Merriam & Webster, Inc., 1989.
Abueva, Jose V. *Ramon Magsaysay: A Political Biography*. Manila: Solidaridad Publishing House, 1971.
Agoncillo, Teodoro A. *The Fateful Years: Japan's Adventure in the Philippines, 1941–45*, vol. 1. Quezon City: University of the Philippines Press, 2001.
———. *The burden of proof: The Vargas-Laurel collaboration case*. U.P.-Jorge B. Vargas Filipiniana Research Center, 1984.
——— and Milagros C. Guerrero. *History of the Filipino People*. Quezon City: Malaya Books, 1970.
Agpalo, Remigio. "Under the Third Republic". In *The Philippine Senate*, edited by Petronilo Bn. Daroy. Manila: DBE, 1997.
Alatas, Masturah. *The Life in the Writing: Syed Hussein Alatas: Author of the Myth of the Lazy Native*. Marshall Cavendish, 2010.
Alegre, Edilberto N. and Doreen G. Fernandez. *The Writer and his Milieu: An Oral History of the First Generation Writers in English*. Manila: De La Salle University Press, 1984.
Almario, Simuon. "Radio Gossip". *Graphic*, 26 December 1940.
Anand, Ram P. *Legal Regime of the Sea-bed and the Developing Countries*. Thomson Press (India) Limited, 1975.
Anderson, Benedict. "Hard to Imagine: A Puzzle in the History of Philippine Nationalism". In *Cultures and Text: Representations of Philippine Society*, edited by Raul Pertierra and Eduardo F. Ugarte. Quezon City: University of the Philippines Press, 1994.

———. "Hard to Imagine: A Puzzle in the History of Philippine Nationalism". In *The Spectre of Comparisons: Nationalism, Southeast Asia and the World*. Quezon City: Ateneo de Manila University Press, 2004.
———. "Rereading Rizal: The translator as propagandist". *Manila Chronicle*, 26 September – 2 October 1992.
———. " 'Noli' Bowdlerized". *Manila Chronicle*, 3–9 October 1992.
Annual Report of the Embassy Spain for the Fiscal Year 1962–1963. Madrid: Philippine Embassy, 1963.
Annual Report of the Embassy Spain for the Fiscal Year 1963–1964. Madrid: Philippine Embassy, 1964.
Annual Report of the Embassy Spain for the Fiscal Year 1965–1966. Madrid: Philippine Embassy, 1966.
Anonymous. "They like thrillers". *Philippines Free Press*, 10 September 1932.
———. "His honor, the author". *Philippines Free Press*, 15 February 1936.
———. "Cebu incident clarified". *Philippines Free Press*, 16 May 1936.
———. "News of the week: Not guilty". *Philippines Free Press*, 26 October 1940.
———. "Front page faces: He saved himself". *Philippines Free Press*, 2 November 1940.
———. "Hartendorp vs. the Ateneo". *Philippines Free Press*, 1 February 1941.
———. "Guerrero answers critics". *Philippine Liberty News*, 1 May 1947.
———. "Again, Guerrero". *Philippine Liberty News*, 3 May 1947.
———. "Bayanihan in London". *Sunday Times Magazine*, 17 April 1960.
———. "Guerrero's Translation of the 'Noli' ". *Philippines Free Press*, 29 July 1961.
———. "Dr. Alfredo Leon Guerrero". *Science for Schools* 6, no. 11 (November 1962): 8.
———. "RP shows renewed enthusiasm for Spain". *Examiner*, 19 August 1963.
———. "Leon Ma. Guerrero". In *Biographic Register*. Manila: Bureau of Printing, 1970.
———. "PROC envoys make their first appearance at Freedom Day rites abroad". *DFA Review* 2, no. 7 (1975): 1.
———. "CPR to launch Guerrero book". *DFA Review* 2, no. 8 (1975): 1, 8.
———. "Guerrero to Cuba". *DFA Review* 2, no. 9 (1975): 1.
———. "CPR Speaks". *DFA Review* 2, no. 10 (1975): 6.
———. "FL proposes world code of ethics at UN". *DFA Review* 2, no. 10 (1975): 1.
———. "The unseen Indian hand in Manila's Moscow diplomacy". *India eNews*, 21 August 2006.
———. "La herencia de las manitas". *El diario de hoy*, 12 November 2006.
An anthology of Carlos Palanca Memorial Awards winners. Manila, 1976.
Aquino, Benigno Jr. "Jabidah! Special Forces of Evil?". In *A Garrison State in the Make and other Speeches*. Benigno S. Aquino, Jr. Foundation, 1985.
Arcellana, Emerenciana Y. *The Social and Political Thought of Claro Mayo Recto*. Manila: National Research Council of the Philippines, 1981.
Arcilla, Jose S. S.J. "Ateneo de Manila: Problems and Policies, 1859–1939". In *The Jesuit Educational Tradition: The Philippine Experience*, Raul J. Bonoan, S.J. and James A. O'Donnell, S.J., eds. Budhi Papers no. 9, Ateneo de Manila University, 1988.

Arguilla, Manuel E. *How my brother Leon brought home a wife, and other stories*. Philippine Book Guild, 1940.
Ariff, Mohammed bin Dato Othman. *The Philippine Claim to Sabah: Its Historical, Legal and Political Implications*. Kuala Lumpur: Oxford University Press, 1970.
Azarcon-dela Cruz, Pennie. "David's Goliath". *Sunday Inquirer Magazine*, 6 January 2002.
Ateneo de Manila Preparatory School Class. *Graduates, Awards, Honors 1924/1927*. Manila: Ateneo, 1924/1927.
Ateneo de Manila. *Ateneo de Manila Annual Commencement 1920–1921*. Manila: Ateneo, 1921.
———. *Ateneo aegis 1931–1935, 1940*. Manila: Ateneo, 1931–1935; 1940.
———. *Ateneo Monthly Commencement Number 1923–1927*. Manila: Ateneo, 1923–1927.
"Authors' Vignettes". In *Philippine Prose and Poetry Volume Three*. Rev. ed. Manila: Bureau of Printing, 1961.
Avellana, Daisy H. *The drama of it: A life on film and theater*. Manila: Anvil, 2009.
Bacareza, Hermogenes E. *A History of Philippine-German Relations*. Quezon City: Self-published, 1980.
"Bachelor of Arts course". *Ateneo Monthly* (Commencement, 1926).
Barranco, Vicente F. "Leon Ma. Guerrero: The Hot Rod Driver as a Tourist Guide par excellence". *Philippine Panorama*, 11 July 1982.
Baviera, Aileen S.P. and Lydia Yu-Jose, eds. *Philippine External Relations: A Centennial Vista*. Pasay City: Foreign Service Institute, 1998.
Bernad, Miguel A. *Dramatics at the Ateneo: A history of three decades 1921–1952*. Manila: Ateneo Alumni Association, 1977.
Bonner, Raymond. *Waltzing with a Dictator: The Marcoses and the Making of American Policy*. Timesbooks, 1987.
Bonoan, Raul J. S.J. "Ateneo de Manila: Past and Future". In *The Jesuit Educational Tradition: The Philippine Experience*, edited by Raul J. Bonoan, S.J. and James A. O'Donnell, S.J. Budhi Papers no. 9, Ateneo de Manila University, 1988.
Bordas, Jane. "Diplomats' Wives also sweat it out'". *DFA Review* 1, no. 4 (1974): 8.
Buencamino, Felipe III. "The law and the non-lawyer". *Philippines Free Press*, 26 April 1941.
———. "Let's get rid of lawyers and lawyer-judges". *Philippines Free Press*, 21 June 1941.
———. *Memoirs and diaries of Felipe Buencamino III, 1941–1944*. Makati City: Copycat, 2003.
Camagay, Maria Luisa T. *Kasaysayang panlipunan ng Maynila, 1765–1898*. Manila: The Author, 1992.
Canivel, Virgilio. "Exposé of oratory". *The 1933 Ateneo Aegis*. Manila: Ateneo, 1933.
Carlyle, Thomas. "History as biography". In *The Varieties of History: From Voltaire to the Present*, Fritz Stern, ed. New York: Vintage Books, 1973.
Catholic Hour Pamphlets, 1939–40. Manila: Chesterton Evidence Guild, 1940.
Census of the Philippine Islands Taken under the Direction of the Philippine Legislature in the Year 1918. Vol. 4, part 2. Manila: Census Office of the Philippine Islands, 1920.

Chua, Jonathan, comp. and ed. *The Critical Villa: Essays in Literary Criticism by Jose Garcia Villa*. Quezon City: Ateneo de Manila University Press, 2002.

Cline, Howard F. *Latin American history: Essays on its Study and Teaching, 1898–1965*. Austin: Published for the Conference on Latin American History by the University of Texas Press, 1967.

Collantes, Manuel. "Diplomacy for Development [Speech delivered at the discussion series on national development, AIM, Makati, 26 September 1973]". In *From Mabini to Collantes: The Filipino Diplomat*. Manila: Foreign Service Institute, 1984.

Collier, Simon, Thomas E. Skidmore and Harold Blakemore, eds. *The Cambridge Encyclopedia of Latin America and the Caribbean*. New York: Cambridge University, 1992.

Combat History Division G-1 Section, Headquarters AFWESPAC. *Triumph in the Philippines*, edited by Celedonio A. Ancheta. Manila: National Bookstore, 1977.

Constantino, Renato. *The Making of a Filipino: A Story of Philippine Colonial Politics*. Quezon City: Malaya Books, 1969.

Coquia, Jorge R. *The Philippine Presidential Election of 1953*. University Publishing, 1955.

"Contemplating Soedjatmoko's Thought about Intellectuals." <https://ugm.ac.id/en/news/5531- contemplating.soedjatmoko%E2%80%99s.thought.about.intellectuals> (accessed 1 February 2016).

Cornejo, Miguel R. *Cornejo's Commonwealth Directory of the Philippines*. Manila: 1939.

Cruz, E. A. "Leon Ma. Guerrero — the writer". *Times Journal*, 26 June 1982.

Cruz, Gemma. "People I have known — II: 'Uncle Leoni was fun' ". *Manila Chronicle*, 24 September 1964.

Cruz, Isagani R. ed. *The Best Philippine Short Stories of the Twentieth Century*. Manila, Tahanan Books, 2000.

Cruz-Araneta, Gemma. "A reluctant exile". *Sunday Times Magazine*, 20 August 1989.

"Cultural Agreement between the Government of the Republic of the Philippines and the Government of the Socialist Federal Republic of Yugoslavia". In *Philippine Yearbook in International Law* 6 (1977): 206–209.

Day, Beth. *The Manila hotel: The heart and memory of a city*. Manila, 1986.

de Asis, Leocadio. *From Bataan to Tokyo: Diary of a Filipino Student in Wartime Japan 1943–1944*. Center for East Asian Studies, University of Kansas, 1979.

de la Costa, Horacio S.J., *Light cavalry*. Manila: Catholic Bishops' Conference of the Philippines, 1997.

———. *Readings in Philippine History: Selected Historical Texts Presented with a Commentary*. Makati: Bookmark, 1992.

———. Papers. Ateneo de Manila University Archives.

del Castillo, Teofilo T. *A brief history of Philippine literature*. Progressive Schoolbooks, 1937.

del Rio, Alma [Simuon Almario]. "Guerrero in Radio: Once a Newspaperman, He finds scripts and magazine stuff equally stimulating to write". *Graphic*, 26 December 1940.

Dizon, Josue S. "The Foreign Policy of the Philippines with special emphasis on the Macapagal Administration, 1961–1965". PhD dissertation, American University, 1969.
Domingo, Benjamin. *Philippine Treaties Index 1946–1982*. Manila: Foreign Service Institute, 1983.
———. *The Making of Filipino Foreign Policy*. Quezon City: University of the Philippines Asian Center, 1983.
———. *The Re-Making of Filipino Foreign Policy*. Quezon City: University of the Philippines Asian Center, 1993.
Edgerton, Ronald K. "The Politics of Reconstruction in the Philippines". PhD dissertation, University of Michigan, 1975.
Enriquez, Elizabeth L. "Appropriation of Colonial Broadcasting: A History of Early Radio in the Philippines, 1922–1946". PhD dissertation, University of the Philippines Diliman, 2005.
———. *Appropriation of Colonial Broadcasting: A History of Early Radio in the Philippines, 1922–1946*. Quezon City: University of the Philippines Press, 2008.
Far Eastern University. *Green and Gold Law Annual*. Manila: Senior Class, Institute of Law, 1948.
Fernandez, Erwin S. "The originary Filipino: Rizal and the making of Leon Ma. Guerrero as biographer". *Philippine Studies* 57, no. 4 (2009): 461–504.
———. "Rereading *The First Filipino*: Interrogating León Ma. Guerrero's Rizal". *Danyag: Journal of Humanities and Social Sciences* 14, no. 1 (2009): 51–60.
———. "Decolonizing the Filipino: Cultural-Intellectual Revolution in Contemporary Philippines". *Proceedings of the Asia Youth Culture Camp 2: "Doing Cultural Spaces in Asia"*, 26–29 October 2006, edited by Kim Shin Dong et al. Gwangju, Korea: Asia's Future Initiative, 2006.
Foreign Affairs, Department of, Republic of the Philippines. *Biographic Register*. Manila: Bureau of Printing, 1970.
Francisco, Vicente J. assisted by Leon Ma. Guerrero. *Legal Thesis Writing and Forensic Literature*. Manila: East Publishing, 1950.
Galdon, Joseph. *Essays on the Philippine novel in English*. Quezon City: Ateneo de Manila University Press, 1979.
Garraty, John A. *The Nature of Biography*. New York: Alfred A. Knopf, 1957.
Gatmaytan, Augusto. "The case against Spanish". *Philippines Free Press*, 31 March 1962.
Gleeck, Lewis E. Jr. *Dissolving the Colonial Bond: American Ambassadors to the Philippines, 1946–1984*. Quezon City: New Day Publishers, 1988.
———. *The Third Philippine Republic, 1946–1972*. Quezon City: New Day Publishers, 1993.
———. *The American half-century (1898–1946)*. Quezon City: New Day Publishers, 1998.
Golay, Frank H. *The revised United States-Philippine trade agreement of 1955*. Ithaca, New York: Southeast Asia Program, Dept. of Far Eastern Studies, Cornell University, 1956.
Guerrero, David. *LMG: The Leon Maria Guerrero Anthology*. Manila: Guerrero Publishing, 2010.

Guerrero, Leon Ma. "First year A". *The Atenean*. Manila: Ateneo, 1928.

———. "Second year A". *The Atenean*. Manila: Ateneo, 1929.

———. "Dramatics". *The Ateneo aegis: A literary quarterly*, March 1930.

———. "Library". *The Ateneo aegis: A literary quarterly*, March 1930.

———. "The datu's jewels". Staged on 6 August 1930. In Bernad, *Dramatics at the Ateneo*. See supra.

———. "Dramatics". *The Ateneo aegis: Commencement*, March 1931.

———. "Will o' the wisp: A commencement short short story of one who chose to tread on the path of glory". *Graphic*, 18 March 1931.

———. "The country beyond". *Graphic*, 15 April 1931.

———. "I did not know", "Student Days", "My Dream-Blue Lagoon", "Lines on an ancient Chinese fan" and other poems and articles. In *Wings: A Literary Semi-Annual* 1, no. 2 (March 1932): 21, 69 passim.

———. "'Sure we envy him' say critics of Villa". Letter to the editor. *Philippines Free Press*, 19 November 1932.

———. "A legacy in stone". *The 1933 Ateneo aegis*. Manila: Ateneo, 1933.

———. "Etc...". *The Guidon*, 2 August 1933 – 9 March 1935.

———. "Hello! Miss Information? A short story". *Philippines Free Press*, 23 September 1933.

———. "Taps (In memoriam of Rev. Fr. Richard A. O'Brien, S.J.)" [A poem]. *The Ateneo Aegis Jubilee Number 1859-1934*. Manila: Ateneo de Manila, 1934.

———. "Pirates ahoy! A short story". *Philippines Free Press*, 13 January 1934.

———. "Happy racing: A short story". *Philippines Free Press*, 24 February 1934.

———. "The foreign menace: A short story". *Philippines Free Press*, 14 April 1934.

———. "30,000 suspects: A short story". *Philippines Free Press*, Part I, 7 July 1934; Part II, 14 July 1934.

———. "An enemy of Caesar". *Philippines Free Press*, 20 April 1935.

———. "Time out for murder". *Philippines Free Press*, Part I, 11 August 1934; Part II, 18 August 1934.

———. "All questions answered: A short story". *Philippines Free Press*, 29 September 1934.

———. "The power of suggestion: A short story". *Philippines Free Press*, 20 October 1934.

———. "Snatch: A short story". *Philippines Free Press*, Part I, 19 January 1935; Part II, 26 January 1935.

———. "Business for art's sake: A short story". *Philippines Free Press*, 9 March 1935.

———. "Double exposure: A short story". *Philippines Free Press*, 30 March 1935.

———. "The high cost of dying". *Philippines Free Press*, 13 April 1935.

———. "An enemy of Caesar". *Philippines Free Press*, 20 April 1935.

———. "My grandfather as I knew him: An intimate glimpse of the life and manners of the greatest Filipino botanist, Leon Ma. Guerrero written by his grandson". *Philippines Free Press*, 27 April 1935.

———. "The high cost of babies". *Philippines Free Press*, 4 May 1935.

———. "How Japan looks at Ramos". *Philippines Free Press*, 1 June 1935.

———. "Life a la Tokyo". *Philippines Free Press*, 8 June 1935.

———. "One-man revolution: A short story". *Philippines Free Press*, 15 June 1935.
———. "The travel racket". *Philippines Free Press*, 22 June 1935.
———. "A letter to Queen Angelina". *Philippines Free Press*, 22 June 1935.
———. "The best man never wins: A short story". *Philippines Free Press*, 29 June 1935.
———. "Mussolini goes lion-hunting". *Philippines Free Press*, 20 July 1935.
———. "Escolta miner: A short story". *Philippines Free Press*, 10 August 1935.
———. "What can we expect from the League of Nations?". *Philippines Free Press*, 28 September 1935.
———. "China's contribution to the Philippines". *Philippines Free Press*, 12 October 1935.
———. "San Beda cops collegiate title". *Philippines Free Press*, 19 October 1935.
———. "Along the galleon route". *Philippines Free Press*, 30 November 1935.
———. "His Dishonor, the Mayor". Chapter I, *Philippines Free Press*, 14 December 1935; Chapter II, *Philippines Free Press*, 21 December 1935; Chapter III, *Philippines Free Press*, 28 December 1935; Chapter IV, *Philippines Free Press*, 4 January 1936; Chapter V, *Philippines Free Press*, 11 January 1936; Chapter VI, *Philippines Free Press*, 18 January 1936.
———. *His dishonor, the mayor*. Manila: Philippines Free Press, 1936.
———. "The guardian angel of the UP". *Philippines Free Press*, 1 February 1936.
———. "Setting the national pace". *Philippines Free Press*, 15 February 1936.
———. "History — as sometimes written". *Philippine Magazine*, March 1936.
———. "With a kiss in a garden: A short story". *Philippines Free Press*, 4 April 1936.
———. "Vacation fever". *Philippines Free Press*, 18 April 1936.
———. "Cebu goes round and round". *Philippines Free Press*, 9 May 1936.
———. "Cebu — correction". *Philippines Free Press*, 16 May 1936.
———. "Escape: A short story". *Philippines Free Press*, 23 May 1936.
———. "Amateur hour by Baron Unterheizen himself as told to Leon Ma. Guerrero Jr.". *Philippines Free Press*, 30 May 1936.
———. "Education under the Commonwealth". *Philippines Free Press*, 6 June 1936.
———. "Eating up the fields". *Philippines Free Press*, 27 June 1936.
———. "Girls without boys as told to Leon Ma. Guerrero Jr.". *Philippines Free Press*, 25 July 1936.
———. "Turning off the jazz". *Philippines Free Press*, 18 July 1936.
———. "Bullets after ballots in Spain". *Philippines Free Press*, 1 August 1936.
———. "United we fight". *Philippines Free Press*, 17 October 1936.
———. "They like to weep". *Philippines Free Press*, 24 October 1936.
———. "The first step". *Philippines Free Press*, November 14, 1936.
———. "Was Bonifacio a Sakdal?". *Philippines Free Press*, 28 November 1936.
———. "Child in search of Xmas: A short story". *Philippines Free Press*, 12 December 1936.
———. "The Siamese inquisition as told by Arsenio Lacson". *Philippines Free Press*, 23 January 1937.
———. "The inconstant people". *Philippines Free Press*, 30 January 1937.
———. "Pintakasi time". *Philippines Free Press*, 27 February 1937.
———. "Found: The lost horizon". *Philippines Free Press*, 12 June 1937.

———. "The battle of the gods". *Philippines Free Press*, 19 June 1937.
———. "Midnight in Spain". *Philippines Free Press*, 17 July 1937.
———. "Yellow fever". *Philippines Free Press*, 24 July 1937.
———. "The phantom president". *Philippines Free Press*, 7 August 1937.
———. "Shanghai encore". *Philippines Free Press*, 21 August 1937.
———. "The forgotten president". *Philippines Free Press*, 28 August 1937.
———. "The silent speaker". *Philippines Free Press*, 11 September 1937.
———. "Apostle of Malacañang". *Philippines Free Press*, 18 September 1937.
———. "More enduring than bronze". *Philippines Free Press*, 9 October 1937.
———. "The private life of a bill". *Philippines Free Press*, 16 October 1937.
———. "The fourth r". *Philippines Free Press*, 27 November 1937.
———. "3 wives". *Promenade*, January 1938.
———. "Conversation with the devil". *Philippines Free Press*, 8 January 1938.
———. "The merry go-round broke down". *Philippines Free Press*, 12 February 1938.
———. "Ninth endorsement". *Philippines Free Press*, 12 February 1938.
———. "Solomon without a sword". *Philippines Free Press*, 19 February 1938.
———. "Everybody's money". *Philippines Free Press*, March 1938(?).
———. "Synonym in Celebes". *Philippines Free Press*, 23 April 1938.
———. "Java Express". *Philippines Free Press*, 7 May 1938.
———. "Left-hand man". *Philippines Free Press*, 14 May 1938.
———. "Bali-hoo". *Philippines Free Press*, 14 May 1938.
———. "Bali Faces". *Philippines Free Press*, 21 May 1938.
———. "No, no, a thousand times no!". *Philippines Free Press*, 4 June 1938.
———. "4,000,000 midases". *Philippines Free Press*, 16 July 1938.
———. "Life of the party". *Philippines Free Press*, 30 July 1938.
———. "Man who knew too much". *Promenade*, July 1938.
———. "Forgotten story". *Philippines Free Press*, 13 August 1938.
———. "Rice and fall". *Philippines Free Press*, 20 August 1938.
———. "Dreamer, not demagogue". *Philippines Free Press*, 17 September 1938.
———. "The old-fashioned virtues". *Philippines Free Press*, 24 September 1938.
———. "The miraculous lawyer". *Philippines Free Press*, 8 October 1938.
———. "Enter through a trap door". *Philippines Free Press*, 22 October 1938.
———. "Garden of the dead". *Philippines Free Press*, 29 October 1938.
———. "California, here we come". *Philippines Free Press*, 3 December 1938.
———. "Early Christians in Bali". *Philippines Free Press*, 10 December 1938.
———. "Easter fashions". *Philippines Free Press*, 1 April 1939.
———. "Rich boy joins the army as told to Leon Ma. Guerrero". *Philippines Free Press*, 29 April 1939.
———. "Curtain up!". *Philippines Free Press*, 29 April 1939.
———. "Reelection for Quezon? As his enemies see it!". *Philippines Free Press*, 6 May 1939.
———. "Buenavista — pleasant prospect? An experiment in human reconstruction". *Philippines Free Press*, 20 May 1939.

———. "Street scene". *Philippines Free Press*, 20 May 1939.
———. "A smile for Manila". *Philippines Free Press*, 10 June 1939.
———. "Mabini: Forgotten hero". *Philippines Free Press*, 17 June 1939.
———. "Labor-saving time". *Philippines Free Press*, 24 June 1939.
———. "Most celebrated Filipino love story". *Philippines Free Press*, 15 July 1939.
———. "Weaving a future". *Philippines Free Press*, 29 July 1939.
———. "The valley of a million smokes". *Philippines Free Press*, 23 September 1939.
———. "All for sportsmanship!". *Philippines Free Press*, 28 October 1939.
———. "Woman suffrage comes of age". *Philippines Free Press*, 4 November 1939.
———. "The year of second thoughts". *Philippines Free Press*, 11 November 1939.
———. "Hitler faces death". *Philippines Free Press*, 18 November 1939.
———. "Screen test for the 'colegiala'". *Philippines Free Press*, 25 November 1939.
———. "Case history". *Philippines Free Press*, 2 December 1939.
———. "Still small voice". *Philippines Free Press*, 9 December 1939.
———. "Initiation in Mindanao". *Philippines Free Press*, 16 December 1939.
———. "First Pampanga menace". *Philippines Free Press*, 13 January 1940.
———. "Peace! Peace! ... But there is no peace!". *Philippines Free Press*, 20 January 1940.
———. "She grew up with the movies". *Philippines Free Press*, 20 January 1940.
———. "Pampanga peacemaker". *Philippines Free Press*, 27 January 1940.
———. "Chip on his shoulder". *Philippines Free Press*, 27 January 1940.
———. "The lone ranger". *Philippines Free Press*, 3 February 1940.
———. "The housekeeper's daughter". *Philippines Free Press*, 10 February 1940.
———. "But the living do not rest in peace". *Philippines Free Press*, 10 February 1940.
———. "The dead end kids". *Philippines Free Press*, 17 February 1940.
———. "Citizens by judicial decision". *Philippines Free Press*, 24 February 1940.
———. "The royal family". *Philippines Free Press*, 24 February 1940.
———. "The great man's daughter". *Philippines Free Press*, 2 March 1940.
———. "If she were a song...". *Philippines Free Press*, 9 March 1940.
———. "The magnificent brute". *Philippines Free Press*, 16 March 1940.
———. "Why I'll vote yes". *Philippines Free Press*, 15 June 1940.
———. "The dictatorship of greed". *Filipiniana Reference Shelf*. Manila, 1940.
———. *Catholic Hour Pamphlets, 1940-1941: The usurer*. Manila: Chesterton Evidence Guild, 1941.
———. *Catholic Hour Pamphlets, 1940-1941: Unite*. Manila: Chesterton Evidence Guild, 1941.
———. *Catholic Hour Pamphlets, 1940-1941: Huelga!* Manila: Chesterton Evidence Guild, 1941.
———. *Catholic Hour Pamphlets, 1940-1941: The two brothers*. Manila: Chesterton Evidence Guild, 1941.
———. *Catholic Hour Pamphlets, 1940-1941: No, Mr. Russell*. Manila: Chesterton Evidence Guild, 1941.
———. "The language of the law". *Philippines Free Press*, 10 May 1941.

———. *Partyless Democracy*. Manila: Chesterton Evidence Guild, 1941.

———. "Rizal and the New Order". *Voice of the New Philippines: A Collection of Lectures on Current Topics* 2 (February 1943): 43–46.

———. "Water for the thirsty of Corregidor". *Shin seiki*, March 1943.

———. "The Last Days of Corregidor". *Philippine Review*, May 1943. Reprinted in *Philippine Review*, March–April 1955, *The Voice of the Veteran: An Anthology of the Best in Song and Story by the Defenders of Freedom*, edited by Manuel E. Buenafe. Republic Promotion, 1946; in *Philippine Prose and Poetry*, Vol. 4. Manila: Bureau of Printing, 1951 and in *The Fall of Bataan and Corregidor*. Manila: Philippine Educational Promotion, 1975.

———. "The Fall of Corregidor". *Philippine Review*, July 1943.

———. *Twilight in Tokyo: The Inside Story of Laurel during the Last Days of Imperial Japan*. Manila: Manila Times Publishing Company, 1946. Translated into Tagalog as *Takipsilim sa Tokyo* by Adriano P. Laudico. Manila: Manila Times Publishing, 1946. Republished in *Manila Times as Twilight in Tokyo*, 19 August – 1 September 2003.

———. "Review of *Children of yesterday* by Jan Valtin". *Pacific Affairs* 20, no. 1 (March 1947): 87–88.

———. "The Passion and Death of the USAFFE". *Evening News*, 9 April – 3 May 1947.

———. "Author says his point was: Bataan was a fight by and for Filipinos". *Evening News*, 14 April 1947.

———. "Guerrero rebuts critics on 'Passion'". *Evening News*, 16 May 1947.

———. "Claro M. Recto: A Study in Filipino Nationalism". *Philippine Trends*, 15 June 1949.

———. "Senator Vicente J. Francisco in 'The Bench and Bar in News'". *The Lawyers Journal*, 25 December 1949.

———. *The Young Rizal: A Translation of Memorias de un Estudiante de Manila by Jose Rizal with Translations of Rizal's Early Poems, Along the Pasig and the Council of the Gods*. Manila: Bardavon Book Co., 1950. Some excerpts were published in *Philippine Prose and Poetry Volume One*. Rev. ed. Manila: Bureau of Printing, 1960 with the title "My Home" by Jose Rizal, translated by León Ma. Guerrero, and in *Philippine Prose and Poetry Volume Three*. Rev. ed. Manila: Bureau of Printing, 1961, "Chapter IV: From '72 until '75" with a footnote: translated by León Ma. Guerrero.

———. "What are Filipinos Like?". In *Essays: English, American, and Filipino*, by Arturo G. Roseburg. Bardavon Book, 1950.

———. "The Philippine Law School as school of law and not of men". *Manila Chronicle*, 19 March 1950.

———. "Our choice of heroes: We Filipinos must be one of the most peace-loving nations the way we choose our heroes". *Sunday Times Magazine*, 30 December 1951.

———. "Rizal's First Love". *This Week*, 17 June 1951.

———. "Heritage from Spain". *Sunday Times Magazine*, 7 October 1951.

BIBLIOGRAPHY 329

———. "What are Filipinos like? A frank and refreshing appraisal of the native character". *Philippines Quarterly*, December 1951.
———. "The Philippines and the Vatican: The Diplomacy". *Sunday Times Magazine*, 31 August 1952.
———. "The Philippines and China: The Diplomacy". *Sunday Times Magazine*, 7 September 1952.
———. "The Philippines and Indonesia: Diplomacy for a competitor". *Sunday Times Magazine*, 14 September 1952.
———. "Diplomacy of atonement". *Sunday Times Magazine*, 21 September 1952.
———. "The Philippines and Thailand: Wanted — Rice diplomacy". *Sunday Times Magazine*, 12 October 1952.
———. "The Philippines and Italy: Diplomacy for a closed market". *Sunday Times Magazine*, 19 October 1952.
———. "The Philippines and the United States: Diplomacy of readjustment". *Sunday Times Magazine*, 25 October 1952.
———. "The Philippines and Australia: Diplomacy of Isolation". *Sunday Times Magazine*, 3 November 1952.
———. "The Philippines and Britain: Diplomatic Might-Have-Beens". *Sunday Times Magazine*, 9 November 1952.
———. "The Philippines and India: Diplomacy for Peace". *Sunday Times Magazine*, 16 November 1952.
———. "The Philippines and the Netherlands: Diplomacy and Law". *Sunday Times Magazine*, 7 December 1952.
———. "The Philippines and Belgium: Diplomatic Listening-Post". *Sunday Times Magazine*, 23 November 1952.
———. "The Philippines and Argentina: Diplomacy and politics". *Sunday Times Magazine*, 30 November 1952.
———. "Del Pilar". *Philippine Free Press*, 13 December 1952.
———. "Diplomacy for a transition". *Sunday Times Magazine*, 14 December 1952.
———. "The Flower of Happiness". *Journal of the Philippine Pharmaceutical Association* 40, no. 2: 83–85.
———. "The American Influence". *Saturday Mirror Magazine*, 8 August 1953.
———. "A Christian Mistake". *Weekly Women's Magazine*, 14 August 1953.
———. "Carlos P. Garcia". *Weekly Women's Magazine*, 2 October 1953.
———. "Is the UN necessary?". *Saturday Mirror Magazine*, 7 October 1953.
———. "Past and present". *Manila Chronicle*, 15 September 1953 – 4 January 1954.
———. "Two kinds of political leadership". *Weekly Women's Magazine*, 6 November 1953.
———. "Statue for a scientist". *Sunday Times Magazine*, 6 December 1953.
———. "Youth in government". *Sunday Times Magazine*, 10 January 1954, p. 10.
———. "Asia and America". *Manila Daily Bulletin*, 8 February 1954. Also published in *Philippines Herald*, 7 February 1954, and *Philippine Review*, 12 February 1954.
———. "Dangers of Charity". *Sunday Times Magazine*, 14 February 1954.

———. "Man and his environment". *Saturday Mirror Magazine*, 27 February 1954. Reprinted in *Pamana*, October 1977.

———. "Something up Russian sleeve? Soviets have new strategy in Asia". *Manila Daily Bulletin*, 29 March 1954.

———. "The Reparations Plan". *Manila Times*, 21 April 1954. Also published in *Manila Daily Bulletin*, 21 April 1954, and *Philippines Herald*, 21 April 1954.

———. "The Filipino Nation". *Manila Times*, 4 July 1954. Also published in *The Diplomatic Record*, 5 July 1954, and *Manila Chronicle*, 5 July 1954.

———. "Retail trade nationalization and US nationals". *Manila Times*, 18 July 1954.

———. "What are Filipinos Like?". In *Katha: Philippine writing in English I*. Philippine Writers Association, 1955.

———. "The Philippine experiment". *Sunday Times Magazine*, 10 April 1955.

———. "The Philippines export". *Sugar News*, April 1955.

———. "Extracts from a report on the Suez Canal situation to the Council of State and the National Security Council". Manila, 1956.

———. "A Personal View of the International Situation". Manila, 1956.

———. "What are Filipinos Like?". In *Looking at ourselves: A study of our peculiar social traits as a people,* by Delfin F. Batacan. Philaw Pub., 1956.

———. "Visit to Shakespeare's hometown". *Kislap Graphic*, 2 October 1957.

———. *Alternatives for Asians: The Philippine Experiment.* London: Philippine Embassy, 1957.

———. *An Asian on Asia: Three B.B.C. "Third Programme" Talks.* London: Philippine Embassy, 1958.

———. "Free for all". *Kislap Graphic*, 1 April 1959.

———. "The cult of personality". *Kislap Graphic*, 29 April 1959.

———. "The Kaiser and the Philippines". *Manila Chronicle*, 24–28 August 1960. Also published in *Philippine Studies* 9, no. 4 (October 1961): 584–600.

———. "Recto and Filipino Nationalism". *Manila Times*, 7 October 1960.

———. "The importance of being small". *Manila Times*, 12 October 1960.

———. "Our countryman Claro Mayo Recto". *Philippine Panorama*, November 1960.

———. "The First Asian Nationalist". *Asia Magazine*, 5 November 1961.

———. "Rizal: after 100 years". *Manila Times*, 31 December 1961. Also published in *GAO Journal* 9, no. 3 (December 1961): 6–8, 19.

———. "What are Filipinos Like?". In *Philippine contemporary literature* by Asuncion Maramba. Bookmark, 1962, 1982.

———. "Seven years in London". *Manila Times*, 13 January 1962.

———. *The first Filipino: A biography of Jose Rizal.* Manila: National Heroes Commission, 1963.

———. *The first Filipino: A biography of Jose Rizal.* Manila: Guerrero Publishing, 1998.

———. *El Sí y El No (Estudios Historico-Sociales).* Madrid, 1963.

———. "Seriously speaking". *Manila Chronicle*, 31 August 1963, p. 4.

———. "Rizal and Bonifacio". *Manila Chronicle*, 29 December 1963.

———. "Bonifacio's democracy and Rizal's warning". *Manila Times*, 29 December 1963.
———. "Rizal and Bonifacio". *Philippine International Law Journal* 2, no. 4 (October–December 1963): 534–44. Also published as "The Sixth Jose Rizal Lecture: Rizal as a Liberal; Bonifacio as a Democrat". *Comment* 20 (4th Quarter 1963): 3–12.
———. "Las Dos Muertes del General Aguinaldo". In *Homenaje a Emilio Aguinaldo*. Madrid: Embajada de Filipinas, 1964.
———. "The Legacy of Claro M. Recto". *Manila Chronicle*, 3 October 1964.
———. "Policy of Indecision". *Philippines Free Press*, 7 November 1964.
———. "What young Filipinos should know". *Manila Chronicle*, 8 March 1965.
———. "Will parity be forever?". *Daily Mirror*, 12 March 1965.
———. "Parity Forever?". *Manila Times*, 16 and 18 March 1965.
———. "Votive lights on a dark river". *Manila Chronicle*, 6 August 1966. Also published in *Manila Times*, 5 August 1966.
———. "The Secret of Taj Mahal". *Sunday Times Magazine*, 6 August 1967.
———. "Common people can learn to get along with one another". *Manila Times*, 24 March 1967.
———. "Letter to the Times of India". New Delhi, 1967.
———. "Spanish friars in exodus". *Philippines Free Press*, 9 December 1967. Also published as "Nozaleda and Pons: Two Spanish Friars in Exodus". In *Studies in Philippine Church History*, edited by Gerald H. Anderson. Ithaca and London: Cornell University Press, 1969.
———. "The Right to Sabah: Reply to Malaysia". *Manila Times*, 24 July 1968.
———. "The Malaysian game". *Philippines Free Press*, 27 July 1968.
———, ed. *Philippine Approaches: A Monthly Review of Writing in the Philippines* 1, no.1 (January 1968); 2, no. 1–2 (January–February 1969).
———. "Was Rizal an un-Catholic Christian?". *Weekly Graphic*, 19 June 1968.
———. "Rizal and the Faustian generation". *Manila Chronicle*, 1 January 1969. Also published in *Manila Times*, 1 January 1969.
———. "A little iron for our soul". *Weekly Graphic*, 22 January 1969.
———. "A crisis of confidence". *Philippine Free Press*, 25 January 1969.
———. "Political revolution and evolution". *Sunday Times Magazine*, 15 June 1969.
———. "The strange ratooning of Filipino nationalism." *Philippine Quarterly*, December 1969.
———. "Is the Filipino indolent?". *Examiner*, 21–28 November 1970.
———. "The United Nations: king log". *Sunday Times Magazine*, 10 January 1971.
———. "Our 7000 shores". *Sunday Times Magazine*, 7 March 1971.
———. "Ambassadors and politics". *Philippines Herald*, 27 June 1971.
———. "Development alternatives: alignment or non-alignment". *Manila Chronicle*, 27 June 1971.
———. "The Pensacola Syndrome: Is the United States really committed to the Philippines?". *Pacific Community*, March 1972. Also published in *Philippine Free Press*, 3 June 1972. Republished in *Philippine Free Press*, 29 October 1988.

———. "Corregidor Revisited: Wainwright's bravest act". *Manila Times*, 7 May 1972.
———. "Corregidor Revisited: Posting on Rock was a blessing". *Manila Times*, 8 May 1972.
———. "Corregidor Revisited: The day Manila wept". *Manila Times*, 9 May 1972.
———. "The challenge of Mindanao". *Philippines Free Press*, 13 May 1972.
———. *Prisoners of History*. New Delhi: Embassy of the Philippines, 1972.
———. *Encounter of cultures: The Muslims in the Philippines*. Manila: Office of Press and Public Affairs Department of Foreign Affairs by the National Media Production Center, 1972. Also published as BNFI paper no. 2 by the Bureau of National and Foreign Information, Department of Public Information, Manila. Also published in *Philippine Quarterly*, September 1973; *Archipelago*, May 1974, and *Pamana*, March 1975 and as "Philippines: Conflict of Cultures", *The Asian* (Hong Kong), 14-20 January 1973.
———. "What are Filipinos Like?". *Philippine Literature in English*, edited by Esperanza V. Manuel and Resil B. Mojares. Cebu: Cornejo & Sons, 1973.
———. "A Model for ASEAN?". *The Ambassador*, August 1973.
———. "Pricking the American Conscience". *New York Times*, 24 November 1972. Also published in *DFA Review* 1, no. 2 (1973): 3.
———. "A voyage to Europe". *Sunburst*, December 1973.
———. "The last days of Jose Rizal; intellectual dissent brought him martyrdom". *Archipelago*, January 1974.
———. "Today began yesterday". *Daily Express*, 21-29 September 1975.
———. *Today Began Yesterday*. Manila: National Media Production Center, 1975. Reprinted as *Why Martial Law: A Historical Approach to Martial Law in the Philippines*. Manila, 1975.
———. "The boy who was nothing". *Bulletin of American Historical Collection* 6 (January-March 1978): pp. 7-10.
———. "Filipinization of a Hoosier Lady". In *Perspective of a diplomat's wife*, by Beth Day Romulo. Manila: Foreign Service Institute, 1981.
———. *We Filipinos*. Manila: Daily Star Publishing, 1984.
———. File. Personnel Files 201. National Archives of the Philippines, Paco.
———. Papers. Dasmariñas Village, Makati City.
——— and Horacio de la Costa. "Another crack at Villa's verse". Letter to the editor. *Philippines Free Press*, 29 October 1932.
———, Gilberto Zamora and Jose J. Reyes. "The case of the seven suspects". Chapter I, *Philippines Free Press*, 9 February 1935; Chapter II, *Philippines Free Press*, 16 February 1935; Chapter III, *Philippines Free Press*, 23 February 1935; Chapter IV, *Philippines Free Press*, 2 March 1935; Chapter V, *Philippines Free Press*, 9 March 1935; Chapter VI, *Philippines Free Press*, 16 March 1935; Chapter VII, *Philippines Free Press*, 23 March 1935; Chapter VIII, *Philippines Free Press*, 30 March 1935; Chapter IX, *Philippines Free Press*, 6 April 1935; Chapter X, *Philippines Free Press*, 13 April 1935.
Guerrero, Roberto Ma. "David Guerrero: Preserving a father's legacy". *Manila Times*, 29 June 1995.

Guerrero, Wilfrido Ma. *The Guerreros of Ermita (Family History and Personal Memoirs)*. Quezon City: New Day Publishers, 1988.
Gruenberg, Estrellita V. "The canon of Philippine Literature according to teachers of Metro Manila". In *Manila: History, People and Culture, Proceedings of the Manila Studies Conference*, edited by Wilfrido V. Villacorta, Isagani R. Cruz and Ma. Lourdes Brillantes. Manila: De la Salle University Press, 1989.
Hartendorp, A.V.H. *The Japanese Occupation of the Philippines*, vol. 1. Manila: Bookmark, 1967.
———. *History of industry and trade of the Philippines*. American Chamber of Commerce of the Philippines, 1958.
Hayden, Joseph R. *The Philippines: A study in national development*. New York: The Macmillan Company, 1955.
Hernandez, Jose M. "Passion and Death of the USAFFE Full of Errors, Spokesman Maintains". *Evening News*, 13 May 1947.
———. "USAFFE Record will stand scrutiny of entire world, writer asserts". *Evening News*, 15 May 1947.
Hidalgo, Cristina P. *Creative Nonfiction: A Manual for Filipino Writers*. Quezon City: University of the Philippines Press, 2005.
Hill, Homer M. "Philippine-Mexican relations, 1960–1970". MA thesis, Philippine Center for Advanced Studies, University of the Philippines, 1975.
Homenaje a Emilio Aguinaldo. Madrid: Embajada de Filipinas, 1964.
Hsiao, Shi-ching. *Chinese-Philippine diplomatic relations, 1946–1975*. Manila: Bookman, 1975.
Ibabao, Victor B. S.J. "Aspects of Catholic social action in the Philippines prior to World War II: The contributions of Fr. Joseph A. Mulry, the Jesuits, and the Ateneo alumni". MA thesis, Ateneo de Manila University, 1986.
In Memoriam: León Ma. Guerrero, Lawyer, Writer, Diplomat, Historian and Nationalist (1915–1982). Manila: Office of Press & Public Affairs, Ministry of Foreign Affairs, 1982.
Ingles, Jose D. *Philippine Foreign Policy*. Manila: Lyceum of the Philippines, 1982.
Ira, Luning B. with Isagani R. Medina. *Streets of Manila*. Manila: GCF Books, 1977.
I.T.R. "Atty. Leon Ma. Guerrero in The Bench and Bar in News". *Lawyers Journal*, 21 December 1949.
Japanese Occupation. Papers. University of the Philippines Main Library.
Javier, Ignacio [Leon. Ma. Guerrero]. "Not as Enemies but as Elder Brothers". *Sunday Tribune Magazine*, 18 October 1942.
———. "The Philippines and Burma: A Parallel". *Philippine Review*, September 1943.
Jenkins, Shirley. *American Economic Policy towards the Philippines*. Stanford: Stanford University Press, 1954.
Joaquin, Nick. "The First 50 Years Were the 'Most!'". *Philippines Free Press*, 30 August 1958.
———. "1974 and all that". *Philippines Free Press*, 20 March 1965.
———. "The Guerrero Family's Ambassador". In *Gloria Diaz and other delineations*. National Book Store, 1977.

———. "708 Avenida Rizal". In *Joseph Estrada and other sketches*. Manila: National Bookstore, 1977.

———. *Doveglion and other cameos*. National Book Store, 1977.

———. "The Mysterious Guerrero Bishop". In *Nora Aunor and other Profiles*. Quezon City: National Book Store, 1977.

———."Pop Culture: The American Years". *Filipino Heritage*. Alfredo Roces, ed. Vol. 10. Manila: Lahing Pilipino, 1978.

———. *Manila, my Manila*. Makati: Bookmark, 1999.

Jocano, Felipe Landa. *Philippines-USSR Relations: A Study in Foreign Policy Development*. NDCP Foundation, 1988.

Jose, Ricardo T. "Manuel L. Quezon and the Commonwealth, 1935–1944". In *Philippine Presidents: 100 Years*, edited by Rosario Mendoza Cortes. Quezon City: New Day Publishers & Philippine Historical Association, 1999.

———. "Test of Wills: Diplomacy between Japan and the Laurel Government". In *Philippines–Japan Relations*, edited by Setsuho Ikehata and Lydia N. Yu-Jose. Quezon City: Ateneo de Manila University Press, 2003.

Jose Rizal National Centennial Commission Papers. National Historical Commission of the Philippines, Manila.

Jose Rizal Biography Contest Manuscripts. Lopez-Bantug Collection. De la Salle University Library.

Kahin, George McT. and Milton L. Barnett. "In memoriam: Soedjatmoko, 1922–1989". *Indonesia* 49 (1990): 133–40.

Kessler, Richard J. Jr. "Development Diplomacy: The Making of Philippine Foreign Policy under Ferdinand E. Marcos". PhD dissertation, Fletcher School of Law and Diplomacy, 1985.

Keith, Agnes N. *Bare feet in the palace*. Little Brown, 1955.

Kneedler, Martin C. *An Introduction to Latin American Politics: The Structure of Conflict*. New Jersey: Prentice Hall, Inc., 1983.

Labrador, Juan. *A Diary of the Japanese Occupation*. Manila: Santo Tomas University Press, 1989.

Legarda, Benito J. Jr. *Occupation '42*. Manila: De la Salle University Press, 2003.

Legge, J.D. *Intellectuals and Nationalism in Indonesia*. Ithaca: Cornell University Press, 1987.

Leifer, Michael. *The Philippine claim to Sabah*. Zug: Inter Documentation, 1968.

Lichauco, Alejandro. *The Lichauco Paper: Imperialism in the Philippines*. Monthly Review Press, 1973.

Litiatco, A. E. "Giving beginners a break". *Graphic*, 1 February 1934, p. 11.

———. "Dictatorship in Literature". In *Literature Under the Commonwealth*, by Manuel Arguilla et al. Manila: Alberto S. Florentino, 1973.

Locsin, Teodoro M. "The church under attack". *Philippines Free Press*, 5 May 1956.

Lopez, Salvador P. "Salvador P. Lopez to Leon Ma. Guerrero, Jr.". *Historical Bulletin* 11, no. 3 (September 1967): 340–43.

———. "New Directions in Philippine Foreign Policy". Lecture given under the auspices of the Department of Political Science, at the Faculty Center, University of the Philippines, 10 June 1975.

———. "Authority and Liberty". *Mr. & Ms.*, 18 August 1981.

———. "Capsule Story of a Life". *Mr. & Ms.*, 1 September 1981.

———. "The Laughter of Leoni". *The Times Journal*, 23 June 1982.

———. *Elpidio Quirino: The Judgment of History*. President Elpidio Quirino Foundation, 1990.

———. Papers. University Archives, University of the Philippines Main Library.

Lumbera, Bienvenido L. and Cynthia N. Lumbera. *Philippine Literature: A History and Anthology*. Manila: Anvil, 2005.

———. *Philippine Literature: A History and Anthology*. Manila: National Book Store, 1982.

Lyceum of the Philippines. *The Lycaean*. Lyceum of the Philippines, 1954.

———. "History of the College of Law". *College of Law Catalogue*. Lyceum of the Philippines, 2006.

Mabini, Apolinario. *The Philippine Revolution*. Translated by Leon Ma. Guerrero. Manila: National Historical Commission, 1969.

Macapagal, Diosdado P. *A Stone for the Edifice: Memoirs of a President*. Quezon City: Mac Publishing House, 1968.

Macaraeg, Feliciano. "Envoy Discusses Plans: To solidify Philippine-Spanish ties". *Mirror*, 30 May 1964.

Madrona, Severo C. "Respectable Independence: The Foreign Policy of Carlos P. Garcia, 1957–1961". MA thesis, College of Social Sciences and Philosophy, University of the Philippines Diliman, 2003.

Majid, Abdul. *The Filipino Novel in English: A Critical History*. Quezon City: University of the Philippines, 1970.

Malay, Armando J. *Occupied Philippines: The Role of Jorge B. Vargas during the Japanese Occupation*. Manila: Filipiniana Book Guild, 1967.

Malaya, J. Eduardo and Jonathan E. Malaya. ... *So Help Us God: The Presidents of the Philippines and their Inaugural Addresses*. Manila: Anvil, 2004.

Mangahas, Federico. *Maybe, Incidentally: The satire of Federico Mangahas*. Essays selected and edited by Ruby K. Mangahas. Quezon City: University of the Philippines Press, 1998.

Manlapaz, Edna Z. *Angela Manalang-Gloria*. Quezon City: Ateneo de Manila University Press, 1993.

Manuel, E. Arsenio. *Dictionary of Philippine Biography*. Quezon City: Filipiniana Publishing, 1955.

Mapile, R.V. "The Spanish Law Controversy". *Weekly Graphic*, 15 April 1964.

Maramag, Ileana. "An urban history of Manila, 1898–1934". PhD dissertation, University of the Philippines, 1988.

Maramba, Asuncion D. *Early Philippine Literature: From Ancient Times to 1940*. Manila: Anvil, 2006.

Marquardt, Frederic S. *Before Bataan and after: A personalized history of our Philippine experiment*. New York: The Bobbs-Merrill, Co., 1943.

———. "Remembering Leoni Guerrero". *Bulletin of American Historical Collection* 11, no. 2 (April–June 1983): 34–39.

McCawley, Peter. "Sumitro's life mirrors the turbulence of Indonesian history". <http://www.thejakartapost.com/news/2001/03/31/sumitro039s-life-mirrors-turbulent-indonesian-history.html> (accessed 1 February 2016).

Meyer, Michael C. and William L. Sherman. *The Course of Mexican History*. New York: Oxford University Press, 1987.

Meyer, Milton W. *A Diplomatic History of the Philippine Republic: The First Years 1946–1961*. Claremont, California: Regina Books, 2003.

Moreno, Virginia. "A Critical Study of the Short Story in English Written by Filipinos from 1910 to 1941 with an Anthology of Representative Stories". MA thesis, University of the Philippines, 1952.

Morton, Louis. *The Fall of the Philippines*. Washington, D.C.: Center of Military History, United States Army, 1989.

Nadel, Ira. *Biography: Fiction, Fact and Form*. New York: St. Martin's Press, 1984.

Nakpil, Carmen G. *Woman enough and other essays*. Quezon City: Ateneo de Manila University Press, 1999.

———. *Whatever: A new collection of later essays, 1987–2001*. Quezon City: Ateneo de Manila University Press, 2002.

———. *Myself, Elsewhere*. Metro Manila: Circe Communications, Inc., 2006.

———. *Legends & Adventures*. Metro Manila: Circe Communications, Inc., 2007.

———. *Exeunt*. Manila: Nakpil Publishing, 2009.

Navarro, Nelson A. *What's happening in our country: The life and times of Emmanuel Pelaez*. Makati City: Emmanuel Pelaez Foundation, 2008.

———. *Maximo V. Soliven: The man and the journalist*. Manila: Solidaridad Publishing House, 2011.

Noble, Lela G. *Philippine Policy Toward Sabah: A Claim to Independence*. Tucson, Arizona: University of Arizona Press for the Association for Asian Studies, 1977.

"Notes on the authors". In *The Voice of the Veteran: An Anthology of the Best in Song and Story by the Defenders of Freedom*, edited by Manuel E. Buenafe. Republic Promotion, 1946.

Office of Public Information, Malacañang. *Republic of the Philippines Government Manual 1950*. Manila: Bureau of Printing, 1950.

Ohno, Takushi. *War reparations and peace settlement: Philippines-Japan relations 1945–1956*. Solidaridad, 1986.

Ongpauco, Fidel L. *They Refused to Die: True Stories about World War II Heroes in the Philippines 1941–1945*. Canada: Levesque Publications, 1982.

Onorato, Michael P. *Frederic S. Marquardt: Philippine memories*. Fullerton: Oral History Program, California State University, 1986.

Ordoñez, Elmer A. "The Filipino Short Story in English: From the Commonwealth through the War years to the Post-war Decade, 1935–1955". MA thesis, University of the Philippines, 1956.

Orosa, Rosalinda I. "Her Parties make news in London". *Woman and the Home*, 19 June 1958.
Padilla, Pedro. *Arsenic & I*. Manila: Self-published, 1962.
Palma, Rodolfo. "Ex-USAFFE Captain says Guerrero Opus a Desecration of Dead Heroes". *Evening News*, 11 April 1947.
Parpan, Alfredo. "A Study of Church and State Relations during the Japanese Occupation: The Jesuits in the Philippines 1942–1945". MA thesis, University of the Philippines, 1979.
Paterno, Roberto M. "The Young Horacio de la Costa: A Biographical Background 1916–1945". In *Horacio de la Costa: Selected Writings of his Youth 1927–1945*, edited by Roberto M. Paterno. Manila: 2B3C Foundation, 2002.
Pelaez, Emmanuel. "Philippines' Role in Asia". *Philippine International Law Journal* 2, no. 3 (1963): 364–65.
Philippine Claim to North Borneo Volume I. Manila, 1964.
Philippine Embassy in India Annual Report for the Fiscal Year 1966–1967. New Delhi: Embassy of the Philippines, 1967.
Philippines, The. New Delhi: Embassy of the Philippines, 1972.
Philippines, Republic of the. *Official Directory of the Republic of the Philippines 1946–1968*. Manila: Bureau of Printing, 1946–1968.

———. Congressional Records, House of Representatives, Third Congress, First Regular Session (January 25, 1954 – May 20, 1954), First Special Session (July 19, 1954 – August 3, 1954), *1954 Index and History of Bills and Resolutions*. Manila: Bureau of Printing, 1965.

———. *Philippine Diplomacy: Chronology and Documents 1972–1981*. Manila: Foreign Service Institute, 1981.
Pineda-Ofreneo, Rosalinda. *Renato Constantino: A life revisited*. Foundation for Nationalist Studies.
People's Court. Papers. University of the Philippines Main Library.
Post Report 1967. New Delhi: Embassy of the Philippines, 1967.
Quirino, Carlos. *Amang: The Life and Times of Eulogio Rodriguez, Sr*. Quezon City: New Day Publishers, 1983.

———. *Apo Lakay: The Biography of President Elpidio Quirino of the Philippines*. Manila: Total Book World, 1987.

———. "Introduction". In *The First Filipino*, by Leon Ma. Guerrero. Manila: Guerrero Publishing, 1998.
Quirino, Elpidio. *The Memoirs of Elpidio Quirino*. Manila: National Historical Institute, 1990.
Recto, Deanna O. "A Critical Survey of Literary Criticism in English in the Philippines". MA thesis, University of the Philippines, 1969.
Reed, Robert R. *Colonial Manila: The context of Hispanic urbanism and process of morphogenesis*. University of California Press, 1978.
Reyes, Narciso G. *Memories of Diplomacy: A Life in the Philippine Foreign Service*. Pasig City: Anvil Publishing, 1995.

Reyes, Norman. *Child of Two Worlds: An Autobiography of a Filipino-American or vice versa*. Manila: Anvil, 1995.

Reynolds, Craig J. "Introduction". In *Thai Radical Discourse: The Real Face of Thai Feudalism Today*. Ithaca: Cornell University, 1987.

Rizal, Jose. *Noli Me Tangere*. Translated by Leon Ma. Guerrero. London: Longmans, 1961.

———. *The Lost Eden*. Translated by Leon Ma. Guerrero. Asian Society, 1961.

———. *The Subversive (El Filibusterismo): A Sequel to The Lost Eden*. Bloomington: Indiana University Press, 1962.

———. *El Filibusterismo (Subversion): A Sequel to the Noli Me Tangere, A Completely New Translation for the Contemporary Reader by Leon Ma. Guerrero*. London: Longmans, 1965.

———. *El Filibusterismo*. Translated by Leon Ma. Guerrero. Guerrero Publishing, 2004.

Rodao, Florentino. "Spanish Language in the Philippines: 1900–1940". *Philippine Studies* 45, no. 1 (1997): 94–107.

Romani, John H. *The Philippine Presidency*. Institute of Public Administration, University of the Philippines, 1956.

Romulo, Carlos P. Papers. University Archives, University of the Philippines Main Library.

——— and Beth Day Romulo. *The Philippine Presidents*. Quezon City: New Day Publishers, 1988.

Ronas, Malaya C. "Philippine Foreign Policy, 1946–1972" and "Philippine Foreign Policy, 1972–1986". In *Philippine Politics and Governance: An Introduction*, edited by Teresa S. Encarnacion-Tadem and Noel M. Morada. Quezon City: Department of Political Science, College of Social Sciences and Philosophy, University of the Philippines Diliman.

Rye, Ajit Singh. "A Survey of Philippine-India Relations in the Post-Independence Period". *Asian Studies* 6, no. 3 (December 1968): 271–85.

Rye, Lourdes. "Philippines-India Bilateral Relations (1950–1980)". MA thesis, University of the Philippines, 1990.

Salanga, Alfrredo N. "The Great Switcheroo of Eighty-Two: Was there a mistake about the Romulo & the Guerrero Awards?". *Mr. & Ms.*, 13 July 1982.

Salt, Alexander E.W. *An introduction to the history of Manila: Notes on the historical origin of the names of the districts, barrios, streets, monuments, etc., of Manila, with some account of the fortifications of the Walled City*. Manila, 1912.

Santiago, Tomas. "Open letter to Solicitor General Lorenzo Tañada". *Philippine Liberty News*, 1 May 1947.

Santos, Emmanuel T. *The Constitution of the Philippines: Notes and Comments*. Manila: Self-published, 2001.

Saulo, Alfredo. *"Let George do it": A Biography of Jorge B. Vargas*. Quezon City: University of the Philippines Press, 1990.

Savory, Theodore H. *The Art of Translation*. London: Cape, 1957.

Scott, Thomas. *The Diplomacy of Liberation: The Foreign Relations of the African National Congress Since 1960*. London: I.B. Tauris, 1996.

7 years of the PAG: a report covering seven years of Philippine contemporary art as noted through the Philippine Art Gallery. Manila, 1958.

Sevilla, Lina O. "Guerrero in 'cerrada' at Madrid reception". *Manila Times,* 28 June 1963.

Sicam, Paulynn P. "A man for all seasons". *Goodman: General Motors Philippines Publication* 2 (April 1977): 11–15.

Singleton, Fred. *A Short History of the Yugoslav Peoples.* New York: Cambridge University Press, 1985.

Sison, Marites N. and Yvonne T. Chua. *Armando J. Malay, a guardian of memory: The life and times of a Filipino journalist and activist.* Manila: Anvil, 2002.

Sobritchea, Carolyn I. "Reflections on the Development of Philippine Studies in the Philippines: The U.P. Asian Center Experience". *Asian Studies* 38, no. 1 (2002): 99–109.

Spence, Hartzell. *For Every Tear a Victory: The Story of Ferdinand E. Marcos.* New York: McGraw Hill Book Co., 1964.

Steinberg, David J. *Philippine Collaboration in World War II.* University of Michigan Press, 1967.

Supreme Commander's Annual Report and Yearbook 1962. Manila, 1962.

Sussman, Gerald. "The Sabah Claim and Maphilindo: A Case Study of Philippine Foreign Policy Decision-making". MA thesis, Philippine Center for Advanced Studies, University of the Philippines, 1975.

Taylor, John R.M. *The Philippine Insurrection against the United States: A Compilation of Documents with Notes and Introduction.* Pasig: Lopez Foundation, 1971.

Thee Kian Wie. "In memoriam: Professor Sumitro Djojohadikusumo, 1917–2001". *Bulletin of Indonesian Economic Studies* 37 (2): 171–81.

Thompson, Mark R. *The Anti-Marcos Struggle: Personalistic Rule and Democratic Transition in the Philippines.* Quezon City: New Day.

Torres, Cristina E. "The Americanization of Manila, 1900–1921". PhD dissertation, University of the Philippines, 2001.

———. *The Americanization of Manila 1898–1921.* Quezon City: University of the Philippines Press, 2010.

Totoy [Leon Ma. Guerrero]. "Totoy to Momoy" "Momoy to Totoy". *The Guidon,* 6 July 1929 – 9 March 1935.

———. "The Times in Rhymes". *Philippines Free Press,* 21 April 1934 – 10 December 1938.

———. "Thanks for the present". *Philippines Free Press,* 14 December 1935.

———. "The terrific and tear-jerking tale of the toothpick containers". *Philippines Free Press,* 13 January 1940.

———. "*Tatang*". In original typescript. University of the Philippines Main Library, 1972.

Vargas, Jorge. Papers, Jorge Vargas Museum and Filipiniana Research Center, University of the Philippines Diliman.

———. "Sugamo Diary". In Agoncillo, *The burden of proof.* See supra.

Ventura, Sylvia M. *Mauro Mendez: From Journalism to Diplomacy.* Quezon City: University of the Philippines Press, 1978.

Villarin, Mariano. *We Remember Bataan and Corregidor: The Story of the American and Filipino Defenders of Bataan and Corregidor and their Captivity.* Baltimore: Gateway Press, Inc. 1990.

Vitug, Honesto T. *I shot the presidents.* V.G. Puyat, 1989.

Worthen, John. "The necessary ignorance of a biographer". In *The Art of Literary Biography,* edited by John Batchelor. Oxford: Clarendon Press, 1995.

Yabes, Leopoldo Y. *Philippine literature in English: 1898–1957.* Quezon City: University of the Philippines, 1958.

———. "The Filipino Novel in English". *Herald Mid-week Magazine,* September 1941.

———. "The Filipino Essay in English: A Critical Study with an Anthology of Representative Essays (1912–1941)". MA thesis, University of the Philippines, 1949.

Yu-Jose, Lydia N. *Filipinos in Japan and Okinawa 1880s–1972.* Research Institute for the Languages and Cultures of Asia and Africa, Tokyo University of Foreign Studies, 2002.

Yusuf, Abdulqawi. *Legal Aspects of Trade Preferences for Developing States: A Study in the Influence of Development Needs on the Evolution of International Law.* Brill, 1982.

Zaide, Jose A. *Bababa, ba? Anecdotes of a Foreign Service Officer.* Mandaluyong City: Academic Publishing Corporation, DFA Foreign Service Institute and the Ateneo Alumni Class '60/'64, 2004.

Index

Note: Page numbers followed by "n" denote endnotes.

A
Abad, Gemino, 310n17
Abad Santos, Jose, 69, 203
Abad Santos, Ossie, 203
Abad Santos, Pepito, 203
Abada, Esteban, 115
Abaya, Hernando, 69
Abdel Nasser, Gamal, 159, 175
Abdul Razak, Tun, 205
Abella, Domingo, 194
Abello, Emilio, 90
Abou-Riche, Omar, 236–37, 241
Abyssinia, 49
Afghanistan, 162, 226, 227, 234, 249, 304
Africa, Bernabe, 98
Africa, relations with Philippines, 98
Afro-Asian Writers Symposium, 304
Afternoon Out – Tea at the Philippine Embassy, 159
Agoncillo, Teodoro A., 180
Aguinaldo, Calixto, 68
Aguinaldo, Emilio, 195, 207
Albert, Mariano A., 110
Alcuaz, Federico Aguilar, 275
Alegre, Edilberto N., 7, 296
Alejandrino, José, 180
Algeria, 209, 210
Allied Minorities, 71
Allied Youth, 50, 71
Almagro, Melchor Fernández, 180
Almario, Simon, 80
Alonso, Mariano, 207
Alpha Beta fraternity, 37
Altamira, Rafael, 180
"Alternatives for Asians", 162

Alzate, Manuel A., 224
"American Influence, The", 131
American Jesuits, education under, 30–32
  debating skills, 35–37
  Guidon, student publications, 32–35
  overview of, 30–32
Americanization in Guerrero household, 21–25
Anderson, Benedict, 7, 9n7
Annexation Law, 246
anti-Americanism, 256
"anti-report", release of, 252
Anti-Smuggling Pact, 246
Antipolo, 28
"Antonio Prospero", 70
ANZUS conference, 125
apartheid, 176–77, 242, 259
Apostol, Cecilio, 285
Aquino, Benigno S., 54, 84, 97n23
  arrest of, 94, 96
Araneta, Antonio "Tonypet", 216, 283
archipelago concept, 259–60
Archivo del Bibliofilo Filipino, 180
Argentina, 125, 175
Arguilla, Lydia, 136
Arguilla, Manuel, 136
Arias, Roberto, 219
Armengol, Pedro Ortiz, 180
Arranz, Melecio, 109, 114, 115
Arriba, 195
Art of Translation, The, 168
"Asia and America" speech, 138, 307
"Asia for the Asians" policy, 146, 215, 297, 303–4

overview of, 128–33
reorienting Philippine foreign policy, 138–41
Asia-oriented policy, 300
Asia, spokesman for, 164–66
Asian-African Legal Consultative Committee, 259
Asian Center, 301
Aspiras, José, 244
Association of Southeast Asia (ASA), 302
Association of Southeast Asian Nations (ASEAN), 304
   alignment and non-alignment policy, 264
   founding, 237
   zone of peace and neutrality, 273–74
Aswan Dam project, 160
Atenean, The, 32
Ateneo Aegis, 43
Ateneo Alumni Association (AAA), 58–59
Ateneo Catholic Instruction League, 37
Ateneo de Manila University, 6, 289
Ateneo Players Guild, 43
Atienza, Juan, 200n4
Atlee, Clement R., 156
atomic bombs, 94, 119
Aung Than, 94
Australia, 75, 125, 250n9
Avelino, Jose, 56, 108–10, 113, 115
Avellana, Daisy, 158
Avellana, Lamberto "Bert", 53, 59
Awa Maru, 93
Ayuntamiento, 68

B

Baguio Conference, 302
Bali, 53, 54
Ballesteros, Antonio, 180
Ballesteros, Manuel, 207
Bandung Conference, 3, 301
Bangkok, Philippine and Malaysian delegation in, 243–46
Bangkok Talks, 245, 246, 268, 308
Bantug, Jose P., 194
Barcelona, 208
Barnett, Milton L., 4
barong tagalog, worn at official function, 156
Barrett Browning, Elizabeth, 265
Barretto, Alberto, 115
Barretto, Tomas, 115
Barrister, The, 50
Bataan
   Filipino campaign in, 297
   surrender of, 75
   writing Filipino history of, 100–103
Baviera, Aileen S.P., 8
Bayanihan Philippine Dance Company, 179
Belgian-Philippine relations, 125
Belgrade, 285, 290, 292
Bell Trade Act, 124, 142, 146, 301
Bellarmine Guild, 51, 57, 69
Belloc, Hilaire, 35
Ben Hur, 52
Bengzon, Cesar, 58
Bernabe, Manuel, 285
Bernad, Miguel A., 43, 46n15
Beta Sigma Lambda party, 110
Biardeaus, Madeleine, 224
bicameral legislature, 109
Bilibid Prison, 78, 79
Biography as an Art: Selected Criticism, 185–86
Blumentritt, Ferdinand, 180, 181
Boguslav, David "Dave", 94, 100
Bombay Rotary Club, 234, 235
Boncan, Maria Virginia, 200n4
Bonifacio, Andres, 132, 181, 198, 199, 224
   centenary, 206
Borges, Jorge Luis, 274
Borja, Jacinto C., 98, 209
Borobudur, 54
Boy Scouts Association, 169

INDEX 343

Boyle, Charles "Chuck", 78, 82n5
Bracken, Josephine, 182
Brezhnev, Leonid, 292
Brillantes, Hortencio J., 277
British Broadcasting Corporation, 164
British Club, 78
British Legion of Hammer Branch, 154
British North Borneo Company, 199, 244
Brownell, Herbert, Jr., 215
Bryant, William J., 23
Buckingham Palace, 153
Buencamino, Felipe, 74, 76
Bundy, William P., 214–15
Bureau of Internal Revenue (BIR), 129
Burgos, José, 83n19, 180, 256, 257
Burgos trial records, 202–3
  Guerrero's efforts to recover, 205–6
  Spanish resistance, 208
Burke, Margaret
  learning diplomatic protocol, 272
  marriage to Guerrero, 271–72
  meeting with Fidel Castro, 284
  private secretary, 180, 182
  return to Philippines, 293
Burma
  Greater East Asia Co-Prosperity Sphere, 84
  military takeover, 165, 166
  squabble between Siamese and Burmese counsellors, 86
Burnham Plan, 20

C
Cabili, Tomas, 115
Caldera, Rafael, 275, 277
Calderon, Felipe, 256
Calingo, Mauro, 219, 223
Calle Nueva, ancestral house on, 21
Camasura swindles, 68
Camp O'Donnell, 78
Cancún Summit, 296
Carlos P. Romulo Papers, 6
Carlyle, Thomas, 2, 132

Carpentier, Alejo, 274
"Case of the Seven Suspects, The", 42, 299
Castelo, Oscar, 129–30
Castiella, Fernando, 196, 197
Castillo, Andres V., 197–98
Castro, Fidel, 279, 284
Castro, Fred Ruiz, 74, 76, 77
"*catálogo razonado*", 194
"Catholic Hour", 57
Cavanna, Jose Ma., 180
Cavite Mutiny, 83n19
Cea, Edmundo, 132, 146
Cebu Carnival, 52
Cenizal, Josefino, 55
Central America mission, 272–73
Central Intelligence Agency (CIA), 130, 140
Chamberlain, Neville, 55, 214
Chaudhuri, Nirad C., 237–38
Chavez, Federico, 275
Chen Chih-Ping, 99
Cherian, P.V., 234
Chesterton Evidence Guild, 51, 57, 58, 69, 70, 306
Chesterton, G.K., 35, 40
China, 140
  member of Greater East Asia Co-Prosperity Sphere, 84
  relations with Philippines, 247, 248
  struggle with India, 228
Chinese immigration racket, 131
Chitang (Carmen Maria Vicenta Guerrero). *See* Guerrero, Carmen Maria Vicenta (Chitang)
Christian Filipinos, 266–67
Christmas Day, 26–27
Christmas story, 55–56
Chua, Yvonne T., 4
Churchill, Winston, 146, 154, 160, 214
Civil Liberties Union (CLU), 70
Clark Air Base, 140, 141
Clifford, James L., 186
Cobb, Irvin S., 39

Cohan, George M., 43
Colayco, Manuel C., 32
Cold War, 99, 119, 121, 223, 235
Collas, Juan, 49
College Editors Guild (CEG), 39, 41–42
Colombia, 273, 275, 277
Commonweal Hour, 57
Commonweal Service, 69, 70
Commonwealth national elections, 50
Communist China
    Philippines coexistence with, 247–48
    recognition of, 140
    relations with, 140
Communist Manifesto, The, 4
Compagnia Generale Impianti, 124
Conlu, Pedro Hernaez y, 54
"Conference that Fell Asleep, The", 234
Conference on the Law of the Sea, 259
Constantino, Renato, 4, 260
"constitutional crisis", 114
Copenhagen, 156, 157
Cooper Act, 19
Corominas, Anita (Annie)
    away from Manila, 213
    death, 265, 269n6
    dinner parties, 154, 166
    fund-raising activity, 167
    illness, 193, 254, 260
    in Japan, 88–89, 94–95
    during Japanese Occupation, 79
    in London, 153, 227
    marriage to Leoni, 53–54
    non-alcoholic, 231
    role in *Salazar*, 70
    sixth wedding anniversary, 85
    Taj Mahal visit, 236–37
    valedictorian, 52
Corregidor, fall of, 76–77
Costa Rica, 270, 273, 275, 277
Court of Industrial Relations, 52
Court of Saint James
    defending Garcia and Philippine elections, 163–64

East Asian Association, 161–62
European Common Market, 162–63
Germany and Scandinavian countries, 156–57
overview of, 153–54
Paris visit, 158–59
reporting on Suez Canal crisis, 159–61
secret weapon, 166–67
Southeast Asia Treaty Organization, 167–68
spokesman for Asia, 164–66
Sugar Council, 167–68
translation business, 168–69
US-UK military bases agreement, 162–63
"we Filipinos are one Asian people", 154–55
Court of Social Justice, 57
Creightonian, The, 39
Cristobal, Adrian, 5, 306
Critique of Rizal's Concept of a Filipino Nation, 180
Cruz, Gemma Teresa Guerrero, 92, 184
    arrival in Mexico, 283–84
    Miss International, 210
    marriage in Spain, 216
Cruz, Isagani R., 309n14
Cruz, Ismael, 79
Cruz, J.V., 160
Cruz, Roman, 67
Cruz, Toto, 92
Cuba, official visit to, 284–85
Cuenco Law, 207, 208
Cuenco, Mariano Jesus, 109, 113–15, 123, 132
Cuna, Elpidiforo, 49, 59
Cyrano de Bergerac, 44
Czechoslovak Socialist Republic, 230

D

Dagohoy, Francisco, 36
Datos para mi defensa, 180
Datu's Jewels, The, 43

David, Pablo Angeles, 115
Day, Beth, 275, 296
de Asis, Leocadio, 84–86
de Castiella, Fernando María, 212
de Cervantes, Miguel, 209
de Guzman, Pedro, 200n4
de la Costa, Horacio, 6, 31–33, 35–36, 40, 45, 132, 179, 180, 181, 192n25, 204
  death, 288
  last request, 289
  martial law regime, 282–83
  Provincial Superior of the Philippine Province of the Society of Jesus, 241
  reunion with Guerrero, 258
  wrote *Salazar*, 70
  as Skeezix, 36
  translation of Rizal's poems, 15
de la Cruz, Apolinario, 202
de la Rosa, Rogelio, 55
de Leon, Diony, 92
de Leon, Lily, 52, 53
de Leon, Manuel "Manny", 74
de Madariaga, Salvador, 180
de Mas, Sinibaldo, 202
de Rodriguez, Maria Josefina Caminero, 200n4
de Ungria, Jose, 92
de Villaverde, Marques and Marquesa, 212
de Zuñiga, Martinez, 202
Death March, 76
"Decay of Democracy, The", 36
del Pilar, Marcelo H., 131, 180, 181
del Rosario, Rosa, 55
del Sol, Mila, 55
Delgado, Francisco, 139, 141, 172, 173, 175
democracies, Philippine and Indian compared, 238–39
"Democracy, an Exposé on Rhetoric", 36
Democratic group alliance, 115

Denmark, 156
Desidirio, Jose, 92
"development diplomacy", 277–78
DFA Review, 6
Diccionario de Historia de España, 180
Dick, Robert McColluch, 49, 56, 59
"dictatorship of greed", 49
Diokno, Ramon, 112
"diplomacy of development", 304
  Philippine-American economic relations, 234
  Philippine foreign policy, 233
  Philippine *vs.* Indian democracies, 238–39
  speeches, 234–36
  visit to Taj Mahal, 236–37
"Diplomacy of Food, The", 235
diplomacy of isolation, 125
diplomat
  as intellectual-bureaucrat, 252
  role of, 188
Diplomatic Agenda of Philippine Presidents, 1946–1985, 6
Division of Protocol, 98
Dizon, Victor, 196
Djojohadikusumo, Sumitro, 2, 3, 4
Djokjakarta, 54
Domingo, Benjamin, 8
Dominguez, Aurora, 21
Dorojski, Steven, 290
Dorticós, Oswaldo, 284
Duque, PA, 100
Dutch embassy, in Philippines, 125
DZRH, 139

E
Eagle, Joe, 85
East Asian Association, 161–62
"Easter fashion", 54
Eastern Europe, 214, 249, 264, 293
Echeverría, Luis, 273, 274, 278–79
Economic Commission for Asia and the Far East (ECAFE), 302

Economist, The, 183
Ecuador, 273, 275, 277
Eden, Anthony, 153
Egypt, 159
El Debate, 44
El Filibusterismo. See *Fili*
El Galeón de Manila, 284
El Porvenir Restaurant, 49
El Salvador, 273, 275, 278
Elizabeth II, Queen, 153
Emergency Powers Act, 112
Enciclopedia Espasa, 180
Enverga Report, 247
Epistolario Rizalino, 179
Erlinda, 74
Ermita, birth and boyhood in
   bourgeois atmosphere, 20
   charm-and-wit practitioner, 26–28
   Guerreros' settlement, 20–21
   Hispanization and Americanization, 21–25
   siblings, early life with, 25–26, 28n8
Espino, Federico Licsi, Jr., 151
Estadismo de las Filipinas, 202
Estrada, Jose S., 200n4
Eucharistic Congress in Manila (1937), 51
Europe, relations with Philippines, 98
European Common Market, 162–63, 189, 214
European Community, 119
Evangelista, Teodoro E., 90–91, 98
exports
   British *vs.* Philippine, 183
   Philippine-Yugoslav relations, 291

F
Face of Thai Feudalism, The, 4
factionalism, in Philippine Senate, 109, 112
Fall of the Spanish American Empire, The, 180
Far Eastern University (FEU), 109–10, 138

Faustian generation, 246–47
Feliciano, Florentino, 244–46
Feniquito, 84
Fernandez, Doreen G., 7, 296
Ferrer, Jose Figueres, 275
Fili, 178, 181, 190
Filipinization, 186
"Filipino First" policy, 173, 183, 186, 302
Filipino Muslims, 266–67, 302
Filipino nationalism, 103, 184, 256–58
Filipino students in Madrid, 197
Finland, 156
First Filipino, The, 6, 7, 179, 298, 307
Florante at Laura, 54
Fonteyn, Margot, 159, 219
Foreign Affairs Officers (FAO), 135
foreign affairs, undersecretary of, 133–38
foreign policy
   debate, 121–23, 139, 300
   independent, 248
   Philippines, 98, 233, 234, 248, 258, 260–61, 268, 304
   spokesman, 123–26
Foreign Service Act, 134, 135
Foreman, John, 180
Formosa, 84, 93, 154
Fort Santiago, 78
Francisco, D.L., 49
Francisco, Filomena, 25, 59
   agent of tradition, 23
   Catholic teachings, 23–24
   clothing styles, 25–26
   death, 258
Francisco, Gabriel Beato, 24
   "Lolo Abeng", 24
Francisco, Guillermo B., 52
Francisco Law School, 110–11
Francisco, Vicente J., 67, 108, 111, 113
Franco, Generalissimo Francisco, 194–96
   diplomacy, 213–14

visit to Philippines of Marques and
  Marquesa de Villaverde, 212–13
Frederick IX, King, 156
Free Press, 6, 42, 48, 56, 59
French Revolution, 132
Fuentes, Carlos, 274

G
Gaitskell, Hugh, 156
Gandhi, Indira, 224–25, 254, 265
Ganges River, 230
Garces, Luis, 114
Garcia, Carlos P., 7, 163–64, 173, 183,
  263, 302
  vice presidential candidate, 130
  meeting with Ohno Katsumi, 142–44
  Secretary of Foreign Affairs, 133–35
Garraty, John A., 181
Gaston-Roces Publication Company, 50
Gawad Mabini, 1, 305
Germany, promoting trade in, 156–57
Ghazali Bin Shafie, Tan Sri, 245–46
Gibbs, Gibbs, Chuidian and Quasha,
  107
Gleeck, Lewis E., Jr, 7
Gokhale, Gopal Krishna, 224
Gomburza, 83n19, 219, 256
Gomez, Mariano, 83n19, 256
gout, 204
Grand Cross of the Lion, 193
Grand Cross of the Order of Isabela la
  Católica, 219
Grand Cross of the Order of Quetzal,
  273
Grand Cross of the Order of the
  Yugoslav Flag, 293
Grand Cross, Order of Dannebrog, 193
Graphic, 33, 56, 58
"great debate" on Philippine foreign
  policy, 122, 139, 300
Greater East Asia Co-Prosperity Sphere,
  79, 84, 89, 143, 300
Greater Malayan Confederation, 303

Grey, Zane, 42
Grupo Escolar Islas Filipinas, 218
Guatemala, 270, 273, 274, 277, 278, 291
Guerrero, Alfredo León, 21, 183, 184
  agent of modernity, 24
  collection of weapons, 22
  Manila College of Pharmacy, 22
  death of, 197
Guerrero, Carmen Maria Vicenta
  (Chitang), 24–28, 32, 34, 40, 79,
  123, 213, 277, 295–96, 304
  husband's death, 92
  "My Humble Opinion", 131
  National Historical Commission,
  246, 282
  visit to London of her daughters,
  184
Guerrero, Cesar Maria, 53, 79
Guerrero, David (Leon Xavier), 272,
  273, 306
  anthology about Leon Ma. Guerrero,
  7
  in Belgrade, 292
  Benedict Anderson rebuttal, 9n7
  birth, 182
  childhood days, 272–73, 275
  fascination with advertisements, 296
  relationship with father, 285, 292
Guerrero, Efrain Ma., 107
Guerrero, Fernando María, 33
  La Independencia, 23
Guerrero, Gemma
  death of, 25, 28n8
Guerrero, León Jorge, 20, 48
Guerrero, León Maria, 21
  telling fantastic tales to Leoni, 24
Guerrero, Leon Maria (Leoni)
  alcoholism, 295
  budding Americanization, 30, 32, 35
  basketball fan, 49, 51–52
  death, 305
  detective short stories, 42
  Doctor of Humanities degree, 260

export promotion, 291
failing health, 290
fascination with international affairs, 49, 51
fiftieth birthday, 216
first marriage, 53–54
Guidon, editorial work at, 39, 41, 44
Hispanic leanings, 59
honeymoon in Bali, 53
humour sense, 39–40, 42
law school, 48–50
least enjoyed assignment, 291–92
legal counsel, 112–14
and Mario, 32
poetic ability, 33
preparatory years, 31
radio work, 56–58
retirement, 295
second marriage, 271
secretary to Jorge Vargas, 79, 80
senatorial candidacy, refusal of, 264–65
and Skeezix, 40, 45
spokesman for Asia, 164–66
theatre acting, 43–45
"Totoy to Momoy", 39, 41, 58
translator role, 114–16
writing style, 40
in youth politics, 50
Guerrero, Lorenzo Maria, 25, 282
Guerrero, Margaret Burke. *See* Burke, Margaret
Guerrero, Mario Xavier, 25–28, 32, 90, 128, 207, 296
   Philippine Artists Gallery board of directors, 128
   Philippine Heart Center for Asia, 282
Guerrero-Robertson affair, 173–74
Guerrero, Wilfrido Maria, 7, 25, 28n8, 283
Guidon, The, 6, 32–35
Guillén, Nicolas, 284
Gustilo, Loreto "Baby", 85

H

Hajk, Jiri, 180
Hakone, diplomatic evacuation centre at, 94
Hare-Hawes-Cutting Bill, 45, 50
Hartendorp, A.V.H., 70
Harvard Club, 120
Havana, appointment to, 284–85
Hechanova, Rufino, 196
Heidelberg, 157
Hermita, 19
Hernandez, Jaime, 144
Hernandez, Jose M., 102
Heuss, Theodor, 157
"higher laws of vision", 40
Hilario, Gil, 156
Hilario, Vicente M., 40
"Hindi-English Conflict, The", 237
Hinduism, 224
Hinulugang Taktak, 28
Hiroshima, 94
His Dishonor, the Mayor, 51, 299
Hispanic culture, 197, 270
Hispanization in Guerrero household, 21–25
Hispanization of the Philippines, The, 180
Hispano-Luso-American-Philippine Assembly on Tourism, 219
Historia de España, 180
Historia General de Filipinas, 180, 202
History of India, A, 224
History of Spain, A, 180
Historia Política de la España Contemporánea, 180
Hodobu (Japanese Department of Information), 6, 79, 81, 84
Honduras, 273, 275, 278
Hodza, Fadilj, 291
Honma, Masaharu, 77, 81, 101
Hontiveros, Daisy, 59
Horiguchi, 86–87
Horacio de la Costa Papers, 6

INDEX

Hua Guofeng, 292
Huelga, 57
Hunting Aerosurveys, 154
Hurley, John F., SJ, 73

I
"I Did Not Know", 33
Ikonic, Branislav, 291
Imperial, Gloria, 55
Imperial Rule Assistance Association (1945), 89
Impresiones, 180
Ince, Wallace, 82n5
independence day
   celebration in London, 156
   change of date, 195–96
independent foreign policy, 248
India
   "anti-report," release of, 252
   banquets and state dinners, 230–31
   bi-alignment, 228
   democracies compared, 238–39
   exploring, 229
   financial aids, 229
   Indira Gandhi's policies, 224–25
   new chancery, 226–27, 254
   Rashtrapati Bhavan, 225–26
   relations with Philippines, 223–24
   relations with USSR, 249
   secular state, 166
   struggle with China, 228
   UNCTAD II co-chair, 242, 250n4
Indian Council of World Affairs, 238
Indian School of International Studies, 233
Indochina, 73, 125
Indonesia, 124, 302
Informe sobre el estado de las Islas Filipinas en 1842, 202
Ingles, Jose D., 7, 157
Ingrid, Queen, 156
Institute of Asian Studies, 301
Institute of Atomic Information, 157

International Bar Association, 161
International Cultural Exchange Programme, 161
International Meeting of Parliamentary Representatives and Exports for the Development of International Trade, 108
International News Summary, The, 75
International Parliamentary Union Conference, 108, 119
International Sugar Council, 167–68, 177, 219, 253
International Sugar Organization (ISO), 243
Iran, 120
Iraq, 165, 166
Iribarne, Manuel Fraga, 207
Irwin, Henry L., SJ, 44
Isidoro, Francisco "Doro", 78, 79, 82n5
Islam, 224
Israel, 302
Italian-Philippine relations, 124

J
Jabidah Massacre, 243, 250n9, 304
Japan
   Greater East Asia Co-Prosperity Sphere, 84
   investments in abaca, 42
   Philippine ambassador to, 209
   reparations mission, 142
   resentment against Filipinos, 91–92
   sponsored Philippine Republic, 84
   surrender, 94
Japanese Foreign Office, 84
Japanese Imperial Navy, 89
Japanese Occupation, 74, 81, 109, 257
Japanese Occupation Papers, 6
"Japanophobes", 73
Javier, Ignacio, 57, 73, 78, 79, 176, 300
Joaquin, Nick, 6, 22, 205
Johnson, Lyndon, 217, 229
Jones Law, 20

Jordan, William, SJ, 44
Jorge B. Vargas Papers, 6
Jorge Vargas Museum, 6
Jose Rizal National Centennial Commission (JRNCC), 179, 187, 190n2, 191n22
Jova, John Joseph, 277
Juan Luna Centennial Commission, 200
Julius Caesar, 44
Junior Alumni Association, 50
Junior Coalition League, 50

K
Kahin, George McT., 4
Kalaw, Teodoro M., 179, 180, 253
Kangleon, Ruperto, 132
Kapisanan ng mga Pilipino sa Nippon (KAPINI), 86
Kapisanan sa Paglilingkod sa Bagong Pilipinas (KALIBAPI), 80
Kaul, T.N., 225, 229
Kennan, George, 164–65
Kennedy, Raymond J.H., 43
Kensington Gardens, 153
Kessler, Richard J., Jr, 7
King Henry IV, 44
King Lear, 44, 45, 158
Knight Grand Cross of Rizal, 193
Knight of the Blessed Sacrament Sodality (KBS), 36–37
Korean War, 121
Kuroda, Shigenori, 84, 87
Kussela, Armi, 156
KZIB, 57
KZND, 80
KZRF, 57
KZRH, 57, 70, 77, 79, 80
KZRM, 44, 56–57, 69, 78, 82n5

L
La Batalla de Lepanto, 200
La Defensa, 36
La Loba Negra, 180
La Política y Los Políticos en el Reinado de Carlos III, 203
La Revolución Filipina, 253–54
L'Aiglon, 43
Lacson, Arsenio, 114–15
Lacy, William B., 133
Lake Lanao, 78
Lara, Guillermo Rodriguez, 275, 277
Larrarte, Araceli, 200n4
Latin American experiences, 273–75
Laurel, Jose P., 65, 68, 84, 89, 93–94, 108, 110, 139, 163
  arrest, 94, 96
  financial adviser plan, 86
  Twilight in Tokyo, 99–100, 299
Laurel-Langley Agreement, 242, 301
Lavides, Francisco, 84, 86, 110
Law of the Sea, 259
Leacock, Stephen, 42
League of the Sacred Heart (LSH), 36–37
legal counsel, 112–14
Legge, J.D., 4
Leogardo, Clara, 21
Leon Ma. Guerrero Papers, 6
Leon Ma. Guerrero Personnel Data Papers, 6
Liberal Party, 109, 110, 113–15, 130, 141, 204, 217, 239, 264
Liberia, 157, 158
Lim, Manuel, 69
Lim, Vicente, 75
Literary Apprentice, 58
Litiatco, A.E., 58
Lizardo, Quirino, 67
Lloyd, Selwyn, 166
Locsin, Teodoro M., 49, 56
Lodge, Henry Cabot, 175
London
  banished to, 144–47
  Guerrero's seventh year in, 186–87
London Times, 169, 183
Longmans, 168, 178

Lopez Arellano, Oswaldo, 275, 278
Lopez-Concepcion, Pilar, 80
Lopez, Fernando, 108, 218
Lopez Foundation, 260
Lopez-Jaena, Graciano, 131, 180
López Michelsen, Alfonso, 278
Lopez, Pedro, 100
López Portillo, Jose, 286
Lopez-Rizal, Leoncio, 185
Lopez, Salvador P., 6, 57–58, 73–74, 82n5, 90–91, 97n16, 111, 172, 175, 209, 301, 306, 310n20
    ambassador to the U.S., 242
    Herald writer, 41
    letter to Guerrero, 134–37
    in Padre Faura, 205–6
    Philippines-India relations, 242
    permanent representative to the United Nations, 241
    Romulo's speechwriter, 122–23
    secretary of Foreign Affairs, 206
    visit to Spain, 196
Lumbera, Bienvenido, 7
Lumbera, Cynthia N., 7
Luna, Antonio, 23, 131, 180, 256
Luna, Juan, 131–32, 196
    Centennial Commission, 200
Luneta Park, 20
Luz, Arturo R., 128
Lyceum School of Law, 129–30, 260

M

Mabanag, Alejo, 132
Mabini, Apolinario, 54
    "internal revolution", 281
    memoirs, 180
    nationalism, 256
    translation of works, 253–54
Mabuhay magazine, 296
Macapagal, Diosdado, 139, 163, 203, 301, 303
    newly elected president, 188
    visit to Spain, 195–96

MacArthur, Douglas, 75, 89
McCawley, Peter, 4
Madrid
    embassy in, 197–200, 209
    "Great Pampango's" visit, 194–97
    preparation for, 189–90
    welfare of Filipino students in, 198
Magda or Mohammedan Revenge, 52
Magsaysay for President Movement (MPM), 146
Magsaysay, Ramon F., 301
    death, 163
    dissatisfaction with Recto, 141–44
    election and candidacy, 130, 132–33
    Undersecretary of Foreign Affairs, 133
Mahendra, King of Nepal, 238
Majul, Cesar A., 180
Makassar, 53
Malacañang, 50, 98, 99, 133, 140, 246, 261
Malari Incident, 3
Malay, Armando J., 4, 41–42
Malaya-Indonesia confrontation, 204
Malaysia
    Federation of, 204
    relations with USSR, 249
    Sabah claim, 243–46
Maloles, Julius G., 200n4
Malolos Constitution, 270
Manalang-Gloria, Angela, 5
Manansala, Vicente, 285
Manchester Guardian, 163
Manchuria, 73
Manchukuo
    in Greater East Asia Co-Prosperity Sphere, 84
Manglapus, Raul S., 146, 160, 275, 276, 277
Manila, 198
    Americanization of, 19–20
    devastation, 95–96
Manila Accord, 205

Manila Chronicle, 131, 135
Manila Grand Opera House, 44, 45
Manila Hotel, 20, 53
Manila Overseas Press Club, 119, 139, 247
Manila Rotary Club, 160
Manila Summit, 204, 205
Manila Times, 115, 178
Manlapaz, Edna Z., 5
Manuel L. Quezon Educational Institution, 122
Mao Zedong, 140
Maphilindo, 205, 303
Maramba, Asuncion D., 7
March of Time, 45, 69
Marcos, Ferdinand E., 1, 7, 139, 140, 221, 246, 247, 301, 303–5
  murder case, 67–69
  new directions in foreign policy, 271
  "New Society", 281–82
  newly elected president, 217, 218
  Senate President, 213
Marcos, Imelda, 265, 268, 292, 305
Marcos, Mariano, 67
Marcos, Pio, 67
Maria Christina Hydroelectric contract, 124
Mariño, Salvador L., 203–4
Marquardt, Frederic S., 49, 217–18
Marquez, Gabriel Garcia, 274
martial law
  disillusionment with, 306
  as "historical necessity", 282
  proclamation of, 275–76
  propagandist, 281–86
  raison d'être, 281
Marx, Karl, 4
Mayans, 273
McLaughlin, Hugh J., SJ, 33
Medalla, David, 178
Memorias de Un Estudiante de Manila, 115
Men of Bataan, The, 65

Mendez, Mauro, 52, 135, 209, 218
Mendez, Pacita, 218
Mexico, 198, 270–75
  insurgency, 277
Meyer, Milton W., 7
Mi Ultimo Adios, 86
Military Bases Agreement, 212, 256
Military Intelligence Service (MIS), 74
Mindanao Independence Movement, 267
Mindanao State University, 266
Miss International, 210
Miss Visayas, 52
Mitra, Ramon P., 173
modern diplomat, features of, 126
Molina, Arturo Armando, 274, 278
"Momoy to Totoy", 39
Monrovia, 157
Montano, Justiniano, 115
Montero y Vidal, José, 180, 202
Montgomery, Robert, 45
Montilla, Gil, 52
Montilla, Luis M., 179, 180, 194
Moreno, Rosario, 55
Moro Province, 266
Morocco, 210
Mossessgeld, Enrico, 90
Mother, 92
Movement for Free Philippines, 275
Mulry, Joseph A., SJ, 36, 43, 51, 57, 59
Mundo Hispánico, 216
Murata, Shozo, 84, 144
Muslims as Filipinos, 266–67
Mussolini, Il Duce, 49
Mutual Defence Treaty, 255–56
Myth of the Lazy Native, The, 4

N

Nacionalista Party, 70, 71, 130, 141
Nagasaki, 94
Nakpil, Carmen Guerrero, 7, 20
  see also Guerrero, Carmen Maria Vicenta (Chitang)

Nakpil, Nina, 184
Nalundasan, Julio, 67
Nara, 93, 94
National Collegiate Athletic Association (NCAA), 49
National Defence System, 70
National Historical Commission, 246
National Movement for Free Elections (NAMFREL), 120
National Waterworks and Sewerage Authority, 158
nationalist, diplomat as, 188–89
Nature of Biography, The, 181
Navarro, Nelson A., 5
Nehru, Jawaharlal, 138, 165, 224, 228
Nepal, 238, 249, 304
Neri, Felino, 133, 135, 145
New Delhi. *See also* India
  building chancery, 226–27
  historic city, 229
New Delhi Conference, 302
"New Directions in Philippine Foreign Policy", 271
"New Society", 281–82
New York Times, 175
New Zealand, 125, 229, 250n9
Nicaragua, 270, 273, 275, 278
Nihongo, 85, 91
Ninay, 180
Nippon Times, The, 90
Nixon Doctrine, 304
Nixon, Richard, 215, 255, 304
No, Mr Russell, 57
Noble, Corazon, 55
Noli Me Tangere, 169, 178, 190
Non-Aligned Foreign Ministers Conference, 290, 305
Non-Aligned Movement, 291, 305
non-alignment policy, 227–29
Norris, Kathleen, 92
North Atlantic Treaty Organization (NATO), 163, 167
North Borneo, 153, 189

North Korea, 189
North Vietnam, 189, 225
Norway, 156, 157
Nostradamus, MD, 58

O

Office of Political and Economic Affairs, 98
Ohno Katsumi, 142–43
oil crisis, 285
"One China, One Taiwan", 266
"One Fate — One Destiny" speech, 89
Orantes, Adolfo Molina, 273, 291
Order of Sikatuna, 197
Osias, Ben, 100
Osias, Camilo, 54, 94, 95, 96, 108, 123, 129, 130
Oslo, 156, 157
Osmeña, Sergio, 50, 52, 53, 69, 71, 75, 92, 170n20, 224, 257, 264, 271
Osorio, Carlos Arana, 274, 277, 278
Othello, 158
"Our Foreign Relations", 123
"Our Mendicant Foreign Policy", 121
Ozaeta, Roman, 67

P

Paasikivi, Juho, 156
Pacific Treaty Organization (PATO), 142
Paco, 20, 79
Padmini, Queen, 239
Padre Burgos, 261
Padre Faura, 36, 248, 261
  new head in, 205–6
  reshuffle in, 209–10
pagtitiis concept, 247
Pakistan, 165, 166, 226, 302
Palacio de Oriente, 194
Palestine, 302
Palma, Rafael, 180
Palma, Rodolfo, 101–2
Pampanga, 20

Pangasinan, 53
Pandit, Vijaya Lakshmi, 162, 236
Paredes, Jesus A., Jr, 31
Paredes, Quintin, 115, 123, 139, 203
Paris, 138, 158–59, 200, 291
parity rights, 214–16, 234
Parsons, Chick, 73
Parti Gerakan Rakyat Malaysia, 4
Parti Keadilan Masyarakat Malaysia, 4
Partido Nacionalista Democrata, 50
Partido Nacionalista Pro-Independencia, 50
"partyless democracy", 69–70, 281
Pasay Lions Club, 146
Passion and Death of the USAFFE, The, 100–103, 299, 307
Pastrana Borrero, Misael, 277, 278
Pasudeco mills strike, 56, 68
Paterno, Pedro A., 180
Payne-Aldrich Act (1909), 23
Paz, Octavio, 226
Pearl Harbour bombing, 73
"Pearl of the Orient" exhibition, 155
Pecson, Geronima, 138
Pelaez, Emmanuel, 5, 132, 151, 198, 199, 204, 205, 303, 306
Pensacola Syndrome, 256
pensionados, 85–86, 94, 131
People's Court Papers, 6
People's Republic of China (PRC)
    admission to United Nations, 265–66
    Philippine diplomatic relations with, 278
    see also China
Peralta, Macario, 115
Pérez, Carlos Andrés, 278
Perez, Eugenio, 139
Perfecto, Vero, 80
Phelan, John Leddy, 180
Philippine Academy of Sciences and Humanities, 216
Philippine-American relations, 99, 102, 173–74, 213, 217–18, 233, 234

Philippine-American War, 23, 257
Philippine Approaches: A Monthly Review of Writing in the Philippines, 241
Philippine Artists Gallery, 128
Philippine-Belgian relations, 125
Philippine Book Guild, 79
Philippine-British relations, 153, 189
Philippine Chamber of Commerce, 247
Philippine Civic Action Group (PHILCAG), 234
"Philippine Experiment, The", 155
Philippine Herald, 119
Philippine Historical Association, 138
Philippine-Iberian American kinship, 270
Philippine-India relations, 223, 225, 242, 250n4
Philippine Institute of Spanish Culture, 208, 219
Philippine Insurrection against the United States, The, 260
Philippine Islands, The, 180
Philippine Law School, 146
Philippine Liberty News, 102
Philippine Magazine, 70
Philippine-Malaysia relations, 243
Philippine Masonry, 180
Philippine-Mexican relations, 270–79
    negative balance of trade, 285–86
Philippine Republic inauguration, 84
Philippine Review, 80
Philippine Revolution, 23, 202
Philippine Society of London, 155, 183, 190
Philippine-Spanish relations, 124, 194, 196–97, 199, 219–20
Philippine Sugar Association, 145
Philippine-Thailand relations, 124
Philippine-US relations, 103, 124, 255–56
Philippine War Damage Bill, 303

Philippine-Yugoslav relations, 291
Philippines
  bargaining position, 249
  civilization, 237–38
  delegation, 243–44
  democracy in, 69
  foreign policy, 98, 233, 234, 248, 258, 260–61, 268, 304
  independence, 195–96
  Indian democracies vs., 238–39
  Latin America and, 198
  legal history, 67–68
  publicity, 187, 189, 190
  relations with socialist countries, 247–49
  Spain's legacy in, 52
Philippines Free Press, 6, 40, 42, 46
Philippines Today, The, 79
Phumisak, Chit, 2, 4
Piñar, Blas, 207
Pineda-Ofreneo, Rosalinda, 4
Poblador, Filemon, 69
Poe, Fernando, 55
poems, translation of, 116
Ponce, Mariano, 180
Portugal, 210
post-war politics, 110
Priestley, J.B., 234–35
Prisoners of History, 267
prisoners of war (POWs), 76–78
publicist, role of, 188–89
Puyat, Gil, 263
"*puyo-puyo*", 53

Q
Quezon, Manuel L., 42
  authoritarian tendency, 70
  death, 92
  Guerrero a Quezon loyalist, 69–71
  "partyless democracy", 281
  social justice programme, 50–51, 69
Quiapo, 20, 27
Quirino, Carlos, 7, 180, 199

Quirino, Elpidio, 98, 103, 108, 110, 121, 128, 300, 302
  foreign policy blunders, 130
  as Secretary of Foreign Affairs, 139
Quirós, Daniel Oduber, 277
"Quo Vadis? A Seminar on Modern Literature", 35

R
Rackety Rax, 51
Radhakrishnan, Sarvapalli, 225
Radio Peiping, 140
radio speaker, in social justice service, 44, 56–58
"Rah-jah Guerrero", 37
Ramon Magsaysay Award for International Understanding, 3
Ramos, Benigno, 48
Ramos, Ely, 55, 243
Ramos, Godofredo P., 139–40
Ramos, Narciso, 135, 223, 243, 306
Rashtrapati Bhavan meeting, 225–26
Rasilla, J. Antonio, 200n4
Reading, Lord, 156, 161, 162
Readings in Philippine History, 210
Reagan, Ronald, 296
Recto, Claro M., 42, 58, 84, 89, 105, 121–23, 174, 215, 261, 295, 298, 300, 302
  death, 184
  dissatisfaction with Magsaysay, 141–44
  Guerrero's appointment, 129, 133, 138
  knighthood, 116
  Romulo's appointment, disapproval for, 145–47
religious fanaticism, 41
"Remember Erlinda!", 74
repatriation, applying for, 94–96
Retail Trade Nationalization bill, 145
Retana, Wenceslao, 180
Revolt of the Masses, The, 180
Reyes, Jose J., 42

Reyes, Narciso, 135–37, 234
Reyes, Norman, 78, 82n5
Reynolds, Craig J., 4
Rinehart, Mary Roberts, 51
Rise of the Spanish American Empire, The, 180
Rivas, Vicente Guzman, 200n4
Rizal and the Philippines of His Days, 180
Rizal Day speaker, 187–88
Rizal, Jose, 23, 86, 115–16, 168–69, 190n1, 193, 298, 307
   biographies, 178–81
   centenary, 187–88
   commemorative markers, 208
   Faustian generation, 246–47
   national hero, 289
   pagtitiis concept, 247
   "social regeneration", 281
   translation of poems and memoirs, 115–16, 307
   relationship with Josephine Bracken, 182
Rizal, Maria, 79
Rizal, Paciano, 181
Rizal Presidential Award, 198
Robles, Jose, 115
Robertson, Walter, 302, 308
   allegations against Guerrero, 175–76
   verbal tiff with Guerrero, 172–73
Roces, Helen, 128
Rodrigo, Francisco "Soc", 36, 59
Rodriguez, Eulogio, 115, 123
Rodriguez, Teodoro, 85
Rogers, F. Theo, 295
"Role of Mass Media in the Development of Southeast Asia, The", 264
Romero, Jose, 145
Romero, Redentor, 285
Romualdez, Alberto Z., 53
Romulo, Carlos P., 1, 56, 73–74, 82n5, 121–23, 134, 157, 172, 195, 246, 248, 249, 253, 254, 295, 306

College Editors Guild, 39
"great debate" on foreign policy, 122, 139, 300
martial law regime, 275–76
Permanent Philippine Representative to the United Nations, 111
Today Began Yesterday, 281
United States ambassador, 145–46, 156
Ronas, Malaya C., 7
Rosado, Bautista J., 200n4
Rostand, Edmond
   Cyrano de Bergerac, 44
   L'Aiglon, 43
Rotary Club of Cebu, 121
Rotary Club of New Haven, 120
Rotary Club of San Fernando, 120
Rotary Club Philippines, 68
Rotor, Arturo, 58
Round Table Conference, 3
Roxas, Gerardo, 264
Roxas, Manuel A., 7, 65, 78, 94, 99, 108, 114, 203, 300
Roy, Ram Mohan, 224
Royal Geographical Society, 155
Russia, 119, 263

S
Sabah
   claim, 198–99, 201n20, 209
   Philippine policy towards, 243–46
Sabatini, Rafael, 42
Sabido, Pedro, 194
Salvador P. Lopez Papers, 6
Salazar, 70
Salazar, Antonio de Oliveiro, 70
Salonga, Jovito, 264
Sampaloc, 20
San Francisco, 75, 120
San Jose Seminary, 36
San Miguel, 20
Santa Ana, 20
Santa Mesa, 20

Sanz, Felix, 200n4
Sarasin, Pote, 167
Sauer, Kenneth, 75
Saturday News, The, 174
Savory, Theodore H., 168
Scandinavian countries, trade promotion in, 156–57
School of Oriental and African Studies, 204
See You in Manila (SYIM), 74
Sendenbu (Propaganda Corps), 79
Serantes, Josefina, 200n4
Serrano, Felixberto, 134, 156, 168, 172, 173, 176, 263, 302
Seven Keys to Baldplate, 43
Severino, Rodolfo, 200n4
Shah Jahan, 236–37
Shell Company, 155
Sikhism, 224
Sinsuat, Mama, 92
Sintesis de Historia de España, 180
Sison, Marites N., 4
Sison, Teofilo, 94–95
Sjahrir, Sutan, 4
Skeezix, 36, 39, 40, 45
   see also de la Costa, Horacio
social justice programme, 50–51, 69
"social regeneration", 281
socialist countries, 247–49
Soedjatmoko, 2, 3, 4
Soekarno, 165
Soldevilla, F., 180
Soler, Arturo, 200n4
Soliven, Maximo V., 5, 65
Somoza Debayle, Anastasio, 275
Song of India, 49
South Africa, apartheid in, 176–77, 259
South Korea, 229, 263
South Vietnam, 229, 263
Southeast Asia Treaty Organization (SEATO), 160–61, 167–68, 172, 189, 301

Spain. *See also* Madrid
   Franco diplomacy, 213–14
   legacy to Philippines, 120
   post-civil war, 195
Spanish-Philippine relations, 124, 194, 196–97, 199, 219–20
Spear, Percival, 224
Spence, Hartzell, 71n2
Spoliarium, 196
Spruance, Raymond E., 140, 142
Stage of the World, 44
Star Reporter, 114
"Still Small Voice", 55–56, 299
Stonehill, Harry, 203–4
Storm over Nuevaluz, 57
Stroessner, Alfredo, 275
"Student Days", 33
Study of Poetry, 33
Subandrio, 205
Sudan, 165, 166
Suez Canal crisis, 159–61, 170n19
Sugamo Prison, 94
Sugar Quota office, 112
Suharto, 3
Sukarno, 3
Sultanate of Sulu, 199, 201n20, 244
Sumulong, Lorenzo, 115, 173
Surabaya, 53
Sweden, 156, 169
Sy-Changco, Faustino, 84, 85
Syed Hussein Alatas, 2, 4
Symington Report, 255–56
Symington, Stuart, 255

T
Tabuena, Romeo, 128, 285
Taiwan, 189, 266
Taj Mahal, 236–37
Tamayo, Rufino, 278
Tañada, Lorenzo, 101, 129, 130, 132, 142, 174
Tatang, 283, 307
Taylor, John R.M., 260

Teehankee, Claudio "Ding", 296, 306
terno, worn at official function, 156
Thailand, 124, 249
    Greater East Asia Co-Prosperity
        Sphere, 84
    military takeover, 165, 166
    squabble between Siamese and
        Burmese counsellors, 86
Thee Kian Wie, 4
Thein Maung, 88
"Third Programmes" talks, 164
Thompson, Francis, 35
Tibet, 172, 174, 175, 302
Tilak, Bal Gangadhar, 224
"Times in Rhymes, The", 42, 299
Times of India, 226, 237, 244
tinikling, 159, 168
Tito, Joseph Broz, 285–86
    funeral service, 292–93
    hunting aficionado, 290
Tjokroadisumarto, 145
"To a Modern Poet", 40
Today Began Yesterday, 105, 281, 306
Togle, Enrique V., 200n4
Togo, foreign minister, 93
Tokyo
    Filipinos' life in, 86, 91, 92
    Philippine Embassy in, 87
Tokyo Rose, 176
Tondo, 20
Totoy (pseudonym), 39, 41, 42, 51, 299
"Totoy to Momoy", 39, 41, 58
Town Meeting of the Air, 57
Toynbee, Arnold, 164
translation of poems and memoirs, 115–16
Treaty for the Prohibition of Nuclear Weapons in Latin America (Treaty of Tlatelolco), 273–74
Tribune, 44, 79
Tristan, Dr, 92
tuberculosis, 71
Tunku Abdul Rahman, 302
Turkish ambassador in Japan, 88
Tutay, Filemon, 49
Twilight in Tokyo, 99–100, 299, 306
Two Brothers, The, 57
"Two Chinas" policy, 265–66
Ty, Leon O., 49

U

U Thant, 229
U.N. Ad Hoc Political Committee, 175
UN Security and Economic and Social Councils (SC-ECOSOC), 175
UNCTAD II, 242, 250n4, 261
Undersecretary of foreign affairs, 133–38
Underwood–Simmons Act (1913), 23
"unfinished revolution", 165
Ungria, Jose de, 92
UNICEF, 258
Unite, 57
United Nations
    bridging division between countries, 230
    "people's UN", 258q
    verbal tussle in, 172–77
    as world government, 259
United Nations Conference on Trade and Development (UNCTAD), 230
United Nations Educational, Scientific and Cultural Organization (UNESCO), 137
United Nations Sugar Conference, 217
United States, 119, 255–56
United States Army Forces in the Far East (USAFFE), 73, 76
United States Forces in the Philippines (USFIP), 76–77
University of Santo Tomas (UST), 128
US military bases, 142, 213, 256, 258, 301, 303
    dismantling, 305
US-Philippine relations, 124–25, 255–56

INDEX

US-UK military bases agreement, 162–63
USSR, 99, 209
   trade links, 247, 249
   see also Russia
Usurer, The, 57

V

Valdes, Emmanuel, 85
Van Dine, S.S., 42
Vanguard, 58
Varanasi, 230
Vargas, Jorge B., 52, 78–81, 84, 203
   arrest, 94, 96
   comparison with other envoys, 87–88
   Guerrero's speeches for, 89–90
   tea party for *pensionados*, 85
Vargas Llosa, Mario, 274
Vargas, Marina, 78
Vargas, Roberto, 84
Vargas, Teresita, 84, 85
Vatican, The, 124
Venezuela, 273, 275, 277
Victoriano, Marcelo, 80
Vidas, Kazmir, 291
Viernes de Dolores, 85
Vietnam, 162, 212, 217, 225, 228, 230, 235, 255, 261, 302
Villa, Jose Garcia, 57, 136, 299
   "How to Tell: Poem for Cecile", 40
"Villa-Lopez controversy", 57–58
Villanueva-Kalaw, Pura, 55
Villareal, Cornelio, 139, 140, 263
Viola, Maximo, 180
Virata, Cesar E.A., 305, 306
Visayas, 20
Voice of Freedom, 74–75, 78

W

Wadsworth, James J., 173
Wainwright, Jonathan (Skinny), 76–77
Wallace, Ted, 78, 82n5
"What are Filipinos like?", 2, 298, 299
Why Martial Law?, 281, 306
"Will o' the Wisp", 33
Wodehouse, P.G., 39
Women Writers Club, 54
Worthen, John, 5
Wright, Willard Huntington, 42

Y

Yamamoto, 81
Yamashita, 81, 87, 90
Yao Kuang, 278
Yasuda mansion, 85
Yokohama Police Academy, 92
Young Philippines party, 71
Young Rizal, The, 115
"Young Turks", 115
Yu-Jose, Lydia, 8
Yugoslavia
   economic crisis, 288, 290
   export promotion, 291
   Guerrero's last post, 304
   least enjoyed assignment, 291–92
   Tito's funeral service, 292–93
   World Bank loans, 288
Yulo, Jose, 84, 203

Z

Zacarias, Antonio, 107
Zafra, Nicolas, 185
Zamora, Gilberto, 42
Zamora, Jacinto, 83n19, 256
Zobel, Fernando, 128
Zobel literary prize, 207–9, 285
Zone of Peace, Freedom and Neutrality (ZOPFAN), 274
Zulueta, José, 129

About the Author

Erwin S. Fernandez is an aspiring biographer and a Pangasinan historian with graduate and baccalaureate degrees from the University of the Philippines Diliman. Recipient of international and local fellowships, he has published widely on a number of topics from Arab-Israeli conflict, multilingualism, Rizal, decolonization in universities, Philippine diplomacy, social movements and military to Philippine-Malaysia dispute over Sabah, Pangasinan history, literature and poetry. He has written two children's short story in Pangasinan, one of which he illustrated himself. He is currently looking for publishers for his two unpublished manuscripts, one on the early history of Pangasinan and the other on the history of his hometown, Urdaneta City. Founder of the Abung na Panagbasay Pangasinan (House of Pangasinan Studies), an independent research centre promoting Pangasinan studies, he advocates the preservation and dissemination of Pangasinan language, literature and culture and supports federalism and parliamentary form of government.

Leon Ma. Guerrero, Leoni's paternal grandfather and namesake, during his late years.
Rights reserved, courtesy of the Manila Bulletin Publishing Corporation, Manila, Philippines.

Leoni (fourth from left, second row) stands for a class picture along with his classmates and teacher on his first year high school, 1928.
Reproduced with kind permission of Chalcot Press.

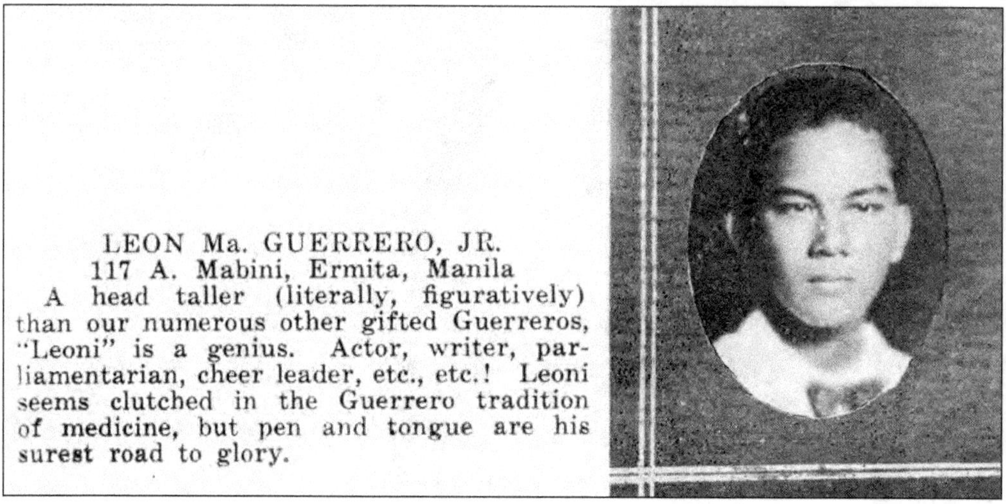

LEON Ma. GUERRERO, JR.
117 A. Mabini, Ermita, Manila
A head taller (literally, figuratively) than our numerous other gifted Guerreros, "Leoni" is a genius. Actor, writer, parliamentarian, cheer leader, etc., etc.! Leoni seems clutched in the Guerrero tradition of medicine, but pen and tongue are his surest road to glory.

Leoni graduates from the Ateneo de Manila high school in 1931.
Reproduced with kind permission of the University Archives, Ateneo de Manila University.

Leoni Guerrero (third from left) attends AB Seminar on the Trend of Modern Literature in 1932 along with Jesus A. Paredes Jr. (fifth from left) and Horacio de la Costa (second from right) under the guidance of their professor, Rev. Hugh J. McLaughlin, S.J. (leftmost).
Reproduced with kind permission of the University Archives, Ateneo de Manila University.

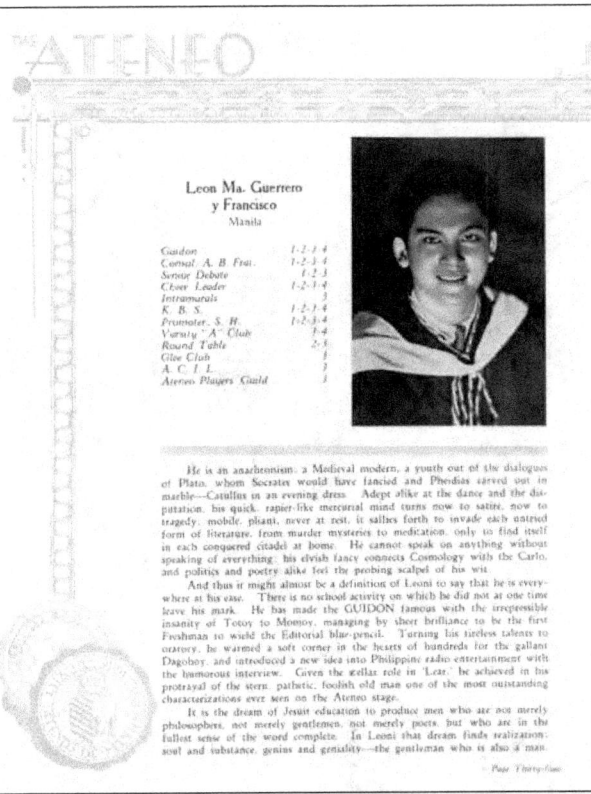

Leoni Guerrero graduates top of his class, *summa cum laude*, in 1935. Here is the write-up about him and his picture in graduation attire from the Atenean yearbook, *Aegis*.
Reproduced with kind permission of the University Archives, Ateneo de Manila University.

The Guerrero family from left (standing) Carmen, Mario Xavier, (seated) Mrs Filomena Francisco Guerrero, Alfredo Leon, Anita Corominas and Leoni.
Reproduced with kind permission of Chalcot Press.

Leoni Guerrero marries Anita Corominas at the Ermita Church on 31 March 1938. They went to Bali for their honeymoon.
Reproduced with kind permission of Lopez Museum & Library Collections.

Ambassador-designate and Mrs Guerrero are seen here outside the embassy at Palace Green, Kensington on their way to the Buckingham Palace for the presentation of credentials on 13 October 1954.
Reproduced with kind permission of Enrique L. Locsin and Teodoro L. Locsin Jr. of Philippines Free Press.

At the opening of the photo exhibit on the Philippines, Ambassador Leon Ma. Guerrero and wife, Annie, chat with J.W. Platt, a Royal Dutch/Shell group of oil companies managing director, in March 1955.
Reproduced with kind permission of Enrique L. Locsin and Teodoro L. Locsin Jr. of Philippines Free Press.

Asian chiefs of mission in London attend reception in honour of Earl of Selkirk. Sitting from left: Dr Sunario, the Indonesian ambassador; Mr Ngo Dinh Luyen, the Vietnamese ambassador; the Earl of Selkirk, the British Commissioner for Southeast Asia; Ambassador Guerrero, dean of the Asian ambassadors and high commissioners in London; Sir Robert Clarke, former British Commissioner for Southeast Asia; U Aung Soe, the Burmese ambassador; Tunku Ya'acob, the Malayan High Commissioner. Standing from left: Prince Kammao, the Laotian ambassador; Mom Luang Peekdhip Malakul, the Siamese ambassador; Lt General Mohammad Yousuf Khan, the Pakistan High Commissioner; Mr PR Gunasekera, the Ceylon High Commissioner; Mr Au Chheun, the Cambodian ambassador.
Reproduced with kind permission of Enrique L. Locsin and Teodoro L. Locsin Jr. of Philippines Free Press.

Ambassador Leon Ma. Guerrero shakes hand with Marquess of Reading, Minister of State in the British Foreign Office.
Reproduced with kind permission of Enrique L. Locsin and Teodoro L. Locsin Jr. of Philippines Free Press.

The London embassy under Ambassador Guerrero establishes rapport with the Filipino community. From left: Miss Joyce Schonfield, Mrs Alicia Atienza, Miss Jean Carr, Mrs Josephine de Guzman, Mr Restituto de Guzman, Miss Teresita Romero, Mr Juan Atienza, Dalisay, Mr Vicente I. Singian, Ambassador Guerrero, Mr Dominador Salazar, Mrs Guerrero, Mr Rodolfo Romero, Mrs Nieves Singian, Mr Armand Fabella, Miss Elsa Villanueva, Miss Alison Ritblat, Dr Asuncion Fernando and Mr Federico Barrera Jr.
Reproduced with kind permission of Enrique L. Locsin and Teodoro L. Locsin Jr. of Philippines Free Press.

Ambassador Leon Ma. Guerrero in *barong tagalog* and Mrs Guerrero in *terno* entertain British Foreign Secretary Selwyn Lloyd at the Fourth of July reception in 1958 at the London embassy.
Reproduced with kind permission of Enrique L. Locsin and Teodoro L. Locsin Jr. of Philippines Free Press.

Biographer-to-be and Ambassador to London Leon Ma. Guerrero briefs President-to-be, Vice-President and concurrent Secretary of Foreign Affairs Carlos P. Garcia on the Suez Canal crisis.
Rights reserved, courtesy of the Manila Bulletin Publishing Corporation, Manila, Philippines.

Ambassador Leon Ma. Guerrero (seated on the left) confers in February 1959 with members of the International Sugar Council as vice-chairman, Mr D.A. Bruce Marshall (Canada) (seated on the right), chairman, (standing from left to right) Dr M. Tarrab (Cuba), Mr Eric Roll, executive director of the council, Mr D.J. Muir (Australia), immediate past chairman, and Mr W.A. Nield (UK).
Reproduced with kind permission of Enrique L. Locsin and Teodoro L. Locsin Jr. of Philippines Free Press.

At the reception of Rizal's birth centenary at the embassy in London in June 1961, Ambassador and Mrs Guerrero honour Miss Visaya Regidor and Mr Cristobal Regidor, children of Rizal's contemporary, Antonio Ma. Regidor whose house in London Rizal would frequent.
Reproduced with kind permission of Enrique L. Locsin and Teodoro L. Locsin Jr. of Philippines Free Press.

Philippine ambassador to Madrid Leon Ma. Guerrero presents his credentials to Generalissimo Francisco Franco with Foreign Minister Fernando Ma. Castiella (leftmost) witnessing on 3 May 1962.
Rights reserved, courtesy of the Manila Bulletin Publishing Corporation, Manila, Philippines.

Ambassador Leon Ma. Guerrero commemorates the 1963 birth centenary of Andres Bonifacio (1863–97) (his portrait on the wall), the father of the Philippine revolution and founder of the revolutionary organization, with two unidentified gentlemen.
Reproduced with kind permission of Enrique L. Locsin and Teodoro L. Locsin Jr. of Philippines Free Press.

Ambassador and Mrs Guerrero exchange pleasantries with Gregorio Marañon Moya, the director general of the Instituto de Cultura Hispánica, at the Philippine Independence Day celebration in 1964 in Madrid. Ambassador Guerrero arranged a cultural programme featuring a Philippine folk dance presentation and a lecture by National Library of the Philippines Director Carlos Quirino instead of the usual cocktails. Reproduced with kind permission of Enrique L. Locsin and Teodoro L. Locsin Jr. of Philippines Free Press.

Ambassador Leon Ma. Guerrero poses beside the statue of Felipe II whence the Philippines and Filipinos got their names. Reproduced with kind permission of Enrique L. Locsin and Teodoro L. Locsin Jr. of Philippines Free Press.

Ambassador Leon Ma. Guerrero, at the rostrum, delivers a lecture at the Sixth Public Plenary Meeting of the Philippine Academy of Sciences and Humanities (PASH) at the Abelardo Hall auditorium in the University of the Philippines in Diliman Campus in March 1965. At the back are UP college deans, UP President Carlos P. Romulo, former UP President Vidal A. Tan and Director Eduardo Quisumbing.
Reproduced with kind permission of Enrique L. Locsin and Teodoro L. Locsin Jr. of Philippines Free Press.

Ambassador Leon Ma. Guerrero is sworn in as regular member of the Philippine Academy of Sciences and Humanities (PASH) before UP President Carlos P. Romulo (rightmost) with wife Annie, Philippine Secretary of Foreign Affairs Mauro Mendez (third from left), and Philippine Vice President and former Secretary of Foreign Affairs, Emmanuel Pelaez witnessing.
Reproduced with kind permission of Enrique L. Locsin and Teodoro L. Locsin Jr. of Philippines Free Press.

Michael Goldenberg of the Philippine Booklovers Society (second from right) presents a plaque to former Senator Geronima T. Pecson at her residence in the presence of Ambassadors Leon Ma. Guerrero (rightmost) and Salvador P. Lopez (leftmost).
Reproduced with kind permission of Lopez Museum & Library Collections.

Philippine ambassador to New Delhi Leon Ma. Guerrero delivers the Annual Rizal Lecture at Fort Santiago on 30 December 1968.
Reproduced with kind permission of Enrique L. Locsin and Teodoro L. Locsin Jr. of Philippines Free Press.

Ambassador Leon Ma. Guerrero, now the dean of the New Delhi diplomatic corps, talks to Sardar Swaran Singh, Indian Minister for External Affairs, at the Independence Day celebration held at the Philippine embassy in the 1970s.
Reproduced with kind permission of Enrique L. Locsin and Teodoro L. Locsin Jr. of Philippines Free Press.

Ambassador Leon Ma. Guerrero talks to Indian Prime Minister Indira Gandhi.
Reproduced with kind permission of Chalcot Press.

Ambassador Leon Ma. Guerrero marries Margaret Burke in a church ceremony in London. Reproduced with kind permission of Chalcot Press.

Leoni on his evening attire types out on his typewriter with David beside him smiling. Reproduced with kind permission of Chalcot Press.

Philippine ambassador to Mexico Leon Ma. Guerrero presents his credentials to President of Mexico Luis Echeverría.
Reproduced with kind permission of Chalcot Press.

Ambassador Leon Ma. Guerrero, appointed as President Marcos's special envoy, shakes the hand of General of the Army Alfredo Stroessner on his fifth term as president of Paraguay in Asuncion.
Reproduced with kind permission of the Department of Foreign Affairs (DFA), Republic of the Philippines, through the DFA Archives.

Ambassador Leon Ma. Guerrero attends the 28th session of the United Nations General Assembly with Foreign Affairs Secretary Carlos P. Romulo (front row, rightmost) as chairman, Narciso G. Reyes (front row, second from right) as vice-chairman along with other members of the Philippine delegation who were ambassadors, consuls and vice-consuls.
Reproduced with kind permission of the Department of Foreign Affairs (DFA), Republic of the Philippines, through the DFA Archives.

Ambassador Leon Ma. Guerrero and second wife Margaret Burke pose beside Leoni's favourite caricature of himself.
Reproduced with kind permission of the Department of Foreign Affairs (DFA), Republic of the Philippines, through the DFA Archives.

Ambassador Leon Ma. Guerrero, accompanied by the President of El Salvador Colonel Arturo Armando Molina, greets schoolchildren after the presentation of his credentials.
Reproduced with kind permission of the Department of Foreign Affairs (DFA), Republic of the Philippines, through the DFA Archives.

Portrait of Leon Ma. Guerrero by the prize-winning Filipino painter, Federico Aguilar Alcuaz. Reproduced with kind permission of Chalcot Press.

Ambassador Leon Ma. Guerrero (rightmost) and Mrs Guerrero in Muslim *malong* (leftmost) host Freedom Day reception at the embassy with U.S. Ambassador John Joseph Jova (second from left) and Ambassador Hortencio J. Brillantes.
Reproduced with kind permission of the Department of Foreign Affairs (DFA), Republic of the Philippines, through the DFA Archives.

Ambassador Guerrero chats with ambassador of the People's Republic of China to Mexico Yao Kuang on 12 June 1975 upon the opening of relations between the Philippines and PRC.
Reproduced with kind permission of the Department of Foreign Affairs (DFA), Republic of the Philippines, through the DFA Archives.

The Philippine delegation to the UN with First Lady Imelda R. Marcos (rightmost). Mrs Marcos addressed the General Assembly on world code of ethics on 23 September 1975. Seated from left: Ambassador Narciso G. Reyes, Philippine permanent representative to the UN and Foreign Affairs Secretary Carlos P. Romulo. Seated behind, from left: Ambassadors Alejandro Yango, Leon Ma. Guerrero and J.V. Cruz.
Reproduced with kind permission of the Department of Foreign Affairs (DFA), Republic of the Philippines, through the DFA Archives.

Philippine ambassador to Cuba Leon Ma. Guerrero exchanges views with Oswaldo Dorticós, President of Cuba.
Reproduced with kind permission of Chalcot Press.

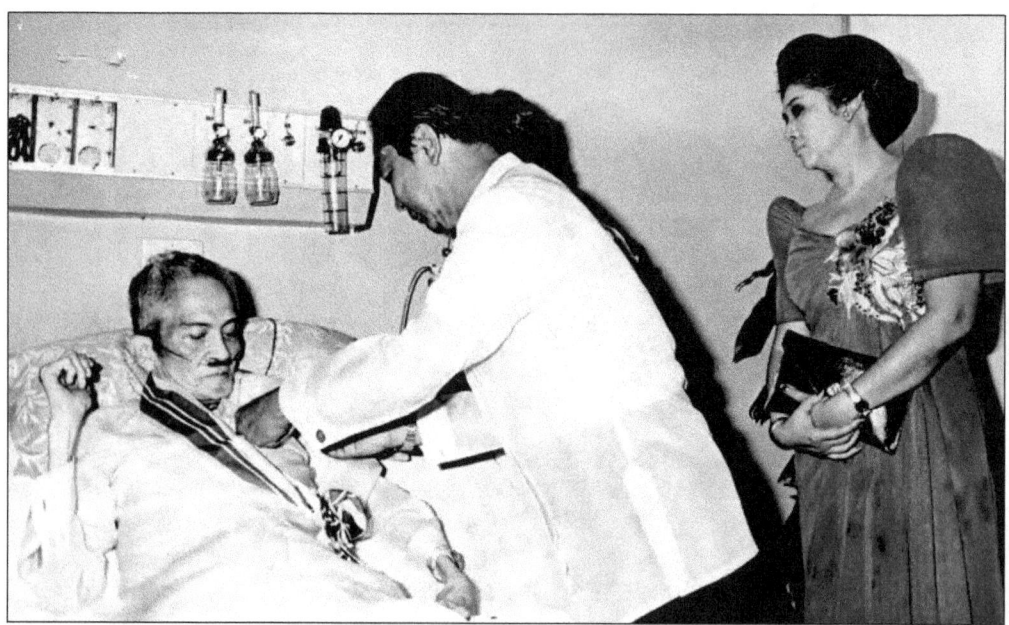

Philippine ambassador to Yugoslavia Leon Ma. Guerrero presents his credentials to Yugoslavia Vice President Stevan Dorojski.
Reproduced with kind permission of Chalcot Press.

President Ferdinand E. Marcos bestows on Leon Ma. Guerrero the *Gawad Mabini* at the Philippine Lung Center with First Lady Imelda R. Marcos looking on.
Rights reserved, courtesy of the Manila Bulletin Publishing Corporation, Manila, Philippines.

www.ingramcontent.com/pod-product-compliance
Lightning Source LLC
Chambersburg PA
CBHW072118290426
44111CB00012B/1702